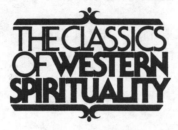

# THE CLASSICS OF WESTERN SPIRITUALITY

# Sharafuddin Maneri
## THE HUNDRED LETTERS

TRANSLATION, INTRODUCTION AND NOTES
BY
PAUL JACKSON, S.J.

PREFACE
BY
SYED HASAN ASKARI

FOREWORD
BY
BRUCE LAWRENCE

PAULIST PRESS
NEW YORK • MAHWAH

Cover art
The artist LIAM ROBERTS was born in Ireland and now lives in New York. After attending the National College of Art in Dublin for five years, he studied at the Academy of Fine Arts in Florence, at the Royal Academy of San Fernando in Madrid, and at the Academy of Fine Arts in Rome for one year each on scholarship. In his cover art Mr. Roberts used gouache pigment (opaque water colors) and fluid lines to portray his sense of Sharafuddin b. Yahya Maneri as a holy, retiring mystic whose essential qualities cannot be concretely captured.

Design: Barbini, Pesce & Noble, Inc.

Library of Congress
Catalog Card Number: 79-56754

ISBN: 0-8091-2229-4

Published by Paulist Press
997 Macarthur Boulevard
Mahwah, NJ 07430

Printed and bound in the
United States of America

# Contents

## The Editor of this Volume

Born on June 11, 1937 in Brisbane, Australia, PAUL JACKSON was the first child of Frederick Jackson, an army officer, and his wife Violet. Father Jackson attended a number of Catholic schools in Queensland, spending the last seven years at the Marist Brothers' College, Ashgrove, Brisbane.

In 1956 he joined the Society of Jesus in Melbourne where he did his novitiate and philosophical studies. In 1960 he was assigned to the Hazaribagh Region in India where he taught for three and a half years. He studied Hindi in Ranchi for one year and did four years of theology at Kurseong.

Father Jackson was subsequently appointed headmaster of a Hindi-medium middle school in Maheshmunda and also became chaplain in Giridih. A year later he was appointed teacher and games superintendent in a Hindi-medium high school in Mahuadanr. In 1972 Father Jackson traveled to Delhi to earn an M.A. in history and to complete a diploma in Urdu. In 1974 he went to Shiraz, Iran to study Persian and to act as Catholic chaplain.

Returning to India in 1976, he did his tertianship in Hazaribagh and then went to Patna to begin doctoral studies on the life and teaching of Sharafuddin Maneri. Father Jackson has just completed his thesis for submission to Patna University.

Author of the Preface

SYED HASAN ASKARI, born in Khujwa, Bihar, India in 1901, earned his A.B., M.A. and B.L. degrees from Patna University in Bihar state (North India). He later went on to teach at the same university, distinguishing himself as the foremost Indian scholar on the cultural, literary and religious history of his native region. He has published over 150 research papers, edited and translated numerous medieval texts, and continues to be very active as a research scholar at the Khuda Bakhsh Oriental Library in Patna. An honorary degree of D. Litt. was conferred on him by Magadh University, and the Government of India recently awarded him a special stipend for his outstanding contributions to medieval Indian history and culture.

Author of the Foreword

BRUCE BENNETT LAWRENCE, born in Newton, N.J., in 1941, is Professor of the History of Religions at Duke University. A specialist on Indo-Muslim culture and medieval Sufism, he earned his A.B. at Princeton University in 1962, and his Ph.D. from Yale University in 1972.

Professor Lawrence has been the recipient of several academic awards, including a Kent Fellowship for graduate study (1967-71) and an American Institute of Indian Studies Senior Faculty Research Fellowship (1974-76). He serves on national committees for both the American Institute of Indian Studies and the Association of Asian Studies. His editorial/advisory responsibilities include the Indo-Persian segments of the *Journal of South Asian Literature* and *Encyclopaedia Persica*, as well as the Islamic component of the *Abingdon Dictionary of Living Religions*.

Professor Lawrence has published numerous research articles and three books: *Shahrastani on the Indian Religions, Notes from a Distant Flute: The Extant Literature of Pre-Mughal Indian Sufism,* and *The Rose and the Rock: Mystical and Rational Elements in the Intellectual History of South Asian Islam.*

# Preface

Many years ago I went to Bihar Sharif and met there the learned Shah Najmuddin, father-in-law of the *sajjadah nishin* or spiritual successor to Sharafuddin b. Yahya Maneri. He told me that he had translated half of the *Maktubat-i Sadi* [The hundred letters] into Urdu, and that a few years earlier he had sent a copy of the original Persian text to the famed British scholar R. A. Nicholson, hoping that the latter might undertake its translation into English. Unfortunately, he did not.

This conversation made me think that, however incompetent I might be for the task, I ought to try to write something about the life, times, and teaching, as well as the letters and discourses, of Sharafuddin. I have made liberal reference to Makhdum al-Mulk, as he is popularly known, in several articles published in the *Journal of the Bihar Research Society* from 1948 to 1956, but I have never undertaken a systematic translation of any of his major writings.

I was very glad many years later when, in 1976, I came across Fr. Paul Jackson in the Khuda Bakhsh Oriental Public Library, Patna. He expressed his desire to take up the work of translating *The Hundred Letters*. Hence the present translation from his pen has been placed before a wider public than would have been reached by the original Persian or recent Urdu and Bengali renditions. Up till now only one translation of Makhdum al-Mulk's writings has appeared in English, consisting mainly of excerpts from *The Hundred Letters*, totaling less than 10 percent of the work and excluding all the verse and

xi

nearly all the Quranic citations. Baijnath Singh, a Hindu gentleman of Gaya, first published his work in 1908 under the title *Letters from a Sufi Teacher*. He deserves credit for his pioneering endeavor, and Samuel Weiser of New York has recently (1974) reprinted the book in its original format. The present translation by Fr. Jackson gives us the full text in English for the first time.

*The Hundred Letters* was prized among all the Sufi circles of medieval India, having been quoted by the Mughal traditionist and biographer Abdul Haqq in his classic account of Indo-Muslim saints, *Akhbar al-akhyar*, and also by the renowned seventeenth-century revivalist Sheikh Ahmad Sirhindi in his copius letters *Maktubat-i Imam Rabbani*. Abul Fazl, author of the *Ain-i Akbari*, mentions reading portions of *The Hundred Letters* to the great Mughal Akbar while Hamiduddin, secretary to Aurangzeb, relates that the last major Mughal dynast kept a copy of the work with him at all times. A still more remarkable index of the fame of *The Hundred Letters* is their inclusion as a compulsory text in medieval Indian *madrasas*, where they were not only read but fractionally memorized as part of the education of the future leaders of North Indian Muslim society.

Many Sufi orders came to Bihar—the Chishti, the Shattari, the Qadiri, and the Naqshbandi. But Makhdum al-Mulk Sharafuddin b. Yahya Maneri eclipsed the leaders of all these orders. He still enjoys immense popularity in religious and official circles among Hindus as well as Muslims, a tribute that has been denied to other medieval Sufi masters and that explains the popularity of the order he introduced to Bihar, the Firdausiya.

There are many writings by and about Sufis in India, but one has to be able to read Persian in order to benefit from them. A few Urdu translations of medieval classics also exist. Many such works could be cited by name, but their titles would be of little interest to the general reader of this remarkable series. Suffice it to say that the most famous treatise on Sufism produced in India and widely known on account of its English translation (by R. A. Nicholson; London, 1911; repr. 1976) is the *Kashf al-Mahjub* of Sheikh ʿAli Hujwiri. Written in Lahore circa A.D. 1060, it is the earliest known Sufi treatise in the Persian language. While similar to Makhdum al-Mulk's collection of letters in some respects, the *Kashf al-Mahjub* is more a work *about* Sufism, while *The Hundred Letters* is a work *of* Sufism.

Dr. Zakir Husain, the late President of India, had once suggested to me a project of rendering into English all that was philosophi-

# PREFACE

cal, doctrinal, or mystical in the works of Makhdum al-Mulk, in short, all that indicated the distinctive outlook of this unrivalled Bihari saint. Dr. Zakir Husain made this proposal when he was governor of Bihar, and he himself volunteered to finance the project, but, unfortunately, it did not materialize.

Fr. Jackson undertook the present translation in order to comprehend the spiritual teaching of Sharafuddin, a teaching that flowed from the wellsprings of the saint's profound inner experience of God. The reader may judge for himself or herself to what extent Fr. Jackson has succeeded in conveying the Muslim saint's experience to a largely non-Muslim audience. It is for me a work of inspiration comparable in breadth and subtlety to the original Persian text.

I am most grateful to Mr. Richard J. Payne for including this volume in the series Classics of Western Spirituality, published by Paulist Press. It will enable numerous people to become acquainted with the mature insights of a Sufi who not only originated the Firdausi order in Bihar but enjoyed a long life, during which he initiated devotees into the mystical way, wrote letters to numerous disciples, and delivered stirring discourses before the audiences assembled at his humble center in Bihar Sharif.

Syed Hasan Askari
Patna, Bihar
November, 1978

# Foreword

The tradition of letter writing among Sufis has a long history both within and beyond South Asian Islam. The early ascetics of tenth-century Baghdad corresponded with one another, and Abu Nasr Sarraj (d. 988) from Tus in eastern Iran refers to their literary activities in his compendium of Sufi doctrine, *Kitab al-luma*ᶜ. P. Nwyia has also described in detail the letters of spiritual direction circulated among North African Sufis from the twelfth through the fourteenth centuries (*Un mystique predicateur a la Qarawiyin de Fes, Ibn ᶜAbbad de Ronda [1332–1390]*; Beyrouth, 1961). And both the illustrious Ghazzalis, Muhammad Abu Hamid (d. 1111) and his younger brother Ahmad (d. 1126), corresponded with contemporary Sufis on a wide range of topics, though neither of their compilations contains the explicit, intimate detail relating to mystical practice, including dream interpretation, which we find set forth in the literary exchange between two early fourteenth-century Iranian Sufi masters, Nuruddin ᶜAbdurrahman Isfaraini (d. 1317) and ᶜAlauddawlah Simnani (d. 1336) [see H. Landolt, ed., *Correspondence spirituelle echangee entre Noroddin Esfarayeni (ob. 717/1317) et son disciple, ᶜAlaoddawleh Semnani (ob. 736/1336)*, Teheran & Paris, 1972].

South Asian Sufis exercised their pens as well as their tongues in communicating spiritual insights to one another. Two thirteenth-century saints from Nagor, a city in present-day Rajasthan, wrote numerous letters to fellow North Indian Muslim mystics: The correspondence of Qazi Hamiduddin Nagori (d. 1244) has been arranged and preserved as a commentary on the ninety-nine beautiful names of God entitled *Tawaliᶜ ash-shumus*, while the letters of Sufi Hamiduddin Nagori (d. 1274) have been transmitted, together with the letters to which he was replying, in a disparate compilation of the saint's literary outpourings (including poetry, topical essays, invocatory prayers and notable conversations) called *Surur as-sudur*.

Among the major Sufi saints of pre-Mughal India whose collections of letters have been partially or wholly preserved to the present day are Nizamuddin Awliya (d. 1325), Masᶜud Bakk (d. 1387), Nur Qutb-i ᶜAlam Pandawi (d. 1415), Sayyid Muhammad Husayni Gesu Darraz (d. 1422), Sayyid Ashraf Jahangir Simnani (d. 1425), and ᶜAbdulquddus Gangohi (d. 1537). All of them belonged to the dominant Sufi order of the Delhi Sultanate or pre-Mughal period (1206–1526), the Chishtiya. But non-Chishti spiritual masters were equally prone to, and adept at, corresponding with fellow sheikhs, or disciples, or even lay acquaintances. The aforementioned Qazi Hamiduddiin Nagori was a member of the Suhrawardi order, while Shah 'Bu ᶜAli Qalandar (d. 1324), who authored an impressive set of letters—at once lyrical and evocative—was a nonaffiliated saint from the Punjab. A less extensive but still notable ream of correspondence has also been attributed to the premier saint of Kashmir, the Kubrawi sheikh, Sayyid ᶜAli Hamadani (d. 1385).

By comparison with their medieval predecessors and contemporaries from other parts of the Asian subcontinent, the Firdausis were numerically small and delimited in influence; though linked by genealogy to the Kubrawi order, they never alluded to, or elaborated on, their connection with Central Asian Muslims, and their growth within India appears to have been restricted to northern and western Bihar. For this reason, it is all the more remarkable that their contribution to the tradition of letter writing among South Asian Sufis was second to none. Their astonishing achievement may be traced directly to the subject of this book, *The Hudred Letters* of Sharafuddin b. Yahya Maneri; but it ought to be noted that both the immediate successors to Sharafuddin in the Firdausi order, Muzaffar Shams Balkhi (d. 1400) and Husain b. Muᶜizz Balkhi (d. 1440), were not only spiritual masters of a high level but also skilled literary craftsmen; they produced collections of letters that complemented and extended the many insights set forth in the correspondence of their illustrious predecessor Makhdum al-Mulk [see B. Lawrence, *Notes from a Distant*

# FOREWORD

*Flute: The Extant Literature of pre-Mughal Indian Sufism*, Tehran, 1978;
pp. 77–78].

Makhdum al-Mulk Sharafuddin b. Yahya Maneri wrote many
letters. In addition to *The Hundred Letters*, which have been fully and
brilliantly translated into English for the first time in this volume by
Fr. Jackson, the Bihari saint wrote a series of two hundred letters,
many dealing with topics similar to those covered in *The Hundred Letters*, and also a small collection of twenty-eight letters addressed to
his principal disciple and eventual successor, Muzaffar Shams Balkhi.
By no means, however, should we assume that the literary output of
Makhdum al-Mulk has been preserved in its entirety. Preceding *The
Twenty-eight Letters* is an introduction in which it is reported that the
sheikh's correspondence with Muzaffar was confidential and originally consisted of more than two hundred letters sent from Sharafuddin
to his beloved disciple over a twenty-five-year period. Muzaffar, however, directed that they were to be buried with him, and only one
small bundle was "kept apart in a bag"; it is they that now comprise
*The Twenty-eight Letters*.

The above anecdote is interesting beyond what it says about the
prized literary legacy of the principal Muslim saint of medieval Bihar.
It also hints at one of the many paradoxes that characterize Sufism.
Sufism is the inner dimension of Islam and, therefore, cannot be captured in even the most subtle verbal or literary exchange. It must be a
felt experience, shared relationally and transmitted generation after
generation from spiritual master to disciple. Those who stand outside
Sufism—and, in the case of many of the readers of this volume in The
Classics of Western Spirituality, outside Islam altogether—can understand the thought world, the ideational structure, the normative categories of Sufism, but its real intent, its own inner life and fullest legacy, still must be transmitted from spiritual master to disciple, and in
that sense what Sharafuddin intended to say in the two hundred
"lost" letters will always be buried with Muzaffar Shams Balkhi.

The same anecdote has another interpretation. It is also integral
to the Sufi experience that the written communications of the masters could be—and often were—misunderstood by those not initiated
into the Way. The younger Ghazzali, Ahmad, corresponded with an
intensely devout Sufi who began as his disciple and was executed for
the fervor of his discourse in 1132. The fate of this Iranian mystical
genius, ᶜAynulquzat Hamadani, together with that of an early Sufi

martyr to love, Mansur al-Hallaj (d. 922), were well known to Shara-fuddin and his fellow Firdausis. A poem in *The Twenty-eight Letters* bluntly warns the reader (i.e., Muzaffar):

> Beware, do not utter a secret in public,
> If you be truly a lover of secrets.
> Have you not seen how in the flush of love,
> Hallaj spoke the secret and went to the gallows?

Despite the emphasis on esoteric truth in Sufism, both for doctrinal and security reasons, what Sharafuddin did disclose in writing to another disciple, Qazi Shamsuddin of Chausa, in *The Hundred Letters* provides us with a consistently brilliant and magnificently systematic overview of mature Sufi thought.

*The Hundred Letters* are not personal. Makhdum al-Mulk gives us no insight into his own spiritual formation or private states, nor is he pointedly polemical: The names of adversaries and friends alike are most often disclosed only by indirection. In this sense, *The Hundred Letters* contrasts with the other famous collection of spiritual correspondence from medieval India, the *Maktubat-i Imam Rabbani*, an enormous corpus of 524 letters from the pen of Sheikh Ahmad Sirhindi (d. 1621), a Muslim revivalist and founder of the Naqshbandi-Mujaddidi order. Sirhindi does not hesitate to speak of his own spiritual preeminence or to explain how he attained it, and he details points of disagreement with fellow Sufis, lay Muslims, and, occasionally, contemporaneous Hindus [see Y. Friedmann, *Shaykh Ahmad Sirhindi*, Montreal and London, 1971; pp. 72–74].

*The Hundred Letters* might better be compared *not* to another compilation of spiritual correspondence, either from Islamic India or elsewhere in *dar al-Islam*, but rather, as Professor Askari has suggested in his valuable Preface, to the *Kashf al-Mahjub* of Sheikh ʿAli Hujwiri. In *The Hundred Letters* Makhdum al-Mulk treats the same topics on the same broadly descriptive scale that was already demarcated in the eleventh-century treatise of Hujwiri. *Kashf al-Mahjub* has long been known to English readers of matters Islamic, thanks to the excellent translation of the Cambridge Persianist R. A. Nicholson (London, 1911; repr. 1976). The work has been rightly praised for its author's vast knowledge of theoretical Sufism and detachment from any sectarian viewpoint. Yet *Kashf al-Mahjub* reads more like an encyclopedia of mystical Muslim practitioners, their thought and terminology, than like an everyday manual on elements and aspects of the Sufi life.

# FOREWORD

What distinguishes *The Hundred Letters* from *Kashf al-Mahjub* is its art-ful balance—between reflection and conduct, between explanation and advocacy, between attachment to the Law and pursuit of the Way, between sobriety and ecstasy, bondage and freedom, death and life. *The Hundred Letters* of Makhdum al-Mulk Sharafuddin b. Yahya Maneri may be less personal than the correspondence of Sheikh Ahmad Sirhindi, less comprehensive than the *Kashf al-Mahjub* of Sheikh ᶜAli Hujwiri, less revealing than the saint's own twenty-eight letters to Muzaffar Shams Balkhi, but they are unrivalled—and cannot be surpassed—as an invitation to experience the Sufi Way as a Sufi master experienced and described it, to join him in the endless struggle, which has been ordained for man alone in the whole created order, to seek perfection while clinging to the pain of love.

Bruce B. Lawrence
Durham, N.C.
May 1979

# Introduction

This introduction will deal with (1) the biography of Sharafuddin b. Yahya Maneri, (2) the text of *The Hundred Letters*, (3) its translation, and (4) the notes and indices.

## Sharafuddin b. Yahya Maneri

The future saint was born in Maner, a town about twenty miles west of Patna, in Bihar, a state adjacent to Bengal in northeast India circa August 1263. His father, a famous Sufi in his times, was named Yahya. Hence the full name of the saint is Sharafuddin Ahmad ibn Yahya Maneri. He later became known as Makhdum ul-Mulk, "The Spiritual Teacher of the Realm," and at present people in Bihar simply refer to him as Makhdum Sahib. He is still venerated as the most famous Muslim saint ever to have lived in Bihar. The anniversary of his death is annually celebrated, as is the custom among Sufis, and the occasion draws large crowds to Rajgir, where there is a shrine consisting of a small cave in which he used to live, a well from which he used to obtain his water supply, and a small mosque where he used to pray. Crowds also visit Bihar Sharif, the township in which he spent the last forty years or so of his life and where he now lies buried.

Sharafuddin attended a local mosque-school for his early education. He then accompanied a noted Delhi traditionist, Abu Tawwama al-Hanbali, to Sonargaon, near modern-day Dacca in Bangladesh, where he remained for some time and received a thorough education in all the standard branches of Islamic learning current at the time.

1

He also married the daughter of his Hanbali mentor (though against his wishes, according to tradition) and had one son with whom he returned to Maner on receiving word of his father's death. He left his young wife behind in Sonargaon and adopted a life of celibacy. After his father's funeral, having entrusted his small son to the care of his mother, he set out for Delhi, in search of a spiritual guide, probably during the late 1280s.

It was in Delhi that he met a number of Sufi masters, including the renowned exemplar of his age, Sheikh Nizamuddin Awliya (d. 1325). But Sharafuddin did not become his disciple nor the disciple of any other Sufi master. Finally, as he was about to return to Bihar disappointed, his brother managed to persuade him to visit yet one more guide, the little-known Najibuddin Firdausi. An immediate, overpowering attraction drew the two men to one another, and Sharafuddin became the disciple of Najibuddin. On his way back to Maner the Bihari saint disappeared into the forest of Bihia and from there went to the Rajgir Hills, famous for their association with the Buddha and the countless Buddhist and Hindu monks who reside there. Many years later he was coaxed to come to the Friday prayer in Bihar Sharif, about twelve miles away, and after much coaxing, he was finally persuaded to take up residence there. The reigning Sultan of Delhi, Muhammad ibn Tughluq (1325–1351), gave him a land grant for his maintenance and ordered a center to be constructed for him. The saint continued to live in Bihar Sharif until his death on Wednesday evening, January 2, 1381.

There is much uncertainty about the chronology of Sharafuddin's formative years, and the few dates given above are to be viewed as tentative conjectures. I hope to produce shortly a study of the life and teaching of Sharafuddin, which will present a coherent account of his formative years, based on original Persian manuscript sources. His later years, after he settled in Bihar Sharif, are amply documented due to the profusion of *malfuzat*, that is, written accounts of what he said and did, recorded by his own disciples. The person to whom we are most indebted for these writings is Zain Badr Arabi, the indefatigable, self-effacing compiler of *The Hundred Letters*, to which he has added his own introductory preface.

## The Text of The Hundred Letters

In his preface, Zain Badr Arabi states clearly that Qazi Shamsuddin, the governor of Chausa in western Bihar, had frequently petitioned Sharafuddin to send him written instructions for his spiritual

# INTRODUCTION

advancement because his many responsibilities prevented him from attending the audiences regularly held in Bihar Sharif. Sharafuddin complied with the Qazi's request, writing him a number of letters on various spiritual topics throughout the year A.H. 747 (A.D. 1346–1347). Zain Badr and others in attendance on the saint copied out these letters and made a collection of them, which was subsequently arranged in the order now presented to the reader. *The Hundred Letters* rapidly gained fame beyond as well as within the Sufi circles of Bihar. The above-mentioned Sultan Muhammad ibn Tughluq wrote a letter to Sharafuddin, inquiring about some further advice on a point raised in *The Hundred Letters*. Sharafuddin's reply to the request of the reigning Deli monarch is still extant, providing dramatic confirmation of the early popularity enjoyed by his correspondence wtih Qazi Shamsuddin Numerous are the manuscripts of *The Hundred Letters* in all parts of the Asian subcontinent ruled and influenced by the Indo-Persian elite through the Mughal period (1526–1857). During the last century, two printed Persian editions were brought out, one in Kanpur, the other in Lahore. In 1908, about 5 percent of *The Hundred Letters* was translated into English at Gaya. In 1973, a complete Urdu rendition appeared in Bihar Sharif, while in 1976, the first forty letters were published in Bengali from Dacca, with the remaining sixty due to be published soon from the same place.

The present translation was made from a manuscript predating the reign of the Mughal Emperor Akbar (1556–1605) and now belonging to the Khuda Bakhsh Oriental Public Library, Patna. The two printed Persian texts were also utilized, as well as the Urdu translation. When the revised translation was completed, I was thrilled to be able to check it with the Balkhi manuscript, a copy of *The Hundred Letters* that belonged to Sharafuddin's chief disciple and spiritual successor, Muzaffar Shams Balkhi, who has made copious annotations in the margins. The manuscript dates from the very lifetime of Sharafuddin, as references are made to him on several occasions with blessings that are used only for the living. Other evidence can also be adduced to prove that the manuscript is what it is purported to be: the personal copy of Muzaffar Shams Balkhi. It remains in the possession of Muzaffar's descendants, who now live in Patna and were kind enough to allow me to consult it. Written in a delicate *naskh* style, the manuscript has been slightly damaged by worms, and the last two letters are missing. Yet it is a work as beautiful as it is rare, the commentary alone being a priceless source of further insight into *The Hundred Letters*. After consulting this, the most authoritative known manuscript of *The Hundred Letters*, I was able to make a number of correc-

3

tions, especially of the verses, all of which have enhanced the accuracy—and, I trust, the value—of the resulting translation.

## The Translation

The principles underlying this endeavor are those enunciated by the translators of the *New English Bible*. In other words, a serious attempt has been made to grasp the meaning of the original Persian text, making use of all available aids, and then to express it in modern English. With this in view, no Persian words, except for proper names, appear in the text. Anyone familiar with the number of translations of the Bible available these days will realize that there is no such thing as *the* translation. All that a translator can hope to do is to provide his readers with an intelligible—and, if possible, literate—version in the secondary language, always keeping in mind his duty to be faithful to the intent of the original author and reflective of the idioms used in the primary language.

## Notes and Indices

Some readers may prefer to ignore the notes entirely and let the text speak for itself. This can be exciting, for questions will arise and judgments gradually be formed that are of greater import because they relate to the particular mind set and religious disposition of each reader. It can be confidently asserted that all the major spiritual questions that arise will be answered, to the extent that Sharafuddin addresses them, simply by reading on. The general index, however, is intended to help the courageous reader who would like to find out, for himself or herself, what Sharafuddin teaches about particular topics, such as grace, self-struggle, repentance, and so forth, referring him or her to the various passages in *The Hundred Letters* where the subject is treated.

Other readers might feel the need to consult some notes because they are entirely unfamiliar with Islamic spiritual writing. The notes are meant to be hints indicating two or three things that might prove useful for someone who feels he recognizes the terrain as vaguely familiar, but would like to have some of the vagueness removed.

Finally, there are some footnotes dealing with certain technical Persian expressions of Arabic origin. These are meant for interested scholars, and the general reader, having neither the benefit nor the

# INTRODUCTION

disadvantage of knowing either Arabic or Persian, is advised to skip these notes.

The Quranic references indicated in the text form an additional index that will be of interest to some. Brief explanatory notes have also been added to indices of books and peoples cited or quoted in the text.

# Sharafuddin Maneri
## THE HUNDRED LETTERS

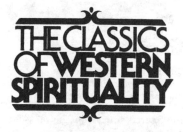

THE CLASSICS
OF WESTERN
SPIRITUALITY

Above is a specimen from the Balkhi manuscript of *The Hundred Letters*, the oldest extant copy of this work, having been transcribed by Husain Muiz Balkhi, the nephew and successor to Muzaffar Shams Balkhi, himself the principal successor to Sharafuddin, probably before 1400 A.D. The page is from Letter 33 "Fasting", and the marginal note by Muzaffar explains Sharafuddin's 'hint' on the value of bodily suffering: it is the externalist *ulema* who will receive a 70-fold reward for their fasting, while the true faster, i.e., the Sufi, will be rewarded with the sight of God Himself.

*In the name of God, the Merciful, the Compassionate!*
*May He enable me to complete this work in a fitting manner!*

Boundless praise and abundant glory be to the Most Pure Lord who adorned the hearts of the mystics with the lights of the manifestation of His perfect beauty and the revelation of His unfading glory and who, at every moment, held them spellbound as they gazed upon the marvels of His hidden secrets! In every age He ordered the pure wine of incessant illuminations to be poured into the cups of their souls, so that they became so intoxicated that He took them out of themselves and revealed the light of witnessing to Unity before both their bodily and spiritual eyes, and showed himself to them outside themselves, with the result that, in the intensity of the manifestation of that light, it was as though they themselves, their souls, and the whole world had never been born or brought into existence! They saw nothing but Him, went nowhere except toward Him, accepted nothing that did not come from Him, spoke to none apart from Him!

Here there is no we or I or this or that:
He remains, He remains, He remains!

A hundred thousand graces, blessings, and perfect salutations be upon the soul of the leader of lovers and the foremost of all mystics, the Prophet Muhammad! The beautiful garment of the prophethood of the prophets appeared because of him, while the garment of sanctity fitted snugly on the bodies of the saints due to his righteousness. If he had not existed, who would have existed? There would have been no heaven or angel! If he had not come, who would have come? Neither Adam nor mankind! He was such a prophet that God had ordained for him an abode without roof in the very proximity of Himself, as well as a hundred thousand miracles, and a hundred thousand signs of intimacy completely unknown to any angel, prophet, or saint. He pitched the tent of His glory in the desert of the existence of this world. He made the creatures of both worlds His servants. May an abundance of blessings and saluations descend upon his descendants, and upon his family and companions! Each of them was in front of that resplendent full moon, like a star diffusing his light and scattering it as each moved about. Blessings also upon those well versed in the Way and upon the men eloquent in explaining Truth who have taken possession of his inheritance!

Special blessings from the eternal threshold of the Everlasting One upon the one engrossed in witnessing manifestations and revelations, the gift of the age, our lord, master, teacher, and guide along the way to God, the axis of all the mystics, the pride of Truth and Reality, of God and of Religion, Ahmad Yahya Maneri! May God Almighty grant his long life to be a blessing for Muslims and may He exalt the believers with the favor of seeing Him!

After all this praise and blessing, this unworthy slave, Zain Badr Arabi, relates how one of the disciples, Qazi Shamsuddin, the governor of the township of Chausa, time and again presented petitions, the fundamental intention and scope of which was that, on account of the vicissitudes of fate in an unholy age, he was too far away to be able to attend the assemblies of the Master. Also, on account of his diligence in service, which necessitated the acquisition of both religious and worldly knowledge, he had to forgo much. He has presented this helplessness along with his petition that something might be written, according to the capacity of the slave, concerning each aspect that pertained to the knowledge of the Way. This would be, for him, a source of both pleasure and profit.

On account of this need, the Revered Master put to writing, by means of his indulgent pen, a few lines according to what needed to be acquired in order to meet the expectations of the petitioner. He has described the ranks and stages of the travelers, the states and affairs of the disciples, such as repentance, discipleship, belief in the Unity of God, mystical knowledge, passionate and affectionate love, turning back and going ahead, attraction and effort, servitude and service, solitude and seclusion, security and blame, spiritual guides and novices, and other similar things, in accordance with the needs of novices and travelers, as well as stories of our predecessors that could serve both to verify and to render palatable this teaching, in addition to a slight allusion to their states and works.

At various times, from the region of Bihar, in the year A.H. 747 (A.D. 1346–1347), he ordered them to be sent to the aforesaid township to the petitioner just mentioned. This is the collection the servants and attendants who were present in that dwelling place compiled from those letters, arranging them in the following order so that, on the day and at the hour when grace befriends them, they might put into practice what they have read. In addition, they hope that seekers after mysteries and the just men of the age might obtain capital from this collection and esteem it as an eternal blessing and enduring wealth. Such men would also realize that these letters are an expedient to advancing in the ranks of the world to come, and make them a companion during the period spent in this world, esteeming them as a grace from God.

> The judge received hints of the secret, and ordinary people
> Bore off all the money of this hidden treasure.
> O Lord, grant me but a small coin from all this treasure,
> Even though my heart be worthless and I, full of faults!

Also:

> O God, Your mercy is a boundless ocean:
> I would be satisfied with only one drop of it.
> If the impurity of all sinful creatures
> Were to be immersed but once in that vast expanse,
> It would not darken such a timeless ocean:
> Rather, the work of the world would turn into light!

# MANERI

*In the name of God, the Merciful, the Compassionate!*

May the bounty of God be upon you, my brother Shamsuddin, both in this world and the next! It should be known, at the very beginning,[1] that belief in the unity of God can be divided into four stages.[2] In the first of these a person proclaims "There is no god but God!" (Q47:19)[3] but his heart is devoid of faith. Such belief is hypocrisy and will prove profitless in the next life. In the second stage a person both proclaims "There is no god but God!" and believes in his heart that this is so. This type of belief can be either conventional—as is true for ordinary people—or supported by rational proofs—as is the case of the learned. This is the way belief normally manifests itself. In truth it can be said: Come, open your eyes and see that each particle of dust, if you look carefully, contains a world-revealing cup. Sufis say that such faith prevents people from falling into crass polytheism and saves them from languishing eternally in hell. It also ensures entrance into paradise. Although this type of belief is more beneficial and enduring than the first, there is still an element of instability about it. The highest form of belief is for you, my friend, not this, which is fit for old women!

The third stage is said to be reached when a person's soul is illuminated in such a way that he is able to perceive every action flowing from a single source and deriving from a single agent. This firm belief is different from the faith of common people and the faith of the learned, both of which are constricted. This elevates the heart. It is the contemplation of a light that effaces creatures! There is a similar difference between the person who believes that a certain gentleman is in an inn because somebody told him (just as the person of conventional faith inherits what he believes from his father or mother or someone else) and the person who, upon seeing the gentleman's horse and servants at the door of the inn, infers that the owner himself must be inside. This is the view and belief of the learned, but it contains a great amount of imitation. From the vantage point of someone who has actually seen the man, however, both beliefs are on the same footing; that is, they are equally defective. A believer who has attained the third stage is like the man who actually sees the gentleman in the inn. He is a Sufi who, in this stage, sees creatures and experiences the Creator, in the sense that he perceives that they all come from Him. This very discrimination, however, indicates that the state of complete unification has not yet been attained.

Sufi masters are of the opinion that, in the fourth stage, such a surfeit of the dazzling divine light becomes manifest to the pilgrim that every single existing particle that lies within his vision becomes concealed in the very luster of that light just as particles in the air are lost to sight on account of the brightness of the light emanating from the sun. This occurs not because the particles have ceased to exist but rather because the intensity of the sunlight makes it impossible that anything other than this concealment should result. In the same way, it is not true that a person becomes God—for God is infinitely greater than any man—nor has the person really ceased to exist, for ceasing to exist is one thing, and becoming lost to view quite another![4]

> Before your Unique Being, there is neither old nor new:
> Everything is nothing, nothing at all! Yet He is what He is.
> How then can we remain separate from You?

When "I" and the "You" have passed away, God alone will remain!

When you look into a mirror you do not see the mirror for the simple reason that your attention has become riveted on your own handsome reflection. You would not, however, go on to say that the mirror has ceased to exist, or that it has become beautiful, or that beauty has become a mirror. In a similar fashion, one can contemplate God's almighty power in the whole gamut of creation, without any distinction. Sufis describe this state as that of being entirely lost to oneself in contemplation of the Unique Being!

> A person who attains such a blessed state says:
> "His very brilliance blinds me to whatever descends!"

Many have lost their balance here; for without the ever-present help of God's grace and favor, as well as the assistance of a spiritual guide, no one can traverse this wilderness. The guide should be a person who has passed through the ups and downs of the Way and tasted the unique sweetness of his all-demanding Majesty, as well as the pleasure of his intoxicating Beauty, and himself have attained enlightenment. This is the meaning of the following story. One day, Mansur al-Hallaj[5] saw a famous Sufi, Ibrahim,[6] wandering about in a wilderness. He inquired what he was about. "I am treading the path that leads to perfect trust in God," he replied. Mansur exclaimed, "If your whole life were to be passed in doing justice to this stage of trusting in God, then how would you ever reach that of being lost in divine contemplation?" It has been noted that fostering any sort of desire is really a waste of time, since it will be but a hindrance to contemplation.

Some people are admitted into the royal Presence for an hour a week; others, for an hour or two a day; while yet others are absorbed in divine contemplation for the great part of their time. Beyond these four stages is one known as "losing consciousness of being lost in divine contemplation." This is due to the total absorption of the understanding of the pilgrim, which leads him to forget himself altogether, in the heightened awareness of the King who is unsurpassable in beauty and power! In an instant, the pilgrim is himself borne off to the concealment of nothingness! Everything slips away from him for, if he were to know anything else, then, in the opinion of Sufis, it would be a sign of the distinction between seeing God apart from creation and seeing creation rooted in God! Hence we can understand how a person can lose sight of both himself and the entire creation in the dazzling light of God! The last vestige of self-awareness is itself lost in the rapture of this union.[7]

> When you lose yourself in God, you proclaim the divine Unity.
> Lose the sense of "being lost"—that is complete detachment!

Hence it is that he forgets himself and the entire creation on account of this dazzling divine light. On account of this forgetfulness, all awareness of self is lost. There is no calling upon the name or observance of customs; awareness of whether one exists or not; explanation, allusion, or divine throne! In this world, all things pass away (Q55:26). There is no splendor except at this stage. Here, "everything perishes except His essence" (Q28:88). Here alone is God actually seen face to face. Apart from here, one finds no trace of the Truth! "I am the Holy One!" The absolutely unhampered realization of the Unique Being occurs only in this stage.

> Do not delude yourself, instead remember,
> Not everyone who gets lost in God becomes God!

Consider an example from the world around us: the nut consists of (1) the outer shell, (2) the inner skin, (3) the kernel, and (4) the essence of the kernel itself, its oil. All four constitute the nut, but each is different in its importance and possible uses, as anyone can easily see. In a similar fashion all the aforementioned refer to belief in divine Unity, although in degrees, fruits, benefits, and gains there are thousands of distinctions. This letter should be given careful, detailed consideration, for it will be found to be the foundation of all stages, states, activities, and ecstatic phenomena. It will also help the reader to understand the sayings and allusions of religious leaders, when he peruses their writings, for that is what God is like. They will not fall into error. Also, it can throw light upon the foundation and lawfulness of verses dealing with divine Unity and its various degrees, a matter in which one and all can be deceived and in which contradictions may arise.

Brother, you are now but an ant, yet you can become a Solomon. Do not be preoccupied with your sinfulness. Though you might now be fainthearted, you can develop great courage. Do not lay stress on your present impure and mean condition, but rather on what it is possible for you to achieve. For many long years there have been followers of the Way. Consider Adam; he came from mud and water. Though an orphan raised by Abu Talib, Muhammad became the messenger of God. From Azar the idol-maker came Abraham, the Friend of God. Consider also how polytheists have become monotheists; unbelievers, believers; sinners, followers of the Way, and mischief-makers, peacemakers![8] Neither is God's might dependent on man's obedience, nor is His Grace determined by man's sin. [A conversion story follows.]

*Peace!*


LETTER 2: REPENTANCE

*In the name of God, the Merciful, the Compassionate!*

Dear brother Shamsuddin, God's bounty be upon you! Realize that sincere repentance is like a beautiful carpet on which you perform your devotions. God has said: "Turn toward God in repentance, believing that you might triumph!" (Q24:31). This verse was revealed to the companions of the Prophet and all repented and became models of abjuring infidelity and embracing faith in the one true God. Turning their backs on sin, they submitted themselves entirely to God, Who has ordained repentance for all. Some of the more noted companions asked what the revelation meant. The Prophet replied that repentance is incumbent upon all, at every hour and at every moment. Infidels should renounce their infidelity and become true believers; sinners should turn aside from their sins and observe God's commandments; those already doing good should progress from what is good to what is still better; those standing still should not linger in the courtyard but come straight up to His door; while those immersed in the affairs of this world should not sink lower into them, but rise to the pinnacle of detachment. It would be a sin for a pilgrim who has already ascended to a certain stage if he were to descend to a lower one. One should turn away from all sorts of greed. There is no room for complacency, since there is always a higher state than the one the pilgrim happens to be in. He must always press on! There is a command in the Law: "Walk ahead of those who travel alone."

Moses said, "I have repented before You" (Q7:143). That is to say, I turned from myself to You because of my passionate desire to see Your Face.[9] This is an example of turning away from something good in itself to something infinitely better. The Prophet said, "I beg for pardon seventy times a day." For him, seeking pardon meant advancing from what was of some merit to what was of much greater merit; to proceed from one stage to a higher one—this is the divine command. A person in the first stage cannot hope to have the repentance of someone in the second. "The virtues of the righteous seem to be sins for those closest to God."

The actual meaning of repentance is "turning back." There are, however, many ways of turning back, which vary according to the stages, the actions, and the stations of those who repent. Ordinary people, out of fear of punishment, turn from oppressive behavior to being sorry. The elect turn away from their evil deeds because they have become cognizant of their obligation to revere their Master. The elect of the elect, perceiving the insignificance and instability of all creatures and, indeed, their nothingness in the light of the glory of the Maker, are able to turn away from all that is not God.

Once this has been grasped it should be noted that repentance, although it does not happen "once and for all," does not thereby cease to be genuine. If a penitent person, after resolving not to fall into a particular sin again, through negligence actually does so, he can heed the command to repent, consider its merit, and rejoin the ranks of the penitent. Once a man made a resolution in this fashion but again fell. Immediately he went to the shrine of a saint. One of the sheikhs there told him: "By the mercy of God I repented seventy times and each time I fell again, but after I begged pardon for the seventy-first time, I fell no more!" He also told him of another person who had made a similar resolve and after falling again, he hesitated to return to the shrine. "How do I know what is my present spiritual state?" he asked himself. He then heard a voice within him say, "You submitted yourself to Me and I forgave you your sins. Again you were unfaithful and spurned Me. Now I have given you time to repent. If you wish to return, I shall receive you in peace."

Zu'l-Nun Misri expressed the collective view of the great Sheikhs when he said: "The repentance of ordinary people is from sinning again, the repentance of the elect, from being negligent again, but the repentance of prophets consists in seeing clearly their own paltriness, and in realizing that they have arrived at the state of prophethood without having done anything to merit it." Khwaja Suhail Tushtari, with many others, is of the opinion that people should not forget the sins of the past but keep them continually in mind so that, despite having much to boast about, they will not grow proud. Khwaja Junaid, along with many supporters, thinks that repentance means forgetting entirely about sins of the past, since the penitent person should become a lover, and for the lover the mere remembrance of an injustice is itself an injustice. If we look only at the outward expression of these two positions there is an apparent contradiction, but actually they say the same thing, for the meaning of "forgetting" is to expunge the attraction of sin from our hearts to such an extent that one could say that it is as if no sin at all had been committed! As Khwaja Junaid said, "I have read extensively but found nothing as profitable as this couplet:

When I asked about my sins, Love replied:
"Your very existence is a sin beyond comparison to any other."

O brother,[10] the hour of death lies in ambush! Every moment of reprieve is precious, for the angel of death will suddenly show himself. An old man came up to a saintly man and said, "O man of God, I want to repent of the many sins that afflict my conscience." "You have waited too long," replied the saint. "But I came quickly," protested the old man. "Explain yourself," ordered the saint. "If a man finally repents before dying, even though he has delayed for years, it is quick [i.e., expedient]," replied the old man.

O brother, take heart, no matter how sin-stained you may be, you can be sure that you are not more stained than Pharaoh[11] was with all his magic nor more defiled than the dog of the Sleepers of the Cave, nor harder than the stone of Mt. Sinai, nor of less value than a slat of wood!

Even if a slave is purchased from Abyssinia, what harm is there if his master calls him "Snow White"!

[An anecdote about angels follows.]

You saw my faults from head to toe, but still purchased me:
How shoddy are the goods, how gracious is the buyer!

*Peace!*

## LETTER 3: RECONCILING OFFENDED PARTIES

*In the name of God, the Merciful, the Compassionate!*

Brother Shamsuddin, may Almighty God grant you eternal peace and the perfection of His grace! Prayers and greetings! Study the words that follow and try to grasp their meaning, namely that, after repentance, the task that falls to the lot of the beginner is the reconciling of people who have fallen out with one another. This next step is important since all sins are of three kinds. The first is the abandonment of what has been required of you, such as prayer, fasting, and so on. A person ought to perform all of these to the maximum extent possible. The second category of sin is that between the creature and the Lord. Examples of these are wine drinking, usury, listening to musical instruments, and similar activities. A person should strive to extricate himself from these sins and to attain the state of repentance, and he should also resolve firmly not to commit them again in the future. The third type of sin is between you and other men. This is still harder and more difficult to correct than the sins already mentioned. There are various kinds of conflicts—some concern property, others one's soul and body, still others women and slave girls, and also religion!

With regard to goods, it is necessary, whenever possible, to return anything illegally obtained to its rightful owner. If you are not in a position to return his goods, you should ask the owner to remit your debt to him. If he is dead, do some deeds of charity for the welfare of his soul. If you cannot do this, perform other good deeds, seeking pardon for him as he stands in judgment. Turn your heart to the Lord, humbling yourself and pleading for help so that He, of His bountiful generosity, might be pleased with you on the Day of Resurrection.

As for what concerns your soul, consult one of God's saints; he will know whether punishment or pardon awaits you. If this is not possible, turn to God Himself in supplication and lamentation, so that the One against whom you have sinned may become your friend on the Day of Resurrection.

As for what is done through the body, such as backbiting, blaming, or troubling others in various ways, it is necessary for you to admit your backbiting to the person concerned and to seek his forgiveness. If you sense that he may become angry with you, it is still good to grasp at the opportune moment, and to remain calm. If, however, he becomes incensed whenever you speak, then turn back to God and implore forgiveness on his account! If he has died, perform some good work for his soul.

With respect to the treatment of women and slave girls, it is not opportune to ask for forgiveness and bring the matter into the open. That situation should be handled by turning to God so that He may be happy with you on the Day of Judgment. Remain calm, even in the face of God's increased anger—though such is rare—and seek His forgiveness.

As for what concerns religion itself, such as making another person into an unbeliever, or leading him astray in matters of faith, this also presents difficulties. You must first of all accuse yourself of having lied and ask forgiveness of the person whom you have misled, if this is possible. Otherwise, turn back to God Almighty and plead with Him continuously until God Himself fills that person with happiness!

What needs to be grasped in the present chapter is this: As far as possible, make your peace with anyone who has a legitimate grudge against you.[12] If you cannot do this, turn to Almighty God, humbling yourself and crying out for help from a righteous heart so that, on the Day of Resurrection, God Himself might be happy with you. Be confident that, when the Lord realizes how sincere-hearted His servant is, He, out of the infinite treasure of His mercy, will make your adversary happy.[13] If you act in accordance with what has been said and wholeheartedly turn away from sin, all will go well. But if you have omitted obligatory duties in the past and done nothing about it, or if you have not taken pains to be reconciled to your enemies, then punishment awaits you. Unforgiven sins, you should realize, form a chasm that is difficult to cross and fraught with baneful consequences and dangers! [A tradition from Khwaja Abu Ishaq Isfahani follows.]

O brother, the slave of sin faces a veritable calamity. First comes the sin of hardening one's heart, which ultimately leads to unbelief and wretchedness. May God protect us from such things! And do not forget the wiles of Satan and Balaam! The works of both were sinful from the very beginning and, at the end, both became unbelievers. A pious person once said that a black heart comes from indifference to committing sin, coupled with the absence of any desire to submit oneself to God. If you heed sound advice, however, this baneful effect will not afflict you. For goodness sake do not act like a fool, be swift to repent! No one knows the hour of death. And if after repenting you chance to be defeated and fall again, hurry back to the state of repentance, saying to yourself, "It is possible for me to die before sinning again!" In the same way after the second, third, fourth, and indeed after each and every relapse, repent! Do not be more sluggish in repenting than you are in sinning! Be aware of not succumbing to Satan's attempt to prevent you from repenting of your sins! If you say "What's the point of repenting this time? I know very well that I shall sin in the future by failing to remain steadfast in my sorrow for sins! How does repenting profit me?"

Know that such ideas are really the way Satan deceives people. Who has informed you that you will remain alive until such time as you do not sin again? You could easily die before then. The very fact that you are afraid of sinning again indicates that you do sincerely repent, even though it is God alone who can effect the radical transformation of a person's heart. If this is your desire but you have, in point of fact, only turned incompletely from your past sins, then, providing you are aiming at complete holiness in your life, no sins will actually stain your soul, except the fresh ones that you might commit! This is greatly to your advantage.

Even should you yield to fear and sin again and so fail to remain in a state of perfect repentance, at least one of two possible benefits will accrue to you. Have you never heard that the Prophet once said, "The best of you is he who, when he sins much, repents much"? The heart of the matter of repentance is that you earnestly resolve to abandon sin. Only God knows if you will sin again in the future but, as far as possible, you should appease anyone whom you have offended and adhere to those of His ordinances that you have neglected. As for the rest, return to God with lamentation and supplication. Take a purificatory bath, put on clean clothes, and perform four prostrations of formal prayer—and make sure all this proceeds from the core of your heart! Then, in some deserted place where no one except God Almighty can see you, put your face to the earth; throw dust on your head and rub your face in it too! With tears in your eyes and a heart filled with compunction and grief, recite, one by one, the sins of your whole life and rebuke your soul in this fashion: "O soul, the time has come for you to repent and turn to Almighty God." Since you do not have enough strength to bear patiently the divine punishment, nor do you have the means to save yourself from it, raise your hands in supplication and pray words such as these: "O Exalted One, your servant flees to your door! Your sinful servant makes peace. He comes forward with his humble request for forgiveness. Graciously accept me! Look mercifully upon me! O Lord, forgive me, and wipe away all my sins, for goodness belongs to You alone, O forgiving and merciful One!"

If a drop of sin should appear,
How could it possibly be seen in such an ocean?

[Other prayers follow.]

Pray and seek forgiveness for all Muslims and occupy yourself with worship till you experience a heartfelt sorrow and emerge purified from your sins—as though this were the very day your mother gave birth to you! God will befriend you and lavish rewards and merits upon you, as well as blessings and mercies beyond description. Thus you will finally be purified from the affliction and calamities of both this world and the next.

O brother, if you wished to be accepted without faults, you should not have been created with defects! Know for certain that Adam was not expelled from paradise for eating wheat[14]—he himself wanted to be expelled! On the Day of Resurrection, thousands upon thousands of sinners will find rest in paradise whereas Adam, for one small fault, was expelled from it. If you say that Adam, in paradise, was disobedient in order that he might be expelled, then what did our Prophet do "at the distance of two bow lengths" (Q53:9) that he was brought back from there to here? Although he was taken to the highest heaven in order that the angels might learn reverence from his prayers, he was brought back here so that men might learn from his mode of worship how the Law was meant to be observed! There he said: "There is no limit to the praise due You." Here he said: "I am the most eloquent of the Arabs. Bow down in worship in every possible way. Bring before God any petition or desire you might have!" There he said, "It is You whom I worship, O God Most High." God replied, "Accept everything that has been given." When he said, "We implore help from You!" (Q1:4) God replied, "Give him whatever he wants!" The Royal Treasury will be a source of joy to beggars, among whom none is more aware of his indigence than this particle of dust!

Heaven and earth, throne and footstool, all exude His fragrance, but He does not decrease by a single particle! Indeed, there is no treasury like God's! From it, the needs of every creature are met a thousand times over. He has given and will continue to give every possible dispensation to those who are penitent.

*Peace!*

## LETTER 4: THE RENEWAL OF REPENTANCE

*In the name of God, the Merciful, the Compassionate!*

Brother Shamsuddin, may God bless you with the special blessing granted to the penitent! Many requests have come that something should be written on a variety of topics and that some warnings be given. I was also somewhat weary for a time, too, and this will account for the fact that a number of letters on the same topic were written in succession. They should be studied very carefully and the meaning of their contents verified with Qazi Sadruddin. The meaning of this injunction is simply that, since Qazi Sadruddin is there at the moment, consulting him will remove any difficulty you may experience. As far as possible, press on, for the real task is not to fail for a single hour in the task of renewing one's penitence for sin. Maintain a high resolve[15] in this task, for it is Almighty God Who helps a man achieve genuine repentance. The basis of spiritual work is repentance, just as its crowning achievement is faith.

Who travels this path? It is Faith! And who is it that bears this burden, if not Faith? Who cuts through the engulfing wilderness? Faith does! And who but Faith could traverse this bottomless ocean?

The very sweetness you taste is that of Faith! To whom does this pain you endure belong if not to Faith? Who reveals the way of seeking? Faith! Whenever repentance appears, there too is Faith. Indeed, the sun of Faith warms each breast to the extent that it is penitent. It is as though the door to the threshold of repentance, once it is flung open, allows the sun of Faith to warm the interior.

The reality of repentance requires a radical shift in one's basic nature. Whoever commands a novice to undergo a forty-day retreat commands it for the sake of this change, in order that his very nature might be transformed. When he has been fully converted, he becomes another person, not in the sense that a different man appears in front of you but, since his qualities have changed, he too has changed. His essence remains the same yet it hardly matters, for now a completely different faith, a real faith, appears in him.

Before his conversion, there had been nothing but conventional faith and movement of the tongue, as is the case with most people. On this point someone said:

How long will you worship God only with your tongue?
That amounts to worshiping the air!
Until you become a Muslim inwardly,
How can you be a Muslim outwardly?

This lame-ass of conventional faith and empty utterances that you and I possess cannot suffice for traveling along the Way; nor can it bear the burden or cut through the engulfing wilderness; nor can it taste the divine sweetness. It would be like a mosquito trying to carry the load of an elephant! As the poet said:

Not everyone knows how to deal with wealth;
Not every ass can carry the Messiah's weight!

Who but Rakhsh, for instance, could bear the weight of Rustam?

Due to the vast scope of this stage and the genuinely terrifying aspect of this work, O brother, you should not let yourself grow slack, nor allow aversion to show its face and tempt you to flee from the fray altogether! Recall the teaching of the prophets: Keep away from things that are beyond your strength! This fear should not be discussed, either in speech or in writing. No one, no matter what state he is in, should be fainthearted! Here terms like "work" make no sense, nor is there question of "paying" for what you get! For instance, we could cite cases of people who had been raised so swiftly from idolatry that the place of protestation before the idol was still warm and yet they went beyond the angels and the spheres of heaven, and were endowed with such virtues that even if men, jinn, and angels were to go in search of them, no trace of them would be found! Turning back, the men, jinn, and angels would ask: "What's going on? What has happened here?" The blessed ones would reply, "He does what He pleases!" (Q85:16). In His Presence, "how" and "why" carry no weight! "Motive" finds no entry here! Return these terms to the world of men from which they came! There they have meaning. May the Most High God grant my brother this vision of himself, exalting him beyond himself with the same mercy and favor shown to the Prophet and his descendants! Every time you feel low, take heart!

O brother, the courage of real men does not descend upon just anybody. Neither heaven nor earth, nor throne nor footstool, nor even hell itself could bear the burden of this resolution of theirs! It has been said:

> Neither the pain of hell nor the pleasure of heaven affects
>     them.
> Members of this group have been so molded
> That they grasp only for the very presence of God,
> And what is not "He" they fling far behind!

The high resolve of these men is like a devout consummation, or a holy desert devoid of either inhabitants or their refuse, a veritable place of rest! Nothing holier than this can be created, just as no desert can match the expanse of the divine Unity. Such courage is not found at the Kaaba or in Jerusalem, nor does it revolve in unison with the heavens and earth. God be praised for this wonderful work, that a man can be sitting at home, feet tucked up under the folds of his robe, his head placed on his knees as he ponders the divine secret! Though it is beyond the boundary of such a high resolve, you cannot find it except in dust and water! In this sense it has been said that Sufism permits no stasis. Remember that water left to stand becomes stagnant! A man should retire to his own corner, settle there, and the divine secret will appear to him in both the realm of death and the realm of activity.

Rapid movement, as you know, appears different from what it really is. A millstone, for example, if it picks up good speed, could easily be taken as being stationary by a person glancing at it! Some friends asked Khwaja Junaid why he did not participate in musical assemblies. In response, Junaid quoted them the Quranic verse: "You think the mountains are firmly fixed, but they will pass away like clouds (Q27:90). Because of its speed, you do not perceive my experience of ecstasy: How do you tell someone who has never seen it about the morning breeze?"

*Peace!*

## LETTER 5: SEARCHING FOR A SPIRITUAL GUIDE

*In the name of God, the Merciful, the Compassionate!*

My brother Shamsuddin, may God honor you in both worlds! You should know that according to the unanimous opinion of famous saints of the Way, a novice, after undergoing genuine repentance, should seek a spiritual guide. He should be perfect, well versed in the vicissitudes of the Way, and firmly established in his high state. In short, he should be a man who has experienced both the horror of God's majesty and the delight of His beauty. "The learned are the descendants of the prophets." With regard to the spiritual guide, all these qualities should have been realized in his person. He should be a physician skilled in the knowledge of medicines and the types of treatment to be applied to the defects and ailments for which the novice is seeking a cure. God Himself has said: "Associate with the righteous" (Q9:119), that is, associate with the prophets. After them come the great sheikhs, who are the successors to the prophets, since "the learned are the descendants of the prophets." It is a Tradition of explaining the process of succession. "My learned ones are like the prophets of the People of Israel" is a related Tradition as is the declaration that "a sheikh in his community is like a prophet in his." This is especially true if the people have no means of acquiring instruction in the path of religion from a prophet. [Three illustrative quotes follow.]

In the beginning, there was no need either for a prophet or a sheikh, because the seed is such that it requires nothing except the divine grace in order to fall into the soil of one's heart: "God guides whomsoever He wishes!" (Q42:52). Wherever that seed is found, some form of guidance, either through the role of a prophet or that of a sheikh, the prophet's deputy, is necessary. As the Quran has attested:

25

"Surely you guide to the straight path" (Q42:52). And also one finds many theological arguments in Sufi works on this topic. Among them we have created a group who guide with the truth (Q7:181). One runs as follows: It is beyond dispute that the road to the Kaaba is clear and well known but, without a guide, someone who himself knows the way, a person cannot travel along it. It is not enough to be able to see the road with one's eyes and have enough strength in one's legs. Imagine what it must be like on that Road along which 124,000 prophets have traveled, and yet no trace of their journey remains! Without a guide who knows the way, it is impossible to travel along this Road.

Remember, too, that an ordinary road is infested with thieves and robbers, so that one cannot travel along it without an escort. As for the mystic Way, the world, one's ego, devils, men, and jinn all infest this Way, thus making it impossible to travel along it without an experienced, holy man as one's escort. Remember, further, that there are many slippery places where it is easy to fall. And one can be plagued with misfortune and dangers from behind! Many philosophers and worldly minded people, as well as others lacking faith, piety, or any semblance of morality—have become followers of their own base desires. They have gone without a perfect sheikh or leader who has reached his goal on this Way, and have instead trusted in their own intellectual powers. They entered the wilderness where they fell and perished, losing even their faith.

> You are an ant; the Way is like the long tresses of beauty.
> Beware, O man, of merely guessing or blindly following
>  others.

But the blessed ones, protected by the riches of the saints, have passed beyond those hidden dangers and arrived safely at their destination. They managed to progress without mishap and, along the way, have themselves seen where each has fallen, and also the extent of his corruption. Other travelers who managed to avoid misfortunes and pass successfully through various trials at last succumbed to lassitude! If the sheikh is possessed of supernatural powers, he will be able to protect the novice from either falling or languishing during his struggles. The explanations and subtle hints of the sheikh can also guide the novice to the proper way of acting. Otherwise, the novice will fall into dissipation or formalism and will lose whatever he has labored to gain!

Seek the shade of a guide, O blind one!
He will serve you better than any staff.
Humble yourself like straw! Shatter the mountain of pride
That the guide may become a magnet for you!
If you do not do this, then heed the words of Attar:
"Every sorrow you endure will be lost to the wind."

The pilgrim treading this Path will have to pass through several spiritual stages.[16] When his soul is stripped bare of its outer garment, a ray of the divine light will illumine it, and the soul might even, in this state, perform a miracle as an agent of God. In the experience of divine union, such as was expressed in the "I am the Truth" of al-Hallaj, and the "Praise be to me" of Bistami, it is possible to become proud of being blissfully united to one's Goal. It becomes apparent that, although endowed with intellect, knowledge, and understanding, such a person is nevertheless unable to exercise true perception. If, in this condition, a sheikh who is well versed in spiritual matters does not guide him, there would be great fear that he might lose his faith and fall into the wilderness of imagining himself as God incarnate or as one identical with God! In the course of his pilgrimage, he should expect to be assailed by spiritual crises. Also, various types of mystical experiences might occur; some might be satanic, others might be produced by his own ego, still others could come from the Merciful One Himself. This is all entirely new to the novice and he cannot discern the source of these spiritual experiences. He needs the assistance of one well versed in discerning these various spirits, in the same way as cocks alone understand the crowing of their peers. In the words of a poet:

How can you comprehend the language of cocks,
Since you have never met a Solomon?

At this stage the novice can by no means make progress unless he has a God-assisted sheikh to help him, a teacher who is widely experienced in the understanding of spiritual matters.

If someone is keen on gaining admission to the presence of the king in order to acquire rank and position or a province or palace or a post near the king, and if he has nothing to merit such gifts from the hands of the king, then he will have to make friends with one of the close associates of the king and bind himself to that person because the latter is a confidant of the king. When the confidant advocates the case of another, the king does not pay attention to the absence of genuine claims and services rendered by the petitioner, for his attention is on the acceptable qualities of his confidant. The king cannot ignore what he says but, on the contrary, accedes to his request. If the petitioner by himself had tried for many long years he would not have obtained what he wanted. In a similar way, the sheikhs are kings close to the King, and their requests are acceptable to Him. All those who come to the sheikhs and bind themselves to the sheikhs attain what they desire. The sheikhs, by their clear glances and purity, learn many secrets and grasp the suggestions contained in the Quran and the traditions of the Prophet, such as references to the Path, the Heart, and the Way. In order to help novices, the sheikhs draw conclusions from first principles and, according to these conclusions, issue instructions to guide them.

The first instruction applies to the moment when God Almighty opens the eyes of someone to his deeds so that he can judge the good as good and the evil as evil. There then wells up within him the intention of expunging the latter, but he does not know how to set about doing so. What must he do? He should visit some holy person who lives in a religious sanctuary and bind himself to him with the determination of changing his way of life. He hopes that one of God's cherished ones will accept him, fallen and lost as he is, and release him from the vice of ungodly selfishness that grips him. Second, if any blemish or defect comes to light, the guide should, in a gentle and compassionate manner, induce the novice to abstain from such things. Third, the guide should keep him away from bad acquaintances and unsuitable companions, and should also forbid him to listen to their conversation. All that it would take the novice a year to accomplish by himself can be finished off in an hour with the proper guide! The same holds true in other matters.

It is only possible for the novice to reach an advanced stage with a spiritual guide through whose assistance he obtains his desire. The novice might have to associate with two, three, four, or even more guides in order to reach his Goal. Each guide and each association would become for him the revelation of a stage, but it would be better if he made no slur about the guide's own stage of spiritual growth. Nor should he point out that the guide has only attained to some particular stage. He should say: "It was allotted to me to get this far from my association with him. He must have gone higher than this!" This is a more polite way of talking. The really mature ones of the Way of the Lord Most High do not preoccupy themselves with stages and states. If you are associated with a guide, you should not depart from that place without his permission nor, on your own initiative, dissociate yourself from him. This condition should be kept in mind. If the novice goes to another guide, or sets out on a fruitless search without the permission of his own guide, he will not achieve what he desires! Everyone who acts in such a manner becomes a renegade of the Way. According to the understanding of the sheikhs, such a person has really abandoned the Way.

When a novice begins to associate with a spiritual guide, he will have to spend three years in three types of training. If he stands firm in obeying these orders, he can then don the real garb of the seeker, and not merely the conventional one. Unless this procedure is followed, experienced guides insist that the novice cannot be accepted into the Way. The three requirements are: one year's service on behalf of other people, one year devoted to God, and another year spent in watching over one's own heart. A novice's hands should be wide open in prayer and his tongue moving in supplication, for the prayers of those who weep and moan find favor in God's eyes. At such times, the veil of modesty is lifted, and what one desires should be asked for importunately. Ask for whatever you wish, and do not get caught up with trifles! Do not leave the divine threshold or cut yourself off from Him! You should know that He has lavished everything freely upon men. Faith, as well as the forgiveness of sins, has been freely bestowed. He is the One who can bestow the whole world if He wants to. "Is there anyone who begs to be heard? Is there anyone who seeks? Is there anyone who implores forgiveness?" Something within stirred me up: "Ask Me; for my generosity knows no bounds! I command you to ask! If you do not, I shall press you for being lax. I give even what has not been asked for."

> Even what is not asked for He grants;
> If you ask, imagine what He will give.
> He is a King: If He so wishes,
> He can bestow both worlds upon a beggar!

O brother, all this flows from the divine bounty. There should be no talk of claims here, since His generosity means that He gives without making any claims. Where there is a question of "what is due" one cannot talk of generosity, since claims make us feel obligated to someone. Once obligation enters, debt comes as well and requiting a debt cannot be considered generosity! [An anecdote of Ali's generosity follows.]

*Peace!*

### LETTER 6: THE QUALIFICATIONS OF A SHEIKH

*In the name of God, the Merciful, the Compassionate!*

Dear brother Shamsuddin, may God honor you in both worlds! It should be noted that the foundation of the qualifications and claims to rank of a sheikh or religious leader rests, in brief, on five supports. These have been extracted from the following Quranic verse: "They [Moses and a companion] found a servant [Khizr] from among Our servants to whom We had shown mercy and blessed by granting him whom we had taught knowledge" (Q18:65). From ourselves when God sent Moses to Khwaja Khizr for his initiation and instruction, Khizr taught Moses the five stages to becoming a sheikh, a religious leader, and a teacher! The first is the submission of servanthood common to our servants; the second is an aptitude to receive truths directly from God without any intermediary; the third is a submission distinguishable from the first submission by a very special grace; the fourth is the honor of receiving divine knowledge of God without any intermediary; and the fifth is the riches of receiving infused knowledge. These five stages, taken together, comprise all that is meant by perfection in its various levels, explanations, and details, even though it cannot be set forth in a single letter like this.

The sheikh should be experienced in these specialized affairs. He becomes well qualified in them by having passed through them all himself. Generally speaking, each stage has its own goodness and is well supported by various traditions. Much material is available for the first stage, and is readily accessible to the sheikh. Until he is freed from servitude to all that is not God, he cannot become a servant of God. The second stage—the capability of receiving truths directly from God without any intermediary—is impossible until you emerge completely from the natural man with all his disordered inclinations. This is also the precondition for experiencing God's special mercy.

But the special favor of closeness to God that constitutes the third stage is not granted to those who simply imitate what other people do. More is required before the luster of divinity can shine on a person's head and enable him to attain this high post of intimacy with God. At the fourth stage one acquires knowledge of God without any intermediary. So long as the tablet of the heart is not wiped clean of knowledge obtained by the intellect, or by hearing, or by sense perception, it remains impure and cannot receive knowledge without an intermediary. The special aspect of the fifth stage is that it conveys infused knowledge inclusive of not only the essence and actions of God but also the divine essence. The Prophet has said: "I recognized my Lord by means of my Lord." Jesus the Prophet also said: "A man cannot be reckoned among the host of angels in heaven and on earth, that is, those who have attained divine illumination, unless he be born again!" This stage is not obtained simply by the act of being born from a human mother; a once-born person sees only this world, but everyone who is born again from himself, that is, one who emerges from bondage to his human inclinations, will see the other world. Both this world and the world to come are evident—that is what it means to be born again.

It has also been said that the hierarchy of stages and the various ranks of religious leadership are not contained within limits and numbers. Being a sheikh is not a question of personal appearance, that is, the contour of one's face or beard, by which people may discern that such-and-such is a sheikh. To be a sheikh is to experience great intimacy with God. As has been said, "The saints dwell under My domes. Except for Me, no one can recognize them."

> Those who travel along this Way live by the life of Another;
> The birds flying in His air come from the nest of Another.
> Do not look at them with your earthly eye, since they
> Belong neither to this world nor the next but Another.

Here a question arises: Where will a novice find a sheikh like this, and how can he submit himself entirely to him? By what means can he recognize him as being *the* man? This is no easy matter, for it is unseemly that a novice go around weighing men of God in the scale of his feeble intellect, or should hope that he can see by his limited vision who has attained divine communion and become intimate with God! Nor is it fitting that anyone should follow another on the mere assertion of a third party. How, then, can the novice know that such-and-such a sheikh is a genuine teacher, a seeker who has become perfectly proficient and already attained his goal?

The answer given is this: Each one of those who seek God has been allotted all that is necessary for him and in the measure that is required! It is fitting that he should be completely unable to go beyond what has been destined for him exactly as it has been decreed and measured out for him, since along this Way not even a straw falls by the wayside. The lot of each student has been measured out from the very beginning and no one can place a hindrance of any sort in his path.[17]

Another question arises: Is there any sign to distinguish a pretender from a genuine teacher, or one who is capable from one who is incompetent? The answer given is that there are many signs, but it is difficult to interpret them; there is no sign that subsumes all the others, nor is there a single one to which we could point and say, "This certainly shows he is a sheikh!" or, if it is not present, that he is not a sheikh. In short, it has been said about someone who has been previously favored, "God has favored his servants before the creation of earth and water!" Those people who struggle on Our behalf (Q29:69) and place their feet on the path of seeking due to the irresistible attraction of the divine favor should turn their hearts away from their all-too-familiar sloth and the sinful delights of their soul, as has been divinely decreed from the beginning of time. The beauty of the sheikh who has attained his end and become perfected is mirrored in his heart. The seeker desires that the sheikh be a pilgrim himself, not an ecstatic, since such people do not make suitable sheikhs, although they, too, may experience ecstasies. But the ecstasy of sheikhs is of a different order. It hallows them, enables them to teach and guide others, and is quite different from unrestrained ecstasy. When a righteous novice perceives, in his own heart, the beauty of a sheikh, he becomes enamored of the beauty of his saintliness, draws peace and contentment from him, and begins his search. The origin of all goodness is a certain uneasiness; this is how a lover is born. Until the novice falls completely in love with the beauty and saintliness of the sheikh, he will not come under the full influence of his guidance. The novice should follow the wishes of the sheikh, not his own! In this respect it has been said: "Discipleship is the abandonment of all one's own desires."

O heart, if you seek the pleasure of the Beloved,
It is necessary to do and say what He commands.
If He says, "Shed tears of blood!" do not ask, "Why?"
If He says, "Give your life!" do not quibble about protocol.

Sheikhs who have attained differing stages are in disagreement about whom they should call "novice" and whom they should call the "desired one" or sheikh. Some say this: The person who enters the company of great and saintly persons and submits himself to their orders regarding activities and meditations can be called a novice, while the other person is the desired one, that is, the sheikh. Others say that you can call anyone a novice when a perfect sheikh, a saintly man, a mystic, or a learned man takes a pair of scissors in his hand and, having run it over the novice's head, accepts him. Such a person becomes a novice, while the one using the scissors is called a desired one, or a sheikh. In truth, when God's servants submit to the Prophet and, moving ahead, find that they get lost in the resplendent qualities of His beauty and His majesty, then they reach the stage described in the tradition: "When I make him my friend, I become his ears, eyes, hands, and tongue."

If you cast a kindly and inspiring glance toward a stranger, he becomes one of you; and if your glance falls on a sinner, he submits; and if it falls on one who has already submitted himself to God, then he will be placed on the throne of saintliness.

It is said that there is no nook or cranny where a saintly teacher cannot be found. Even if such a place were to exist, it would still be under the protection of the shadow of His bounty and there will remain no distinction between his will and the will of God, and he will breathe the divine inspiration in every breath, to such an extent that he comes to exemplify the tradition "Whoever is for God, God is for him." There is only one caliph and sultan for an age, but ordinary teachers, like vegetable sellers, are found in every town. [An expression of the intercessory power of the saints follows.]

O brother, know for certain that this work has been going on since long before you or I appeared! Each person has arrived at his resting place and the stage he has attained has been made clear. There is no one who has begun a completely new work. That which was ordained has now become manifest in its entirety. Do you think that any of the 124,000 prophets who entered this world brought a new revelation with him? Not at all! On the contrary, they have stirred up what was in your heart and turned your attention to what God has ordained. The purpose of books and prophets and intermediaries is merely to propel you forward to the established goal. [A saying of Abul Hasan Kharaqani is quoted.]

*Peace!*

LETTER 7: DISCIPLESHIP

*In the name of God, the Merciful, the Compassionate!*

Brother Shamsuddin, discipleship is a matter of wanting something from the heart. Our inner musings are related to some particular thing. As a result of our thinking about it, a certain uneasiness arises in our hearts. This produces the determination to seek the thing itself. The more esteemed the desired object, the better and nobler it is to seek it. The desire of God is wholly pure, stripped of anything base, untainted by selfishness, and free from inconstancy. It will be enriched by God Himself, Who will remove any obstacle that might obstruct its attainment. In this way a person can enter the divine world.

As long as heaven and hell clutter your mind.
How can your soul become aware of this secret?
When you have been liberated from both these places,
Will this wealth burst forth like down from the shades of
    evening?

A determined man will have to face up to a number of obstacles and impediments. They may be caused by weakness of purpose, or frailty, or something else that hinders the attainment of the desired Object. Even the desire for a good name or praise can become an impediment. A sincere novice is one who resolves to be purified of all pleasures and self-interest. If he turns away from the whole world but remains hesitant about one object, then that will remain as an obstacle for him! "If a slave requires only one silver piece for his manumission, he still remains a slave!" Purposefulness in the Way is like intentionality in the Law, for the Law says that all worship performed without an intention [to praise God] has no value. Similarly, in the

Way, every enterprise that is without a purpose or desire has no consequence. There are three kinds of desire:[18]

1. Desire of the world. When a man is totally immersed in seeking the world, his desire is an unmitigated calamity, a mortal illness! When it clouds the heart of the beginner, it is an obstacle to all virtuous deeds. Troubles appear on his way and, on the Day of Resurrection, everyone whose intention has been engrossed by desire of the world will be deprived of comfort and eternal happiness, as has been said, "There is an obstacle between them and what they desire" (Q34:54). Experienced saints have noted that no probity can be expected from a novice who remains inclined toward the world from the outset. Everything that is beyond the minimum necessary for strength and sustenance will turn out to be the cause for their repentance and sighing on the Day of Ressurection!

2. Desire for the things to come. This desire manifests itself when a man's heart progresses beyond the present world and eternal bliss becomes his fervent desire. He undergoes many austerities, adopts ascetic practices, and purifies his life all for the sake of his heart's desire, that, on the Day of Resurrection, he might attain the coveted Object. This is what ascetical and devout people want and hence it has been called "longing and fearing." The Quran has alluded to both kinds of desire: "There are those among you who seek this world, and those among you who seek the next world" (Q3:15). The latter is eternal, while the former is merely ephemeral. Covetous people become the disciples of this world; pious folk, disciples of the world to come.

3. The third desire is for God Himself. It arises when the vision of God is disclosed to a man and he courageously passes beyond all creatures, indeed beyond all things that are under the sway of the divine command, but remain merely created signs of the Master. By groping after something trifling and created, a person exalts nothing but his own baseness. But whoever seeks the shade of the canopy of the Honor of both worlds himself gains honor in both; as the Quran says: "Tell the person who desired honor that all honors are from God" (Q35:10). The God-seeking novice has gone beyond this world but at the same time is not content with the world to come. Everything that comes between himself and the Object he desires and yearns for is reckoned as a Brahmin's thread[19] or an idol. Someone asked a saint: "What is an idol?" The saint replied, "Whatever diverts you from God is your idol." Everything that preoccupies you with

other than God is, therefore, an idol. A person should gird up his loins in preparation for this quest and set out manfully along the path of religion, following some compassionate spiritual guide so that the latter might help him to tread the Way and inform him of the dangers of each stage, and thus prevent him from being cut off at any stage, or from falling into any sin or fault. For such a novice nothing is more important than a compassionate guide.

People say that a tree that springs up by itself does not give fruit, and if it does, the fruit is tasteless. The activities, states, and all the works of a novice who lacks a guide are devoid of originality and become routinized. They do not help him to mature or progress since a novice, at the beginning, is like an undifferentiated mass of sound and corrupt elements. When a sick person, out of contempt for others, tries to cure himself, he falls into destruction. He should seek out an experienced physician who can provide a remedy for his illness. Just as people need a prophet; a child, a nurse; a sick man, a physician; a thirsty person, water; and a hungry one, bread—so too a novice needs a compassionate guide. He should be a man who has experienced the divine Presence and is acquainted with the intricate questions concerning the various stages of the Way, so that he can appreciate what facilitates and what impedes progress along it. When there is someone at hand who grasps the nature and causes of sicknesses and knows what syrups and potions should be prescribed, how does it benefit a novice to rely on himself? It would be like a person who, though ignorant of the Way, acts as a guide and is thus destroyed. It is said that, if a novice wants to learn all about these states from books, he becomes exactly like someone who associates with the dead—and he too becomes dead at heart!

All knowledge is based on this premise, that students follow the instructions of their teachers, and that people are obedient to their prophets. So, too, a novice should show respect to a righteous spiritual guide in order to obtain salvation. They say that everyone who sets out upon the Way thinking that he is self-sufficient and is content with his own company, that man remains a proud idolater and will never delve deeply into the treasure trove nor attain a prominent position.

In this connection, take note that by no means is it within the power of any guide to make an unruly novice into an earnest seeker, just as the Prophet could not make a rejected people into sincere believers. Moreover, since God Almighty Himself has laid the foundation for the treasure of Islam, this very foundation becomes manifest when a person heeds the call of the Prophet. Similarly, the benefits of Sufism and the secrets of the Way will be manifest only while the novice is living with his guide and being of service to him—provided that the requisite foundation already exists!

Once you have understood what discipleship is, then know further that the desire of the righteous and the intention of the sincere do not come from you or me nor are they your work or mine! For you or for me, to wear the sacred thread or to worship idols is equally inappropriate. A church or a temple is not a place fit for us, nor would any idol or idol shrine accept us. What are we to do? We cannot falsely lay claim to being disciples. Nor can we boast about being Muslims. What place do we have among righteous and sincere believers? It may well be that they draw us into the crowd of liars and boasters.

> Even if no bouquet can be made from us,
> Still, we may be fit brambles for the fire-pot!

This saying is completely true: "It is better to be in this sanctuary, even under false pretenses, than to be anywhere else!" If nothing ever happened to you, how could you grow in goodness? Look how many people there are who set out on the road and suddenly the One referred to in these sayings comes and throws the halter of yearning for Himself around their necks—something they had never imagined or desired! If this is not His wish, then do not bother entertaining even the slightest hope. But if He wants it, you have no reason to be afraid. Look, the verdict has already been written down and the unseen Judge has signed it!

*Peace!*

LETTER 8: SAINTHOOD

*In the name of God, the Merciful, the Compassionate!*

Dearest brother Qazi Sadruddin, may the blessing of God and the love of the saints be yours! [A depiction of sainthood with reference to Arabic grammar is set forth.] A saint, then, is a person who continuously enjoys the divine favor in all his activities and becomes one of those protected by God. In general, the states of his soul are free from troubles, but the difficult state for him to sustain is sinlessness. God Almighty continues to keep him free from base and serious sins! Just as a prophet is preserved from sin, so too is a saint protected. The difference between a "preserved" and a "protected" one consists in this: The preserved one [i.e., a prophet] is completely preserved from committing sins, but a protected one [i.e., a saint] may commit a sin from time to time, without, however, persisting in that sin. Surely repentance with God is intended only for "those people who sin out of ignorance and immediately repent" (Q4:17).

Every quality needed for giving counsel and explaining things is granted to the saint. Indeed, all these qualities necessarily are present in him, just as there is necessarily absent from him defects in his relationship with God, or in his constancy in interceding before God on behalf of His creation. The saint is also obedient, but not out of fear of the next world, or due to hope for reward in paradise. He has no regard for his own soul nor does he measure his own actions.

> Those who have seen the path to the world of divine Unity
> Have unconsciously been running toward It!
> When in denial they see the ultimate meaning of affirming,
> They abandon affirmation altogether, and embrace negation!

The hints of the sheikhs in this connection contain the following. According to Khwaja Abu Usman Maghribi, "Even if a saint becomes famous, he will not be seduced by fame!" Another sheikh has observed that a saint should remain hidden; but if he happens to become famous, then the saying that "he abstained from publicity" should be taken to mean that publicity could lead toward a temptation to find glory in fame but, of itself, it is not sinful, since by means of his sanctity a saint can resist temptation and remain just. It is related that Khwaja Ibrahim Adham said to someone: "Do you want to be one of God's saints?" When the man replied that he did, the sheikh exclaimed: "Then don't go hankering after this world or the next! Free your heart for the sake of friendship with God, and turn your heart toward Him. You will become a saint when these conditions are present within you!"

> Go beyond yourself. And then
> Journey in My world toward Me!
> Shut your eyes tightly, and then,
> In My Presence, look at Me!

Give up that precious soul of yours
And then, O Khwaja, learn from Me!
Whatever you prize in your little world,
Bring it forward and place it at My door!

The aim of this is to enable you to experience God Almighty Himself! It is fitting that the lives of saints are changed into ones of special friendship and sanctity. The saints of His kingdom realize that they are His chosen ones. By means of a variety of special miracles, they become both signs and the radiant manifestation of His own activity. He frees them from natural calamities and from dependency on the natural inclinations of their souls, thus demonstrating that neither their courage nor their love exists apart from Him. This is what has put them ahead of us and that is where they will be on the Day of Resurrection. In this matter, we have two opposing groups. One is the Mutazilites,[20] and the other is the common people. The Mutazilites deny that anyone has a privileged position among the faithful, while the common people allow room for special favors, but at the same time allege that no such privileged people now exist. (Others say that saints have an influence in this world.)

Place your steps manfully on this Way,
Since the heavens themselves revolve in your service.
You are blissfully asleep, while those upon His Way
All kiss the dust that marks His threshold!
They proceed in silence, with their heads bowed low,
Their tongues cut out and strewn along the Way!
In comparison to that mine where souls are His jewels,
The firmament has always been but dust upon His threshold!

Among them are four thousand "concealed ones" who do not recognize one another and who do not know the beauty of their own state. In all their states they remain hidden from both themselves and the people. News comes from this and the saying of the sheikhs is understood in this, that there are those who are authorized to loose and to bind and are the guards at the gateway to God. [A description of the Sufi hierarchy follows.]

In their activities, all of these both recognize and depend on one another. The speakers who relate this Tradition are unanimous in affirming its correctness. At this stage someone might dissent saying, "You claim that they recognize one another and know each other to be saints. If this is so, then it would be necessary to postulate that they are at peace concerning their future life—but this is inappropriate." The answer to this objection is that knowledge of one's sanctity does not imply complete reassurance, just as a believer who becomes Sufi as a result of his own deep faith cannot thereby be perfectly at ease about the future. In a similar way, it is fitting that a saint should be aware of his own sanctity, yet not completely at ease. It is good, nonetheless, if, by way of a miracle on the part of the Almighty, he can be assured of his end and remain secure in God, experiencing both the correctness of the state of his soul and his protection from opposition. There are examples of such people, namely, the ten people about whom the Prophet testified that they are among the people of paradise. Because of his assertion, they were at peace and not at all anxious about their end. They are among the group of saints. Yet their contentment about their final end did not impair their religious practice.

You might object that they claim this knowledge from the Prophet, but revelation, by which he himself had this knowledge, came to an end with him. How can people nowadays know without revelation? The answer is that they are aware of their own saintliness by means of the fact that God Almighty has put within them a very fine sense, a special gift that, except for the saints, is not found elsewhere, and certainly not in His enemies. It is proper that God Almighty[21] should effect this peace within them, and that they should discover His own secret, in order that they might realize that it is a miracle and a gift from Him, and that which it purports to predict really will come about. In such people there is no deception, pretext, or vacillation.

On the other hand, a person who is beguiled and deceived would be one who, as soon as anything of a miraculous nature comes to light, is content with the miracle itself, and considers himself a miracle worker. Anyone who considers that he is a temple of sanctity, however, does not rest content with what is miraculous, nor does he pride himself with being a miracle worker. The two attitudes are contradictory, and we know that a mutual contradiction cannot be sustained, since the nature of one would highlight the contradictory demands of the other. This is the way the venerable Sufis look at miracles, as one of them has said: "There are many idols in the world, one of which is miraculous concurrences." Just as infidels, because of their attachment to some idol, are enemies of God but can become saints by cutting themselves off from their idols, so too do Sufis have their idols, namely, miracles! If they become satisfied with miracles, they will be put to shame and be dismissed from the divine Presence, but if they cut themselves off from miracles, they move closer to God and become united to Him!

> For the ascetics, heaven and paradise are places to be reached;
> For lovers, there is no delight but in the depths of a prison.
> The common and the elect, good and bad, all enjoy His grace,
> But to confront His violence is the work of the manly.

From this it is clear that when God Almighty confers something miraculous upon them, submission and humility increase in their hearts, at the same time that docility and courtesy, along with dread and fear, are also enhanced. The king of mystics, Abu Yazid Bistami, at one stage on his journey came to the edge of a large expanse of water that needed a boat to be crossed. He did not have one, but he began to experience that he was crossing it without a boat. In this state, he traversed a path that appeared in the water until, coming to his senses, he exclaimed, "Fraud! Fraud!" and returned. There is a delicate mystery here, and it is this: Genuine sanctity is connected with rejecting all that is not the Friend. Everything must be abandoned for the sake of God. Abandoning and seizing are opposites, as are acceptance and rejection. Whenever a person accepts miracles, allowing himself to be captivated by them, and putting his trust in them, he is not rejecting but is accepting something other than the Friend! There can be no sanctity without rejection.

O brother, there is no room for despair! As the Quran testifies, "Say, O you My servants, who have dissipated your souls, look at God's mercy and do not despair! (Q39:53). O you who gaze reverentially on the sanctity and purity of prophecy, look at some of those immersed in the impurities of sin, and convey the secrets of my love that washes away their sins in the water of forgiveness. "Pardon them, and ask God to forgive them and accept their repentance" (Q3:159) so that they might not turn aside from the door on account of the shamefulness of their sins but, with all the strength of their hearts, grasp the rope of hope. Then they will know that the waves of the ocean of His mercy purify sinners from the impurities of their sinfulness as well as from the attraction of things prohibited. These waves of forgiveness both purify them and enable them to attain the wealth of His vision. "Surely God forgives all sins" (Q39:53). A tested saint has hinted at this condition in the following quotation:

If you are caught in the harness of love,
Yet manage to pass beyond desire, you will be happy.
Your being will be purified from its garment of sin,
And you will become fit to receive the divine secrets!

Listen to what is said in the Psalms of David: "O David, warn the righteous ones that I am very sensitive, but give sinners the good news that I forgive sins!" This divine fire consumes the root of hopelessness and destroys the young shoots of despondency and pessimism, bringing to light the secret of "Don't despair of the mercy of God" (Q39:53).

*Peace!*

LETTER 9: SAINTLINESS

*In the name of God, the Merciful, the Compassionate!*

Dear brother Qazi Sadruddin,[22] may you be honored by God! You should know that commonplace saintliness is rooted in faith. Every person who embraces the Muslim faith becomes a member of the congregation of God's saints! Often, however, there is more than a suspicion that, along with this type of saintliness, there is sin and the commission of forbidden things. There are others who fulfill what is commanded and shun what is prohibited. People doing this should be counted among the saints. The various groups are like the squadrons of an army—a special one in front, ordinary troops to the side, and a very special one in the center! These hand-picked troopers not only obey commands and shun prohibited things, they also bring to heel their own desires. Their regard is not on what is due them; instead, whatever their Friend wants is the very thing they themselves desire! Giving priority to what He wants, they disregard their own desires. They understand what is idolatrous, since they know that the basis of all idolatry is connected with yielding to our own selfish desires. The Quran hints at this when it says: "Have you seen him who makes a god of his own desires?" (Q25:43). Here it is necessary to understand exactly what idolatry is in order to avoid falling into some fault in this matter.

One kind of idolatry is called "manifest"; it occurs when a person substitutes something else for God. This form of idolatry is forbidden by the very principles of the faith. May God preserve us from it! The second type is called "covert"; it occurs when a person considers something other than God as necessary, and seizes upon that thing as desirable. Some say that, for Sufis, idolatry is to take note of the existence of anything but God! Others say that covert idolatry is tantamount to relying upon oneself in all circumstances; desiring with one's own power; and accepting advice and stratagems in any undertaking that comes up. Such covert idolatry is prohibited by the perfection of divine Unity, if not by the explicit principles of the Law!

> When I fell into the abyss of Your Unity,
> The thought of no other came to me,
> Neither of men nor angels, in Your Unity:
> I, a slave, gazed on You and became free!

Everyone knows that you need friends if you want to become great! It is fitting that there are groups of the elect, of common people and of those who observe "command and prohibition." Beyond these, however, there is a special group worthy of becoming boon companions. And beyond these is the class that is fit for divine secrets. And beyond these comes the group of those on terms of intimate friendship with God. Here, if either party wants anything that belongs to the other, his inclination will be simply to give it, for the mutual usage of goods is such that everything is considered common. In this way, any trace of mistrust departs from them. There is an example of this in the Law. The venerable Sufis have said: "There are commands for common people and matters of license for the elect, since the Prophet[23] himself has condoned the latter." For example, he said to an Arab who had broken his fast in the month of Ramzan: "Eat and also feed your wife and children! It is lawful for you, but not for anyone else." This was clearly an abrogation. For ordinary people, he paid attention to the actual extent to which things are commanded or prohibited. But for foreigners he amended the Law, giving them permission to keep some of their customs, even in face of the claims of the Law and thus showing, in a special way, his friendship toward them. "I am one of that elect who can do as he sees fit with respect to their possessions." [A poem of Khwaja Sanai is then quoted.]

There is no doubt that all prophets are equal in respect to prophecy, yet they differ from one another in the matter of grace, just as all believers, though on the same level with respect to faith, vary in virtue. One group has attained only the common level, while others rise to a privileged rank. Anyone who denies this is denying what can be plainly seen. Consider an earthly king who has soldiers in abundance, men who are bound completely to his orders and dependent on him for their sustenance. Among them some are grooms, while others are carpet layers, doorkeepers, chamberlains, treasurers, cupbearers, army commanders, ministers, and boon companions. Still others reach such privileged positions that the king entrusts the seal of the kingdom to them, so that whatever such a person commands becomes the command of the king himself. The same is true of any prohibition or appointment he makes. All this is clear to an intelligent man.

Similarly, believers, with respect to their faith, occupy graduated, orderly ranks. When they are in these grades we have described, then each, in his position, is "special," since there are people below him, but, at the same time, he is "ordinary," for there are others above him. The particular rank of the saints becomes apparent when they have become the elect of God. This stage is attained when the apparent merges with the hidden and they become one. The elect neither oppose, think, nor discuss things with their inner selves. In seeing the Master, they forget about their own needs. They would not exchange their Friend even for both worlds. They are so immersed in gazing upon Him that the question of hope no longer arises, so immersed in fear of Him that they are afraid of nothing else, so immersed in love of Him that his absence makes them desolate, so immersed in remembering Him that nothing except Him enters their memory. Everything about them, visible and hidden, within the sphere of their spiritual powers, becomes so absorbed in the Friend that nothing remains in them except Him!

> If, in love, you are despoiled of your qualities,
> You will go beyond your self and become a lover!
> Some quality may appear and then disappear,
> So do not put any stock in it, lest you be ashamed!

When a person reaches this stage with respect to his desires for himself, the hold of his self, and even his spiritual and personal qualities, he becomes utterly lost to himself; he is rooted and fixed in the qualities and desire of his Friend! Everything he wishes is fulfilled, not because the desire of something other than his Friend has arisen in him, but because his own desire has become the desire of his Friend. Indeed, it is in him that the friend manifests His own desire and whatever makes its appearance is really the Friend's desire, not his own. People might judge that he wants something or other but, as far as he himself is concerned, it would mean that his Friend desired something in a special way. This privileged rank cannot be denied; and yet some say, "It's your groundless boasting! It is not genuine!" [A poem follows.]

When they reach the stage under discussion, saints become aware that they are God's elect in accord with the famous saying "The absence of any desire is the precondition of saintliness," and they see themselves as desireless. If saintliness requires a lack of self-control, then they consider themselves to have no say in their actions. All desires come from their Friend while they, of themselves, desire nothing, as the King of the Prophets has testified: "If they swear by God, then what they want will surely be granted." But the presupposition of this is that they do not swear, yet if they do they will get what they ask for in God's name. The Prophet was also indicating that although the saints get whatever they want, they actually do not want anything! [A poem follows.]

The regard of the saint is always on his Lord. "The saint is protected from self-interest; therefore pride does not enter him." In other words, all those who attain this stage do not become self-seekers since, at this stage, their attention is not on themselves. If the foundation of this stage is lost, however, then the whole work disintegrates.

> As long as anything remains with you, you are in your own
>    essence;
> The Kaaba, due to your worship, becomes a tavern!
> If anything emanates from your essence, you are still far off:
> You are like a temple facing the Kaaba![24]

"Saints have been despoiled of human qualities." A saint should withdraw from human company, for weeping is an antidote to fame! "May they not be put to the test!" In other words, let the people find nothing to reprove in them that might make them stumble! Dependency on other people comes from two things, their reproach or their praise, both of which are inimical to true religion. There is a mystery in the fact that anybody who venerates, as the sign of the soundness of his worship, becomes blind to any other than the One venerated. If pride is interwoven in this veneration, then a person has really seen his own soul, not God. He is venerating that, not God. Whenever hypocrisy is found along with veneration, mankind has been seen, not God. The person is venerating them, not God. Since he worships his own soul and mankind and desires things other than

God, it is all deceit—"A saint is protected from the evils of human nature and yet the form of his human nature remains rooted within him." Keeping himself untainted by earthly things does not occur simply by the fact that the desire of something is no longer in him. Nor is it sufficient reason for praising and blessing him for, if such were the case—that is, that he had no desire for anything unseemly—this could simply mean that, from the beginning, he had been impotent and bereft of the means required for acquiring such things. Strictly speaking, it would not be an instance of something prohibited but of something precluded. How could he be praised, blessed, or given a reward for refraining from doing something he was unable to do in the first place?

For men, there is a reward for obedience to God and a punishment for rebellion against Him. Angels, on the other hand, do not have the means of disobeying: For them there is no question of abandoning rebellion or of practicing obedience. They can neither reward nor punish. Man, however, has a human nature and takes pleasure in the things he wants. For the common man this would mean that he prefers what he wants to what God commands. Saints, however, prefer the command of God to what they themselves desire. The difference, O brother, consists in this: You should not remain unaffected by the pain of this human condition and the impulse to escape it, but should not, at the same time, be without hope, for justice and grace are His qualities. He is just. He keeps watch over what He commands. He knows our weakness. And since His justice makes Him interested in His own commands, it is He who does the work of the people, from the first to the last! Since He also insists on showering his grace-filled glances upon our helplessness, our work gets done, our sins are transformed into good deeds, and our faults become virtues. What place is there for lack of hope? A destitute creature has said:

Do not be without hope today, O heart, for
Tomorrow His glance will be on His own command!

O brother, whoever among us has been stained by the impurities of sin or has consented to forbidden things will be cleansed by water from the cloud of grace and benevolence Himself! Who can disgrace us tomorrow in the presence of the prophets and the saints, and the whole host of God's creation? A mature saint has said:

Even if a lover be captured by sin,
Or become enamored of the cup of intoxication, still
Why should he fear a multitude of blunders,
For the Beloved is One who keeps secrets and veils sins!

*Peace!*

### LETTER 10: THE MIRACLES OF SAINTS

*In the name of God, the Merciful, the Compassionate!*

[N.B. For the sake of convenience, the word used to denote a prophetic miracle (*mujizat*) is translated with a capital *M*, whereas the word for the miracle of a saint or the miraculous in general (*karamat*) is translated with a small *m*.]

Dearest brother Shamsuddin, may God's blessings be upon you! The orthodox doctors of the Law agree with the mystics that the miracles of the saints are admissible, even if they occasionally attain the status of Miracles. The Mutazilites, however, do not admit them, except as something that could be common to both sinners and obedient Muslims. They say it could be an answer to prayer, for example, if someone in a desert, perishing with thirst, finds a spring of water; or if someone gives him a glass of water to drink; of if a host offers bread to a ravenous person. They maintain that when one of God's slaves acquires faith, he advances from the stage of hostility to that of holiness, and since holiness can lay claim to miracles—on the argument that equality is implicit in the meaning of holiness—then it should be that all have equal power to command!

The answer to the Mutazilite position is that the holiness that comes with faith does embrace all, and at this stage, both he who sins and he who submits are equal, as are the prophet and the nonprophet. But real sanctity is something different, and it requires special miracles. Just as a king has an army and all are equal insofar as they have postings, yet the prime minister and the chamberlain will have a thousand miracles to display, while a doorkeeper or a carpet layer will not. One could say that if God Almighty wants a prophet to display his prophethood, he should do so by a miracle. Yet if a nonprophet were also capable of such Miracles, doubt would arise. How could genuine prophethood be displayed? The net result would be that a prophet would not be distinguishable from a nonprophet. The answer to this difficulty is that a genuine saint says exactly the same thing as a prophet and desires the same thing he desires. In addition to this, he states clearly, "In whatever I have discovered, I have found confirmation of Him, but note, I myself am not a prophet!" The display of miraculous powers on the part of a saint is a confirmation of the Prophet; the truth of his claim is thus borne out, and no doubt should arise. [A legal example is cited.]

One might say: "How can it be that a saint can perform miracles? It is a forcible breach of the natural order for him to reach the very boundary of Miracles! Will he then make a claim to prophethood?" But this is impossible, since truthfulness of speech is a precondition of saintliness. A claim against what is genuine would be a lie, and no liar can be a saint! Someone might say, "How can you assert that a Miracle goes contrary to the laws of nature and yet is an indication of the genuineness of a prophet? If you admit the same thing for a nonprophet, its occurrence would become routinized and it would no longer remain the sign of a genuine prophet."

I would not agree with your persistent concern, namely, that the miracles of the saints could usurp the proper role of the Miracle of the prophet, which is defined as an act contrary to the natural course of affairs. The reason is that the miracles of the community are The Miracle of the Prophet. Just as the Law continues to remain, so should the proof of its authenticity! We can say that the saints bear witness to the genuineness of the gift of prophecy that the Prophet exercises until the very Day of Resurrection. If you ask what the difference between a Miracle and a miracle is, it should be stated that in a Miracle, one finds the revelation of the condition, whereas in a miracle, it remains hidden. Also, the prophets know that a Miracle is to occur and give news of it in advance, whereas saints do not have information about a miracle before it comes to pass.

This is the basis for saying that there is really no proof that a saint has acquired saintliness until he considers himself the lowliest of all creatures.[25] If he sees himself in this fashion, how could he go around claiming to perform miracles? Since there can be no such claim, a fortiori how could he give news of the coming occurrence of such? It is also said that those who seek anything from God except God Himself can never attain genuine saintliness. If a person claims to be a miracle worker, it means that he has sought something other than the Friend. This would banish saintliness rather than prove its existence.

When you have grasped so much, ponder it carefully! It is not fitting for God to grant Miracles, which He reserves for just men, to any liar who lays claim to prophethood. A prophet is a just man and a confirmer of the truth. It is therefore necessary to put one's faith in him, whereas a false prophet is a liar and a mutilator, in whom it is not proper to put one's faith. A speaker of the truth should be separated from one who defaces it, and that would be by a Miracle. If, however, Miracles were to emanate from both, nothing would remain by which to distinguish the mutilator, nor would it be clear to the people whom they should trust. Thus a resemblance would arise between the truthful man and the liar. What a dreadful prospect! Moreover, the sheikhs of this group[26] and all the Sunnis agree that it is appropriate that any act that constitutes a forcible breach of what normally occurs, like a Miracle of the prophets or of the saints, even if it occurs at the hands of an infidel, should produce no doubt in anyone's mind that might lead to deception. [The example of Pharaoh is cited: Though he laid claim to divinity through his miraculous deeds, any intelligent man could perceive that he was not God.]

Deception means that someone pretends to save, but actually destroys. The deceiver confers honor, but brings subjection. He points out the way, but induces error. With enemies there is this defect: No matter what they give, it is all obstinacy and deception! Thus we have three forms of behavior: For the prophets, there are Miracles; for the saints, miracles; for enemies, deception and obstinacy. [Yet another list is mentioned.] An obstinate and fraudulent sinner prides himself on what he does and places his trust in it. He considers himself deserving of praise and displays arrogance toward others. A genuinely good man, however, flees from miracles and is afraid of them. He cries out to God for help, and even holds his own body in contempt. The venerable Sufis have noted that in most cases, preoccupation with miracles indicates the extent to which a person is satisfied with what is not God. Eventually a withdrawal from God Himself will appear.

Consider, for instance, the mother who wants her child to get away from her or to go outside. She gives him some sweet to eat. If the child is intelligent, he prefers to cling to his mother's skirt; but if he is foolish, he takes the sweet, rejoices, and goes outside, where he either falls into the water or under the feet of some passing animal. His attention is only on the sweet and not on how far away from his mother he is. Taking the sweet, the foolish child left his mother; but if he had continued holding on to her skirt, the sweet would also have been his.

A group of venerable Sufis has said that miracles are simply color and decoration, meant to help people a little. Every camel that people look after carefully, decorate and parade around the town, is honored by the people during this display, at the same time that the knife for the sacrifice is being quietly honed. If its throat were not destined to be cut, then all this preparation would be for nought. A sheikh has said: "There are many idols[27] in the world. A miracle is one of these." As long as infidels are associated with idols, they remain God's enemies. When they turn away from idols and sever all connections with them, they become saints. In the same way, a miracle can become the idol of a mystic! If he is content with miracles, he will one day be filled with shame! By not turning away from miracles, he makes idols of them. Thus he cannot come close to the God who has been revealed to him!

> May it never happen, O dearest "idol" of mine,[28]
> That love of You should depart my heart, or thought of You,
>   my mind!
> Even if You seek my death there will remain
> That taste for You in my rotting bones.

[Further elaboration, a story of Bayazid, and a couplet follow.]

> God forbid that my heart should ever become separated from
>   You,
> Or that it should grow intimate with anyone other than You.
> Diverted from love of You, whom would it love?
> If it were to quit your lane, where would it go?

To conclude, O brother, have you not heard that "there is life at the beginning of love, but death at the end?" And also that "there is deceit at the beginning, but death at the end!" and again, that "in the beginning there are miracles, but grief at the end!" It is with reference to such a situation that someone has said, "Misfortunes are required for love, just as salt is needed in the cauldron."

Comforting it is to experience pain on account of the friend who is also a physician daily visiting the home of his sick.

Do you know who such a person is? It is everyone endowed with beauty who is not a lover of himself, and does not usurp, on account of his own beauty, the praise due to God, for he should be such that, if tomorrow there were to come an announcement, "Look at Me!" he would say, "It is impossible! How could such Beauty be seen by eyes such as mine?" Someone has said:

> No matter how much you try, you will never describe that
>   union.
> It is beyond the reach of the tongue or the power of utterance.

O brother, on that day that the carpet of love will be spread, all will throw their preconceived desires into the fire, for it has been decreed that they all belong to the Beloved! Total absence of desire is the lot of the lover. Hence it is that they say: "He is merciful and compassionate toward ordinary slaves; but with lovers He is a King who accomplishes whatever He wants!" [The sufferings of Noah, Abraham, Jacob and Joseph are briefly reiterated.]

> He does all these things yet, out of godly fear,
> The true man does not utter even a single sigh!
> For His face is like a mirror:
> One sigh would cloud it over!

*Peace!*

## LETTER 11: THE STATES OF THE RIGHTEOUS

*In the name of God, the Merciful, the Compassionate!*

Dearest Brother Shamsuddin, the states of the righteous are an ocean of purity, though it has been said, "If they be an ocean, how can one grasp their meaning?" Those whose souls have alighted at the treasury of favors, and whose hearts are mines of divine secrets experience already the separation of good from bad, which is a special feature of the Day of Resurrection! Promises and threats concerning them are made clear to them here and now. What is a threat for others is a source of peace for them. Both this world and the next obey them, and they are also not bypassed in either this world or the next! One evening, Khwaja Junaid decided to go to the mosque. When he arrived at the door, he saw a glowering person in front of the door. He said, "Who are you, for my heart is set against you?" "I am Satan," he replied, "you wanted to see me." He said, "I have a question to ask you." "Ask away!" He said: "Do you have any power over God's friends?" "No," was the reply. "How is that?" I inquired. He said: "If I want to snare them in this world, they fly to the next. If I want to catch them in the next world, they fly to the Lord Himself, where it is impossible for me to go." One of God's beloved has given us this hint:

> All who have been taught the gambit of love
> Have been set ablaze with love's eternal flame.
> The heart brought to perfection for union with Him,
> Its eyes sewn together, returns not to either world!

Then he said: "O accursed one, who would believe that you could tell us about their secrets?" He replied, "True, but there is one occasion when I know what is manifested in them, and that is when, during a prayer-gathering, they fall into ecstasy." Saying this, he disappeared. Junaid grew perplexed and, wrapped in thought, entered the mosque. A voice came to him from the corner of the mosque: "O son, do not be deceived by the speech of this enemy! Since the saints of God are so precious to Him, why should he reveal to this enemy things He does not even show to Gabriel or Michael?" Junaid saw that it was his spiritual guide, Khwaja Sari Saqati, and he was relieved. [The hidden life of Khwaja Uways Qarani is mentioned approvingly.] Tomorrow, one of the many favors of God for His just ones will be to make them strangers to their own tribes. Thus would the saying be fulfilled: "Have I not caused the memory of you to languish?" In this very lane I have been plundered for your sake so that the night patrol might not grasp the skirt of your name and reputation. A frenzied lover has thrown some light on the meaning of this saying:

> Have you seen what idolaters do in a temple?
> What small hands can do to your narrow mouth?
> I am intoxicated with You, so treat me gently,
> For you know, O idol, what intoxicated people can do?

Sheikh Ibrahim Shabih was, in his time, a man to be imitated. His every prayer for the righteous was this: "O Lord, just as You have made me forgotten in the hearts of the people, so also make me forget them, so that no one will recognize me, nor I them!" From this, leaders endowed with perception say that, if people speak truthfully, they will acknowledge that their mutual acquaintance is unhealthy, except in those friendships that are fostered for the sake of God Almighty, as it is said in the Quran: "On that day, friends will become enemies of one another, except for the God fearing" (Q43:67). [The attitude of Abul Hasan Nuri is then praised.]

O brother, what sort of name would you like to have at your death? The blessed ones have given this precept: Whatever is received and manifested to anyone today should not be promulgated, even by a person admitted to the seven heavens, nor should speeches filled with love be made concerning it! The very place where a person slides away from the faith is where, in the future, the Resurrection itself will be revealed, since the Chosen One gave this information concerning Khwaja Uways Qarani: Among the righteous companions, on the Day of Resurrection, the blessed ones will be told, "You will go into the abode of peace!" But to Uways Qarani, "the sun of the Day of Resurrection today shines fiercely. Come into the shadow of the divine throne and dedicate your righteous tongue to interceding for the sinners of the community, since it is my wish to bring into paradise today as many sinners of the community of Muhammad as there are hairs on the sheep of the tribes of Rabi and Mizar." While he was in the world, Uways conducted himself in such a way before other people that no one in the tribe where he lived was more humble than he. People used to throw large stones at him, play tricks on him, and inflict every sort of indignity on him. The Chosen One, at the height of his prophethood, described the increase of his spiritual wealth in these words: "I detect the breath of the Merciful One coming from Yemen!" The secret of this is contained in what has been said:

> O lover, if you set your foot in my alley,
> Be prepared that moment to lose name and fame!
> How much illumination can you expect
> If you set out with a candle as your light?

When Haram ibn Hayan saw Uways, he said: "O Uways, tell me some tradition about the Prophet of God that I might recollect in your name!" He said, "I do not have the strength for that task, that men should crowd me and make me a traditionist or a judge or a canon lawyer. I have a more important occupation than these. Please excuse me! If even a particle of the divine secret enters my heart, how can I turn around and become a traditionist? I have been sealed with 'There is no god but God.' It does not allow me to pass on to anything else. My regret at not finding Him in the boasting of lordship is like a flame raging within me! That choicest morsel, divine Unity, has made me a stranger to both worlds. The divine secrets have singed my heart with everlasting anguish. The blemish of my penury has undermined my security! The trial of not finding Him has dashed my hopes to pieces! Yet the praise of the Chosen One has fixed upon me the epithet 'endowed with great purity.'" The secret of this Tradition, "I detect the breath of the Merciful One coming from Yemen," is indicated in unending anguish. One troubled at heart has said:

> Union with You does not quell the anguish of my tormented
>     heart,
> Nor is this thirst quenched by your refreshing water.
> Drained of vitality my existence slips away.
> Yet my soul is still stirred by the love of Your beauty.

Sufis say that no sound is closer to the Lord than that of a person wailing over his sinfulness! Today it is fitting that the righteous ones of this Way to the Lord of religion should learn lamentation for sin from Uways Qarani.

O brother, anyone who is not crying and lamenting at every moment of his life is a vain person, full of negligence with respect to the Day of Resurrection. He is as good as dead. He should be full of grief over the opportunities of today that are lost as a result of insatiable appetites. How can there be knowledge of God if life is limited to maintaining and seeking position and dignity, observing commands and prohibitions, practicing disdain and negligence, honor, worldly pride and self-flattery?

> Sacrifice your life; union with Him is not granted to mere
>     friends!
> Only the intoxicated no longer drink milk from the goblet of
>     the Law.
> That place where all men will drink wine together
> Is where no worshiper of self will receive a drop!

O brother, as far as possible, spend your life in tasks of humble repentance and seek protection in the shadow of the bounty of some renowned religious figure. Seek out a saintly friend, for he will be a veritable treasure for you. As for withdrawing from human company, realize that you cannot travel along the road of religion without a friend. If you say, "What should I do? It is not easy for me to find such a friend. Remove from my back the weight of the robe of love that weighs upon my infidel soul!" Do not participate in its infidelity, for it will give your life to the wind and will plunder your religion; it will make you a stranger on the Day of Resurrection; it will make you well acquainted with the world; it will utter secret insinuations concerning your spiritual treasure; it will destroy the mansion of your faith; daily your ardor for it will increase, and hourly your love for it will grow. You should know that, in reality, this soul is the enemy of God's religion! Consider it as your enemy, so that you may turn back and become faithful to your religion. Do not be intimate with people; otherwise the angels will become jealous. One mature Sufi has said:

> When my soul had almost expired out of love for the Beloved,
> I said, "Do not settle for union with yourself, My Guest."
> He replied, "If you want to be fit for union with Me,
> Do not allow a 'you' in yourself! There should only remain an
> 'I'!"

[Some particular prayers, known for their efficacy, are then reiterated.]

*Peace!*


LETTER 12: LIGHTS

*In the name of God, the Merciful, the Compassionate!*

Dear brother Shamsuddin, may God Almighty illumine your soul with the lights of his knowledge! When the mirror of the heart is thoroughly cleansed of the rust of human nature and selfish qualities, it becomes capable of reflecting lights from the extrasensory world. In the beginning, the nature of these lights is comparable to flashes of lightning and illuminations. As purity of heart increases, so too do the power and frequency of these lights. What first appeared as lightning gradually becomes more like a lamp, or a candle, or a torch, or a flaming fire. Then sublime lights appear. At first they appear as stars, both small and large. Then they become more like the moon until, in time, they rival the sun itself. You should know that every light that initially appears as a flash of lightning or an illumination becomes still greater after being blessed by the ritual ablutions and prayers.

Once a disciple of Sheikh Abu Sa'id Abul Khair, after performing his ablutions, entered the place of prayer and there saw a light. "I have seen God!" he shouted. The sheikh, on being told about his state, said: "You have seen nothing. That was the light of your ablution. What a gulf exists between you and that Pure One!" If there were no shadow veiling the wealth of that Ancient One, the unfortunate person who tries to see Him would be utterly destroyed! When, however, lights like those of lamps, candles, or torches and other suchlike things are seen, they then come from the sanctity of the sheikh or from the Lord of Prophecy, and the lamp and candle of the heart are illuminated to that extent. If a person sees lights that are comparable to various types of chandeliers, that would mean that he has seen what was just stated. But if he sees them in the form of sublime lights, such as the stars, moon, or the sun, then they are generally held to be spiritual entities manifest in a pure form on the highest stratum of the soul.

When the heart has been so purified that it can reflect stars as though in a mirror, then the light of the soul appears like a star. If a person sees the moon, and it is full, know that the heart has been completely purified. If it has any blemish, then to that extent it is opaque. When the mirror of the heart attains the perfection of purity, it becomes capable of reflecting the spiritual light, which is seen as being like the sun. As purity increases, so too does its sunlike effulgence until the time arrives when its light is a thousand times more luminous than that of the sun. If a person sees both the sun and the moon on one occasion, he should recognize the moon as his heart illuminated by the reflection of the light of his soul. The sun is his very soul.

Yet till God comes forth from His concealment so that the thought of Him might be compared to the face of the sun, verily the light of the soul remains without form or features! Sometimes it happens that rays of the lights of the divine attributes extend a welcome, as is written, "Whosoever comes to Me, even the distance of a hand, is brought forward a whole yard." From behind the veil of spiritual things and the affairs of the heart, a divine reflection is projected onto the mirror of the heart, which, to the extent of its purity, reflects in turn what it has received. If someone says, "How can we know that the rays are the light of the divine attributes?" the following answer is given: It is due to the lights of divine attributes that the heart becomes illuminated. That very light makes Him known. Yet, in truth, it is He Himself who praises Himself. A sense of inner bliss arises within him so that in that very bliss a person knows that what he is seeing is from God Almighty and not from any other source!

As to the meaning of this bliss, it is difficult to explain. It has been said that the attributes of divine beauty are illuminative but not scorching, while the attributes of His majesty are scorching but not illuminative. Here the mind and intellect are of no help. Sometimes it may happen that this purity of heart attains perfection. "We have given them our signs in the heavens and in themselves" (Q41:53). As a notable Sufi has said: "I have not looked at anything without seeing the Lord in it; and when the light of God throws a reflection on the light of the soul, the vision is mixed with bliss." When, however, the light of God Almighty comes into view without the veil of soul or heart, it becomes perfectly clear. There is no color, quality, limit, comparison, or contrast to it. It itself is the stability and firm support of all existing beings! Here there remains neither rising nor setting, right nor left, height nor depth, space nor time, near nor far, day nor night, neither earth nor world nor heaven itself. Here the pen breaks; the tongue is tied; the intellect sinks into the pit of nothingness, while understanding and knowledge are lost in the wilderness of amazement. You might now be pining out of grief that you are in the stage of being distant from Him. Actually, the grief of not having found Him is better than the pain of being close to Him! In amazement one finds that amazement itself is the prelude to loss, while grief is the means of finding and gaining access to Him. Verily it is imperative to clear one's ego out of the way, while the garment of human nature should be nought but dust. Dust should only be viewed as dust, to remove the danger that a person might esteem himself. Indeed, whoever esteems himself has made a eunuch of himself!

In the time of Adam there was a certain person who called attention to himself repeatedly. He was the leader of the angels. Yet when he preened himself, he became a eunuch who looked like a woman. He was given the embellished house of the world so that in the eyes of base people he appeared clean and respectable. Thus did God do violence to Satan in creating him. Yet He showered His blessings on this handful of dust in also creating him. He exalted the one, while disgracing the other. He demeaned Satan, who became completely unacceptable to Him, while He accepted Adam, pledging never to turn away from him again.

Do you know what this means? Wherever there are handsome people, there must also be some black-faced fellow. Everything that is deprived of something really ugly to throw its own beauty into relief is defective. Wherever there exists a saint reflecting the light of purity, there will also be a soul as filthy as a cesspool to contrast with him. When the soul dons the garment of love, then some speck of tyranny and ignorance comes forward so that a person might not be forgetful of himself and what he is. A peacock realizes what it is when, having gazed admiringly at its plumage and taken delight in the special beauty of each of its feathers, its glance comes to rest on its feet.

*Peace!*

## LETTER 13: UNVEILING THE MYSTERIES

*In the name of God, the Merciful, the Compassionate!*

Dear brother Shamsuddin, may God grant that many mysteries will be disclosed to you! The meaning of *manifestation* is "to come from behind a curtain."[29] An initiated person perceives things that previously he had not been able to understand, as has been said, "I lifted the veil from your sight" (Q50:22) in order that you might perceive what had been concealed until then. This refers to those impediments that veil the sight of God from his servant and make it inaccessible to him. Beauty pertains to different worlds, such as this one and the one to come—whether it be eighteen thousand worlds, according to one Tradition, or eighty thousand, according to another. All of them are present in man's constitution. With reference to each world, man has been given the special vision that will enable him to observe that world and the revelation occurring in it. All eighty thousand worlds can be summed up in two worlds. They comprise darkness and light, earth and heaven, the visible and the invisible, the physical and the spiritual, this world and the next. To summarize requires but one sentence, but to explain, many words are necessary.

When a sincere pilgrim, impelled by his aspirations, turns his face from his lower nature and fixes his gaze on the heights of the Law and, in the footsteps of a just man, takes to traveling the road of the Way, observing the injunctions of the Law, and enjoying the protection of his spiritual guide, then from behind each veil that is lifted—all eighty thousand of them—there is granted him a special vision that is suitable to be observed at that particular stage. It quickly comes into focus for him. The very first special vision to be unveiled

58

is that of the intellect. To the extent that the veil is lifted, a person understands the meaning of anything intelligible that has been revealed to him, and he becomes familiar with the secrets of the particular revealed world. This is called the "revelation of the intelligible world." He should not place too much confidence in this new knowledge, for not everything that swims into sight can be attained. Overconfidence is premature:

Not everything you see, O heart, will He grant you!

O heart, renowned philosophers remain at this stage and think that they have actually attained their desire! When the sincere pilgrim has passed beyond the revelation of intelligible things, then the revelation of the heart becomes manifest. It is called the "revelation of perception." Various kinds of lights shine forth. After this is the revelation known as "revelation of secrets." The secrets of creation and the wisdom contained in the existence of everything become apparent. At this particular stage it can be said:

Grief for You has plundered my heart,
And for You my heart has forsaken all.
The secret unknown even to holy people,
Your love whispered in the ear of my heart.

After that comes the manifestation of the things of the spirit. They are called "spiritual revelations." At this stage, heaven and hell appear, angels are seen, and there is the opportunity to converse with them and also to listen to them. When the soul is completely purified and cleansed of all bodily defilements, then disclosure of the Infinite occurs. He sees the entire circle of what has been decreed for the past and future. Here the veil of time and place is rent asunder, so that what occurred in the past is known in the present. A person can also perceive the very beginning of creation coming into his vision, as well as the various ranks of all creatures. Similarly, he sees what will take place in the future. As Harisa said: "When I look toward the blessed, I see them advancing; but when I look toward the damned, I see them dying." When the veil of the categories of space and time is torn asunder, everlasting time and space are revealed. Here the veil of appearances is also necessarily rent asunder. A person will then experience that he can see from behind as well as he can see from in front. As the Prophet said: "Just as I can see from in front, so too can I see from behind." What people call revelations and miracles occur at this stage. From this exalted state one can know the thoughts of others, be aware of things done at a distance, walk on water or on fire, fly in the air, and do other suchlike miraculous things. Such things are not to be given too much importance, however, for they are found among both believers and nonbelievers!

Once the Prophet asked a man called Ibn Saiyad, "What do you see?" Ibn Saiyad said, "I see the divine throne on water." The Prophet said, "That is the throne of Satan. Beware! Similar things will also accompany the Antichrist." There is a Tradition that says, "The Antichrist will have the power to raise men from the dead." Only that can really be called a genuine miracle which could not exist, except for the followers of the faith, and is hidden in the soul, but revealed during ecstatic contemplation. Both Muslims and infidels have souls, but the concealed things are not meant for anyone except the special companions of the Prophet. They have said that the concealed one is the intermediary between the two worlds—the one of divine qualities, and the other, the spiritual world—so that the heart might be enabled to experience divine ecstasy. The reflection of those virtues reaches to the spiritual world, which is a noble spirit, as has been said: "These are those on whose hearts God has inscribed faith and strengthened them with his own spirit" (Q58:22). Elsewhere it has been said: "By our order did we reveal to you a spirit. You did not know what the book was, nor what faith was. But we made a light for your soul that by it we may guide those among our slaves whom we want to guide" (Q42:52). This verse has also been interpreted thus: "I have given the noble spirit of light to many great men, but not to others, so that by means of that light they might find the Way to the world of divine attributes." A hint about all this is that "only a second Rustam could master Rakhsh," the horse of Rustam. This is called the "revealing of divine attributes." In this state, if the pilgrim is destined for the attribute of the world of things revealed, infused knowledge will appear in him. If the quality of hearing is revealed, he will hear the divine word and address; if that of seeing, then the vision and divine witness become manifest; if the divine beauty, then one gains a foretaste of the spectacle of divine beauty; if the quality of eternity, then genuine permanence is experienced; and if it is the quality of divine Unity that is revealed, then real unity is experienced. One may think of the other qualities in an analogous manner.

When I alight at the head of the street of Your love,
The secret of both worlds becomes completely manifest in my heart.

Having been welcomed at that threshold, my heart
Obtains the desideratum of all the worlds.

O brother, this work has no material cause, so there is no reason to despair. The pleasure associated with the wind is experienced when it blows. At the destined hour it whirls into action. One auspicious evening an order reached the Archangel Gabriel, "Go down to the world tonight and have a look around!" He went and found everyone sound asleep, except for an old man who was an idol worshiper. He was sitting in front of an idol, lost in worship, with his head bowed low. With great devotion he was soliciting the idol for things he needed. Gabriel wanted the divine command to destroy this man and thus wipe his defiling presence from the face of the earth. "O Gabriel," said a heavenly voice, "even if he does not recognize Me as his Lord, still I consider him one of my slaves!" On another auspicious evening an address came to Gabriel, "Go tonight also and see who is asleep and who is awake." Gabriel went and saw, standing on one leg, in the niche of a mosque, and plying the Lord with a hundred petitions, the same old man. "Do you recognize him?" asked the voice. "He is the one who was lost in prayer before his idol. Today, a stranger has become a friend, and one ignorant of Me has become filled with knowledge of Me."

*Peace!*

### LETTER 14: MANIFESTATION

*In the name of God, the Merciful, the Compassionate!*

Brother Shamsuddin, may God deign to manifest Himself to you. Manifestation occurs through revelation of the divine essence and attributes. The soul also has its own glory. Many travelers grow proud at this stage and think that they have attained the divine glory. If one does not have access to a perfect sheikh, a man experienced in mystical matters, then it would be difficult to escape this danger. Everyone who sincerely seeks God should catch hold of the skirt of a mature master so that he may benefit from the blessing conferred on him by the spiritual wealth of that sheikh and thus attain what he desires and yearns for! As the Quran informs us: "Enter a house through the door!" (Q2:189). There is a hint contained here!

If you travel the Way without benefit of any intermediary,
You will fall headlong from the Way into a pit!
Follow a spiritual guide that, by his bounty,
Sooner or later you may reach the realm of the King.

For the moment, grasp the difference between divine illumination and illumination from the soul. When the mirror of the soul is cleansed of the impurities of human existence, it becomes polished in relation to God and its purity becomes perfect. It becomes like the rising sun of the divine beauty, and like Jamshed's cup it reveals the essence of the Lord, as well as His attributes. But not everyone who acquires the luster of polishing is also granted the boon of witnessing. "That is God's grace, which he bestows on whomever He wishes" (Q62:4). Not everyone who runs catches a wild ass, but only a person who is actually running can hope to catch one!

Among travelers there should be a spiritually endowed teacher who purifies the heart not only of deficiencies common to human nature but also of the rust accumulated by each traveler's particular nature. Many spiritual qualities illumine the heart. This is due to the experience of spiritual lights. The soul, in effect, has been illuminated with the beauty of its own attributes. But its full illumination requires the effacement of the effects deriving from the unruly characteristics of human nature. It sometimes happens that the essence of the soul, which is the vicar of God on earth, becomes manifest and claims, "I am God!" Sometimes it happens that a person sees all creatures bowing down before the throne of the vicegerency of his soul and falls into error. He thinks that he is God himself! The situation can be compared to that described in a Tradition: "When God manifests himself to anyone, everything becomes dependent on him." He falls into many faults of this kind and, unless he receives divine grace and assistance from a spiritual guide, he cannot avoid making such errors. Now we come to the difference between divine illumination and illumination from the soul.

Let us first consider the manifestation or illumination that proceeds from the soul itself: It has a tendency to appear as something novel. It does not have the power to do away with unruly tendencies completely, even though at the time of illumination a person is far from their pull. The human soul does not annihilate them, since this kind of manifestation is still veiled. Human inclinations remain. When divine illumination occurs, one is no longer encumbered since, of necessity, the divine illumination leads one to refrain from acting in response to the soul and to suppress all purely human tendencies. "And say: God has come forward, and the existence of what is false has been removed. What is false does not endure" (Q17:81). Illumination from the soul does not bring peace to the heart, neither does it cleanse the heart of impurities or liberate it from doubt and suspicion, nor is the bliss of complete understanding bestowed upon it. Divine illumination, on the other hand, does cleanse and liberate and inform *totally*. Also, illumination from the soul causes pride and self-esteem to appear; haughtiness and preoccupation with self increase; the quest for God is harmed; fear of God and supplication grow less. But divine illumination does away with all these. Instead of preoccupation with self, self-forgetfulness is found; both yearning for God and fervor in seeking Him increase, as does the thirst for God. Above all, a person genuinely experiences himself as a mirror of the essence and attributes of the Exalted Friend! When the mirror becomes clean, it can reflect whatever the Lord wishes to manifest in it, for example, the attributes of speech—"And God spoke to Moses" (Q19:25). And if it is a question of creative power, then reflect on these words concerning Jesus: "And if You, by My command, make birds of clay and breathe into them, they will fly away by My command" (Q5:110)—and so on for the other attributes and their manifestation in man. [The story of a disciple of Abu Turab Nakhshabi follows.]

There is a very subtle difference between witness, display, and illumination. This cannot be perceived without perception and clear insight. God willing, what is here exposited at length may be experienced instantaneously. You should know that *illumination* and *concealment* are two words commonly found among the Sufis. The former means "to be revealed," while the latter means "to be hidden." What this group means to say is that, through illumination, God discloses Himself; whereas by concealment, He hides Himself.

There is no question here of God's essence since variability and alteration are incompatible with the divine essence. It is instead like light, which, once it has been shed on some problem, causes people to say that the problem has been solved. The problem has not really been solved, but one's mind has been illuminated and the problem comprehended. Knowledge is called the solution of the problem, while ignorance is called its obfuscation. When a person becomes engrossed in himself, he finds that vision of the invisible world remains hidden from him. This is called "concealment." When, however, he sees from the divine perspective rather than his own, doing away with his human ego, he then sees what is hidden. This is called "illumination."

O brother, on the day that men were brought into existence, God said: "Come along the Way of seeking, and never despair of finding me!" Man gradually discovers that the meaning of "seeking" is not to seek one's own glory! This is the secret, but how difficult it is to attain! Realize what all this means! Wherever there is beauty, there is both enticement and debasement, as the following quatrain indicates:

> Here am I accepting grief suffered for Your sake as happiness,
> Crying out as I endure oppression for Your sake.
> Despite all this, were I to become dust on Your path,
> I would still not be worthy of being touched by Your feet!

God will give everyone who sets out faithfully along the Way even what was never requested. Yet, if anyone does not direct his feet along this Way, even though he has desires, he will get nothing. A great man related this story: Someone was asked, "Do you wish to see the Lord?" "No." "Why not?" "Because Moses desired to see God, but did not; whereas Muhammad had no such desire and yet saw Him." Is not this garment of mud merely transitory, like all the work of Adam and men? Of the innumerable host of created beings not one is involved in accomplishing the work that is being done in you. If one were, then one could talk about a cause. Reflect for a moment on those spiritual substances called angels who are clothed with the vesture of sinlessness, submission, sanctity, and purity! Not everyone capable of service is necessarily capable of love! Not everyone who exists on the fringes of the wide Expanse can traverse the Expanse itself!

*Peace!*

## LETTER 15: UNION WITH GOD

*In the name of God, the Merciful, the Compassionate!*

Brother Shamsuddin, may God Almighty grant you the blessing of union with Him! Realize that union with the Lord is not of the same kind as when your body is joined to another, nor your accidents with others, or your substance with your body, or knowledge with the thing known, or willing with the thing willed. "God Almighty is more exalted than that!" [ref. to Q17:4, 43]. This word *union* occurs in the Law and public discourse, and is also well known among the Sufis. It means "being joined to the Lord." What does it mean to be joined to the Lord? It means that, for the sake of God, one is cut off from what is in any way base. Being closely united would mean becoming lost in the very depths of God! To this corresponds a great freedom from preoccupation with things other than God. On the other hand, to the extent that a person becomes free from preoccupation with God, to the same extent he becomes separated from Him.

One can learn from this saying of Harisa: "Surely I see the throne of my Master." It so happened that, to the extent that Harisa was not united to this world, he was closely united to the Hidden One. Muhammad the Chosen One was detached from both worlds in order to be intimately united with God. If his secret leaked out, he would say, "I take refuge in You from You!" When he said these words, it was clear that nothing remained in his secret thoughts that was other than God.

Separation from this world restores union with God. Again there is the saying of Abdullah ibn Umar. As he was performing the circumambulation of the Kaaba, he said: "I was lost in the vision of the Lord in that place." This means that his personality was lost in the Law, while his secret thoughts were immersed in the Truth. Absorption in the Law is superseded by absorption in the Truth. A person is no longer aware of either house or greeting. So engrossed does he become in God that he hears no greeting, and his veneration of the Lord of the house reaches such a stage that there remains no memory of even the house! This is the sense of "I see God Himself in that house!" But when the person who had greeted him and not been vouchsafed a reply came, he was full of complaints and reproaches against him. When Umar came to the place, he said nothing. This became an argument in favor of the claim made by Abdullah, since the masters of jurisprudence argue that when it is necessary to speak, no reply becomes the reply. In short, every spiritually endowed person arrives at the point of return to the Lord. "Surely the ultimate point of return is to your Lord" (Q53:42). In the beginning, the first covenant was "Am I not your Lord?" (Q7:171). Just as spiritual nature was prepared for a lump of clay, so on the pinnacle of human nature was showered the leaven of everything leavened! "God created the universe in darkness, but then sprinkled his light upon it." One gulp from the cup of "Am I not" gives so much pleasure to his palate that throughout his entire lifetime it can never be erased from his soul. Indeed, his life consists of that delight and the desire of that Light is like the center and treasure of his own being. He is not inclined toward this world and is unable, even for a moment, to abandon that wine!

> Your lovers have been intoxicated from eternity.
> They have come, their heads swaying with "Am I not?"
> Imbibing this wine and savoring its fragrance,
> They become spiritual sots due to "Am I not?"

Those people are like moths sacrificing their lives out of love—for the yoke of yearning for God himself has fallen upon their necks in the covenant of "Am I not?" Here, many feathers and wings strain after Him. The veils of the beauty of the glorious Candle are shed, so that "whoever comes even a hand's breadth toward Me, toward him do I advance a yard" takes him by the hand! From the many stirrings of a heart, yearning for God Himself is like a rope between the two worlds, for it draws a person to the very edge of union and says, "How far could one reach with these weak wings and feathers? You have drawn aside the veils of My beauty, but you cannot fly in the atmosphere of My divine substance with these paltry wings and feathers!" Those required there are earned on the battlefield by "those people who struggle on Our behalf" (Q29:69). As the Quran goes on to promise, "Certainly I shall show them the way!" Wings and feathers of another hue shall I bestow upon you by scattering my own illuminations—"God guides by His own light whomsoever He wishes" (Q24:35).

If the most exalted of angels, jinn,[30] and men were gathered together, they could not confer on a single slave the enjoyment of the illumination of the Lord God, nor even enough desire for Him to enable a slave to venture a few footsteps upon the Divine Expanse. Undoubtedly this is a better desire than any concerned with creatures, and a form of slavery that is really a liberation from slavery and from oneself. Such people have the habit of directing all their desires toward the Divine World. One breath of theirs is equivalent to all the affairs of both worlds. The following verse hints at the intensity of their renunciation:

> In one breath the Sufis celebrate two feasts,
> While spiders tear flies to pieces!

# THE HUNDRED LETTERS

At every moment a Sufi dies, only to obtain a new form of existence, coming further under the control of the desire of self-effacement and absorption in God. From that effacement one goes for a different type of stroll in the Divine World, under the influence of a strong yearning. "God effaces or establishes whatever He pleases" (Q13:39). At every step absorption and affirmation are obtained, so that the Sufi celebrates two feasts there: one that of absorption, and the other a feast of affirmation. At this stage, it is fitting that he should be called "the Spirit of God" or "the Word of God"; such a title will become like a robe that fits him perfectly.

O brother, this work is scarcely compatible with having the sash of lordship tied to one's turban! For when that beloved one, Adam, came to heaven, he looked around and said: "These itching feet of mine cannot remain in the bonds of a stirrup. And this head of mine, filled with the effects of love, cannot bear the weight of the crown. I have been given an erect stature, that I may stand upright and alone, just like the letter *alif*."[31] Causes and effects are fit only for the fire. He said "Here am I!" to love, and bade adieu to the eight heavens. While he was passing through heaven, along with his crown and robe of honor, Adam was in the rank of those near to God. When he entered upon the Way of seeking, he was not aware of things that still lay concealed. Hence it has been said:

> Do you know the precondition for entering a tavern?
> First lay aside your crown, your belt, and your turban!

Every particle of the being of Adam raised this primeval slogan of love:

> I will sorely try your heart with the anguish of love;
> Even today I shall demand your very life's blood!

*Peace!*


## LETTER 16: THE TRAVELER AND THE ECSTATIC

*In the name of God, the Merciful, the Compassionate!*

Brother Shamsuddin, may God grant you the wonders of travelers! Those who venture along this Way are of two kinds: One is the traveler, the other is the ecstatic. Ecstatics are those filled with a tremendous longing for God; they have attained this stage under the compelling impulse of their zeal. They have passed beyond all other stages, but not much insight has been given to them. They are unaware of the various states of this Way; they have no knowledge of the various stages, nor do they grasp the dangers that could occur along the Way; they cannot distinguish between goodness and wickedness, nor can they discern what is beneficial from what is harmful. Such men are unfit to become sheikhs![32] A sheikh should be a person who, even though he be led by the bridle of a deep-felt yearning, still moves along peacefully and slowly in order that he may profit from what is proper and fitting in each particular stage. Hence it is that the states of goodness and wickedness, of peace and perversity, are all made known to him. At one time the sheikh may travel along the Way, while at another, he may wander off it!

In this manner he experiences what it means both to travel along the Way and to go astray from it, with the result that he is able to point out the Way to others! As to the various signs along the Way, those who have trod it have said: If a traveler is passing through the stage of earthly qualities, he sees things such as lanes and alleys, dark places and dwellings, and comes to ruined and broken-down inns, water-logged expanses, and hilly tracts where he experiences a heaviness of spirit and a gloominess, which, however, is followed by a lightness and pleasantness. Second, he traverses the realm of the watery qualities where he sees greens and pastures, trees and sown fields, running water, springs, rivers, and other similar things. In the third stage he passes through airy qualities; he walks on air, flies through it, ascends to the heights and flies through valleys and similar places. Fourth, he passes through the fiery qualities where he sees lamps, sparks, and flames. Fifth, he passes through the firmament and the heavens, seeing himself traversing them, flying from one to the other, perceiving the firmament of the heavens, and even the angels. Sixth, as he passes through the starry region, he sees stars, the moon, the sun, and other things of this nature. Seventh, as he passes through the animal qualities, he sees in every beastly or ferocious form that he encounters the nature corresponding to that animal. If he sees himself overcoming that particular animal, it means that he has overcome that particular defect; whereas if he sees himself being overcome by that animal, it is a sign of the continuing dominance of that bad quality in him. There are thousands of other similar worlds through which the traveler has to pass. In each of them he witnesses sights and subtleties appropriate to it.

O brother, behold your soul and your God! You should play the man and cry, "I shall reach my Goal, or die in the attempt!" This Goal is a dazzling carbuncle, and its great excellence can be judged from the fact that it is guarded by the waves of a bloodthirsty ocean. One hundred thousand people are in quest of it. For its sake, they sacrifice their lives and, having been ruined, plunge to the bottom of the sea. When anyone foolishly tries to enter that threshold, then the Devil, who guards it, enticingly says: "Don't you recognize me? I am the one from whom the inhabitants of the first heaven learned how to sing God's praises, while those of the second learned how to praise God by proclaiming 'There is no god but God!' The inhabitants of the other worlds have received a diploma in accordance with my teaching by means of which they can attain the very heights of heaven. Because I have abandoned all these riches, they have drawn the mark of the curse on my forehead, and placed me at the head of the lane of the Law of Muhammad. Now, come with the crown of sincerity and enter in, or put your foot in my stirrup. Aren't you a man of religion?" And Satan cannot be budged from this position of his, even for the sake of both worlds! He has great pride and holds his ground—until a just man appears in the kingdom and, relying solely on the strategem of purity, he struts manfully along the Way!

*Peace!*

## LETTER 17: THE SOURCE OF ERROR FOR THE TRAVELER

*In the name of God, the Merciful, the Compassionate!*

Brother Shamsuddin, there are some Sufis who have performed many austerities and, having witnessed much, retired for a period of time that they might devote their hearts to the profession of faith: "There is no god but God!" They have exerted themselves so much in meditation that, apart from remembering God at all times, nothing else finds access to their hearts. They have experienced wonderful states, had angelic secrets revealed to them, and attained the stage of being companions who are endowed with miraculous powers. Having been given information about the hidden world, they are correct in all that they say. If they exert their power in time of sickness, the sick person gets better. They have the power needed to destroy their enemies— and this happens, if they so wish.

At this stage, Satan grows envious and shows them all the secrets of the Law, except for one, which is also hidden from him. (That is why he did not prostrate himself before Adam.) The secret is this: The whole purpose of abandoning sin is to ensure that evil desires are broken, and that the tendencies of human nature are brought to heel, with the result that a person does not turn aside from God! There is one further purpose—that a person's heart may be governed by the thought of remembering God, and having been freed from the shackling tendencies of human nature, the heart might become purified for the task of remembering God and attaining a true vision of Him.

The careful observance of the Law is also a way leading to the Kaaba of union. Anyone who has reached this point can dispense with provisions, beast, and whatever else is needed for the journey. It is to this group that Satan explains: "If you pray, your prayer will become a veil for you, for you have already arrived at the goal!" "We are always experiencing the sight of God!" they reply. "The purpose of the bowing and prostrations of prayer is to bring the inattentive heart into the presence of God. We ourselves are not inattentive even for one hour. We see the angelic world revealed to us and the precious jewels of the prophets are displayed for us quite openly. What need is there for us to perform the canonical prayer?"[33] This line of thinking betrays the activity of Satan, who, even in the stage of perfect nearness to God, is still on the prowl. "What need was there for me to worship Adam?" he asks. "Adam is of lesser dignity than I! What profit is there for me in bowing down before him?" The story about Satan in the Quran is not a mere fable but, on the contrary, is an example for such people, enabling them to understand that no degree of closeness can in any way abrogate obedience to the Law! This is what religious men meant when they said, "Care in observing the Law is also a means of traveling along the Way of Almighty God." They spoke the truth when they said that Satan hid from them another subtle point by claiming that the goal of the Law is nothing other than coming close to God. This view is utterly wrong!

Actually, there is also another purpose in the Law. Canonical prayer, for example, is like the five pins that hold up a door. If they are no longer attached to the door, it falls down, just as Satan fell. If anyone asks what is the reason that makes these five prayers like five supporting pins, and what is so special about them, then the answer would be: Understanding the reason for them is not within the purview of the human intellect. It is something special. It cannot be simply thought through and understood. For example, a lodestone attracts a piece of iron toward itself, yet there is no one who can explain how it is done!

They have said that this group is like a man who built a mansion on top of a hill and filled it with many luxurious articles. When the time came for him to die, he made his son his heir and said: "Do whatever you like with all this, but do not throw out the few handfuls of fragrant grass, even if it becomes dried up." When spring came, the mountains and valleys were decked with greenery and luscious fragrant grass appeared. Some handfuls of that grass were brought into the mansion. Its fragrance, on account of its freshness, was simply overpowering! The son said: "My father ordered this grass to be brought into the house because of its pleasant odor. What is the use of it now that it has become dried up?" He ordered the grass to be thrown out. When the mansion was emptied of grass, a black-headed serpent emerged from its hole and, biting the son, killed him. Why? Because the grass possessed two qualities: one, its pleasant odor—and this was known; and another, that the serpent would not approach any spot where it was found. It had a preventive effect on the serpent, but nobody except the lord of the mansion knew that particular quality, since it was beyond the grasp of an ordinary man's mind. The young heir was destroyed, therefore, because he thought that anything that he could not grasp did not exist, even in the treasury of God's limitless power!

He had not grasped the meaning of this verse, "You have been given but a little knowledge" (Q17:85). The same error befalls the man of miracles and divine visions: When one of the secrets of the Law has been manifest to him, he assumes that there are no others left. Satan thought the same thing! This misconception is one of the most serious sins of travelers and pilgrims. It is a grave error, which leads to the destruction of many. As a poet aptly noted:

At a certain place my heart stood still,
Even a hundred signs could not show me the Way.
Each month there are two thousand lovers, like me,
Who are slain—and not even a sigh escapes their lips!

Realize that this was the source of the error of whatever you heard about people who had attained an eminent rank among the followers of this Way! These people understood only the Law's goals and were unaware of a further secret that might be contained in it.

Even if they did not suspect that a further secret was lodged in it, they should have at least wondered why the Prophet had undertaken so much prayer that his blessed feet grew swollen! You certainly cannot argue that what was necessary for his community was not necessary for the Prophet! Recall that he had nine wives, whereas it was lawful for others to have only four! He also said, "I am not like you!" Moreover, while he himself performed a complete fast taking nothing but water, he forbade others to follow this practice. Everyone well versed in the Law, every sheikh and every Sufi who has attained the degree of perfection, knows that each restriction of the yoke of the Law contains a secret that is also a hint of eternal bliss! Hence it is that religious men, even at the hour of death, do not fail in the observance of any of the details of the Law. This is acutely exemplified by Khwaja Junaid. At the time of his death, after he had been washed, he grabbed the attendant's hand—for he had forgotten to comb the sheikh's beard—and compelled him to honor the prescribed tradition. "O leader," protested the bystanders, "at a time such as this, are not relaxations of the Law permissible?" "Of course," replied the sheikh. "But this is how I hope to reach God!"

Such was the mettle of the perfect, while the proud fell prey to deceit. They thought that anything they did not see or understand simply did not exist! Those in touch with the Truth, however, knew the secret of the established pattern for prayer: namely, why the order of morning prayer has two prostrations; the noonday prayer, four; the evening prayer, three. They also knew the import of the two prostrations after each inclination, for each has a special grace attached to its perfect observance. One must be on one's guard about prayer, that its effect might become clear at the moment of death; otherwise no perfection is of use. When a dying person sees himself about to perish, he will say, "What happened to all that perfection?" They will answer, "It had no linchpin. It was chopped off at the base at the time of death." Such a person becomes like Satan, whose virtues proves to be of no benefit due to one act of disobedience! This error is often committed by travelers; they become proud of their perfection, and hidden from them is this trifling thing of which the poet spoke:

An ignorant traveler will get lost on this Way,
For the Way is long, dark, and full of pitfalls!
Hold the lamp of knowledge and wisdom before you,

Otherwise you will stumble headlong into some hole!
Idols still press upon the Sufi in his dreams,
Even though he is otherwise oblivious to himself!

O brother, these men were given two eyes—one to observe the calamities that can befall the soul, the other to behold the wonders wrought by God! When they see the latter, they become puffed up with pride; but when they see the infirmity and calamities of this earthly substance, they melt away. Time and again it happened that the mad lover from Iraq,[34] because he was consumed by the fire of separation, would exclaim, "O that I were dust and had nothing to do with these affairs!" (Q78:40) At other times he would plead, "Where are the angels of the firmament and those who inhabit the heavenly court, that they might line up before the throne of my wealth?"

Sometimes I am plunged to the depths, at other times raised on high.
Sometimes I experience the scar of separation, at others, the garden of union!
[Further explanation, with concluding couplet]
Your awesome majesty may threaten many of us,
Yet no lips will part in even a sigh of complaint!

*Peace!*

## LETTER 18: THE SOURCES OF HUMAN ERROR

*In the name of God, the Merciful, the Compassionate!*

Brother Shamsuddin, many have fallen from the Way because of a doubt or false opinion. One group says, "God has no need of our worship or devotion; nor is He affected by our sin; so why should we bother ourselves with following the Law?" The answer is that such a view reflects sheer ignorance! It is based on the supposition that the Law enjoins things on men for the sake of God—which is absurd and foolish—for whatever anyone does is beneficial to himself, as the Quran says: "Whoever purifies himself, purifies himself for the good of his own soul" (Q35:18) and "whoever does any good work, it is to his own gain" (Q41:46). An ignorant person of this sort is comparable to a patient who has been prescribed something by the physician, but

73

does not follow the treatment. "What harm is there to the physician if I don't follow it?" he thinks. The harm, of course, is to himself! Even though what he said was true, he is the one who will perish! The physician did not speak in order to please him but to cure him! If he follows the physician's instructions, he will be cured; if not, he will perish. Neither outcome concerns the physician!

Those of the second group rush beyond the bounds of the Law, transgress it, and put their trust in the mercy and compassion of God, thinking that He will exercise His mercy in their behalf. The answer to this is: While their saying is correct, it reflects a deception of the Devil that deflects foolish people from the Way. An intelligent person will give this answer: "Yes, He is merciful and compassionate, and that is why He is also the One who punishes offenses severely!" We see that most people in this world of ours have to undergo many trials and endure poverty, while His treasury is limitless and yet, despite His mercy, He does not create even a single grain of wheat for them, to spare the farmer his trouble. Nor does a person stay healthy if he fails to eat and drink; nor is a sick man cured without treatment. Similarly, the causes of sickness and poverty have been created so that, without them, nothing is acquired.

A similar situation pertains to the world to come. Every soul contains some measure of infidelity and ignorance. Just as a sick man, if he is not treated, perishes, so there is no antidote for the poison of infidelity and ignorance except learning and intimate knowledge. And there is no remedy for the sickness of laziness except prayer and proper observance of all devotions. Whoever takes poison and, at the same time, trusts in God's mercy will perish! The sickness of the heart comes from unwholesome desires. Anyone who does not purify his heart of these desires is in danger of destruction whenever he considers them as sinful; and if he does not consider them as harmful, he is not merely in danger, but has already been destroyed. For this would be idolatry, which is the poison of faith!

The third group engage in ascetical practices and claim that the object of their asceticism is to be suddenly purified of all sexual desire, anger, and every other quality that is held to be blameworthy under the Law, and to bring them under control, since this is what the Law prescribes. When they have afflicted themselves and practiced austerities for some time but are powerless to achieve their aim, they then consider that such an aim is unattainable, and that the Law has enjoined something impossible. "Man is constituted with these impulses; there is no way he can be freed from their clutches, just as a black blanket cannot be changed into a white one. We do not intend to occupy ourselves with something that is impossible."

The answer to this view is: It is ignorance and foolishness on the part of anyone to think that the Law has enjoined the complete extirpation of desires and other human tendencies! The ideal should not be considered in terms of such extremes. Nothing of that sort is commanded. The Prophet of Islam himself has said, "I am a man. I get angry." Indeed, they often saw signs of anger on his face! The Lord commends "those who swallow their anger" (Q3:134), not "those who have no anger"! To what extent does he order that there should be no sexual desire? The Prophet had a harem of nine wives! If anyone loses this appetite, he should seek treatment to have it restored, for it is not forbidden to have a wife and children. There is nothing wrong with something that results from anger during a war against the infidels, or the procreation of children to continue the human race, and to establish a good name. Both arise as a result of human desires, and that is what the Prophet intended. But he commanded that they should be kept under control, such as is enjoined by the Law, in the same way as a horse should be broken in and a dog should be kept under the control of a hunter, lest it pounce upon him! Without a horse, a hunter is handicapped in his hunting, yet if the horse is not broken in, it will throw its rider!

The sexual appetite and anger are like dogs and horses. Without these two, one cannot go hunting for eternal bliss. The precondition is to bring both to heel. If they gain the upper hand, then they can wreak a man's destruction. The whole purpose of austerities is to break the dominance of these two qualities and place them firmly under control. It is possible to do this.

The fourth group are those who are caught up in the folly of their own self-esteem, claiming that all works are preordained from the very beginning. Good fortune and hard times, in their view, are already evident in the womb. Nothing at all occurs from one's own efforts. Why bother to exert oneself? How could it profit anyone?

The answer is: When the Prophet explained this matter, the companions said, "We shall depend upon God, and refrain from exerting ourselves." But he commanded them: "Exert yourselves and then will you be granted what has been promised!" And he added, "Don't withdraw your hand! If eternal bliss has been allotted to you, then good works also have been decreed!" The meaning of his statement is that fortune and misfortune are related to devotion and sin, just as good health and death are related to eating well and starving. All those who were ordained, from the very beginning, to die of hunger simply do not find enough food to eat, whereas those destined for plenty become landlords or traders. Those destined to die in the west will find the way to the east closed to them. They will not be able to proceed in any other direction.

The point can be illustrated thus: Once the angel of death was sent to the court of Solomon. He sat close by a man and stared fixedly at him. The man grew frightened. When the angel disappeared, the man begged Solomon that he would command the wind to carry him off to the west. Solomon bade the wind do so. Then the angel of death reappeared in the court. Solomon asked him why he had gazed so pointedly at the poor man. "I was commanded to take his life in an hour, in the west," replied the angel. "I saw him here and was astonished. How could this be? The command had been to take him in the west, but only an hour was left to him, so I came and gazed at him in order that he might take fright and request you to have the wind bear him off." That action, therefore, was not without purpose!

Anyone for whom bliss has been ordained has his heart illuminated so that he can accept the faith, receive the grace of austerity, and expel all base tendencies from himself, as has been commanded: "Whomever God decides to guide, He expands his breast to embrace Islam!" (Q6:126). God Himself has required that there will be a group that goes to hell. He therefore restrains them from doing good deeds, and puts into their heart the idea that works are not necessary, and that bliss and misery have been ordained from the beginning.[35] Misery exists because it was thus construed at the very beginning, when some were ordained to remain ignorant. Their hearts are overcome, for the rank of leadership is decreed from the beginning and is not obtained by repeated effort and the acquisition of knowledge. If the order has been given, then the robe of leadership is placed over his head. Anyone who does not seek and experience the pain of effort remains ignorant, since the eternal decree for him comprises that which has been cast into his heart; but whoever, from the beginning, is commanded to be a leader must make manifest what is already in his heart. It is like a grain of wheat the destiny of which has been fixed from the very beginning, but the prerequisites for its growth are that the soil should be soft, that the seed be sown, that water be given, and so forth. Unless these conditions and prerequisites are met, the wheat simply cannot grow!

It is a similar situation with regard to faith and devotion in their relationship to bliss and misery. Some fool might say, "What is the relationship between faith and devotion, on the one hand, and bliss and misery on the other?" He thinks that with his puny intellect he can unravel the cause of this mystery. By means of his intellect he wants to know about intricate matters that are not within the ambit of his intellect. Everyone knows that the reason for the fall of that group is their own folly, pure and simple, and not the difficult nature of the doubt. The proof of this is obtained from Jesus, the Prophet, who said: "There is healing for the blind man; I can even bring life to the dead; but I am powerless to help a fool!"

O brother, it is necessary to be prudent, for a person can attain the dignity of the archangels Gabriel or Michael in a flash, but he can just as suddenly appear to be like a dog or a pig! When there is knowledge and the illumination of wisdom, a man may become like an angel—"Lo, this is no man, but a blessed angel!" (Q12:31). As it has been said,

> If your step has been firmly rooted in faith,
> You can extract dust from a river, and cold from fire!

But if a person is completely under the influence of lust and his heart is in Satan's nest, then he is like a dog or a pig. "He is like a dog! Whether you attack it or ignore it, he still pants!" (Q7:176).

> You who are rendered content in a moment
> Are like a grazing ass or a cow chewing her cud!

A revelation came to the Prophet David: "O David, be like the wary bird! Do not be trustful or contented! Everything goes somewhere apart!" There was a bird that was placed in a narrow cage and its heart was as joyous as if it were in paradise. These delicate souls are also in the cage of the body. Every evening they put their heads through the window and sigh, thinking, "When can I fly off?" As the poet has said:

> For that one hidden behind Your veil
> There exists a height still loftier than this cell:
> The height of which I aspire is very high,
> But perchance I will exceed even my own ambition!

*Peace!*

LETTER 19: VISIBLE AND INVISIBLE DISEASES

*In the name of God, the Merciful, the Compassionate!*

Brother Shamsuddin, the peace of God be with you! Understand the truth and know for certain that man is composed of two different substances, one heavenly and one earthly. Just as this earthly body is susceptible to disease, so too is the heavenly one. Just as there are physicians for the earthly body who, by means of their treatment, change a sick person into a healthy one and save people from the danger of death, so too there are physicians for the heavenly nature who, by means of their treatment, understand and distinguish illnesses, causes, and connected experiences, leading the sick person from the house of destruction to the house of salvation. Physicians of the earthly body are experienced in the causes of physical ailments, while the physicians of all that pertains to illness in the heavenly nature are first the prophets and, then, the sheiks, who succeed them. Hence the saying, "The sheikh in his community is like a prophet in his." Just as someone whose body is sick may die if there is no physician, so too the person without a prophet or a sheikh faces the danger of spiritual destruction. "The learned men in the community of Muhammad are the heirs of the prophets." Without help, a sick person may perish. In our days there is a scarcity of experienced physicians; both doctors of the body and doctors of the spirit are needed to attend to the mortally ill.

What is to become of us without proper physicians? What will become of health, life, prosperity, and salvation? "Don't despair of God's mercy" (Q39:53). Be full of hope! God is not restricted by conditions and prerequisites although, in His wisdom, He respects them. We, for our part, should throw dust on our heads and acknowledge our sins. We should realize that there is nothing in the hands of any human being save pride and self-conceit! "Except what God wills" (Q87:7), nothing happens. A physician takes the pulse of a sick man in order to acquaint himself with the cause of the sickness and to be able to prescribe different medicines and mixtures according to the patient's strength. He will prepare a mixture; he will allow one thing but forbid another in order to restore the person's health to normal. The person's need is visible on his face; thus will he be saved from destruction. In this manner the Prophet grew acquainted with the fundamental causes of inner afflictions and, according to the aptitude and receptivity of the man so afflicted, insisted on particular injunctions of the Law. Sometimes two prostrations are prescribed, at another time three, and still another, four. He makes one thing lawful; other things he forbids. All this is done in order that the fundamental cause of perplexity, desires, and sicknesses might be understood, and the afflicted person quickly restored to the balance of the Law and cured. Thus will he be saved from destruction. Herein lies the secret of meekness and the means to acquiring insight!

If a person with a bodily ailment opposes the physician and does something contrary to his order, then certainly the disease involved would daily take a greater toll of him and, without doubt, would eventually destroy him. His death would be attributed to his ignorance. If it is a question of everlasting life, then he would languish in hell, plagued with a pain for which there would be no remedy. If a person well versed in the Law, however, were to come to his aid, and assist him in withdrawing from sin, then his health would continuously improve, rather than deteriorate. "God's saints do not die; they merely change their place of residence from here to there." Even after they seem to die, their intellect remains intact. They make a full demand on that recompense of spiritual nourishment which is their due. After the Day of Resurrection, they will live in paradise forever and ever. This can be considered as certain.

One who is born spiritually improverished and becomes immersed in utter disloyalty has no possibility of finding a prophet, since that door has been closed to mankind. Even reaching a representative of the Prophet is difficult, since such people are few in number and hard to find. Where, indeed, can the blessing of their company be found? And how can this misery and poverty of ours reach the door of eternal bliss and attain the threshold of their wealth? This door also has been closed. Concerning us, God's mercy is like the experience of Khusrau:

> Those intoxicated in the assembly of union with You drank
> deeply,
> But when it was Khusrau's turn, no wine remained in the cup!

What remains here? Just us, a handful of sickly, disease-ridden, lowly, luckless ones who, except for books that describe their faith and actions, have nothing at all. There are accounts of their behavior and the path they trod. All we can do is grab at these aforesaid writings and make them our leaders and guides for, if the sun of bliss has been removed from us hopeless ones, there is still, for the moment, a lamp. "May that suffice for us!"

It is my bad luck that the sun has set;
But I may still use a moonbeam as my lamp!

If, God forbid, this door, too, should be closed, well then what could you or I or Pharaoh or Nimrod or Abu Lahab or Abu Jahl do? There would be no hope for you! What could you do? Grieve deeply and sacrifice yourself! Punish your body, cry aloud and lament, for there is a favorable wind that seeks those who have fallen, and raises them to that stage of divine favor which would take seven million years for the inhabitants of the kingdom of adoration to reach! [Words of warning for the proud, and encouragement for the afflicted, follow.]

*Peace!*

## LETTER 20: THE GRACE OF PROPHETS AND THE GRACE OF SAINTS

*In the name of God, the Merciful, the Compassionate!*

Brother Shamsuddin, at all times and in all states the blessings of God are uninterruptedly showered on all the sheikhs of the Way. Saints follow after the prophets, who are more blessed than they, since great saintliness is merely the starting point of prophecy! All the prophets were themselves saints, whereas no saint could become a prophet.[36] None of the theologians or Sufis would disagree with the above statement, except for those heretics who affirm that the saints are more blessed than the prophets. They adhere to this view because they reason that saints are always engrossed in God, whereas the prophets are mostly concerned with the affairs of men. They presuppose that anyone who is continuously absorbed with God is holier than anyone who is only sometimes caught up in this fashion.

Some foolish people lay claim to having an affection for this group and, cutting away the bridle of goodness, follow them. The stage of saintliness, in their view, is higher than that of prophecy. A prophet is granted the knowledge of revelation, whereas a saint receives hidden knowledge. He knows the secret of things about which the prophets are ignorant. Such knowledge is called "infused knowledge," a title derived from the story of Moses and Khizr.

They say that Khizr was a saint, while Moses was a prophet. While Moses had revelation given to him, apart from which he knew nothing, Khizr was given knowledge infused from above. Khizr knew hidden things, even without revelation, so that Moses had to become his disciple, and a master is always more blessed than his disciple! On the other hand, the spiritual guides of his religion, who are firmly rooted in their faith and fully reliable, all say that no one can attain a stage higher than that of the prophets, or even be on an equal footing with them. The answer to the difficulty is this: Khizr had a particular grace, that of infused knowledge, whereas Moses had a grace that was in no way limited. A grace that is specific cannot outdo one that is limitless. Consider the grace of chaste Mary who, without intercourse, gave birth to a son. Yet her grace does not do away with that of Aisha and Fatima, since theirs has not been restricted among the whole of womankind.

You should know that if all the states and spirits of the entire world of the saints were placed beside one step of the Prophet their worthlessness would be evident! The reason is that they are still seeking and advancing, while the prophets have already arrived. They have found what they wanted, having come by invitation of the royal command. Moreover, they lead a whole people. One breath of the prophets is more blessed than all the breaths of the saints. When the saints reach the height of contemplation, they tell of what they have witnessed, and are liberated from the veil of humanity, even though they remain men. Yet it was the Prophet who took the first step into the realm of witnessing, since he pioneered this path. How can saints be compared to him! Even if they reach the state of a Bayazid, what can be said? About the state of prophets, Bayazid himself said, "Alas, we have no power with respect to them! However much we try to imagine them, we find that we are thinking about ourselves!" Just as the rank of saints is concealed from the understanding of ordinary people, so, too, that of prophets is hidden from the grasp of the saints! So inferior are saints to prophets that the latter, when placed next to the former, seem airborne! Can a pedestrian keep pace with fliers?

It is also related that Bayazid said: "They (the prophets) carry our secrets up to heaven!" He himself paid attention to nothing: He was shown heaven and hell, and he did not even look at them! He simply passed by everything, whether hidden or veiled. "I flew quickly! I became a bird and ascended into the atmosphere of the Divine, until I was on an elevated, limitless plain, where I saw the stage of 'Origins'! When I observed that I was all that, I exclaimed, 'O Mighty Lord God! As long as I am filled with egoism, there is no path from me to Thee! What is more, I cannot pass beyond my own self-consciousness. What should I do?' A command came, 'O Bayazid, your liberation from yourself is bound up with submission to my friend [Muhammad]. Anoint your eyes with the dust upon which he trod! Show diligence in imitating him!' " This is what people of the Way call the "Ascent of Bayazid." The real meaning of "ascent" is "nearness." The ascent of prophets was evidently a matter pertaining to both their persons and their bodies, while that of saints was merely intentional. In its discreteness it amounted to little more than a starting point for the former. Everything that occurs to prophets should be done openly, while for saints it takes place secretly. Also, for prophets, purity and chastity and nearness are experienced in the body, while they remain hidden in the heart of saints. There is a considerable difference between someone who makes the ascent in person, and somebody who merely ascends in the recess of his own heart!

When you have grasped this, realize that the traditionalists and the Sufis agree that prophets and saints are specially protected and more blessed than angels. The Mutazilites oppose this view, saying that angels are more blessed. Angels, in their view, have attained a far more exalted rank, are more refined in nature and also more submissive to God. Hence they must surely be more blessed. In response, we say that an obedient body, exalted rank, and refined nature are not the cause of God's grace. A person's grace depends on how much grace God Almighty bestows upon him. If grace depended on submission, then previous generations would have been more blessed than this one, for they were very obedient. Moreover, if grace depended on exalted rank and nature, then Satan would have been more blessed than Adam, since the latter was made from murky dust, while the former sprang from luminous fire. The grace of any person, it should be clearly realized, depends on what is given him by God.

It must also be understood that angels are forced to submit to God by the binding power of their knowledge of Him. They are not caught up in a lustful nature. There is no covetousness, disasters, hypocrisy, or crookedness in their hearts, nor is theirs a shifty nature geared to trickery. Their food consists of submission, and their drink is obedience to God. On the other hand, the nature of man is commingled with lust, and it is highly probable that he will commit sin. The glamor of the world is firmly entrenched in his heart, while greed and hypocrisy are suffused through his entire being. Satan also has a certain amount of power over a man's person, coursing through the blood that circulates in the veins of his body. His evil, covetous soul invites inside all sorts of depravities. Those who are burdened with natural human defects, including the possibility of lust, and yet abstain from all vice and immorality and, at the same time, in spite of avarice, turn their glance away from the world and, spurning Satan's persistent efforts, divert their hearts from sin, are careful about what befalls their own souls, and occupy themselves contentedly in worship, assiduous submission, and struggle with their own soul in opposing Satan—such persons are, in reality, more blessed than the angels! Submission is easy for the angels because their being is not Satan's battleground, nor is it the abode of lust, nor does their nature desire food and pleasure, nor do they have the cares of wife and children, nor are they preoccupied with self; they are neither uplifted by hopes nor overwhelmed by calamities! Consider the astonishing instance of Gabriel, who for so many thousands of years waited for the robe of worship. His being was at the service of Muhammad so that, on the night of ascent, it was he who cared for the Prophet's mount. How much more blessed would anyone be who had conquered his soul after having struggled with himself night and day, especially if God had been gracious toward him and granted him the grace of seeing Him and had saved him from the danger of hell fire. In short, it is God Who gives grace to whom He wills! Attar has hinted at the meaning of this mystery in one of his poems.[37] [Eight couplets are then quoted.]

In reality, saintliness is one of the divine secrets. It is not born from efforts at self-control or from austerities, and only saints can recognize each other! If the import of this saying were not known to the wise, then it would not be possible to distinguish a friend from an enemy, nor could you pick out one who has attained union from a lazy fellow. God Almighty willed things in such a way that the pearl of friendship was placed inside a small oyster, which was in turn thrown into the ocean of calamity so that the seeker of this pearl, by order of the Beloved, has to put his life in danger: While crossing that formidable expanse, he descends to the very bottom of the ocean in order to obtain the pearl he desires! He lives with the sensation that the condition of this world is pressing in on him. One who has gambled with his life has hinted at the meaning of this undertaking:

> Pass beyond soul and intellect for but a moment,
> In order to heed the commandment of God but once!
> Experiencing the love and rhythm of that World
> Is impossible—unless you sacrifice your life!
> You cannot maintain faith as an adjunct to life:
> The night you die will see the dawn of real faith!
> Any desire that supersedes this
> Call it mere custom or habit; it is not faith!

O brother, remain faithful during all this anxiety, and do not desist from seeking pain! You should not be discouraged by the quantity of your sins, or by the reluctance you may feel! Both angels and men bow their heads in His Presence! [The example of God's elevation of a shepherd to prophecy, and also the example of Balaam, are then cited.]

Dear brother, I swear by God Almighty that heaven and what is contained therein can lead to boasting, while hell and what it contains can lead to renunciation! Hell can, therefore, be a cause of blessing and purification for some. This is why they have been created, not for the sake of unhappiness or to put people at a distance.[38] "God wishes to make things easy for you, not difficult" (Q2:185). Note the following justification for this interpretation: Do you not see that gold is thrown into the fire not to harm it but to purify it and make it perfect? In the same sense, a sinner is taken to hell in order to be purified for the Pure Presence. It has been aptly said by the Lord of the Eternal Covenant, Muhammad: "From the beginning it was known that we would sin. That knowledge was not enough to prevent our creation. Why should the iniquities we committed have been prevented or why should they be obliterated along with our forgiveness?" A heavenly voice was heard to say: "Never despair of God's mercy!" (Q39:53). In every age this is repeated in the ear of the soul, which finds therein a hundred new lives and victories! Consider also the Tradition: "If you had not sinned, then God Almighty would have created another people who would have sinned and then cried out for mercy, and finally been forgiven!" These joyful tidings are a reassurance for all the sinners of the world!

> Do not despair, O hapless sinner,
> For, when the sun's rays come forth,
> They fall not only on the king's palace,
> But also on the beggar's nook.

*Peace!*

### LETTER 21: THE FAULTS OF THE PROPHETS

*In the name of God, the Merciful, the Compassionate!*

Brother Shamsuddin, may God grant you increase! It should be known that there are conflicting opinions concerning the faults of the prophets. The traditional opinion says that they are in fact capable of faults, but only slight ones, not grave! There is complete agreement that the prophets are not capable of infidelity. Abraham said, "O God, preserve me and my descendants from idol worship!" (Q4:35). Since he was incapable of committing faults, this prayer appears to be absurd. What is the answer to the difficulty? This prayer was for his children and not for himself. Although he experienced no personal anxiety in the matter of idol worship, he still included himself along with his children that the prayer on behalf of his children might be answered because of him.[39] Remember, too, that the Apostle was commanded: "Intercede for your own sins and for those of believers!"

The Sufis have this to say about idols: The idolatry of tying the sacred thread[40] or prostrating oneself before some idol is not an issue here, but that of coveting something other than God. It could also refer to fearing something other than God, or relying on something other than God. These are just by way of examples, not real cases, and yet they can be compared to the idols that infidels covet or fear. Though these idols provide no profit or loss for them, they still trust in them and thus destroy the very foundation of faith in God's unity. To turn to this faith, a person must put his whole trust in God Almighty and acknowledge that neither in heaven nor on earth is there anything profitable or harmful apart from Him. When He made correct belief obligatory, no rest remained except in Him; no faith, except in Him; nor was there anything else to fear, except Him. In fact, there should be no recourse to anything other than God! If someone were to do such things as the infidels do—even though no doubt might arise about the authenticity of his faith—it would still be like polytheism. Anything at all should be considered as an idol, whether it be profitable or harmful, if fear or hope is associated with it, even though, in and of itself, it is not an idol. This is what Abraham, the Friend of God, meant when he said; "Look at me! I cannot take any rest except with You; nor do I see anything but You; nor do I hope in anyone except You; nor do I fear anyone except You!"

Since, apart from Him, no one exists in either world,
Who, apart from Him, can be the object of love and desire?

This is the meaning of the prayer: "God's Friend does not repent of infidelity, which is the opposite of faith." It is futile, moreover, to compare such a friend with the mass of believers. Infidelity is the abode of enmity, but faith is the abode of love. Although the infidel, because of his infidelity, is an enemy of God, it has not been made clear to him that God is his enemy. His condition is ambiguous. If he leaves this world with the burden of infidelity upon him, let it be known that the Lord is his enemy. If, however, infidelity has lost its grip upon him, it means that the Lord loves him. On the other hand, although one of the faithful is a lover of the Lord due to his faith, it is still not certain that the Lord loves him! This means that his condition too is somewhat ambiguous. His fate is left in the lurch: Either he leaves this world with faith, in which case the Lord really loves him, or—God forbid—if his faith has declined, the Lord will have become his enemy. Such oscillation between love and enmity is altogether impossible for prophets, since they are dear to God, and special in His sight. There is no stage higher than theirs. As God's favorites, they experience the completeness of His love. They have no fear of infidelity for, while change and alteration are possible in creatures, they are not as far as the divine attributes are concerned.

It must not be thought that every lover becomes an enemy, or every enemy, a lover. Still, God can effect a change. Consider Satan, whom God brought down from the high state of friendship to the rank of archenemy.

Who knows whether, in this deep ocean,
Gravel is prized, or cornelian?

Here we have to understand that both God's love and His enmity have no eternal dependence on any cause, because both have always existed. It is the opposition or acquiescence of God's slaves that is temporal. Love and enmity must precede, while acceptance or rejection are added afterwards. Moreover nothing, which is supplementary, can become the cause of what precedes it.

Hence you should realize that opposition and acquiescence are nothing—simply nothing!

The firmament whispered secretly in the ear of the heart,
"From me you will learn whatever God commands!"
Had *I* control over my own fate,
Would I not have spared myself this end?

But the group that maintains that the prophets were capable of committing serious sin illustrates its point with the story of Joseph's brothers who, like him, were prophets, and yet committed great sins. The traditional group of Sunnis, on the other hand, claims that the prophets are incapable of committing serious sins, expecially infidelity, which is the most heinous of all! All other great sins as well should be impossible. The reason is that, if someone is capable of committing one serious sin, then he could commit any of them. Proof of this is found by considering the mass of believers. By way of reply, adversaries might say: "Whatever emanated from the brothers of the prophet Joseph before revelation descended upon them and this, in turn, resulted in repentance and correction."

It is possible for prophets to commit unintentional venial sins known as "faults." Now a fault means that, before falling into it, there was no intention of committing it, and afterwards, there is no lingering in it. It is like a person who is walking on a slippery road and suddenly falls down. Immediately he gets up. Before he fell, he did not intend to fall, nor did he delay in getting up again. The faults of the prophets are of this nature. Nevertheless, they are reprimanded. "On account of the greatness of their rank and their exalted state, the great are taken to task for trifling matters, while lesser people are not even scolded for notable offenses." The mystery contained in this explanation is that "the sincere ones are in grave danger." Not being taken to task for notable offenses is a proof of one's spiritual inferiority, while chastisement for even slight offenses is a proof of one's spiritual stature! It serves as an object lesson for others, since, if those well advanced in virtue are reprimanded, imagine what will happen to others! They ought to learn from the example of the great not to become God's enemies. One group says that this chiding is done out of an excess of love, so that love might find its full expression through chiding. Among friends, chiding is an ongoing process, as the poet has said:

Where there is no chiding, there is no love:
As long as love remains, so will rebukes.

Have you not heard the story of David? When he committed a fault, for forty days, night and day, his head was bowed in prostration. The result was that the abundance of tears that he shed caused so much grass to sprout that it concealed him and he was lost to view. Still, no news of divine forgiveness reached him. In his pain, he afflicted himself so that all the grass withered from his sighing. He placed both hands over his eyes and went on weeping until both palms became covered with blood. He raised his hands to heaven and said: "O God, even if You do not pardon me, at least show compassion for my tears!" "O David," came the reply, "do you remember your tears, but forget your fault?" You must know that because the faults of the great are more serious, they will be dealt with more severely, as the poet has attested:

Those killed by the Beloved's bloodthirsty lips
Remain till Resurrection Day with bloodstained shrouds!

Note that for those who visit cemeteries—whether they visit the tombs of renowned spiritual persons or those of the ordinary faithful—there are many benefits. As the Apostle of God has said, "Visiting tombs causes tenderness to take root in hearts; tears flow freely; and one is reminded of one's last end." Once a man asked for advice about his hardness of heart. He was told to look at cemeteries and to take them as examples, weeping and wailing the whole time. It is profitable to make a visit each week, as Muhammad was commanded: "O Prophet, visit the graveyard every Friday!" And God alone knows what benefits derive from such visits and what they really mean. [Times to visit and prayers to say are then recommended.]

When you arrive at the cemetery, take off your shoes and, with your back to the west and your face turned toward the tomb, recite the prayers recommended for the dead. "O Muslim men and women who live in the abode of peace, may God bless those who have preceded us and those who will follow us! God willing, we shall one day meet you. We seek peace for you and for ourselves." If it be a martyr's tomb, then say: "Peace be upon you, for you have endured! How good is the world to come!" (Q13:24). And if there be graves of both Muslims and infidels, say: "Peace be upon him who follows the path of guidance!" (Q20:47). Afterwards sit down and pray: "In the name of God and in accordance with the community of God's Apostle." [Traditions referring to the benefits of such visits are then mentioned.]

It has been noted that the most difficult night for the dead person is the very first one. Hence it is necessary to give something to charity in his name. If this is not possible, perform two prostrations. Each time, after the introductory prayer, recite the Throne verse (Q2:255) and ask God to apply the merit of your recitation to the dead person. A thousand angels will bear light to his grave, and he will receive the merit of a thousand martyrs.

*Peace!*

## LETTER 22: THE ORIGIN OF SUFISM

*In the name of God, the Merciful, the Compassionate!*

Brother Shamsuddin, may God bless you! The foundation of Sufism is quite ancient, having been practiced by the prophets and the righteous. The fact of the matter is that the predominance of evil habits in our times makes the Sufis themselves appear evil in the eyes of people. Those associated with this Tradition are divided into three groups: The Sufis, the seekers, and the dissemblers. A Sufi is a person who is completely lost to himself, exists only in God, is freed from the hold of his lower self, and is conjoined to the Truth of all truths. The seeker is one who engages in the struggle with self, undergoes austerities, and disciplines himself by means of various practices. The dissembler is one who, for the sake of position and success, makes himself out to be one of the above, but is devoid of any of their qualities. He is also ignorant of them! Despite all this, there is some hope that he might become one of them and, in the shadow of their riches, pass beyond both worlds, becoming a combatant in the army of God and not merely a camp follower. Each city has one vicegerent and one sultan, while others pass their time in the shadows of these two. Among various peoples there are only a few who affirm the whole truth. When, however, someone begins to resemble others in one particular thing, he finds himself imitating them in other things as well. There is an injunction of the Law that says: "Everyone who makes himself similar to a people in both behavior and belief will end up by becoming one of them."

It has been said that the first Sufi in the world was Adam.[41] God Almighty drew him forth from clay and placed him in the stage of choice and purity. He prepared the royal edict of vicegerency for him. For the first time, between Mecca and Taif, he made a forty-day retreat, thus becoming the inspiration for novices to undertake this practice. "I kneaded the mud of Adam for forty days with My very own hands." When he had completed the forty days of solitude, God Almighty gave him the fullness of spirit, lit the lamp of intelligence in his heart, and brought the light of wisdom from his heart to his tongue. He trembled and said, "Thanks be to God!" The Prophet also hinted at the efficacy of this practice when he said: "Anyone who dedicates forty days to God, God, in turn, will order streams of wisdom to issue forth continuously from his heart and upon his tongue!" Adam resolved to acquire sanctity. At the beginning of his vicegerency, he received the gift of the homage and prostrations of angels. He stood up and, like an intrepid traveler, resolved to reach heaven. He journeyed through all the climes of heaven. He passed far beyond the secrets of these kingdoms. He was told, "Keep control over all your senses! Do not yield to your own inclinations!"

Still a novice, he did not yet have the requisite control. Impelled by boldness and mirth he displayed a grasping attitude. From a hidden ambush he was smitten with this rebuke: "Adam has disobeyed his Lord!" (Q20:121). He was brokenhearted. He became immersed in begging forgiveness for his sins. Tradition dates the repentance of the Sufis from this occasion. He said: "O Lord, we have wronged ourselves" (Q7:23). All his dominion and vicegerency were withdrawn from him. He stood there naked, full of repentance. It was said: "Adam, journey in the world in order to discharge this debt!" The condition of discipleship is that a disciple who commits a fault should go on a journey. Adam resolved on journeying over the earth, alone and naked. Since his body was naked, it was said to him: "Adam, beg!" He begged a leaf from each tree, and receiving three leaves, he sewed them together and made a patched garment with which he covered himself. He then set out on his earthly journey.

For three hundred years he sighed with grief until he was thoroughly exonerated. "Undoubtedly God chose Adam!" (Q3:32), that is,

He thoroughly purified him and made him a Sufi. He greatly esteemed the patched garment[42] that he had made from the leaves begged from the trees. At the end of his life, he clothed the prophet Shish with it and conferred viceregency upon him. This became the Way of Muhammad and the means for conveying the wealth of Sufism to descendants of the prophets.

Sufis should be travelers who belong to some group in this world, that they might be able to assemble for companionship and relate what has occurred to them. Thus the Kaaba made its appearance. It was the very first religious sanctuary. Before that time, there had been no such thing. It appeared in the time of Adam. All that the prophet Noah required of the world was a blanket. The prophet Moses himself always wore the blanket that the prophet Shuaib had conferred on him the first day that he entered his [Shuaib's] service. And this is a very important condition in the Way, that there should be a spiritual guide who clothes the novice with the Sufi garb. Jesus always used to wear a woolen garment. Similarly, both Moses and Jesus themselves built Jerusalem as a place of spiritual trust.[43] Then, in every country and region Sufis built meeting places for themselves, and made fixed abodes for periods of solitude where they could practice inner converse with God. Fellow travelers could also come there and recount the traditions of the exalted, divine secrets. When the time for the foremost of the prophets and the King of the saints, the blessed Muhammad—may the peace of God be upon him and his family—arrived, he himself donned such a blanket. "It was the practice of your father, Abraham" (Q22:78). He also yearned for the religious sanctuary of the Kaaba. The Pride of the world set aside a special corner in his own mosque and from his companions he selected a group of about seventy people who were travelers on the Path. They used to converse there together, while the Arab chiefs and ordinary people were not allowed to enter that space. When the Pride of the world bestowed great honor and dignity upon any of the companions, he would give him his own cloak or shirt. That person would then become a Sufi.

The beginning of this Way came from Adam, and its completion was found in Muhammad, the Apostle of God. It remains in the midst of believers and their community. It requires strength of heart, above all else. One should not pay too much attention to one's unworthiness, for this particular work is dependent on the divine favor and grace, not on the actions of any person!

O brother, many thousands are prostrate in adoration, and many more thousands recite God's praises and laud Him; thousands of others are amazed at His secrets, while others are swept along by His works. He created a fearless people out of mere dust. He chose all these servants and submissive ones even though they had not rendered any previous service to Him. He spoke without introduction of any kind, saying, "O handful of dust, am I not your Lord?" (Q7:172). In a single hour, an intoxicated one is lifted up on the couch of bliss as he witnesses the glory of the Lord. At every moment there are signs that he has become attuned to God and accepted by Him. The exquisite gift of divine union is conferred upon him, together with a certain repulsion, veiling, and a hundred rebukes. Every moment is devoted to silent converse with God, yet grief and anger still have their place. Every moment someone is brought forth from the temple of idols and honored by having the garment of acceptance conferred on him, while another is taken outside a mosque and the rope of the pain of banishment is fixed around his neck—for there is need to experience both His kindness and His rage!

*Peace!*

### LETTER 23: IN QUEST OF THE WAY

*In the name of God, the Merciful, the Compassionate!*

Brother Shamsuddin, may God make a seeker of you! Everyone who is a seeker along this Way must be able to build on the capital of the Law in order to proceed from the Law to the Way. When he has found this path to the Way, he will be able to turn his steps from the Way to the Truth. How can anyone who has not laid hold of the Law be able to find the Way? And if he has not yet happened on the Way, then what can he possibly have to do with the Truth?

Never has permission been granted to any foolish person, who is both bereft of divine knowledge and ignorant of the Law, to place his feet upon this Way. Indeed, there would be the fear that such a person might be destroyed and end up nowhere. If a person undertakes struggles, difficult things, and ill-advised austerities all by himself, and if any of them be displayed publicly, then so much pride, arrogance, self-conceit, and folly would become manifest in him that he would throw his own faith to the wind and become enmeshed in the snares of Satan! Know for certain that God Almighty has never made an ignorant fellow a saint, nor would He ever do so.[44] The sheikhs tell us this, and the Quran testifies that "God did not befriend an ignorant man" (Q17:111)—for ignorance is the root of all baseness!

They say that the Way of travelers devolves on a twelvefold knowledge: divine unity, work, divine knowledge, conditions, ecstatic contemplation of God, witnessing God, being addressed by God, hearing God, realization of the divine existence, knowledge of the spirit, the ego, and the intellect. These types of knowledge are separate but interconnected, for knowledge of one implies knowledge of the others. It should be known that the members of these groups are all devotees of knowledge of the Law, the Way, and the Truth. They were so in the past and will always be in the future. But there were some poverty-stricken ones who perished of thirst in the wilderness. Of what use to them was the Tigris of Baghdad or the Nile of Egypt?

> Some thirsty ones fell in the desert and died;
> How would it benefit them if the whole world were the
>     Euphrates?

The traveler along the Way should mull over such a thought! If this world and all its allurements were given to him, as well as the world to come, with all its joys; or if the calamities of the world were to be rained down upon him; or if all his efforts, substance, and pleasures were to be handed over to strangers; or if the future life, with the joys of paradise, were to be handed over to the faithful, while calamities and misfortunes were reserved for him, then his repentance should be such that, while everyone else repented of having done forbidden things in order to avoid falling into hell, he would repent of lawful things, so that he might not go to paradise! His intention should be such that, whereas all worldly men seek their own desires and ease and pleasure, he remains in quest of the face of the Lord. All men seek an increase in prosperity as a result of their efforts, while he seeks Him in little! If he gets anything, he gives it away; while if nothing comes to hand, he still gives thanks to God!

The sign of the traveler is that he is happy even when he does not get what he wants. In this way he will be free of all bonds. His dealings with his rebellious nature should be such that even if it were to yearn for something for seventy years, he would not give in to it! He should also have pursued the path of acquiescing to the Truth so diligently that calamity or good fortune, denial or affirmation, rejection or acceptance—all are the same for him! He sets out with great trust, not asking anything from men or God, for he considers asking from men to be polytheism, and is too ashamed to ask anything of God. His abstention is such that if all he possesses in the world is a patched garment or a blanket he is so happy with it that others envy his absorption in remembrance of God: seeking Him by day, he spends his nights devoted to His service and labor. If his lower self were to cast a glance at all this submission, he himself would sell the worship of seventy years for a morsel of bread and throw it before a dog in order to escape a prideful sense of astonishment. [An example is then given.]

A traveler should be intelligent. He extinguishes his natural inclinations in the furnace of asceticism in order to open his mind to the gifts of God. If he looks to the right, he sees God; if he looks to the left, he sees God; if he stands up or sits down, he sees God. In his magnanimous vision the kingdoms of this world and the next amount to naught. His body melts away in eagerness, while his heart is blessed by God. Thoughts of wife, children, this world or the next no longer find a lodging place in him. Although his person is still in the world, his heart is with God! His soul remains here, but it has already attained its desired stage, having seen the Friend with the eyes of the heart. This stage can be acquired under the protection of an experienced spiritual guide. Assisted by the sanctity of such a master of the heart, one can safely pass through the calamities that lie along the Way. All the sheikhs of this group, the great men of religion, and scholars are in agreement on this point: that, without an experienced guide, no one (except in rare instances) can reach God. As the poet has said:

> Until the glance of a man of God falls on you,
> Where will you learn about your own existence?
> If you are prone to sitting by yourself,
> You will not be able to travel this Path alone!
> You need a guide for the road, do not go alone!
> Open your eyes lest you drown in this ocean!

Many travelers become puffed up with pride after making some progress; they think they have attained the glory of God! Without an experienced guide, a person will become like Satan, and the duplicity of his lower self will come to light. He will be thinking about worldly matters and his own demands. He will remember a few words someone has spoken and think that he has attained his object! He will consider himself to be in possession of lawful influence in the kingdom of the Lord. He will fall into extravagant and heretical ideas, just as someone has hinted in the following verse:

> They are garbed as Sufis, these immature fellows,
> But they have attained only the babble of beginners!
> Having advanced but a few paces on the path of truth and
>     purity,
> They already indulge in slandering the good name of others!

Anyone who sets out upon this Way and experiences the pain associated with it should find for himself a spiritual guide who is much respected by other guides and sheikhs. There should be general agreement about the man's preeminence as a leader and his lawful exercise of spiritual power. All should concur that he follows the will of God, is a man of noble ancestry, and is experienced in the kingdom of the Lord. The novice should imitate him and bind himself to him so that he might remove every obstacle that lies in his path, point out to him the defects of his lower self, and inform him of the dangers that lie along the Way. Thus the novice will be enabled to come completely out of himself, as the poet has testified:

> When a well-esteemed man comes across your path,
> He will protect you in all your endeavors!
> Since you can never distinguish the Way from its pitfalls,
> How far can you progress without a staff?
> The volcanoes that mark this Way are many;
> It is not for everyone that this work is intended.

The condition of being a novice is that, when someone wishes to bind himself to an experienced guide as his disciple, he will first have to put aside his own desires. The lexical meaning of the word disciple is "to seek, to want," and a disciple is "one who seeks." Among the members of this group, a person is called a novice if he is seeking Him but has not yet obtained his desire. The sheikhs have said, "He is a disciple who, in compliance with his guide, is like a dead man in the hands of the washer—he turns whichever way he is turned! A novice should be so submissive to his guide that, at the slightest hint from the latter, he would gladly offer his life, his spiritual riches, and his worldly goods, but not leave his guide! He would obey him, even if the guide were to command him to drink poison![45] He would not delay but comply at once. He would make no use of his mind or rational knowledge.

The example has been adduced of Shiekh Bu Ali Faramdi. Once he told his guide, Sheikh Abul Qasim Gurgani, about a dream he had had: "You spoke to me in such and such a fashion in the dream: why, O Sheikh?" Abul Qasim Gurgani turned his face away and said: "If there were no room for 'why' in your heart, then it would not have found its way to your lips!" A disciple cannot make genuine progress if he is always seeking the why and wherefore of the injunctions given him! The root of the matter at hand is this: "There are some things close at hand that you do not like, even though they are actually very good for you; and there are other things at hand that you like, but are harmful to you. God knows best; it is you who are ignorant!" Everything is smooth along the path of the disciple who is destined to enjoy eternal bliss and becomes an heir to everlasting wealth. Everything that he needs is at hand. The malicious glance of his enemy falls harmlessly on his beauty, and misfortunes are far from the wealth piled up in his lap. On the other hand, that poor fellow who is destined for misery falls into all sorts of thorns and is attacked from behind as he proceeds along his way. At every step a hundred obstacles and dangers arise to confront him!

O brother, everyone who has had the bridle of favor placed around his neck will find himself in the position of being "a felicitous one who is born thus from his mother's womb." He will repel all rage and vehemence, banishing them from within himself as well! On the other hand, a miserable person is born thus from his mother's womb, as the poet has hinted.

This misfortune did not befall us today:
The color of our blanket comes from Gilan!

Now what will you do? You should place hope before you and tolerate misfortune. Even though household goods are defective and not befitting the sanctuary, your hope should still be that whatever God finds, He will buy! [Some examples are given to confirm this teaching.]

*Peace!*

# THE HUNDRED LETTERS

LETTER 24: THE FUNDAMENTALS OF THE WAY

*In the name of God, the Merciful, the Compassionate!*

Brother Shamsuddin, may God help you attain the Object of your desires! The fundamentals of the Way are set forth in this Tradition: "My servant is diligent in approaching Me through supererogatory prayers, till I love him, and when I love him, I become the ear by which he hears, the eye by which he sees, the hand by which he holds, and the tongue by which he speaks." When God holds someone in special affection He behaves toward him in the same way as a kindly mother does with her small son. She is ever on the alert for whatever might harm him. She is careful to attend to all his needs without his having to say anything about them. In truth, it should be known that, when God Almighty looks with favor on someone, He turns him into a focal point for the needs of the people. The dust trodden under his feet becomes a soothing ointment for the eyes, and a fragrant scent for travelers on the Way.

There is a story that the people of Basra had come out of the city to beseech God for rain. Their prayers and lamentations produced not a drop of rain. Then a traveler happened to pass by. He saw the large crowd with upraised hands, closed eyes, and mournful voices. A sense of empathy arose within him. "O God Almighty, by the secret which is in my eyes, send rain," he prayed. Immediately it began to rain. When someone from the crowd heard what he had said and saw what he had done, and noted that his prayer had been answered instantaneously, he followed the traveler to his house and said: "O Sheikh, I have a request to make of you." "Tell me!" he replied. "What is that secret in your eyes," he asked, "which made them able to offer an intercession resulting in rain?" "These eyes of mine," he replied, "have seen Bayazid! You should know that the dust he treads upon becomes a collyrium for the eyes. His tongue also is like spring rain, producing life. Just as spring rain clothes the dead earth with a vesture of new life, and turns a thorn-infested tract into a rose garden, so a word from the lips of Bayazid can bring back to life the dead hearts of men." And he spoke in such a way that his words came straight from the heart. Because his deeds and qualities had been united, his mercy and kindness could shine upon all. He was the sort of man who himself does not eat, but feeds others; who wears little himself, but clothes others. Nor does he pay attention to the wounds inflicted by others. Where there is oppression, he brings trust. He opposes abuse with prayer to God and praise of Him. Do you know the reason for all this? It is because he is protected. Nothing except gentle breezes waft across the plain of his heart toward others. His compassion is like the sun, which shines equally on friend or foe. His humility is like the earth, upon the face of which all creatures tread. He takes in hand no lawsuit against another. No one could even talk of his anger toward his fellowman. All are his dependents, though he is beholden to no one. His bounty is like a river. He blesses his enemy, concentrating all his mercy upon his foe. Most men, though free, see everything from one viewpoint, but his outlook is universal. He accords everyone equal treatment. A person who does not partake of this quality should not take a single step on the Way. He would be a seeker after money and fame, and the speech he uttered would be of no avail for, whenever God Almighty raises up someone, He raises him up completely, so that He gives him a tongue and hands and eyes and ears and a pure heart.

Unfortunately, you and I know orators whose very tongues and hands bear witness against them as, indeed, do all their members! They cannot retrieve a morsel they have already placed in their mouth, and yet they cannot remove the Sufi garb from themselves. Their desire is that the world should acknowledge that it is beholden to them and that the Friday prayer should be read in their name, to their own advantage. A man who throughout his life is unwilling to go into the bazaar wearing a sash or a simple vest or an ordinary hat, because he fears being disgraced in the sight of the tailor, appears to a perceptive person as a worshiper of self rather than a worshiper of God! By the same token, a man who sits in a hermitage and adorns himself with prestige and self-seclusion so that people might consider him a man of probity and pay attention to him is acting like a woman of ill repute who spends the whole day adorning herself in order to attract the glances of men.[46]

It is fitting that all a man's members should become tongues, and that his tongue should support his heart—but that it should be cut out with the sword of modesty if it ever wants to speak anything but the truth concerning Him! His heart also should become a mirror reflecting in front of him whatever has happened in his past, so that he feels tongue-tied! He is unable to say what he wanted to say, and he murmurs: "Such a tongue is unable to make a single statement about God," and from that moment he ceases to talk.

It has been said that everyone who comes out of his own home knows the way back so that, if need be, he can return home. The speech of such a person is not fully grounded in the Way! For a Sufi, the heart takes precedence over the tongue, while for a scholar, it is the tongue that has precedence over the heart. A Sufi is impelled to action by his heart. Orators, however, and those who pursue this world of ours are going along with staves. What are they doing? They are blind, for like a blind person each uses his tongue like a staff, striking the ground here and there as he goes along. In this way he shows that he is a blind man! (This saying is not acceptable to scholars, since they uphold only what is attested by Tradition. Yet it is a widely respected opinion of one belonging to the brotherhood of Sufis!) In sum, Sufis put their trust in their heart, rather than in their tongue. Do you not see that if what outwardly seems to be infidelity springs from the fullness of a person's heart it is in fact genuine faith? "For he who has been compelled to recant while his heart remains faithful" (Q16:106) is still a believer. By the same token, the faith that proceeds from an evil heart is really a form of impiety. As God declared: "Those people say: 'We bear witness that you are the messenger of God.' And God knows that you are indeed His messenger; and God bears witness that the hypocrites are inveterate liars" (Q63:1). The tongue is the master of the household of the Law, command and prohibition become known through it, and religion is proclaimed by it. When someone becomes dedicated to God's work, then the tongue becomes something good. Do you not see that it was the nightingale of the rose garden of the Law who said, "I am the most eloquent among Arabs and non-Arabs," and yet at the end of his work even he exclaimed: "I cannot calculate the praise that is due You!" Such was the extent of the Prophet's astonishment.

O brother, why should the person who displays eloquence in the stage of thanking God hesitate in the stage of Unity? A dear friend has offered the following explanation:

In love the best way to proceed
Is to remember that you have erred!
No wonder that in praising and glorifying You,
Even the most eloquent speaker of both worlds was
    dumbstruck!

Normally a person talks continuously about something he likes very much. But in the design of love it is only when a person steps beyond conversation and then returns to the world that he reaches

Him! "The beauty of those who are furthest from God are loudest in their remembrance of Him!" appears to him:

> If I were wise, I would talk less about You.
> I would close the path of conversation.
> I would gather together a few scorched hearts.
> And then I would weep over my talking and lament it.

O brother, a man who has become a full-fledged believer is very precious indeed, but most people simply put their hands into the throat of faith and move them around a bit. Not everyone who reaches the king's door finds admission to his presence! "Surely the idolaters are unclean" (Q9:28). Purity of heart is a condition for admission. In hell there will be many thousands of tongues that call upon God but not one heart that knows Him. You will see many thousands of eloquent tongues that have become mute, but you will not find a single heart in the clutches of the guardians of hell. O brother, you might not have this rich crown upon your head at the moment, but this is no reason to brand your heart with hopelessness! The Quran attests: "God does not impose on any soul more than it can bear" (Q2:286). The weight of the commands given to each is in accordance with his or her strength. If our heads are empty of any crown, while our hearts bear the mark of hopelessness, these misfortunes are separate and at least not compounded. If there is no step which befits religion then let us turn to shouting slogans by groups of ten, saying: "No one would purchase people with afflictions like those whom God purchases. Who else would pay the price for you that He does?" As the poet has observed,

> Behold us, full of faults, and you the buyer:
> How shoddy the goods, but how generous the Buyer!

It has been said: "If you turn to a sanctuary in your old age, I shall put every kingdom at your disposal; but if you follow my injunctions during your youth, I shall make a way for you in the midst of the angels. Just as you know My right to command and prohibit, so too realize that your justification is dependent on My own generosity. I do not in any way hold the breaking of your promise against you. If you have been afflicted with any grief, I would wish to apologize again for it, on My own behalf." I shall tell you the secret of all that you have heard: God speaks out of His own generosity. It is impossible for His truth and generosity to have limits! If all the renegades and devilish people of the world, together with their offspring and dependents, were to be exalted to the utmost, and the eternal, kingly crown were to be placed on their heads—still His truth and generosity would barely have been tapped!

*Peace!*

## LETTER 25: THE LAW AND THE WAY[47]

*In the name of God, the Merciful, the Compassionate!*

Brother Shamsuddin, may God show you the straight path! The Law is a path established by prophets in the midst of a people, with the help of the Lord. The call issued by all the prophets is, first and foremost, to acknowledge the unity of God. In this, they concur. Moreover, there is only one religion, one call, and One worthy of adoration. All have said, "Your God is one God!" (Q2:163). But Muhammad said, "Fear God, and obey me!" (Q3:49). From Adam to Muhammad there has been no disagreement in the teaching of the prophets, since the call is simply the divine revelation that God Almighty accomplished through Gabriel, having it imprinted in their minds and sounded in their ears. There have been different words, interpretations, metaphors, and supports for different Laws, but what is essential in the call and constitutes the real origin of a community and its laws is the divine invitation. In this there is no contradiction.

The second call of the prophets is to service, by virtue of the fact that they are physicians to the people. At all times, according to the exigencies of the particular people, prophets lay the foundation that governs and regulates that people, through the revelation of the Lord. The acceptance by the prophets of the divine utterances is called "revelation." When they explain things on the basis of that revelation, it is called the "invitation." Those who listen to them and follow them form a "community." The collection of commands and prohibitions, of principles and their institutionalized expressions, comprise the "Law." Following this path is called "submission." Accepting the burden of all this is "Islam," while showing constancy in all these matters is called "faith." So, then, a Law is a path established and maintained by a prophet. This wide road is called a "Highway." The Law should be a wide road, for many roads branch off from it; as the

Prophet said: "My people will be divided into seventy-three different sects, among whom seventy-two will be deviations, and one the path to salvation."

The Way is a path that stems from the Law. The Law expounds divine Unity, purity, prayer, fasting, pilgrimage, the holy war, religious tax, together with other obligations and concerns, while the Way seeks the reality behind all these prescribed things. Works are adorned with purity of conscience, and moral activity is purified of the evil propensities of nature, such as hypocrisy, avarice, oppression, idolatry, and similar things. In short, everything that is connected with outward purity and sanctification pertains to the Law, while everything connected with inner purification and sanctification pertains to the Way.

For example, washing before prayers is prescribed by the Law, while the effort to remain perpetually clean derives from the Way. The Law prescribes that at the time of prayer one should turn toward the Kaaba, while the Way endeavors to turn our gaze toward the Truth (behind the Kaaba). In general, the observance of all that pertains to the senses comes under the ambit of the Law, while the observance of all that is concealed in the inner purity of the body has to do with the Way.

All the prophets command their own communities to do what they themselves do, but there are some matters of conduct and works they do not insist upon, in order to make things a bit easier for the people. They themselves, however, as well as the elect, observe them all, such as praying throughout the night, refusing alms, eating little, turning away from the world, remaining calm in the face of great calamities, displaying simplicity in what concerns food, dwelling, and clothing, and all such similar things. In short, what brings difficulty to people is the Law, but what lightens their burden—whether it is enjoined or merely recommended—constitutes the Way. Hence, if anyone resolves to progress on this Way, he ceases to belong to the class of the common people and enters the category of the elect.

The election of the prophets is of two kinds: One is forbidden and dangerous, as the Quran has said, "This is especially for you, and not for the believers!" (Q33:50). The second type is expressed in a pleasing Tradition: If anyone grows renowned in that speciality and advances along this Way, then how can there be any talk of excess? He would be making progress in his own perfection. Yet no dispensations are granted for anything along the Way, for such are granted on account of the weakness of a person's condition, just as others are allowed for the purpose of mitigating the lot of the needy and the infirm. The masters of the Way, however, should be noted for their strength, courage, application, and diligence. Anyone in earnest must necessarily hold that there are no dispensations for him from anything. He should view what is permissible as forbidden to him. Even in what is lawful, he should not display greed or cupidity. The Law opens the door to ease and comfort, while the Way leaves no loophole for it! It also forbids whatever leads to ease or originates in the sensual soul.

Whenever a disciple allows himself liberties in things that are permissible, his soul then becomes emboldened and he is prompted to follow his appetites. From these he goes on to greater and greater excesses, till he is finally borne off to what is forbidden and there perishes. Everyone who resolves to follow the Way without the Law is like someone who wants to climb onto the top of the roof but breaks the ladder and then tries to scale the wall without it. No matter how hard he tries, he will keep falling down. Such a person may also be compared to someone who tries the trick of throwing many stones up into the air, but no matter how much deception he practices or how hard he strives, the stones will still fall on him even more quickly than he throws them into the air!

Or again, such a person would be like someone who wants to go on a pilgrimage but turns away from the direction of prayer and so, inevitably, turns his back on the Kaaba as well. If he then sets off, no matter how many years he travels with the purpose of reaching the Kaaba, he will never reach it. Every end has its appropriate means, and every intention has conditions attached. In each society people have to be fit for this enterprise and have some affinity for it. The conditions and requirements of the Way are the full complement of God's commands and the Law. When a disciple becomes well versed in the path of the Law and reaches the stage where he discharges, as far as possible, all the duties of the Law, then the divine grace becomes his intimate friend. In this manner will he be found to have been specially chosen from among ordinary men, and will be worthy of becoming a companion to those who tread the path of the special Way.

O brother, when you have grasped what the Law and the Way are, set out as best you can like someone who hobbles and stumbles along in imitation of, and conformity to, those pure souls! Come forward as a pauper who has absolutely nothing and yet presents his petition from afar to the One who cares for the needy! Know that if a few particles from the alchemy of kindness that is found in the treasury of divine grace were to be sprinkled on the idolatry of the idolators or the infidelity of the infidels, then that very idolatry or infidelity would turn into faith in the Unity of God! And if a few drops of the soul-animating sherbet contained in the cup of the Invisible One were to drop into the throats of people, then you would not see anyone in the whole world opposing or denying God! What He did not do to you was determined from all eternity and cannot be ascribed to the agency of some creature. If He had acted as a creature does, then there would be no question of divine grace! Even if every hair of your head were to become an angel of death, and every limb a Pharaoh, and every particle of you a Nimrod, and if hell were to surround you on all sides, still, whenever He wants you, absolutely nothing anyone can do will stand between Him and you.[48]

*Peace!*

## LETTER 26: THE LAW AND THE TRUTH

*In the name of God, the Merciful, the Compassionate!*

Brother Shamsuddin, may God make you prosper! The Law and the Truth are two expressions. For the Sufis the reality of the external state is measured by the Law, while soundness in the internal state is encompassed by the Truth. The outer and inner are joined together; indeed, at root, they are inseparable! Believing, without profession by word of mouth, is not real faith; nor is profession of faith complete without the inner resonance of belief. "There is no god but God" is the Truth, "and Muhammad is the Apostle of God" is the Law. If someone, in the soundness of his state of faith, wants to separate them, he will not be able to do so. His very desire would be futile! One can, however, separate the injunction of the Law from the Truth, in the sense that there is a manifest difference between speaking and really believing, but the externalist scholars say, "We do not make any distinction! The Law is itself the Truth, and the Truth means the Law!"

This is false! Whoever says that it is possible to have one without the other follows the religion of the pagans. There are those who claim that when the state of the Truth is revealed, the Law is no longer needed. Cursed be such a belief and such a religion! It should be known that the Truth has to be interpreted to mean that there can be no annulment with respect to it. From the time of Adam till the end of the world, the command concerning the mystical knowledge of God remains the same. Yet in the Law there is scope for annulment and change. This presents no difficulty, for the Law deals with explicit commands. There was a time when there was no Law, and there will be another time when Law will be no more, but there never was, nor could there ever be, a time without the Truth!

The Law is an action of Man, while Truth belongs to the Lord and is in His safekeeping and protection.[49] Almighty God says: "Those who strive hard for Us, We will certainly guide them in Our ways" (Q29:69). Struggles pertain to the Law: One finds divine guidance through the Truth. The former is the preserve of man and refers to commands that concern him, while the latter is the preserve of God and concerns the various states that a man can experience. The Law pertains to things acquired, while Truth is a matter of God's gifts. The Law is like matter, Truth like the heart. It is the heart that gives consistency to matter. The Law is like the body, Truth like the soul. In the life of man it is impossible to have one without the other: just as the Law is indispensable for the attainment of Truth, so the Truth is necessary to complete the legal requirements of faith.

This group [i.e., the Sufis] is especially well versed in knowledge of the Law and the Truth as applied to real-life situations and not merely verbal ideals. Knowledge of the Truth rests on three pillars: first, knowledge of the essence of the Lord, His unicity and precepts, and also the negation of any likeness to Him whatsoever; second, knowledge of the attributes of the Lord and His commands; and third, knowledge of His deeds and wisdom. Knowledge of the Law rests on these three pillars: the Book of God, the Custom of Muhammad, and the consensus of the community. Dwelling on knowledge of the Truth without insisting on observance of the Law is heresy, while dwelling on knowledge of the Law without attesting to the Truth is hypocrisy. The saints of God acquire, by the sincerity of their quest, the knowledge of instruction, that is, that knowledge of the Law which can be learned from the teaching of others, through diligent application. But the saints also purify their own actions by the knowledge that is given to them and is something inherited, having been bestowed on them as a gift and not acquired through teaching or learning: "Whoever has acted according to what he knew, it is God who made him an heir to knowledge that by himself he did not possess." Hence it is that externalist theologians seek knowledge acquired by instruction—for that is their stage—and yet they do not find this knowledge. Necessarily they become apostates saying, "This is against Tradition!" or, "Where is such a Tradition to be found?" They do not realize that the absence of something from the house of a beggar does not explain why it is also absent from the palace of Sultan Muhammad Shah![50]

The Tradition of Almighty God in his dealings with His own saints is that He dislikes them to manifest more than is fitting. Whatever they get from God is their secret, and their tongue is the instrument used to interpret that secret. The tongue should restrict itself to manifesting the secret in a manner appropriate to, and consonant with, God Almighty.

Their tongue mirrors their knowledge and action;
It is a balanced scale, showing neither more nor less!
United to God, they are distraught with themselves;
Even their own feelings are unknown to them.

If someone sees in a distorted manner, it is because of the crookedness of his being. A squint-eyed person sees double, yet he is convinced that he sees correctly! As far as this group is concerned, those people are all external, squint-eyed persons scanning the world in vain, yet they number themselves among those whose vision is correct! This group is ready to excuse them, because a person with clear vision should be extremely tolerant toward one who is blind. "Turn away from the ignorant!" (Q7:199) is the same command, but the people with this knowledge have departed and their works have come to a standstill. In this religion all who were men of Truth have become hidden and have concealed what they had. Anybody who held himself knowledgeable in this religion hid the Truth from the hearts of the people. So this religion at once came to a standstill, for the people said, "But this is not the Truth!" There used to be adepts of the Truth among them, but they disappeared from their midst, taking their knowledge along with them. No one was left who could describe this religion. Deeds were no longer found in their midst, for they, too, need to be described, and description requires knowledge that must be obtained from those who are capable of understanding! When such people can no longer be found, neither can knowledge! Without it, there is no description, and when description ceases, so too do deeds. Not only this—there is also a decrease in knowledge of the Truth. There is a similar falling off in knowledge of the Law. You should know, therefore, that since this group does not countenance the abandonment of even one of the finer points enjoined by the Law, how could they possibly advocate the neglect of what is obligatory?

The stories of the sheikhs concerning Traditions about the niceties of the Law are recorded in books and repeated on the tongues of all, for the most famous of the great men of religion used to say: "I desired everlasting life of the Lord that all peoples might be brought to the joys and delights of Paradise, and that I might be in the heights of the world and show the fine points of the Law as firmly established, and so that they might know the extent to which the Law benefited them." Thus they can learn the finer points so well that whatever they acquire is found in following the Law.

O brother, do not break your heart, but neither be remiss in carrying out what God has ordained! The goal is reached by His assistance, not by your efforts! [This teaching is then illustrated with reference to Adam and the angels.]

*Peace!*

## LETTER 27: THE IMITATION OF THE MESSENGER

*In the name of God, the Merciful, the Compassionate!*

God's blessing be with you, brother Shamsuddin! For a servant of God, eternal bliss and glory consists in love of the Lord! It is a sign of riches and honor for a creature if he is concerned with imitating the leader of the Muslims, as the Quran attests: "Imitate me [Muhammad] and God will befriend you" (Q3:31). Place the necklace of compliance upon your neck, and bend your ears to his directives; show yourself ready to obey what he commands, and flee far from any rejection of him! Hold on firmly to the citadel of faith with all its pillars and, as you pass each one of them, take note of the rights of each with punctiliousness. Thus the pact of friendship and the knot of love for the Creator, through the guidance of Muhammad, will remain firm. When you depart from here, you will be able to bring your fidelity and firm trust to the abode of the Beloved Himself, as promised in the Quran: "The abode of the righteous is near the All-Powerful King" (Q54:55).

The first stage of Paradise is filled with beautiful damsels, mansions, streams, trees, and purified wine, as has been said: "Paradise is where those people will alight" (Q18:107). When you step into the second stage, the Gift that is beyond description and the Wealth that eludes the imagination will show Its face to you. "For good people has been prepared a place such as no eye has seen, nor has any ear heard its praise, nor has it entered into the heart of man to conceive what it will be like!" This is an explanation concerning it. In the third stage, that of those who meet and who attain union with the Friend, this is what will happen to you: "Who will taste death in the country of the One who lives forever?" There are no limits to the vast expanse of Your dwelling place, just as there are no limits to Your love. One experiences there a stifling like that of a drowning man whose lungs are bursting for the air of Truth!

The explanation of that love is that "He loves them and they love him" (Q5:54), but you and I and others like us, by ourselves, know nothing apart from reports of heaven and hell—which is not much at all! One beloved of God has said: "The Lord, in creating hell, showed greater mercy than He did when He created heaven." Worldly people, although they run after pleasure and indulge their lusts, still hope to reach heaven, yet they foolishly do not cease to grasp after pleasure or to follow their lustful desires. When they think of hell, however, they reduce their sinful pursuits. The reason is that, although they will not desist from the pursuit of transient pleasure for the sake of what is permanent, yet they will do so out of fear of hell, and are thus brought to their final end. On the other hand, one who worships in a spirit of "praising what God ordains" is beloved of God. He hopes to receive his reward from the Lover. What effect will the remembrance of heaven and hell have on his enlightened mind? How could the grief of losing heaven or of going to hell trouble him, for the King of love and desire has come! How could he remain preoccupied with the hope of heaven or the affliction of hell?

> Compared to the refreshment of union, heaven is a pile of
>   rubbish:
> In the path of lovers, it looms as a trivial gain!

As Khwaja Mumshad Dinuri was on his deathbed, a disciple prayed in this fashion: "O God, be gracious to him and grant him the wonder of heaven!" Khwaja Mumshad opened his eyes and said: "Fie upon you! For thirty years now they have been praying that I will enter heaven but I won't even glance at it from the corner of my eye! What sort of prayer is this?" The heart of the matter is contained in this, and the basis of confidence consists in the fact that only pure things have been brought from the world of purity and will be taken back there! This is explained thus: "The abode of the righteous is near the All-Powerful King" (Q54:55). What place is there for reports of heaven and hell? This is a precious secret! "He who knows, understands; he who is ignorant, remains so." Again, if the soul of man, which originates from there, has flown into this hunting ground, then it has come to hunt the pheasant of mystical knowledge and the partridge of love. It will then soar back to the world of its origin to the drumming of "Return to your Lord, joyous, and pleasing in His sight" (Q89:28) till it comes to rest on the branch of the tree of union: "Return is to Him."

O brother, mystical knowledge is the seed of love![51] Everyone who would penetrate further into the world of mystical knowledge will become more inflamed by the fire of love and will receive great delight and preeminence from the face of the Beloved and from the sight of the Desired One. For He is the beloved of souls and the desired of hearts. The souls of lovers are melting in the fire of longing, and whatever He bestowed upon them—life, wealth, wife, and children—they return as they keep treading the Path to the Friend. He gave them consolation and told them of His love for them, and bore witness to the reality of His love for them. "He loves them, and they love Him" (Q5:54). From what we know of Him, He is devoid of contradiction or fluctuation. Without a shadow of a doubt, His testimony is holy. It is in the same vein that the lord of the two worlds said: "God Almighty bestows His splendor on mankind as a whole but on Abu Bakr the Just in particular." In other words, the mystical knowledge enjoyed by Abu Bakr was such that the fragrance of his burning heart used to waft, morning and evening, to the nostrils of the holy ones in their abode of rest. His delight in the Friend was very great. This group asks: "Where in the whole wide world can a particle of this knowledge be found?" One beloved of God has said that a bolt of lightning from the invisible world strikes suddenly. The souls consumed by this astonishing and head-spinning World remain dumbfounded in astonishment; they find no rest anywhere, no stability, no power either to stand firm or to flee. All cry out, "There is no steadfastness with You, nor is there the option to escape from You!"

Such is the saying of the great. One of the seekers came to Abu Bakr and requested him to intercede with God on his behalf so that he might be granted mystical knowledge. That sincere and just man, by virtue of his righteousness and purity, placed the petitioner's request before God; immediately the man became conjoined to God. He was thrown into complete confusion and remained utterly astonished, his head swimming. When he related his condition to Abu Bakr, the latter, out of compassion for him, sought to discern the real state of affairs. A divine decree came to Abu Bakr: "The state of knowledge that you requested of Me on his behalf has been requested formerly by thousands of travelers along the Way. I have bestowed the merest particle of this knowledge upon them. All those who have been favored are in a state of astonishment similar to the one that you are witnessing."

O brother, the inhabitants of the consecrated world say, "We have not been able to render You Your due," and the dwellers of that hallowed world say, "We have not attained the knowledge of You that we should have." Even though this field of battle has claimed many a life (everyone who contests with Rustum falls), it can be traversed by one who strides into this kingdom.

The work really originates from "God bestows His mercy on whom He pleases" (Q3:73). The work does not proceed from you! The magicians of Pharaoh were steeped in infidelity and crime. They believed that their magic could never be put aside, but when the wind of the wealth of the gracious Lover blows, it does not bypass either magic or magician, infidelity, or infidel. Dawn can find a person immersed in the error of infidelity, but by evening, he can be clothed with the robe of faith and repentance. The Lord can open up the Path to peace for a brother by conferring His favor and the perfection of His grace upon him. Know the Truth, that you will not look with a sinful glance at your own devotion, nor place a special claim on your own intrinsic qualities. Do not consider an alley dog to be better than yourself; neither demean yourself in the palaces of the great! Stop heaping thousands upon thousands of the stones and bricks of unfulfilled desires and intentions upon your head! One who stands at a threshold of dust must be humble! He must also be devoid of all claims on his own behalf. If you place thousands of angelic crowns on your head, you still retain a beggar's face with its sullied complexion—it is nothing but mere dust! What will you do? Dust, if it merely cakes your face, can easily be washed off with water, but water cannot wash away your very complexion!

*Peace!*

## LETTER 28: FIXING ONE'S SPIRITUAL ROUTINE FROM THE OUTSET[52]

*In the name of God, the Merciful, the Compassionate!*

Brother Shamsuddin, may God bless you! After a disciple has attained the reality of faith and the soundness of repentance, he should be perpetually occupied with ablutions. Really and truly there should be no time when he is not occupied with ablutions, even though it be dark and cold, and the water itself is cold. After his ablutions let him perform two inclinations as a prayer of salutation. He should never seek to escape from any prayer. Let him perform the five prayers along with the congregation. When one prayer is over let him prepare for the next since "anyone who is waiting to pray is really already engaged in prayer." Then he should occupy himself with prayer and utter those ejaculations that he has determined for himself, or that his guide has told him to say.

When the disciple rises before dawn, he should take a purificatory bath and perform two prostrations in gratitude, saying one hundred times: "I ask God to pardon all my sins, both great and small, apparent and hidden. O God, grant me Your mercy!" With dawn itself, he should perform two prostrations at the customary time. During the first inclination he should recite the one hundred and ninth chapter of the Quran. In the second, he should recite the one hundred and twelfth chapter, on sincerity, which condenses the legacy of the Prophet, that sincerest of men. After this prayer, let him recite: "O God, I pray for Your mercy, which alone can set my heart straight." This is found at the end of the work *Qut ul-Qulub* [Nourishment for hearts].[53] The Prophet used to show great insistence in using this prayer, saying seventy times: "I ask pardon from God, besides whom there is none to be adored; He is alive and remains firmly established for ever. O God, I beg You to pardon me!"

Then comes the dawn prayer, in congregation, which should be offered from the depths of his heart. When this prayer is finished, he should occupy himself with the verse that comes in the *Qut ul-Qulub*. To the extent that it is possible, he should recite the praises of God and beg continuously for forgiveness, earnestly repenting and imploring forgiveness for his whole past life. He should not talk much, except to substantiate God's commands and prohibitions, or to intercede for the welfare of the Muslims, or to speak about things that are profitable for his brother Muslims, or to instruct someone in need of knowledge. All speech of this sort would be beneficial. As far as possible, he should be facing Mecca in all that he does. Let him be occupied in visiting holy tombs or conversing with his spiritual guide, or enjoying the company of a divinely inspired master. This would be better and more profitable than remaining forever on a prayer carpet, preoccupied with the praises of God. Only when he is not occupied with suchlike things should he seat himself on his prayer carpet, in the mosque or at home, and become occupied in remembering God— the most profitable of all activities.

When the sun rises, let him rise up and perform two prostrations of prayer. This is the morning prayer. He should remain seated in the place of prayer until the sun has fully risen. After this, he should perform two more prostrations. This is very profitable. When the sun has risen high, let him perform the mid-morning prayer, which he should make an obligatory practice for himself. He may also perform other prayers joined to these. After all these have been said, let him rise up to attend to the needs of his brother Muslims, such as visiting the sick, carrying biers, or associating with the pious and those who are God-fearing. If none of these activities is possible, he should promptly engage himself in reading the Quran, repeating his prayers and remembering God. After he has done all this, let him recite, "When prayer has ended, disperse in the land and seek God's grace and remember God continuously, that you may succeed" (Q62:10). Then he should attend to his dress and food. If he finds nothing further to do, let him know for sure that "in sleep there is safety!"

When the time for the midday prayer arrives, let him rise from sleep, have a bath, and perform the obligatory four prostrations. After completing that duty, let him perform two more prostrations and remain in the place of prayer, waiting for the next prayer. If his heart is tranquil, let him give thanks till the next prayer. If his heart is not tranquil, he should strive to put it at ease. He should realize that this is genuine remembrance of God. Let him perform the obligatory prayer in the mosque and his spontaneous acts of devotion at home, for the safety of religion, and let all his thoughts be of that nature. When the time for the next prayer arrives, let him perform the four canonical prostrations. After that, let him perform the obligatory prayer. Then let him be occupied in remembering God and in meditation till sunset. Being watchful at this time is just the same as being engaged in praise.

As the sun is setting, he should examine his soul with care, noting that one more day of his life has passed; what has been gained? Has the day been a loss? To what extent has he profited by it? When the sun has set, he should prepare for the evening prayer and when he has said the obligatory prayer, he is free of what Tradition requires. After that, let him perform twenty prostrations, reciting the prayer of repentance, which falls between the evening prayer and the time for going to sleep. If he is diligent, he can perform all these prayers; and he may also impose an added religious duty on himself: "They forsake their beds, calling upon their Lord in fear and in hope" (Q32:16) rightly refers to those who are awake and watchful between sunset and the first watch of the night. When the time for the retiring prayer arrives, he should perform the four canonical prostrations. After that, he should perform the obligatory prayer, then four more traditional prostrations, as well as two final ones for the evening, unless he is in the habit of performing them later on, and is confident that at the very end of the evening he will not omit them. Otherwise, he should perform them at the beginning of the evening. If he does this, he will not be counted among the foolish but will be numbered among those who are in the presence of God. After the retiring prayer, let him read the chapters that come at the end of the *Qut ul-Qulub*. If he is not occupied with these, or he cannot recall them, let him say 250 times the one hundred and twelfth chapter of the Quran, on sincerity, for that is equal to a thousand verses. Afterwards, let him go to sleep in a state of purity, continually remembering God. Also, to prevent sleep from gaining mastery over him, let him rise at the end of the night's rest, before dawn breaks, and begin his work afresh—that is the time to beg for pardon, and prayer is more profitable at this time than at night! If at the end of the night he engages himself in the prayer throughout the night, he should seek God's pardon and recite the Quran. In this way let him show diligence, that the blessing of this hidden way, known as "The Way," might be bestowed upon him. It is incumbent upon him to adjust the Way to the

Law. Anything you perceive in the Way that is not consonant with the Law will not profit you and should be dropped! It is only heretics who maintain that one can stand without the other, and that when Truth is made manifest, the Law then becomes superfluous.

God's curse be upon such a faith! The external, bereft of the internal, is hypocrisy; while the internal, if it lacks external expression, is mere wishful thinking! The outer is joined to the inner at its very roots and cannot be separated by anyone. "There is no god but God" is the Truth, "and Muhammad is the Messenger of God" is the Law. Anyone who wants to be in a state of perfect faith cannot dissociate one from the other. Any such desire would be vain! Day by day a novice should devote himself to traveling along the Way with a pure intention in his heart. He should make a habit of being resolute in his outlook, pure in his actions, radiant in his secret knowledge, and agreeable in his conduct. He should benefit by conversing with the pious and serving the elders. He should realize that this work hinges upon discipleship and austerities. The path of discipleship requires him to yield to the suggestions of his spiritual guide, in small matters and in great, for obeying one's spiritual guide is the cause of many a blessing.

The path of austerity means that a novice should busy himself in opposing the desires of his lower self, for giving in to the natural impulses of one's bestial nature is at the root of all misfortunes. Performing the obligatory duties is a precondition to fulfilling the commands of the Law. In austerity lies the very heart of cutting oneself off from the world, since it entails safeguarding the senses and abstaining from food and drink, as well as from sleep. When a novice commences his work, he should not seek the immediate solution of his difficulties, intentions, affairs, and all that takes place; rather, in all his states of soul he should have recourse to a sympathetic spiritual guide. Let him lay aside any excesses of self, for in this way will he become diligent and straightforward. The hope of union and blessings is like a tree: if properly pruned, it should bear much fruit, but if the sun is kept away from it, and it is not pruned, then it will inevitably wither and perish. A novice should strive, and even though his limbs and members be full of sin, he should never turn back. He should stand firm since faith remains as a quality and adornment of the heart even when disobedience and wickedness are ingrained in a person's members. It is the command of the heart that is correct, not that of one's members. It is the heart that is to be heeded, not one's members. One must keep in mind that "God Almighty does not look at your faces and your works; He looks at your heart and your intentions." Do you think there is only one Mt. Sinai in the world? Or only one Moses? Your body is Mt. Sinai. Your heart is Moses! The strength of both lies in this: "Surely I am God!"

O brother, if you were to worship for many thousands of years and had to suffer many trials and afflictions, you would become purified in the fire of self-searching and striving. Whatever you said would be taken quickly to The Presence where you would experience the recompense for your devotion and labors.

As long as you doubt that I am enamored of Your face,
Regard me as dust clinging to the paw of your alley dog.

[An anecdote concerning Shibli is followed by this couplet:]

Speak but one word to me, and then
Kill me, O King, if that be your wish!

*Peace!*

### LETTER 29: PURITY

*In the name of God, the Merciful, the Compassionate!*

Brother Shamsuddin, remain firm in trying to please Almighty God! Peace and salutations to you from the author of these words! In your own mind be convinced about the answer to this question: "How is a man's worth measured?" It is measured by his purity: In both worlds, purity forms the threshold of riches and happiness, while corruption and pollution are discarded along the Way by all prophets and righteous people.

There is a saying in the Law that runs: "The foundation of peace rests on purity." God does not countenance any corruption, nor does He display His beauty to anyone who is unclean. For a long time punishment has been meted out to the unclean. No one touches it [the Quran] except the pure! (Q56:79). The impure are beyond the pale of Islam, and the dust of misfortune has been poured upon them in their separation.

The first step is to see that one's body, clothes, and food are pure and lawful. All one's senses should be purified of sin and rebellion.

As for one's heart, it should be cleansed of all blameworthy qualities, such as avarice, jealousy, rancor and other similar things. When this first degree of purity has been achieved, then the disciple has taken a step forward on the path of religion; when the second degree of purity has been achieved, he has progress, and with the third degree, three steps. This is the evolving reality of repentance. In this way repentance is gradually realized; hence it is called a "revolution." In other words, the penitent progresses from a state of foulness and uncleanness to one of purity: He is a church that becomes a mosque; an idol-temple that becomes a hermitage; a devil who becomes a man; dust that becomes gold; a dark night that turns into a brightly illuminated day! At that moment when the sun of faith rises on the heart of the disciple, Islam reveals its beauty to him, and he reaches the head of the lane leading to mystical knowledge of God. Without this purity, however, every action that he takes may be called mere habit and custom, performed in imitation of one's parents. That is not Islam! Look attentively at what has been written about this fundamental requirement and study it repeatedly. What is written here should not be overlooked! Many people simply pretend to be Muslims, but they are not. Take care: They are Muslims only according to the external prescriptions of the Law. This, for them, is faith. The mandate of the path called the Way, on the other hand, is that a disciple should both confirm and manifest his purity in two ways. One consists of externalizing what is within his breast. That would, simply speaking, be grace. By itself it is sufficient. It is something rather special. It applies particularly to prophets and righteous men. The second type of purity is that which is connected with what is external and its path is one of struggle. This is the common or ordinary way. The beginning of this purity is concerned with clothes. When anyone wants to attain this purity he should attend first to his clothes. Merely reading and learning about these visible things does not cause them to be realized: It is necessary to bestir oneself as much as possible and show oneself assiduous in renewing ablutions. [Some recommendations follow.] At the end of the night, toward dawn, let him take a bath. Let him consider this a good work. Almighty God will adorn him with a special kind of purity and will remove all external and internal pollution. At every moment he should be aware that God Almighty is there beside him. When someone realizes that God is really his provider, then he should don the robe of humility and be ashamed of the reams of information that his Lord has concerning him. One beloved of God said:

"What is that sign by which you recognize him?" He replied: "No opposition to God should ever arise in my breast!" The One speaking from within my heart says: "Does not your Lord fill you with shame?" [Two references to God's mercy are then cited.]

> One glance from the Friend equals a thousand felicitations;
> I am waiting for the moment when that glance will come!

*Peace!*

## LETTER 30: PURITY—A FURTHER EXPLANATION

*In the name of God, the Merciful, the Compassionate!*

Dear Brother Shamsuddin, may God honor you in both worlds! Purity is of two kinds, external and internal. Just as prayer without purity of body cannot be correct, so too genuine mystical knowledge of the Lord without purity of heart is impossible. Just as clean water is required for purity of the body, so purity of heart is indispensable for true insight into the Divine Unity. It has been said:

> Knowing the divine Unity is not for dust and water;
> It requires something more: a clean heart and a pure soul!

This group is pure not only to the outer eye, but also to the inner eye, since it is rooted in the knowledge of the unity of God. "God loves those who repent. He loves the pure of heart" (Q2:222). This is their wealth. A hint concerning this purity has been given by the Apostle when he said: "O God, make my heart free of hypocrisy!" Know that there was no question even of hypocrisy showing its face in any of the states of his blessed heart. If his glance were to fall on his own favors and high rank, for him it would mean an affirmation of otherness in divine Unity. In the palace of divine Unity affirmation of otherness is shown up as hypocrisy. Though one particle of the miracles of the sheikhs might provide the initial touch of collyrium on the eyes of the disciples, yet finally, in the perfect palace, it too would prove to be a veil, albeit a respected one!

Hence it is that Khwaja Bayazid, the holy one of God, has said: "The hypocrisy of the mystics is better than the sincerity of disciples." In other words, what is a stage attained by a disciple would be a

117

veil for one who is perfect. For a novice, spiritual ambition is expressed in miracles, but for a perfected one it consists in being honored by God. Belief in divine Unity is our duty, and should be acknowledged both in this world and in the next. It should not be affected by either world, that it might remain fit for the divine Presence!

They are neither disturbed by hell nor excited by paradise—
Such is the nature of the people belonging to this group!

[Anecdotes about much bathing are then set forth.]

It is related that Khwaja Bayazid said: "Whenever any thought of the world enters my heart, I cleanse myself, and whenever any thought about the world to come enters my heart, I take a bath." The reason is that the world is polluted and any thought about it is polluting. Hence cleansing or purification becomes necessary. In the life to come there is carnal desire, and one must obtain relief from that ceremonial pollution. While it is necessary to be cleansed from what pollutes, a bath is needed once ceremonial pollution has occurred.

The sheikhs have insisted on the necessity of both external and internal purification and have laid great stress on it. The starting point for those desiring to follow the Way is that their hearts become mirrorlike, so clean and shining that one can see reflected in them an image of the world of creatures and of the divine order. Thus they progress from the ranks of commoners to the rank of the elect. We, however, are unfortunate slaves of the world, bound by habit. We wear the sacred thread of neglect. Except for our devotion to habit, of what else can we boast? In what can we take pride except our neglect? We tread the path like men of religion and lay claim to divine Unity, even though we are impure and our vision blind. Yet Jew and Christian, church and temple are narrower in their outlook than we are. The word *unity* falls from the lips of all who are unitarians, but what a difference between one type of faith in the divine Unity and another! Someone in the world, for example, might know about the duties of ablutions and prayers, and this can be termed "knowledge." On the other hand, Imam Ghazzali also possessed "knowledge." What a difference between his and that of the former! If someone asks, "Why?" the answer is this: "It is a matter of God's grace: He bestows it on whomsoever He wishes."

A person may wonder: Why does God give this wealth to one but not to another, just as a king bestows the post of prime minister on one, while he makes another a doorkeeper? In this way, by giving spiritual riches to someone, He wants to lead him out of his bad habits, whether he be a weaver, sweeper, vegetable seller, oppressor, or one who eats forbidden things. To which of these belongs loveliness? The Quran says: "Are these the ones among us upon whom God has bestowed all this kindness?" (Q6:53). Fuzail ibn Iyaz, although a robber, was ordered to be brought to God, for He desired him. Balaam, son of Beor, on the other hand, was seated on his prayer mat for four hundred years, yet he was finally commanded to be removed from the Royal Presence; he had been rejected. God wanted Umar, even though he was an idol worshiper, whereas the angel of death worshiped for 700,000 years, all to no avail. "He cannot be questioned concerning what He does" (Q21:23).

> From the flock the wolf takes the sheep he wants;
> The wilderness puts each shepherd to the test.

Understand this and be hopeful, for a hundred suchlike things can take place. Once the glance of his graciousness alights on us, all our faults become virtues; all harmful things, beneficent; all evil propensities, things of beauty.

O brother, there was a handful of dust, someone wholly contemptible, fallen by the roadside, banging his feet helplessly! Suddenly, the gracious glance fell upon him and said: "I am going to make a successor in the earth!" (Q2:30).[54] For today endure misfortune and pain, swallow grief and sorrow. Concerning the essence of these works, understand what was said: "If you had not experienced these pains, calamities, griefs, and exertions, and were simply taken off to heaven, not a particle of pleasure would be found therein!" The proof of this is that Adam went to heaven and took no delight in it. He sat on the throne of paradise, but his feet touched the dust. So, one by one, extract the thorns from your foot. If you experience a hundred vexations, you can say: "Why did these thorns, which have pierced my foot, not penetrate into my soul?" Travelers find enjoyment when they arrive at their intended destination. When a disciple attains the object of his desire, it is like water returning to its source, or a bird to its nest. Religions cease, and anxiety about one's work is replaced by this thought: "The servant is with the Lord, the Lord with the servant."

*Peace!*

# MANERI

LETTER 31: RIGHT INTENTION

*In the name of God, the Merciful, the Compassionate!*

Brother Shamsuddin, peace and salutations to you from the author of these words! Know that the powerful deeds and actions of a disciple draw their strength from the intention with which they are performed. Intention is related to deeds and actions as the soul is related to the body, and light to the eye. Can you imagine a body without a soul? Or an eye without light? Well, the same condition would pertain to actions or deeds that lack a pure intention. They would simply be expressions of habit and convention. Venerable Sufis consider habit and convention as pride, not submission, leading to destruction rather than salvation. As long as you tread the path of habit you are a devil, a hypocrite and not a dervish!

The truth of one's intention is evident from its sincerity, like rays from the sun or flames from the fire. When one's intention becomes purified of the dross of the present world, this group calls it the sincerity of the gnostics. They say that the intention of each person is tantamount to his knowledge and perception. It can be of several kinds. One is that desire and love of the world are uppermost: All the actions and deeds that he intends are worldly, even prayer and fasting: "There are some among you who hanker after the world!" (Q3:151). This is their stain. There is nothing left for them except useless labor and frustration.

A second kind of intention is motivated by desire and love of the world to come. All actions and deeds that take their origin from such a person's heart bear the stamp of the life beyond, even eating and sleeping! "The gardens of paradise are for those who have faith and do good works" (Q18:107) refers to them.

There is another people who are known as being royally audacious. Their feet are planted on the earth, but they do not lower their heads even to the level of the next world. They have no purpose or intention in life except to seek the Lord!

Beyond this world there is for us another world;
Beyond hell and heaven we have another home.

All the deeds and actions that come into existence through their agency are purely and simply for God. "It is You alone Whom I worship" (Q1:4) can be fittingly ascribed to these people. "My prayer and sacrifices, my living and dying, are all for the sake of the Protector of the Worlds" (Q6:163). The praise of these people has been aptly depicted in the Quran: "And they desire His face" (Q18:28). They have no desire except to meet God. There is no other reward for them except, "You are our True Friend." Whatever is given to these people cannot be measured out according to the measure of the minds and intellects of men or angels. It is a royal proclamation that runs: "God supplies the needs of whomsoever He wishes without measure" (Q2:212).

Each person is weighed in the scale of his intention, which is dependent on his sincerity. Hence arises the question of punishment, which scorches even the hearts of God's friends: "God does not look at your faces or at your works! He scrutinizes your hearts and your intentions." The awe inspired by this Tradition, "On the Day of Resurrection the fate of people will depend on their intentions," has turned the blood of the just to water! Neither you nor I know how much lamentation will arise from the worldly on that day; it lies beyond the scope of mind or intellect!

Tomorrow you will experience the hangover from today's intoxication!

When the veil is lifted from in front of you, your real state will be revealed to you; belief in many gods, or in One; infidelity, or earnest submission to God.

When the dust settles, you will quickly see
Whether you are astride a horse or an ass!

A disciple should grieve night and day, anxious about whether he will ever emerge from the grip of his habits and conventional actions and be motivated by true intention! When his deeds and actions cease to be routinized, he should look for the shoes of a spiritual guide, that is, he should enter his service. Whatever he does should be at the command of a master of the human heart. When this happens then, even though there be an admixture of elements of dissimulation and hypocrisy and also the habit of thinking of recompense, still it will be a step toward purity of intention. Here is a comparison that can easily be grasped. When a small boy begins to write, he is inevitably a poor writer. As his teacher goes on correcting his writing, however, it will gradually improve. This is self-evident. If, however, he writes poorly and says: "I will put pen to paper when I have acquired the skill of an Ibn Maqla," then he is expecting the impossible!

It is the same with regard to religion, reaching God, and attaining eternal bliss. It has been said that if anyone makes this comment, "I shall not worship until I acquire the righteousness of an Abu Bakr and the intention of an Umar," he could be compared to a fool who says, "I will begin writing on the day that I acquire the grace and perfection of an Ibn Maqla!" If he does not begin with deeds and actions that are mixed with habit, dissimulation, and hypocrisy, he will certainly never reach the stage of human perfection! What does it mean to say to a seven-year-old boy: "Pray and observe the fast"? If it were not for the child's fear of his father, he would not pray or fast. In spite of this, he is tending toward perfection. But there is a precondition: An experienced guide is needed to lead the child from imperfect actions to those that are pure. If there is no guide, then habit becomes like a fatal disease. Nothing comes from such a state. God forbid that it should ever arise!

Do you not see that if a poor writer is not aided by an experienced teacher, his writing will never be perfected, even though he struggles along by himself for fifty years? What we said about looking for shoes did not mean that one should be able to wear the shoes of another! As yet he does not have the ability to do this. He cannot simply step into the shoes of a man of faith. One beloved of God and endowed with virtue said: "I watched a great man for seven years. I was completely incapable of taking up his practices!" If an experienced guide accepts you, your soul will burn with love for him since he accepted you when you were but dust. To be sure, this task of religion is no game! Hence a poet has said:

O lad, the work of love is no mere game,
For this Way is no mere allegory!
Go play, then: love is not your work!

It has been explained that a disciple should be like the earth so that his guide may be like the sky. Sometimes the guide provides him with warmth; at other times with light. Sometimes the guide protects him from adversity, at other times he refreshes him like a breeze. The purpose of all this is to bring the disciple to perfection. If some unfortunate soul is among those blessed by the guidance of a master, all his troubles will be taken care of. If, on the other hand, the disciple is not enriched by a guide, he will not be able to do anything. "You will find no change in God's way of acting" (Q33:62). Yet all this narrative will not be found except in the speech of a just man. Now, what will you do about your intention? "If no rainwater falls upon it, then dew will suffice" (Q2:265). In other words, if someone cannot acquire the blessings of the conversation of this group, then at least he should arrange to read each day from their writings. There is a reference to this in the following:

> Since it is my bad luck that the sun has set,
> May the radiance of your moonlike face be my lamp!

The whole purpose is to have the deeds and actions of a disciple ruled by a right intention. The science of intention is a very refined and subtle one. As far as possible, one should be awake and alert, and try to ascertain the real nature of one's intentions. God willing, this aim is attainable. A person then becomes fearful of his sins and ashamed of his selfishness. It is related that Abu Bakr used to say: "Time and again it happens that I perform two prostrations. When I give the greeting of peace I repent because I have been ashamed and confused at my worship. You could say that I had committed a theft, since a man who does not reach the stage of purity of intention does not attain the pleasure of worship and the joy of his faith." Khwaja Sufyan Suri had walked around the Kaaba with a friend, crying continuously. His friend said: "Are you crying out of a fear of sin?" Sufyan stretched out his hand and plucked a blade of grass. "I have many sins," he said; "and I am worthless when compared to this blade of grass, even though the divine Unity that I confess is the true Unity. Unlike those men who have, but think they do not, we think we have, but in fact we do not!"

*Peace!*

LETTER 32: RITUAL PRAYER[55]

*In the name of God, the Merciful, the Compassionate!*

My brother, Shamsuddin, may you enjoy eternal bliss! O brother, a disciple should show himself diligent in whatever leads to a greater purification and sanctification of his heart, and penetrates its innermost recesses, whether it be prayer, recitation of the Quran, remembering God, or meditating upon Him. This presupposes, of course, that there is no spiritual guide available. Otherwise, the choice should be his, not the disciple's! In prayer there are secrets and works that are over and above the strict task of worshiping God! It has been said: "Whoever has not tasted something knows nothing about it!" The five ritual prayers have been treated in the book *Rawh ul-Arwah* [The comfort of souls]. It is a memorial that was brought back by the Pride of the world from the pure realm of "two bowlengths" from God (Q53:9).[56]

O brother, your worth is quite negligible! You have not yet reached the stage of ascent. You do not possess such magnificence that they bring Muhammad's mount, Buraq, to your door. What should you do? You should don the garb of lustrous purity and run to the glorious heavenly mosque, among the faithful who are clothed with angelic virtues. First enter and then go to the back row of servants. Stand there on the step of petition. At length you will come out in the front row of the friends who have been seated on the carpet of the secret of the Master. It is He who has combined in prayer, according to His own good pleasure, all the pillars of the Law.

In prayer one finds the meaning of fasting, and something more. Fasting is a kind of abstention done for a purpose. In prayer also, restraint is practiced for a purpose. Moreover, it is fitting that you rest there and then go and do other things. In prayer there is purity of intention, and in prayer there is the meaning of the religious tax, because five silver pieces must be given to the poor before one can recite the final prayer. At last let him recite: "O God, pardon me and other believers, that all may be at peace!"

In prayer, too, one also finds the meaning of the pilgrimage. During the pilgrimage, one enters the sacred precincts of Mecca and alights and sojourns there, while in prayer one sanctifies oneself and praises God. In prayer a person can also discover the meaning of the holy war. Ablutions can be compared to donning armor. The prayer leader is like the general, while the people resemble the army. The leader stands in the front line in the sanctuary, where the battle will be joined. The people are drawn up in ranks behind him. United, they come to his aid. When they are victorious in their holy war, they share the booty among themselves. When the leader gives the final blessing of peace, he distributes the grace of the Lord of Glory.

Even though he may not be able to travel to Mecca, a believer who has prayed has also gone on a pilgrimage. Though he has no property, he has also paid the charity tax. Though he may not have had the power to fast, he finds that he has, in effect, fasted. Devoid of the requisite strength, he has nonetheless fought a holy war. Take care, O fearless one! Do not enter lightly into the very heart of prayer, for 124,000 resplendent examples of prophecy and sinlessness have had their heads buried in the dust as they sought this honor. At the same time, many thousands remain in the cemetery because they failed to perform one or two prostrations.

A single prostration, from the heart and soul,
Is of more value than thousands of words!

It has been said that when prayer and supplication become united for a disciple, he advances from the stage of dissipation to the light of the prayer of union. Then his body can be compared to the Kaaba, his heart to the divine throne, while his head is caught up in the Lord! In the *Sharh-i-Ta'aruf* [Commentary on the book about seeking knowledge],[57] those who have gained the divine Presence have been described in these terms: "Their lights have torn the curtains, while their secrets have spun around the divine throne; and their ability will be brought to light in the presence of the Master of the throne." When the light of the faith of a disciple, in the abundance of his zeal, begins to rotate around the divine throne, every mirror reflecting his worth becomes exalted, since those constantly engaged in the prayer of union and holiness attain such a stage as is unattainable except with the help of purity.

"When the Messenger of God prayed, the water of his heart emitted a sound like that of a bubbling cauldron." Then he girded up his loins of service and was garbed in the pilgrim's cloak, with his body in the palace of his heart. His heart rose to the stage of his soul, while his soul soared to that of his head. His head reached the divine Majesty. The face of Truth itself was disclosed to him. His body was in the stage of proximity to God; his heart was nearer still; his soul was very close to God, while his head was immediately adjacent to Him. All that was revealed to him at that stage occurred while he was at prayer.

He heard God's word without any intermediary and was greatly enlightened by the disclosure of hidden things. Sparks shot forth from the fire of zeal burning in his heart. His head was in quest of union. It cried out, "O Bilal, bring me the release of prayer! O Bilal, bring relief to my inner fire, because the direction for the prayer of the lovers is the beauty and perfection of the Friend, not the Rock of Jerusalem, or the Kaaba, or even the divine throne itself!" It is as Khwaja Abu Sa'id said while in a state of ecstasy at the head of the grave of his spiritual guide:

The source of happiness is this mine of bounty and generosity;
Toward the face of the Friend I turn and not toward any
   other!

Due to the ardor of their desire, those who are longing to see the Friend pray much, even without inclination or prostration. They consider all lovers to be the same. They do not single out anyone for signs of special attention, nor do they recognize anyone as notably meritorious.

The prayer of lovers is not a matter of inclinations and
   prostrations;
The very same pain afflicts Muslim, Christian, and Jew.
When the only direction for prayer is the beauty of the
   Beloved,
Love comes and abolishes all other loci of prayer.

One beloved of God has said that before the Rock of Jerusalem or the Kaaba came into existence, the direction for the prayer of lovers was the One without beginning! In place of sacred enclosures and places established by men, the direction of those who long for the Friend has become what it was in the beginning. In this tavern of self-forgetfulness and abode of affliction, the Rock of Jerusalem or the Kaaba has been demarcated to console the hearts of seekers and travelers.

O brother, some things are included in prayer to expand the believer's opportunity to invoke God's name. In this way, his heart will be given enlightenment from God himself, and the awe of Him who is beyond all need will descend upon his head. While his body comes to prayer, his heart will melt away and his soul will be absorbed in the divine secrets. His condition will become far removed from the superstitions of men, as his feet advance further on the carpet of nearness to God. In this state, he will show no inclination toward anything other than God. This is the meaning of what the Lord of the world has said: "If someone who prays were to know the One whose name he is invoking, he would not divert his attention to anyone else." His prayer would be rather extraordinary. While at prayer, all attribution would pass away. It is impossible for anyone who experiences this passing away of attribution to be aware of anything other than God!

It is related that Ali, the commander of the faithful, was engrossed in prayer while an arrow was being removed from his thigh. Because he was lost in his absorbing vision of the Beloved, how could he possibly be aware of the pain of his wound? All attribution had passed away from him! Even if the afflictions of hell had been rained upon his head, he would have been oblivious to them all. Had the pleasures of Paradise been rolled up into a ball and dropped into his mouth, he would have derived no pleasure from them. Behold! The door of generosity is open. The table is laid with good things. Make haste! Discover your true self!

O brother, what can a mere man do in order to seek Him? The generosity of the Bountiful One does not bypass either master or slave, rich man or poor. He is like the sun that rises from its resting place. Even if worldly people gird up their loins in search of this sun, they will not be able to catch hold of even a single particle of its light. The sun, however, in its own generosity, bestows its warming rays on the huts of beggars and the grief-stricken corners of the poor, as well as on the palaces of kings and the mansions of nobles. Do not pay attention to dust and water! Look at His riches! "He loves them, and they love Him" (Q5:54). Or again: "God befriends those who believe in Him" (Q2:257) and "The Lord makes them drink a pure drink" (Q76:21). There is no one who is more intimate with Him than man because of this honor and dignity. The angels around His throne are sinless. They are pure, holy, anointed, and spiritual, but a creature composed of water and clay is quite another matter! A venerable Sufi has said: "This mere handful of dust has been placed like a straight bow in the hands, yet neither Gabriel nor Michael is able to string it!" Wherever the shade of man's Wealth falls, there someone shows forth the beauty of the invitation to come forward. "Surely kings, when they enter a town, destroy it" (Q27:34).

*Peace!*

LETTER 33: FASTING

*In the name of God, the Merciful, the Compassionate!*

Brother Shamsuddin, masters of Truth and Sincerity have said: "Bodily strength depends on food and drink, whereas spiritual strength depends on going hungry and thirsty. In God's domain, hunger is a divine food." It has been said that one of the qualities of the Almighty is this: "He feeds others but is not himself fed" (Q6:14). If a servant becomes distinguished in this practice, then according to the consensus of the wise, he progresses on the carpet of proximity to God. He becomes far removed from the human condition. When somebody fasts in accordance with the order "Make your actions like those of God," then he, too, is able to feed others. In this manner, he will approximate the qualities of the Beloved. He will dissociate himself from human qualities and become honored and greatly enriched in Him, just as the Lord of the worlds has said: "The man who fasts experiences a twofold joy: the breaking of the fast and seeing God."

What is the delight of breaking the fast? This body of ours is composed of many dispositions. The seeker is like a mounted gentleman who is traveling along the road that leads to the Friend. "In order to see Him, fast!" is the command that gives the seeker his cue as to how to reach his Lord. So he fasts from food and drink, while traversing the distance of "the stage whose outer limit extends to the Lord" (Q53:42). At the end of a day's journey, when the time for evening prayer arrives, the horse is brought to a standstill. When it receives some alfalfa and water with which to break its fast, then it becomes, for the rider, the source of his strength. Such delight is suffused throughout his being that, in comparison to it, all other joys become grief and trouble.

The second delight will never be grasped through explanations. It is something that has to be experienced: "Whoever does not taste something understands nothing about it!" "There are 70,000 curtains that veil God. If even one of them is lifted, the rays of His face would consume the intruder. No eye can see Him!" In the stage of the veil of light, everything is consumed. Who can describe it all? This is the meaning of "It is frivolous to talk about what is obvious!"

A certain Sufi sheikh saw Khwaja Ma'ruf Karkhi engrossed in contemplation. He was standing beneath the divine throne, singing God's praise in the abundance of his gratitude. A query came from the Lord of the angels: "Who is this?" though He knew him very well. One of the angels said: "O God, this is Your distinguished servant!" God said: "My servant Ma'ruf Karkhi is intoxicated with the wine of My love. No one can recuperate from love of Me except by seeing Me!" This was also the meaning of what the Lord of the Law said: "Make your bellies hungry, your livers thirsty, and your bodies hungry that you might perhaps see God in this world."

It is said, "He who has seen, has arrived." And whoever has arrived at God Himself has passed beyond the stage of transience of things and even beyond that of permanence. He has been consumed in adoration of the divine face. "Truth has arrived; falsehood has vanished" (Q17:81). Every person who has attained this stage and attempts to describe it says: "I am simply one of those who have lost their way!" Whoever in this state casts his glance toward Him will simply be called "one of the blind." A respected poet has said:[58]

A lover disclosed the secret of the Absolute . . .
And quivered as he proclaimed: "I am the Truth."

It has been written in *Kashf ul-mahjub* [The manifesting of what is veiled] that hunger afflicts the body, purifies the heart, inflames the soul with love, and leads the mind to meet God. Since the heart finds purity, the soul, love, and the mind, meeting, what harm is there if the body must suffer? The Prophet also hints at this when he says: "Every work of man will receive a reward that gradually increases, till it is seventyfold. But a fast that is undertaken for the sake of God will be rewarded by Him." It has been said that the people of Arabia describe virtues and desire to be possessed of them. Imagine that someone was told that a dog could not approach the door of this Wealth, let alone be with the King of the world! The one who fasts is promised: "You are Mine!" and "I am your reward!" And again: "Your reward is to see My face!" Those slain by love are promised: "Whoever My love kills is ransomed by a vision of Me!"

O brother, know the value of what happens when the heart is purified from its murky state and transported from brutish darkness to the seven heavens where the secret meeting is effected by means of fasting!

The practice of fasting is highly esteemed by Sufis. Whenever they wish to hear the word of God in their hearts, they go hungry for forty days.[59] After thirty days have passed, they clean their teeth. It is necessary for them to go hungry for ten more days. Assuredly, the Lord will speak to them in their hearts, because whatever may be revealed openly to the prophets can only be hinted at secretly to the saints. A sheikh has said: "A disciple needs three qualities: Unless he is overcome by drowsiness, he should not sleep; unless urged by necessity, he should refrain from speaking; unless he is starving, he should not eat." For some, two days and nights are enough; for still others, a week; and some may need a full forty days.

# MANERI

O brother, when you are filled with His bounty and a table is laid out with His grace, then abstention from eating is not to prolong the pleasure of His grace, but to find Him in His treasury, as the Beloved. The cycle of eating requires preoccupation with the self, and anyone who is preoccupied with himself becomes hidden from the Beloved. Refraining from eating while sitting on the carpet of the Lord is better than eating in a palace with Him absent or hidden. In short, a man should do as much as he can. One Sufi has observed: "This world is but a day in duration, and what is difficult about fasting for one day?" Someone else has said: "Make a fast from this world, and break it with death!"

Man is the purest of all creatures. His works are full of secrets. They cannot be considered trivial. Heaven and earth, throne and footstool, paradise and hell, are simply like uninvited guests accompanying him to a feast. This is their very purpose! Yet in accordance with the divine command, a person should proceed beyond these stages. When His glance falls upon these occurrences then one will encounter at each stage a gift from His bounty so that, when the friends arrive, they can take possession of their own good fortune and the share allotted them. They say: "Stretch out your hand toward the favor We enjoyed from eternity and toward the bliss We knew before the time of dust and clay."

"O dust and clay! O casket of profound secrets! O unclean dust! O friend and servant, do not imagine that My saying concerning you is simply for the present moment. Before the world existed, before even Adam appeared, My saying concerning you existed; it existed even when you did not! My link with man is through an ancient favor I bestowed upon him!"

One day a man came to the Caliph, but the Caliph did not recognize him. He said: "Who are you?" The man replied: "I am the man whom you honored in such and such a year." The Caliph replied: "I welcome you, for you have made my favor a link between you and me." He commanded that a robe of honor be brought out and presented to that man.

If You water, it is Your own plant that is nourished;
If You crush, it is the work of Your own hands that suffers!
I am a servant of the type that You know well:
Do not throw me away, for it is You who have sustained me!

*Peace!*

130

# THE HUNDRED LETTERS

*In the name of God, the Merciful, the Compassionate!*

My brother Shamsuddin, there is a worship connected with one's body and another pertaining to one's property. The latter is more efficacious than the former, for its advantage accrues to another as well. Sufis simply pay no attention at all to life and property and have no dealings with anyone except God. They say that a genuine dervish is a person who claims no rights with respect to his life and property. If his blood is shed, he is convinced that this shedding comes from God and would count that hour as the culminating point of his life and call it a compensation from the Lord, as it has been said: "Whoever is killed in My love, his blood has been shed by My hands." If his possessions are taken away, he is happy and says, "God be praised! A veil has been removed from my eyes!" Hence they say that giving in alms of the blessings of this world should not be praised by Sufis, since avarice is unpraiseworthy and yet a greedy man is intent on keeping intact two hundred silver coins, even though he must give five of them away after he has had them for a year.

One of the canon lawyers put Shibli to a kind of test by asking him how many silver coins one needed to possess in order to be obliged to contribute alms. He replied: "Do you want me to answer according to the practice of lawyers or according to the practice of God's destitute?" He was asked to reply according to both schools. He said: "According to lawyers, before the expiration of a year, out of two hundred silver coins, five should be given away, while according to God's destitute, the whole two hundred silver coins should be immediately expended! Indeed, as an expression of gratitude, the Sufi should offer up his life." The lawyer said: "We have adopted this practice as a requirement of our religion." Shibli said: "We have taken this practice from the treasury of the Lord of the Worlds, that is, from Abu Bakr, the Just One. He placed whatever he possessed in front of the Prophet and even offered his entire life, as a thank-offering. In *Nawadir ul-Usul* [The book of unusual doctrines], it is written that the Lord divided the special ones of this community into a thousand parts and presented the world before them. Nine hundred parts desired the world. They said: "This world is the field of the world to come. Today we sow in order that, on the morrow, we might reap a harvest." A hundred parts had the world to come placed before them.

Ninety of these parts desired that world. They said: "The Lord has called this a great country. For an insignificant slave, this is something stupendous!" The other ten parts were sorely tried with afflictions and hardships. Nine of them cried out, "Distress has afflicted me!" (Q21:83). Calamity hid even the Object of their yearning from them!

Now only one part remained. The voice of God came: "What is it that you desire? And who is your beloved?" A cry arose: "You are our Lord! You are our Completion! You are What we desire! You are our Beloved!" There was a voice from heaven that said, "Undoubtedly it is you who are My loved ones and My friends!" When a man accepts this faith, he makes a present of his heart; when he prays, he offers his body; when he gives alms, he bestows his goods. Now, all these three qualities are those of lovers and show the genuineness of their claim to love. In other words, everything that has a form is offered up by them as a gift so that their relationship toward us men might be severed completely and their attention fixed upon God. When they approach, the gaze of the Master falls upon them, and they are found free of anything except Him. Even before He accepts them, God has already made them special. He has seated them on the heavenly throne. As for the command to give alms, it implies that the hearts of most men are seen to be preoccupied with calculations concerning goods, and they are absorbed in accumulating goods. It is known by the light of prophecy that anyone who clings to whatever is other than God, insofar as his heart is immersed in that which is not God, it is diverted from the path to God and becomes wholly engrossed in the particular matter at hand. If a person is unable to dispose completely of what he possesses, he can give at least five silver coins out of two hundred to some dervish, taking into account his own weakness. Just look at this generous provision of the Law. "God is more considerate toward those who are weaker!"

It should also be noted that almsgiving is of little practical consequence with Sufis, for their way of life is one of solitude and renunciation. In the time of the Prophet one of the Sufis related that a gold coin was found in his clothes. "On the Last Day you will be branded like a slave!" he was told. There was another incident concerning a Sufi who had two gold coins remaining in his possession. He was told: "There are two marks to be branded on you!" The reason for this severity was that, because they laid claim to a life of solitude and renunciation, even this amount was for them an external sin.

O brother, goods present no difficulty for anyone who, from the very first step, has offered up his life! This is not your work nor mine! Who gave this wealth? Some of us who have been defective from birth will, God willing, gain some resemblance to them. "Whoever becomes like a particular group will be counted as one of them." Tomorrow He will take our hand. There is hope of welfare and prosperity; if not, blood will issue forth from our body. He is always seeking forgiveness for his sins, and his devotion leaves him ashamed, even if there is no question of sin. The point is, there can be defects in his devotion. If the woeful state of your devotion were to be brought before you, you would be more fearful of it than of your sin. The Prophet said, "I seek forgiveness a hundred times a day." The skirt of prophecy should be free of that, for it has been washed of the stain of sin. Still, there would be need to seek forgiveness for defects in one's devotion. Rabia often used to say: "It is for my dereliction in calling upon the name of God that I am obliged to seek forgiveness!" [A tradition from Aisha follows.]

There is none in the city worse than I,
No mother ever bore a son more lowly than I.
I am caught within the circle of creaturely claims,
Yet there is another place outside this circle, closer to Him!
A Magian priest speaks more truthfully to his people than I,
And a dog is more faithful to its fellows than I.
Thanksgiving is proper, for where God's glory shines,
The most forlorn of men has been renewed with hope!

*Peace!*

## LETTER 35: THE PILGRIMAGE TO MECCA

*In the name of God, the Merciful, the Compassionate!*

Brother Shamsuddin, may God's blessings be upon you! The pilgrimage to Mecca pertains to both one's body and one's property. Sufis lay great stress on the pilgrimage. Visiting the Kaaba is undoubtedly a beneficial work, since it is really a visit to the Lord! Wonderful effects are assuredly a sign of God's blessing! The goal and desire of seekers who go on the pilgrimage is the Lord of the house, not the house itself. This is a sort of pretext. The king of gnostics, Bayazid, said: "When I went to the Holy Place and saw the beauty of the Kaaba, I said to myself: 'I have seen much better materials than those employed in the construction of this building!' I desired the Lord of the house. I returned home. The following year when I reached the Holy Place, I opened the eyes of my conscience and saw not only the house but also the Lord of the house. I said: 'In the divine world there is no room for anything except God, in the world of the divine Unity duality is excluded. The Beloved, the house, and I would be three. Anyone who perceived duality would be an unbeliever, and yet I see three: How can I avoid being a heretic?' I returned home. The third year, when I reached the Holy Place, the divine favor swept me into its embrace; the curtain of whatever is not God was removed from my power of discernment; my heart was illumined with the flame of mystical knowledge; my being was inflamed by the lights of divine illumination; and this saying filled my head: 'You have come to visit Me with an honest heart, and the One who is visited has the right to bless the one who visits Him!' "

When I opened my eyes, I saw the light of Your countenance;
When I listened, I heard the sound of Your voice!

For true lovers, the beauty of that house is a sign of the signless Beloved. What should he do? At least the house gives him some consolation, as has been said: "Everyone who is prohibited from seeing the beauty of the Friend consoles himself with a sign of the Beloved. Majnun went around the house of Laila every morning and evening, kissing the dust of the door and walls while he uttered:

I walk around the walls of Laila's house;
I kiss the one who lives in that house.
It was not love of the house that captured my heart,
But the one who was dwelling in the house!

They rub the dust of that threshold with this intention; they wail on account of the pain of their hearts; and they are hopeful that they might pass on from scanning the beauty of the house to catching a glimpse of the Lord of the house and being openly honored by Him. They say that when a lover knows that the object of his affections will come to him from that door and that his Desired One will pass through that door, then if he has to remain in this fleeting world for a while or if there is a moment or two's delay, the Command is given, "Go to the door of anyone you want, and run in the direction of whomsoever you want!" If you touch the feet of the one who speaks to God, that is, Moses, he will not lift you up. If you place your head at the feet of Christ, he will not accept you. All who have life derive it from Him, and everyone to whom the world is due depends upon Him. To underscore this meaning, the Prophet offered the following gemlike directive: "The pilgrimage should be considered as a better court than this world and all that it contains."

If the servant withdraws his affectionate concern from his wife and children and turns his gaze toward the divine court and, after many trials and difficulties have been overcome, sees the beauty of the Kaaba, then every mirror reflects the delight experienced at its beauty. Everything else passes away in the joy of that mercy. And if the gentle breeze of this condition is allowed to blow, and the veil of existence is removed from in front of him, he comes to the divine throne, the Kaaba of the hearts, which is revealed to him. And when the holy pilgrim begins to go around the exalted throne, he will find, at this stage, an indication of the delights of paradise about which he has read. And if his own glance passes beyond the multitude of things and what can be perceived and understood, and attains the vision of the Beloved, then he is indeed fortunate. His state is now far removed from what can be grasped and understood. This is the meaning of "The courts of the pilgrimage are better than the world and all it contains." Indeed, it is better than the benefits of the world to come.

Likewise, the Prophet has said: "Except for paradise, there is no more pleasing reward than the pilgrimage!" In other words, when the lover, out of desire for the sight of the Beloved, departs from his wife and children and devotes himself completely to his heart's Desire, he will undoubtedly be honored with the robe of meeting, for it has been said that, if lovers had not been promised the vision of God in heaven, the remembrance of heaven would not have occurred to their enlightened minds, nor would any of them have turned their steps eagerly toward the heavenly paradise.

O brother, heaven is like an oyster in which is found the good pleasure of the beloved. A diver has to have great courage to plunge into the engulfing ocean and bring up nothing apart from a magnificent pearl! A mystical poet has said:

Heaven is nought compared to the sweetness of divine union;
On the path of lovers, there are many heavens!

There is no such thing as heaven or hell for them;
When the bird has flown, snare and grain are both the same!

Those birds that fly in the atmosphere of the divine Being in the
hope of approaching the Lord of eternity are like birds that, while
they are flying, are free from all cares about food or snares. They
have acquired what they wanted in the place where there is a description of love and earnestness. What can traditions about the pleasures
of heaven or the pains of hell do? Muhammad ibn Fazl says: "I am astonished at those who seek His house in the world. Why do they not
seek His manifestation in their hearts? He might be found in His
house, or He might not, but His manifestation they can always enjoy.
If it is a divine ordinance to visit a stone once a year and to cast one's
glance upon it, how much more obligatory is it to visit the heart
where He can be seen 360 times a day through one's inward glances!
A visit to the heart should take precedence over the canonical pilgrimage!" For us, defective from our birth, there is neither any place
to visit, nor any heart. The dust of misfortune should be thrown upon
our heads; we should weep over our wretched state, and wash our
hands of all tricks and stratagems. It has been well said:

I like the pleasures of morning, but my heart seeks nights of
grief;
How can I make acceptable someone defective from birth?

A seeker should be a person who rejects self and worship of self.
Let him consider his own faith as a sacred thread, account his own
worship as worship of self, and consider himself a veritable Nimrod
or Pharaoh. Let him remain far from any claim, since the carpet of
the honor of the Lord is such that everyone who reaches the edge of it
brings all his requests with him; all his assets are poured out; and his
own perfections begin to appear as backsliding and his devotion as
equivalent to sin. If he is the most eloquent man in the world, he will
become dumbfounded! If he is the scholar of the age, he will find himself ignorant. When you glance at His incomparable glory and honor,
all creatures will appear as nothing. When you look at His kingdom
and power, you will find all things that have ceased to be are still in
existence. If God so desired, He could create one hundred thousand
people like Muhammad every moment so that He could claim, "I am
your greatest and best Provider!" (Q79:24).

There is not the slightest diminution of His beauty and perfection. If He wishes, He could change all the infidelity and polytheism

on the face of the earth into an ocean of mercy. There is no lessening of the quality of His wrath. If He so desires, He could make all men prophets and saints, or He could simply consume them all in a moment of ire and keep them for all eternity in the quality of Her mercy!

O brother, where is knowledge when confronted by this power and might? What dignity can any latent or contingent being, since it is a creature, possess here? A man would be like a small boy who is sent off to school. When he returns home in the evening he is asked what his teacher taught him that day. He replies, "The letter *a* [a simple vertical stroke in Arabic and Persian] has nothing!"

*Peace!*

## LETTER 36: RESOLVING DIFFICULTIES THROUGH INVOCATORY PRAYER AND THE RECITATION OF QURANIC VERSES

*In the name of God, the Merciful, the Compassionate!*

Brother Shamsuddin, may God accept your prayer! There is some disagreement as to whether it is more praiseworthy to pray or to remain silent. The time-honored command [i.e., to pray] is preferable. Some say that prayer within one's soul is worship because of the saying "Invoking God is the essence of worship." It is better to actually carry out something that is an act of worship than to put it aside, even if the petition is not answered and the worshiper himself does not attain prosperity. At some point the worshiper will need to show his firm resolve, for prayer is a disclosure of his own indigence and need before God.

It is related that Khwaja Hazim Araj said: "Not being able to pray is harder for me than being deprived of the necessities of life!" There is a group that says that being silent is the original divine command, and that assent to what has precedence is more praiseworthy. Imam Wasiti used to say: "It is better to choose whatever was established from the beginning. It is also better than collating the contents of books of various periods." The Prophet, reporting what God communicated to him, has said: "I give more to the person who is absorbed in remembrance of Me and refrains from asking questions than to those who perpetually question Me." Those renowned for their learning have discerned that divine guidance is to be gleaned from both these sayings; they say that the more praiseworthy is that which has been deemed more appropriate for a particular time.

In many states of the soul, invocatory prayers are more beneficial than maintaining silence. This is quite fitting. On other occasions, maintaining silence is better than praying, and that also is fitting. What a person perceives should be grasped in the proper time, for knowledge of the opportune moment cannot be learned except at the moment itself! If someone's heart is inclined toward calling upon God, then he will find prayer more satisfying, while if he is inwardly disposed to peace, he will find it preferable to remain quiet. People have said that it is necessary to respect a person's own particular condition. If he finds a great deal of expansion through invocatory prayer, then it is the best thing for him; but if, at the time of prayer, he experiences hindrance and contraction within his own heart, it would be better for him to abandon such prayer and remain quiet. If, at any particular time, he does experience a small degree of either expansion, or restriction and contraction, then both praying and remaining quiet are of equal value. If it happens that mystical knowledge is predominant in someone at a particular time, it would be better for him to pray, because prayer is worship within one's own soul. If, on the other hand, a person is more impelled to the state of mystical contemplation, then it would be better for him to keep quiet and remain in that state.

This is an exposition of the various sayings of the revered ones on the topic of which is more excellent, prayer or silence. It should be examined carefully. One will discover what is good and gain some profit from it. There is much information and advice concerning this affair. According to the Prophet, its meaning is that, really and truly, when a servant calls upon the name of the Lord, and the Lord loves him, He says: "O Gabriel, look after him well! Fulfill the command relating to his needs, for it pleases Me to harken to his plea." It also has to be said that when a servant calls upon the name of the Lord, but considers him as his enemy, He says: "O Gabriel, look after the needs of the one I do not love, so that he might think I listen to him."

It is related that Yahya ibn Sa'id ibn al-Qattan saw God in a dream and said: "O God, I have cried out to You many times, but You have not replied." He said to me: "O Yahya, I like to hear your voice!"

It is also related that the Prophet said: "My soul is in His mighty hand so that whenever I call upon the Lord and He is angry with me, He shuns me. The second time that I call, He does the same thing. The third time God replies through an angel: 'Be resolute, My servant, because you call on no one besides Me! I tell you, this is the real reason why I answer you.' " It has been reported that Khwaja Yahya Mu'az Razi used to speak like this during his intimate prayer with God: "O God, however much I call upon You, I remain a sinner, and however much I do not call upon You, You remain generous!"

O Lord, if You were to unsheathe the sword of your anger from its scabbard of Justice, then the sinless prophets and angels closest to You would prefer not to exist rather than to have to face Your anger! If, on the other hand, You were to bestow the treasure of Your Mercy, then the infidels of Rome and India would don cool garments and offer up their hearts and souls. If, in conformity with Your Apostle, we do not bind stones on our stomachs, neither have we opposed him or thrown stones at him. Accept my devotion, even if it is defective, for You do not drive a hard bargain! Forgive my sins, though they be many, for You seek nothing in anger. We have not been faithful servants, yet we are Your servants. We are troubled and distracted by many works. We have sinned against You, but we also fly to You for protection. Although we are full of faults, still we belong to You!

O God, You have punishment in store for those who deny Your dominion, but what will You visit upon those who are firmly established in You? O Almighty One, the proud are at loggerheads with You, but would You drive away those who pursue faith in peace? You need nothing, and that is why we fear. Yet You do cherish your servants, and in that lies our hope. Those devoted to You have become bashful; give them constancy! Sinners have become grief-stricken; do not restrict them, or trample them under foot! Be forgiving, and do not twist our ear! O Lord, even though we are unworthy, your messenger frees us in Your sight, and thus we become worthy of Your generosity, which alone frees us from the fire of hell! Even if we do not strike manfully, drawn up in battle array, at least each day we prostrate ourselves five times at Your door! You have forgiven sins much worse than ours; do not disappoint us! If You accept the defective worship of anybody, do not dismiss us on account of our deficient worship! If You were not our friend, who could tread the long path through this world? If You did not become our advocate, who would remove our name from the list of the unfortunate? What profit would our condemnation be for You? Forgive us today! Why should You wait until tomorrow? [Two invocatory prayers follow, one of which reads:]

> It is proper for You to forgive and bestow favors,
> Falling down and trembling belong to me!
> Show my lost heart the way!
> Make me sparkle like a gem in the sight of men!
> When You accepted me, my defects were changed to assets,
> But when You abandoned me, my virtues became vices.
> Bind me to Yourself! Remove me from dreams!
> Make me athirst for You! Do not give me water!

It is related that Khwaja Sufyan ibn Ainiyah used to say that one should never give up praying on account of sins and faults, for God—may He be praised and exalted—accepted even the prayer of Satan, that abomination of creatures and instigator of infidelity, when he said: "O Lord, leave me alone until the Last Day!" The word came: "You have been left alone!" Hence there is great hope that the Lord, who heard the prayers of Satan, the foremost infidel, will also listen to the prayer of a sinful believer who calls upon Him!

If you inquire about the benefit of prayer, recalling that what is predestined must come to pass, then the answer is that you should know that even averting some calamity through prayer is itself decreed by God! Prayer is the cause of this aversion because it attracts the divine mercy, which acts like a shield warding off arrows. The result of acknowledging the Lord and His decree should not be that one does not seek advice or, after sowing, not give water. They say that if the decree of grief comes first, other things will strengthen it. Whatever is decreed for man is commensurate with its cause. Examine carefully the removal of a cause, and anxiety about contradictions in the divine plan will evaporate. Now it is necessary to cast a quick glance at prayer and petitions.

If you pray, do so three times. Act in a similar way if you have petitions to make. Ibn Mas'ud relates that the Prophet, when he used to pray and when he would make some request, did so three times. One word more should be noted, namely, that at the beginning of prayer and petitions, one should say the canonical prayer and, at the completion of both prayer and petition, one should perform the canonical prayer as well, just as Abu Sa'id Darrani did and had his hopes fulfilled. [Some Quranic chapters are then quoted for recitation to resolve particular difficulties.]

God will preserve from all sadness, adversity and misfortune until the following Friday, anyone who, after the Friday prayer, and before commencing any work, recites seven times the opening chapter of the Quran and the one hundred and twelfth chapter on Unity, as well as the last two chapters (113 and 114) of the Quran. For the removal of what is irksome, let the sixty-second chapter on Congregational Prayer be recited every evening. After works of supererogation and extolling God, let a person retire somewhere and, holding his hands aloft, say one hundred times: "O Master, O Master!" and he will receive whatever he desires from the Lord. If he says this one thousand times, all his needs will certainly be met.

O brother, although despair is not pleasing to God, hope is acceptable to Him. Because He delights in the hope of His creature, actually being hopeful is an even higher state, since His promise to pardon all sins is well known: "God forgives all sins" (Q39:53).

Since the Lord has promised forgiveness,
Why should I experience fear on account of sins?

O brother, look at one of the explanations of the revelation, "O My servants who have sinned!" (Q39:53). He does not say, "O you who served Me," nor "O you who have repented," nor "O you who have been pious" (cf. Q2:278). This good news is enough for all of you and for all the sinners of the world.

O brother, those noted for being faithful, sober, abstinent, and devoted to God look within themselves and consider that what has been achieved results from their own efforts; but the black-faced sinners, miserable and ashamed of the very blackness of their complexions, do not lift up their heads in either this world or the next, as has been said: "He is more gracious to the weaker."

I do not lack hope in Your presence,
Even though my sins be many,
Since it is Your forgiveness and mercy
Which now and in the world to come are my refuge!

*Peace!*

# MANERI

*In the name of God, the Merciful, the Compassionate!*

Brother Shamsuddin, may God grant you the favor of being one of those who worship Him! Worship is the stock-in-trade of the saints, the way in which the God-fearing conduct themselves, the real business of men, the profession of magnanimous souls, the reason and worth of a man's life, the fruit of knowledge, and the path chosen by those endowed with insight. It is also the way to heaven and eternal bliss, though it means scaling tortuous mountain paths and undergoing countless tribulations. There are many enemies and robbers along the Way. There are few friends or fellow travelers. It is difficult because it is the road to paradise. The Prophet said: "Heaven is attained only after undergoing many trials and tribulations, while one arrives in hell after treading an easy path and having pandered to one's lusts." There are many difficulties—the servant is weak, the times are hard, the enterprises of religion are faulty and languishing, there is no prosperity, life is short, death is near, and the journey is long. Worship is the sustenance without which there is no way to proceed. If it is lost, it is impossible for a person to acquire what he is seeking. This work is not only difficult but hazardous. Hence it is that few people determine to travel this path. Of those who make such a resolution, few actually carry it out. Of those who do so, few attain the object of their desire. Yet one who succeeds becomes beloved of the Lord. His work is brought to completion, and his object attained! He is seated on the sought-after throne, protected from every misfortune. He is secure in the everlasting Country, and speaks in an intoxicated tongue.

> As long as the shadow of the King falls upon us,
> Then both worlds act as our servant and doorkeeper:
> The garden and maidens of paradise are but thorns on our
>     path,
> Since our destiny is beyond both this world and the next.

They say that the real hindrances and veils of the servant are four: the world, creatures, Satan, and one's ego. This world veils the next; creatures, worship; Satan, religion; our ego, the Lord. When a novice undergoes austerities he emerges from the veil of this world. When he embraces the life of seclusion and solitude he emerges from the veil of creatures. When he resolves to follow fully the Tradition of Muhammad he emerges from the veil of Satan; and when he engages in austerities and struggle with self and turns away from following his selfish inclinations, he emerges from the veil of his ego. Then there occurs revelation upon revelation, vision upon vision. In a short time he sees himself in the desert of yearning, toppled upon the plains of love. From there he proceeds toward the garden of paradise and arrives at the meadow of intimacy, where he is given robes of honor and miraculous powers from the gracious and bounteous Lord. His state is now such that, although his body remains in this world, his heart has gone to the next, just as in praise of Sufis, it has been said: "Their bodies are in this world, while their hearts are in the next."

When he is taken from this transitory abode to the presence of the everlasting Lord and sees, in the garden of paradise, his own poor, insignificant, weak soul in the midst of a great country and a mighty kingdom, he experiences a reward and blessing beyond description. What bliss! What wealth! What a blessed servant he is! What a pleasing work he has done! When a seeker after all this places his hands in those of an experienced guide, he will find it easy to devote himself to the service of Sufis and to associate with other Sufis—if he first resolves to forgo criticism, both external and internal. There should not be any internal opposition or external criticism. Both of these would serve only to disturb a novice. He should oppose neither the words nor the deeds nor the state nor the evident virtues of his guide.

Let him consider once again the story of Moses and Khizr, so that he can understand what abandonment of self-control entails; for if a novice rejects the authority of his guide, he becomes an apostate of the Way. None of the guides of the Way will be able to help such a person reach his destination. On the other hand, it sometimes happens that a conscientious novice is not able to acquire training in the service of his spiritual guide and, for some reason, does not make progress. It could also happen that his guide gives him permission, and he then attaches himself to another guide with whom he had no previous association, just as Khwaja Abu Sa'id Abul Khair, after the death of his own guide, Abul Fazl Hasan, attached himself to the service of Sheikh Abul Abbas Qassab.

If a novice detects, in word or deed, anything blameworthy in his guide's conduct, he should flee to the protection of his own helplessness, lest he perish. When all his guide's other affairs are adorned with the precepts of the Law, that single defect is shown in order to test him. He cannot be favored if he himself were to act like that. The whole tenor of his conduct should not be determined by that single defect, nor could he say that his own behavior measured up to his guide's. The novice, upon seeing all this, should pass beyond that single defect and fix his eyes on the beauty of all the other actions of his guide, for it is there that the power of God's forgiveness is made manifest, not in any virtue the novice himself might possess. If, on the other hand, someone's behavior is seen to be totally opposed to the precepts of the Law, or even in general opposition to them, the novice should flee from that place, since such a person would cause him to descend into torments as he tramples underfoot the faith and tears up the path.

In short, there is no alternative: Worship requires knowledge, which serves as its axis and pivot. It is said that knowledge and worship are two substances, the causes of which are everything that you see and hear: the composition of those who compose, the teaching of teachers, and the advice of advisers. Indeed, it is by reason of them that scriptures were revealed and messengers sent. It should be known that whatever is apart from these two works can be considered a useless endeavor leading nowhere. It is simply idle, worthless chatter! This is why Khwaja Hasan Basri said: "The seeking of this knowledge is valuable, for it explains worship; conversely, one should pay attention to worship, since it clarifies knowledge." When the novice has understood the inescapable interrelationship of worship and knowledge he should then realize that, of the two, knowledge is the more exalted. It has priority over worship because it is the source and guide of worship. Thus it is that the Prophet has said: "Knowledge directs action, and action follows knowledge." He also said: "The sleep of a learned man is better than the prayer of an ignorant one." And again: "A person who acts without knowledge does more damage than good." And further: "God inspires the fortunate ones with knowledge, while He deprives the unfortunate ones of it." The misfortune of the latter stems from the fact that they had not gained knowledge, and had acted in ignorance. For such activity there will be no reward in the life to come.

This is the reason why the ascetics of the past used to busy themselves in the pursuit of knowledge more than in any other work, because the task of worship depends upon it. If a man of God worships Him with the devotion of the angels of the seven heavens and of the earth, but lacks knowledge, he will gain absolutely nothing.

O brother, now you should know what to do whenever there is a melting sensation, or whenever pride arises, or an inner burning, for such things befall travelers! There can be a state when, even if the divine throne and footstool were to be bound to the sandal-laces of his courage, a man would not dare peep out of the corner of his eye! Paradise and hell are in abeyance at the threshold of this exalted status. Such a man takes no pleasure in himself. In the very state of his heart's expansion he is beside himself shouting out, "Praise be to me! Exalted am I!" He then enters a state in which he sees himself being overtaken by the pigs and dogs of this world in heaven itself, and fire-worshiping Magi are ascendant over him. He considers whatever is said to ridicule him as correct. He sees all sorts of faults as present within himself. He puts a piece of sugar in the mouth of anyone who throws a stone at him. He prays for whoever curses him. He evinces fidelity in answer to those who are faithless toward him. Have you not heard what was said in perplexity by the man who shouted out, "Praise be to me!" in the world of the perfection of Unity? While he was witnessing the beauty of the divine Oneness when the time came for him to die, he was asked, "O guide of the Way and the Truth, what are you doing?" He replied: "I am throwing away the sacred thread." He also said: "Look, do you not see that I am that Turk who just converted to Islam?"

> Sometimes I experience plenty, at other times penury.
> My heart may burst with joy, or lie grief-stricken.
> Whether people scoff at me or make much of me,
> I have become the chameleon of my age!

*Peace!*

## LETTER 38: SERVICE

*In the name of God, the Merciful, the Compassionate!*

Brother Shamsuddin, may you pass your days in the service and worship of God! O brother, the sons of Adam are the pride of His creation. Their happiness lies in service, their pride is to bow down in worship. It was God's purpose for men that they should be his servants. "I have not created jinn and men except that they should wor-

ship Me" (Q51:56). It is through service that a man attains freedom.[60]
When asked, "What is freedom?" Khwaja Abu Sa'id replied: "Service!" The questioner went on: "The question is about freedom!"
"Until you become a servant," rejoined the saint, "you cannot become free, and until you become free, you cannot experience the joy of union!"

O brother, everyone who has the yoke of service around his neck is master of his world! Those who enquire into the Truth have said: "If there were a greater robe for man in the treasury of the Glorious and Munificent Lord than that of service, then it would have been bestowed upon the Lord of the world when he approached the divine throne." In fact, however, the Lord of prophecy said, at the time that dominion and power were bestowed on him, "I do not want to become a king and a prophet; I want to be a servant and a prophet!" The inspirer of courage placed his service at the gate of the heavenly court—he preferred service to dominion in both worlds. "His eye did not blink, nor did it exceed the limit" (Q53:17). Undoubtedly there will arise a strong desire to be drawn from the Kaaba to the threshold of the divine bridal chamber, and to be taken to the stage that even the imagination of Gabriel, despite his three hundred thousand feathers, did not reach!

At this stage, in the presence of the Glorious and Munificent One, it can be said that it was on account of the honor of his service that Muhammad was clothed with a special robe of honor! "Glory be to Him Who transported His servant by night" (Q17:1). It was in this vein that Khwaja Suhail Tustari said: "The Creator created nothing better than the point of service, for the heart is the treasure house of mystical knowledge of Him." If the Lord had considered anything more precious than the heart of man, He would have manifested himself there. This is the meaning of the saying "Heaven is not a fitting place for intimate knowledge of Us, nor can the earth become Our partner! Only the heart of a believing servant is able to bear the burden of Our stock!" Do not forget that beside Rustam's horse, Rakhsh, none could bear Rustam!

When the sun of His kingdom shone on the mountains of this material world—and there is nothing more firmly established or grand in the world than they—they broke into pieces! Every day, 360 times, the weight of the divine burden shines in the heart of a believer. But the query "Are there any more?" (Q50:30) is raised, as well as the cry, "Pardon! Pardon! I am thirsty!" Though there are countless created beings, there cannot be done for any other existing being what can be done for man. When the Lord of pardon desired that a particle of dust should don the dress of existence and sit on the throne of vicegerency, the angels said: "Will You appoint in the earth one who will do harm?" (Q2:30). The Eternal Grace replied: "In love there is no deliberation"; that is to say, in love, there is no question of arranging things neatly and orderly. What would be the worth of your manifold praise if I did not accept it? What loss would there be from sin, when the one who bears the cup of My pleasure places a vessel of forgiveness in their hands? "God changes their evil deeds into good ones" (Q25:70).

"One of you walks uprightly, while others scatter in every direction: still, when I want those others I spread out the carpet of My mercy, and if any trace of sin is found in them, My love will erase it with pleasure. Do you not see what their relationship to Me is? Do you not realize that in this affair My relationship to them is one of love?"

If a friend arrives with a single sin
I bring forward thousands to extol his good deeds.

It is related that, one day, Abu Ali Daqqaq quoted the Quranic verse "He loves them, and they love Him" (Q5:54). "He says nothing about service or worship; it is love that overcomes everything!" commented the sheikh. One of those present said: "How could we ever claim His friendship?" The sheikh replied: "Ask Him!" "But I am a mere atom of worship!" he protested; "how can I make a request of those holding sway over the seven heavens and the earth!" The heavenly ones said: "We cannot swallow this morsel." The earthly ones said: "The task is beyond the strength of our arm!" When the turn of the creature of clay and water came, he made a mouthful of it and drank it, saying, "Are there any more?" (Q50:30).

In short, the progress and salvation of man depends on the grade of service he has attained. This is the reason why the holy sheikhs have said: "Witnessing is a consequence of self-struggle." It is evident to anyone with a little insight that struggle with self is not restricted to the sons of Adam; it extends also to certain animals that are capable of being broken in. The effects of this are many. After they have been broken in, their price increases a thousandfold. Man is the highest and most perfect of all existing creatures. When he undergoes hardship, there is a still more profound effect. The disciplined man is raised from the depths of brutish and fierce behavior to an exalted angelic state. Indeed, discipline exalts him beyond these angelic realms to the world of sanctity. Undoubtedly angels are holy, but they cannot advance beyond the fixed state in which they find themselves. The situation is different for creatures of mud and water—"Your outer limit extends to the Lord Himself!" (Q53:42). There is no question of remaining in any particular stage, or finding their hearts' contentment even in the two worlds, as it has been said: "Rest is precluded from the hearts of the saints!"

O brother, it is known to those endowed with perception that no link is better than service, or more worthwhile than devotion, whether for joining a weak person to a strong one, or an indigent person to a powerful one, or a poor man to a rich one, or a servant to his Lord! These men consider themselves to be a hundred times more despicable than ordinary Muslims consider pagans, Jews, and Christians to be. Until such a man has swept the dust from the doorway of some pagan and considers himself as being absolutely devoid of attribution, so that no trace of self-esteem could be found in him, the time for you to kiss him has not yet arrived! If even a trace of self-esteem takes hold of the skirt of your heart, it means you are still just beginning! It is the consensus of the people of the Way that everyone who sees something more in himself than was in Pharaoh is foolish. They have said: "It is easy to belittle oneself in the eyes of other people! The real man is he who can appear small in his self-esteem!" If you have not yet been rejected at every door, if you have not become counterfeit coinage in every hand, and if you have not become valueless on every scale, do not think that your service has been tried and found sound!

If the soul of the novice, out of fright or due to some difficulty, turns to laziness, then his protection would consist in not changing his purpose even a hair's breadth, for in the divine Presence a gnat acts like a lion, and an ant becomes a Solomon. You will find it difficult to fulfill your desire to eat and drink. If, however, something is decreed there for you, your first step would be in this world, your second in the next, and your third "in the abode of righteousness, near the Almighty King!" (Q54:55). One beloved of God has said:

Give me a heart, and then look at my boldness!
Call me your fox—and see a lion emerge!

Today, the gaze of all is on their own knowledge and devotion. They are engrossed in their own activities, yet tomorrow they are destined to witness the sway of Lordship. There you will see prophets with all the perfection, beauty, and majesty of their state, yet all that will endure is the statement about knowledge: "Glory be to You! We have no knowledge except what You have taught us" (Q2:32). Look at the angels! They will come and set fire to the temples of worship, saying: "We cannot worship You as You ought to be worshiped!"

O brother, you will see the gnostics and unitarians of this world who come with their empty hands joined in supplication, saying "Even with our mystic insight we didn't really know You!" O brother, His honor wipes out all other considerations of honor! His glory makes all other glory appear to be a stain! His perfection makes all other perfection seem to be positively harmful! His existence draws a line of nonexistence through all other existences! His being clothes the entire world in the garb of servitude and adoration! Open the eyes of your heart! Look at the frustration of Adam! Listen to the cry of Noah! Look at Abraham with no work to show! Listen to the narrative concerning the trial of Jacob! Look at the imprisonment of handsome Joseph. Look at the saw on the head of Zachariah! Behold the sword on the neck of John the Baptist! See the troubled heart of Muhammad and recite, "Everything perishes except His face" (Q28:88).

*Peace!*

### LETTER 39: SERVICE—A FURTHER EXPLANATION

*In the name of God, the Merciful, the Compassionate!*

Brother Shamsuddin, may God adorn you with external and internal worship! Peace and salutations from the author of these words! Take note and be convinced that one should taste the sorrow of service, and that service should be carried out correctly. A seeker should become a servant. If he himself exercises dominion, to what sort of service is he laying claim? Comply with whatever this entails. What does "being a slave" mean? That is what you should be like! Slaves have tongues, but can they ask how and why? Whether you are given sherbet to drink or poison, accept it willingly! Do not assert yourself by saying, "I should have this!" or "I shouldn't have that!" A slave cannot object to his master. No matter what the master does, there is no turning away from him. A venerable Sufi was asked, "What is service?" He replied, "Putting aside all turning aside, and willingly placing before oneself God's decree for you! If you are given something poisonous, drink it like sherbet, without showing the trace of a wrinkle on your forehead!"

O brother, being a servant is itself something exalted. For 700,000 years that wretch Satan was diligent in his attempts to serve, but he could not succeed, even for a moment, in becoming a genuine servant. The genuine servant is he who has been purified of everything that might accrue to himself, and is free from all thought of self or personal favors. Another Sufi was asked, "What is service?" He replied: "When you become free, you become a servant!" A dear one has said: "There are many thousands of Abdul Razzaqs, Abdul Wahhabs, Abdul Rahmans, and Abdul Rahims in this world, but you will have great difficulty in finding one Abdullah [i.e., 'servant of God']!"

O brother, anyone who worships God because He is his portion is called a slave of his own inheritance. He is certainly not a servant of God! Abu Ali Siyah has said: "If you are asked whether you would prefer heaven or two prostrations of prayer, do not utter the word 'heaven'! Say instead, 'Two prostrations of prayer,' for heaven is already decreed for you. Wherever one's portion intrudes, there calamity and subterfuge lie in ambush." [This teaching is illustrated by a story concerning Moses and Khizr.]

If a slave is accepted, well and good; if rejected, well and good; if honored, well and good; if passed over, well and good. Whether he is praised or opposed, it is all the same to him! What can he do? Go to the house of a judge? Or bang his head against a wall?

If you want, kill me or strike me! Otherwise, keep me:
There is only one thing I can do—offer myself to You!

They consider heaven and hell as nothing. Indigent and resourceless, like slaves, they set out on the road. They see nothing except the Lord Himself. Possessing nothing, they desire nothing. One beloved of God saw a dervish and enquired: "Where are you coming from?" He replied, "From God!" "And where are you going?" "To God!" "What is your purpose?" "God!" To every question the reply was the same, "God!"

I write Your name on the palm of my hand;
Fixing my eyes on that Name, I shed tears of blood.

Yet I want nothing but to rivet my attention on You!
No matter where my gaze alights, it is of You that I think!

Seeking a reward for submission, and pondering the reward and merit of one's worship, is a fatal poison. If you spend a thousand years in this fashion at the threshold, and if you perform by yourself all the possible forms of submission and worship known in the world, it will still be said to you: "You are unworthy of Me! Your gift should be total and complete!" A man had spent many long years of his life in submission and worship. He had engaged in a long struggle with himself and had undergone many hardships. A revelation came to the Prophet: "Tell him he is destined for hell! Why should he take such pains?" When the Prophet conveyed this revelation to the man, he simply intensified his various religious practices, in a spirit of great joy and happiness. People were filled with astonishment at the sight! They said: "What is this? Aren't you destined for hell?" He replied: "I considered myself to be totally unworthy of gaining admission into His kingdom. Now that I have been judged worthy of hell, what wealth is mine! What value have I gained!"

O brother, there can be no expectation of proper service from anyone who has not weighed himself in the Scales beyond compare and discovered his own vanity. There is a saying of the venerable Sufis to the effect that the souls of these dear ones were offered to the dogs of a cemetery, yet not a single one paid any attention to them!

A dervish in intimate discourse with God prayed: "O God, if You are not pleased with my love, at least be pleased with my service! If this does not please You, be pleased with my doglike devotion!" The following morning he was walking along the road. A dog, in a state of trance, said to him: "O dervish, you have given yourself a pretty high rank by equating yourself with one of us! What virtue we possess, since not a hair of ours has been raised in opposition to Him!" The dervish threw dust on his head and said:

O that I might become dust on the paw of Your dog!
Since it is not my lot to be a dog in Your lane!

Dust, of itself, is despicable and of no value. After it causes a thousand sins and rebellions, it becomes stained, cruel, and ignorant. Imagine its attire! Then what happened? God cast a glance in the direction of that brother, enabling him to see himself just as he is. Granted more knowledge each day by the grace and generosity of his

Lord, he began to see himself progressively as he is in this abode of dust. If for some days you are sorely tried and without means, do not be sad! At length you will have the pleasure of hearing the divine address, "Come back!" You will again experience His generosity and you will again see yourself honored. Tomorrow, when Adam, along with his children, enters heaven, a voice will arise from the celestial doors from the very extremity of the multitude, and the angels will be filled with astonishment as they watch. "This is the man who was thrust naked out of heaven!" they will exclaim. The men of this Way have recognized the great value of grief and sorrow, in the following verse:

> Such is the heart that, if for an hour it felt no pain,
> It would go to the afflicted, and borrow some of theirs!

There is a tradition current about this: "O worldly people, you receive wealth, recompense, and joy! O dear ones, you have much to endure!" What a span of difference is there here! Reward and comfort are available to all, but calamities and effort are not. Foolish Pharaoh possessed, for four hundred years, kingdom and comfort and, during that period, was unacquainted with scarcity. Still, if he had wanted the pain and burning of the heart of Moses, even for an hour, it would not have been given to him! See what reward the world offers! There is one crown for the proud head, but a thousand for the submissive ones.

Look carefully at the extent of our effort and anguish! Where have they got us? It would be more fitting if we were hit on the head! People have said: If it had been ordained that, at the hour when the saw was biting into the head of Zachariah, someone had asked him, "What do you want?" then, summoning all his energy, he would have exclaimed at the top of his lungs: "I desire that this saw should bite into my head for ever!"

*Peace!*

## LETTER 40: THE EFFECTIVE FORMULA

*In the name of God, the Merciful, the Compassionate!*

Brother Shamsuddin, peace! A novice seeks refuge under the protection of "There is no god but God!" Both in speech and in thought, alone and in company, he should not emerge, even for the twinkling of an eye, from this formula. It is his fortress. The Lord of the world said: "Whosoever has entered the fortress of 'There is no god but God' will receive rest from pain and reproach." It is by virtue of the reality of this that the novice, when he first pursues the Way, experiences fear and a certain dread of encountering robbers. When he enters the fortress that is the stronghold of the Lord, however, he feels secure and his heart is put at ease. Wisdom demands that a fortress should be constructed out of words of both denial and affirmation so that, when travelers along the Way to Unity enter it, they will feel secure from what can obstruct the way: their ego and Satan. When the world of divine Unity has been disclosed to the inner vision of the novice, he finds that any being that has come into existence through creation is "other," and he perceives that the denial of "other" is a precondition for attaining Unity. The fire of jealousy is kindled within us and impels us toward God, because denial and affirmation arise from qualities of our human nature. A novice who has not managed to pass beyond the confines of his human nature will not arrive at the world of divine Unity.

For legal scholars, denial comes after affirmation, whereas lexicographers state that affirmation comes after negation. For a Sufi, both denial and affirmation are idolatry. The reason is that affirmation requires "three" if it is to be a complete affirmation: the thing affirmed, the affirmer, and the act of affirmation. Denial also needs three things for its completion: the act of denial, the one denying, and the thing denied—yet anyone who talks even of two is a polytheist and unbeliever, so how could anyone who sees six be a sincere and orthodox believer? Why are you astonished? Any "other" simply does not exist! Who, then, denies? And since you yourself do not exist, how can you affirm anything? Sheikh Harvi has given us a hint about this:

> Beyond denial and affirmation lies a desert;
> It is a place of profit for members of this group.
> When the lover arrives here, he turns to nothing:
> Not denial, not affirmation, not even "you" exist there!

This is the perfection of divine Unity and the outermost boundary! Having crossed the wilderness of "There is no god" and reached the Kaaba of "but God," they taste the sherbet: "He is the beginning, and to Him do we return." Khwaja Sanai has said:

Until you sweep the Way with the broom of "no,"
How can you arrive at the stage of "but God?"
O pearl-diver in quest of the pearl of "but,"
Place the garment of your soul on the shore of "no"!
Dualism has been preempted from the world of love:
Why ask about this saying? You yourself are the saying!

They have said that an animal, when it falls on a pile of salt, becomes salt. When one creature can have this effect on another, the former altering the latter through its own properties, then why should not the King of Truth be able to achieve this effect? The servant immersed in a mystic state, by witnessing Him, would be changed from his human condition and conducted to the world of possession, and then he would be taken beyond this stage and made a mere nothing, so that only God Himself would remain—He alone would speak and He alone would hear. The man would be simply a sign in the middle. One beloved of God has said:

Say in the city: Either you remain, or I!
If there be two, there will be an uproar in the realm!

Everyone who has looked with the glance of divine Unity and seen the existence of the universe as something other than God, and found that whatever is other than God is transient and destructible, has then rushed toward the world of divine Unity. God has awarded him the prize of paradise, clothed him with the robe of the righteousness of a truthful servant, and given him the wine of fidelity in paradise. He exclaimed, "I have been granted a proof of God!" As the Prophet attested, "When the servant says 'There is no god but God,' the Creator replies, 'My servant has spoken correctly: There is no other god but Me! Bear witness, O My angels, that by virtue of the truth of his speech, I have forgiven all his sins.'" The angels were called to bear witness to the forgiveness of the servant because, by way of testing the divine Wisdom, they had said: "What's this! Will such a creature be made God's vicegerent, one who will come into the world and be responsible for many sins?" (Q2:30). God had replied: "When My love is with them, what can their sin accomplish? Whenever love enters the scene, faults simply vanish!"

If there be but an atom of the pain of God in your heart,
It will profit you more than gaining mastery of both worlds!

The Master of the world was told: "O Prophet of God, know that there is no god but God!" (Q47:19). This is what was said to him, but to others it was said: "Say that there is no god but God!" He was aware that the veil of his humanity was extremely delicate and, through the refinement of the flames of the light that, at the time of the divine manifestation, became active in him, the thin veil of his humanity had been completely effaced. What remains hidden from others was fully revealed to him! For the confirmation of what was hidden, there came a manifestation by word, while witnessing and direct vision came by faith, through knowledge. It has been said that when the Lord of both worlds cast a glance with his perceptive eye from the world of prophecy to that of divine Unity, he was swept off his feet by the intensity of his desire; his existence passed into oblivion in the utmost corner of nothingness; his joints became hidden to all; he passed beyond the realm of humanity. The good pleasure of the Beloved, however, became a superintendent and, for the sake of conveying the message, Muhammad was brought back to the realm of prophecy so that, from time to time, the righteous Aisha would ask him: "Speak to me of your own affairs for a while!" This is an exalted secret! Its purpose is to affirm that there is no other source of protection for the righteousness of a servant except in this sacred formula.

It is known that "when creatures become present in space and time and are installed in the scales of justice, then in that assembly a servant will be chosen." There might be ninety-nine sheets of paper containing charges against him, each one covered with writing from top to bottom. They are presented and placed in one tray of the scales. That would represent all the punishments and afflictions of the servant. After that, one piece of paper would be brought from the divine treasury. On it would be written the words "There is no god but God, and Muhammad is His prophet." This would be placed in the other tray. It would be weightier than all those other sheets! He would be freed from the threats of hell and its deepest pits and would proceed, with great honor and marks of the divine bounty, into paradise. A venerable Sufi said:

> Everyone who has seen the dawn is hopeful of seeing the
> evening!
> [Two examples stressing humility are then mentioned.]

O brother, if it is possible not to bind anything to yourself, that would be a great and good work! The men who have proceeded along this Way have never ceased to struggle with themselves, for there is no peace from that struggle!

*Peace!*

LETTER 41: NAKED FAITH

*In the name of God, the Merciful, the Compassionate!*

Brother Shamsuddin, may God adorn you with right conduct and faith! The Messenger of God has given us this helpful hint: "Faith is stripped bare: Its raiment is fear of God and chastity." For faith, nothing remains closed. It is a key opening up things that are closed, but is not itself closed. The intellect of man is closed, while faith is wide open. A novice should be stripped of everything included in the lower portion of the wide-ranging blessings of faith, and then the full beauty of faith will be revealed to him!

Alas, you are in love with yourself! You do not possess the strength derived from faith that would enable you to doff the cap of lordship; nor can you put up with hearing your good name being dragged into the mud; nor can you exchange your own security for the onslaught of reproaches! Every day you walk pompously out of some school and enter a cloister in order that your cap of lordship, as well as the beginnings of piety, knowledge, and rank, might become higher and more exalted. As your tongue grows longer and you cover an ever-wider range of topics, your despotic rule and killing of people also increases. Simply on the basis of your own knowledge, you bestow excellence on ordinary people while, by means of your touted mystical knowledge, you consider yourself better than the nobility.

O brother, know what the real state of affairs is, namely, that with these counterfeit resources, there is no access for you or me to this divine Presence! A morsel that is suited for a falcon's gullet can scarcely fit into our sparrowlike apertures! A robe that has been sewn to bedeck the torso of some rich nobleman will scarcely fit us, poor and resourceless as we are! Every day our conversation becomes more inconsequential, and our lives grow darker. Genuine delicacy should be expressed in compassion, not in speech. If we foolish talkers were to be called to account tomorrow for what we have said today, we would experience what occurred to Pharaoh, Abu Jahl, and Abu Lahab. Those well grounded in the faith talk little, since they have been emptied of all relationships. They are completely free of pollution from creation that might cling to them. Their hands are clean of any defiling stain. There is the command, "Be!" and it comes into being. This is some sort of manifestation for the heart so that, by the light of this manifestation, they see Him. They become engrossed in the sight of Him. They no longer see themselves, for they no longer exist. They forget themselves as they rejoice in His Being! They, along with all that is theirs, belong to Him. Even though they speak, it is not really they who speak. The same could be said for hearing, walking, sitting, and so on. In their being, there is no being. In their speech, there is no talking. Speakers are struck dumb. There is hearing, but no hearers. They were ignorant of the real condition of creatures, but have now become capable of understanding what it is. In the presence of God, neither the dust of this world nor the dust of the next has any idea of where they have gone! Their hearts are with God, while their bodies are in the midst of creatures. Good things fell to their fellowman but not to them, for they themselves no longer existed!

God does not give man orders for the sake of work, but for the sake of the joy of what is commanded.[61] He does not have to order a bird to fly, but to descend. Even though a vulture soars high, it alights upon carrion. A falcon also soars high, yet its prey is always something alive, for its pleasure is in seizing something with life in it. Life should be sought! Until the soul becomes intimately acquainted with that Life, it cannot live by It! Anyone who lives by the powers of his own soul becomes enslaved by its impulses! By contrast, all the resources of anyone who lives for God become subject to Him. Nobody can live with God except in the world of Unity. This demands the price of not paying attention to oneself. "Whoever looks at himself is a polytheist!" Looking at oneself means giving birth to yourself! There is a debt involved in this birth, which is incurred by birth itself! Do you not see that, as long as the fluid from which God creates children is within the womb of the mother, it is not under the command of the Law? There is no obligation to perform the ablutions. When, however, it leaves its own place and comes into the open world, then the obligation to perform the ritual ablutions has to be fulfilled, whether the child is legitimate or not. Every speaker reveals himself by what he says, either by reciting, "There is no god but God," or by saying, "I am your master, the exalted One!" Try to understand, at this stage, the insight of Imam Shibli when he said: "If I were to pray, I would commit the sin of polytheism; if I did not pray, I would be guilty of infidelity!" Every form of knowledge that is sent to you through your faculties is, for you, a veiling of the Truth; whereas all knowledge sent to you through Him is Truth itself.

Those scholars who have remained confined to their own senses have gained knowledge only by means of the path of the senses. Everyone who remains bound up in things that are felt becomes excluded from the benefits of the hidden world. The knowledge that wells up from the depths of a living stream arises in such a way that there is no need of the senses. Everything that occurs in the world of the senses derives its origin from the events of life. Any form of knowledge that does not make you preoccupied with yourself, or make anyone else preoccupied with you, will not turn out to be a veil along the Way. Abul Qasim Qushairi says: "The knowledge we acquired was acquired when we were resting." On the other hand, anyone who lapses into his own knowledge and is content to remain there should at least realize that he has consigned himself to the veil of words. It is just like someone who has an almond and looks only at its skin, not comprehending that its kernel is hidden from his sight. The life is not in the skin. It is in the kernel. The skin hides the meaning, lest it become apparent to the uninitiated. This saying cannot be clarified with reference to the writings of religious scholars. If you were to read out this saying in front of them, they would tell you that it was foolish and a suspension of the Law. Others would say: "This is the height of compulsion!" Understand that it is neither compulsion nor predestination, nor a suspension of the Law, but the divine Unity in its purest state! A poet gave the following hint about this state:

> The servant reached the place of self-effacement:
> After that, no work remained except God's!

O brother, a church is able to be turned into a mosque, while a rubbish heap can become the site of a royal palace. The raw material for all this is like pieces of iron covered with rust: They can be made into mirrors in which objects can be reflected, but only after a craftsman has placed the whole in a furnace, purified it of its imperfections, and hammered it out on a hard anvil. The polisher is then ordered to rub off any surface rust. The first thing to be seen in it would be the beauty of the polisher! In a similar manner, the constituent elements of human nature should be thrown into the furnace of austerity and be hammered out on the anvil of struggle with self.

The whole should then be entrusted to Love, the Polisher, who will rub off the rust of human qualities. Immediately the reflection of the World of Meaning will appear in it, and it will become a fitting place for the King to gaze upon His own beauty, as someone has said:

> We are simply mirrors while He is the one possessing beauty:
> It is only for the sake of His seeing that we seek Him!

*Peace!*

## LETTER 42: SINCERITY OF FAITH

*In the name of God, the Merciful, the Compassionate!*

Brother Shamsuddin, it should be known that the correctness of one's faith serves to magnify the greatness of the Lord. One of its great fruits is a sense of shame in His presence. When there is faith, there is contemplation; when contemplation is correct, then proper reverence is experienced; when there is reverence for what is hidden, the inner sword becomes operative; and when someone experiences reverence for the Hidden, he becomes ashamed of his own opposition. As far as this group is concerned, contemplation means seeing what is hidden, not looking at what is visible. This has been expressed very briefly, but the knowledge of both worlds lies hidden beneath it!

Total understanding can be gained only insofar as the secret is revealed by God, and everything other than God has been left behind. When the might of God's power is witnessed, all fears about it vanish; when the abundance of His grace flows into a person's soul, he experiences such affection for Him that none remains for anything else; when the grandeur of the all-surpassing excellence of God is contemplated, all actions and even states pass out of sight; when the depth of the divine generosity is perceived, a person becomes so overjoyed with God that the need for either world is no longer felt; when the awesome wrath of God is felt, one is rendered incapable of any opinion or judgment; when God's actions are seen to have no cause, a person places no further reliance on his own actions; and when the glory of God is beheld, one experiences no rest or stability, out of dread of its very absoluteness! This is the secret of he who said:

> The camel-litter is empty, yet still the bells ring;
> There is nothing in the cup, but look at the flies!

The village is abandoned, the countryside deserted:
The abode of nonbeing becomes a meeting place with You.

If someone lacks the sincerity of faith required for such perfect contemplation, there should at least be enough for him to know that even if he has not beheld God, God nonetheless is beholding him forever, and showing such reverence as He receives from His creatures. Whoever thinks it unlikely that creation is seen by Him will not agree that the Creator is seen by creatures! This opinion comes from the tongues of those engaged in worldly pursuits. As far as those who are conversant with the Truth are concerned, it would be infidelity if someone were to be put to shame by God Almighty as much as by creatures. In their view, this would mean that God and creatures were placed on the same level. Whoever places his trust in this would be an infidel! Consider the state of us black-faced ones who are more put to shame by creatures than by God! How can this be? What a difference there is between you and me! Faith can be grasped from this verse:

Since I was not a man of faith, I espoused the Magian creed.
Leaving Islam, I did not see the thread around my middle!

If there had been no explanation on the part of the venerable Sufis in this matter, destruction would have swiftly visited you and me. There is no room even in an idol-temple for anyone who has come from the threshold of Islam!

O Brahmin, take in one who has abandoned Islam!
Or is there no place before an idol for a lost wayfarer like
    me?

In other words, people should always be fearful of those who are base, but rely on the kindness of those who are generous. This lack of proper vigilance by you and me is not due to our lack of respect, but actually stems from the very perfection of the generosity of God. It is the abundance of His generosity and forgiveness that renders His servant's conduct unbecoming. Again, when people do not forgive, then the servant may become afraid of any blame they put upon him. This is what is meant, not that creatures should be established in a position above the Creator. In this single explanation of the venerable Sufis some hope still remains. If not, then with the eyes of self we have been looking at the sacred thread of self, mistaking it for faith. Hence it was that a scorched heart once said:

Everything we have written can be wiped out;
Everything we have taken up should be thrown out!
Everything we thought highly of has proved to be folly;
What pain we experience for having passed our time idly!

This is just what Khwaja Yahya Mu'az said: "It is all the same to Him if He forgives! Doesn't He know everything I have done!" When a person sees this nearness of knowledge, he understands that God sees everything, and he realizes that there are a thousand iron fortresses between the servant and sin, since his state is that of a genuine servant. When someone sins, his action arises out of one of three states. He may have forgotten the majesty of God. The retribution for forgetting is, "They forgot God and He made them forget themselves" (Q59:19). Perhaps he does not know himself, or have any thought of the majesty of God. If this is his state, then he himself has never known God. Or he may know all this and remember it and yet still commit oppression. He is lacking in respect! If he had a hundred thousand faiths, not even one would remain with him! Do you not see that when that venerable Sufi was asked, "How can one recognize God?" he replied, "I resolved never willfully to commit a sin! Moreover, whenever I was close to the Lord, I remembered Him and became ashamed and left." This nearness is called the nearness of power. He sees His power in every breath he inhales, at every moment he lives, and in every danger he faces. His state becomes such that he brings forward no opposition even in his imagination, so how could he possibly oppose God through his limbs? It is fitting that such nearness be that of reverent, mystical knowledge. In the measure of this reverence, there would be respect. In the measure of this respect, there would be shame. In the measure of this shame, there would be a distance from opposition. The person who is not far removed from iniquity has no shame. Hence he has no respect. This in turn is why he has no reverence. It also follows that he does not bear witness to God. Hence it is that he has no mystical knowledge. Realize from this what the Lord of the Law meant when he said: "Shame is a part of faith. He who has no shame has no faith!" He also said: "Shame is to faith what the head of a man is to the rest of his body." Just as no body can endure without its head, no faith can endure without shame.

O scoundrel-hearted fellow, tell me what sort of crime this is!
Evil cannot be considered virtue! What is the meaning of your
    sin?
O unclean one, you lay claim to kindness and fidelity!
Yet you do not reject iniquity! What sort of fidelity is this?

"A believer is master of his heart when he acts as God's deputy."
In other words, at every opportune moment, and in every state, he
should return to the Lord. This is what the stories of the prophets
Solomon and Job are all about! The former received blessings while
the latter had to endure calamities. Blessings and calamities are opposite to one another, yet each prophet, no matter what he received, returned to God. The former, in spite of all his benefits, was in need of
hope, and returned to the Beneficent One. He was blessed with the
praise of "What an excellent servant!" The latter saw some trace of
desire even in his calamity. Through patience he returned to Him.
He did not complain of his calamities. He was blessed with the praise
"Well done, trustworthy servant!" In all things there is a return to
God, because whatever occurs in the life of a servant must be in either of two categories: It is either a blessing, or a hardship. In each of
these he can reach God, and he can also be cut off from God. With regard to the last things also there are only two possibilities—worship-
ful submission, or sinful rebellion. By means of each of these one can
either be cut off from God, or reach Him. Being cut off from God in
each of these would mean that a person sees his worship, but does not
see his sin. When he saw his own worship, he forgot God's bounty.
When he did not see his sin, he forgot reverence for God. Both of
these draw a servant away from God.

On the other hand, God can be reached through both of them. It
would mean that a person does not pay attention to his worship, but
does take heed of his sins. When he does not look at his worship, he
notices his wretched cunning! He brings forward lamentation and
prayers of petition, but not by way of claim. All his attention is focused on God's bounty, not on his own worship. When he sees his
sins he comes forward with sorrow, but not without respect. His gaze
is reverent. He turns away from sin. Both of these become for him a
cause of union.

A sin resulting in repentance is far better
Than that worship which gives rise to pride!

Also:

Who can fall in love with the pattern of a cloak,
If he is one who has already seen the Lord?

No matter how close he comes to God, he would raise the same cry. He would say: "He has not been found, for there are no limits to What is sought!" Although someone is seeking Him, he is not seeking; and although he has found Him, yet he has not found Him! This is what is meant by the saying that a believer who is close to Him burns, while one who is distant cries out, for,

Until the Friend displayed His beauty,
My poor heart found not a moment's peace!

It seems as though the meaning of this would be that he knows there is no such thing for him as nearness or distance, for both refer to God. Just as He does not remain with anyone, neither does His work remain with the work of anyone. It is fitting for the one who is far off to don the cloak of nearness, while he who is near should don that of distance, because analogy is not enough to give a correct appreciation of His work. Since the situation is like this, even though someone might see himself clothed with the robe of nearness, still he would not experience peace due to the deception of distance, and fear turns all blessings into affliction by removing all pleasure from them. It is this fear of deception that causes the pleasure of nearness to depart from him. Hence he finds no rest, even in his closeness. The existence of anything with which no peace is found passes into nothingness. It is in this sense that the lover would be set on fire by being close, while he should cry out from a distance. A scorched one has said:

What dealings can a servant have with You, O Treasure of
    Goodness?
You are a King, while I have been destitute from birth!

O Brother, the orders of God are beyond the bounds of analogies comprehensible to the human mind. What did Adam do that he was clothed with the cloak of purity? And what did that wretch Satan do in order to have the angelic clothing snatched off his body? If purity were the cause of Adam's goodness, then how do you explain that the cause itself was consumed by fire when, in the beginning, he took his very first step in the garden of Eden? And if Satan's sin be taken as the basis for an analogy, then the answer to that analogy is that if Satan was commanded to prostrate himself before Adam, but he did not, then why was his fate worse than Adam's, since Adam was also forbidden to eat wheat, but did? What is the reason for one being given a tassel of liberty upon the cap of freedom of choice, whereas that wretch had to suffer because he utterly refused to accept the option of worshiping dust, saying:

> For me, there is no hope of better days or a place to cry out!
> Nor is there any joy for me at the prospect of union.
> See what has befallen me in the afterlife:
> My fate is that of a beloved in the hands of his enemies!

Adam had not yet eaten the wheat when a cap of purity had been sewn for him. Neither had Satan rebelled when the sword of destruction had been dipped in the waters of poisonous wrath. That wretch said: "If I was commanded to prostrate myself in front of Adam, then he too was ordered not to eat wheat, yet he did! What one gets, the other also deserves!" Hence it has been said:

> Use less analogy, please, O intimate of God!
> The One without cause cannot be grasped by analogy.
> His dealings dazzle the human mind.
> From feebleness it remains clogged up.
> Before His majesty soul and mind are like a decrepit old man.
> The mind is astonished, and the soul dumb struck with awe!

*Peace!*

## LETTER 43: GRATITUDE FOR THE BLESSING OF ISLAM

*In the name of God, the Merciful, the Compassionate!*

Brother Shamsuddin, Islam is the fountainhead of all favors. There should be no time when you are not giving thanks for this blessing! You should consider that if you had been created at the very beginning of the world and were to sing the praises of the blessings of Islam till eternity, you would still not have canceled the debt of gratitude incumbent upon you for this blessing! It was not enough that the herald, when he arrived from Egypt, gave Jacob news about Joseph. Jacob asked: "What religion was he following?" The herald replied: "The religion of Islam." Jacob exclaimed: "Now my blessing is complete!" It is necessary for you not to rest content in this religion for any length of time. There is current a saying of Sufyan Thawri to the effect that "anyone who is content to see the gift of Islam declining will certainly be deprived of it!" It is also said of this great man that he used to repeat with every breath, "O God, make me a Muslim, make me a Muslim," just like someone in a sinking ship who cries out, "O God, save me!"

A Sufi once said that a certain prophet requested the Lord to drive him far from the state of Balaam, son of Beor. This man was then granted so much dignity and knowledge that whenever he lifted up his head, he would reach the exalted throne and see twelve thousand scholars busily taking notes in His assembly. The decree then came: "I have granted him many favors, yet he has not thanked Me for them. If throughout his whole life he had thanked Me even once, he would not have had his blessings snatched away from him!" And losing favors once granted is the most difficult of all punishments to bear! Hence it is noted that separation, after the experience of union, is an intolerable burden. It is also related that wise men say: "We have seen that there are five onerous trials to be undergone in this world: sickness in a foreign land, indigence in one's old age, death in the flower of youth, blindness after the gift of sight, and separation after union." If you ask, "Who has the strength to undergo this difficult work by bringing to bear all the things required for this task?" then know that the Glorious Quran gives this injunction: "Very few of My servants are grateful" (Q34:13). But the Quran also attests: "Those who struggle earnestly for Our sake, We will certainly guide them in Our Ways" (Q29:69). When a weak servant stands firm, no matter what befalls him, what suspicion can the powerful, wealthy, generous, and merciful Lord entertain toward him, a useless sort of person? None at all! And if you protest, saying that the life of man is too short and the difficulties of the Way too burdensome for anyone to live a life of fidelity and meet all the requirements made on him, then know that the difficulties of the Way are indeed many, and its requirements very strict! Nonetheless, whenever God wants a servant to pass along it, He makes this long way short for him, and turns difficulties into things easily accomplished, with the result that someone after passing by all of them may exclaim: "How short is this way, and how easy is this work!"

Hence it is that a number of venerable Sufis have said: "There are two steps on the way to God, and they are quite distinct. It might take someone seventy years to traverse the difficulties of the Way. Another might spend twenty years in overcoming these difficulties. Another might take ten years to do so. Someone else might pass beyond them in a year. It is also possible that someone might do so in a month, or even in a week, or in only an hour. Finally, it might happen that, by a special grace of God, all difficulties of the Way are traversed in a single moment. Do you not see that the companions of the cave required no more than a moment till they saw a change in the country of Daqyanus and proclaimed: "Our Lord is He who gave birth to both heaven and earth"? They saw what truths lay along this Way and traveled beyond them. They entered the ranks of those who put their trust in God and who follow the right path. All of these attained the goal toward which they were traveling. It took but a moment. It was thus also with the magicians of Pharaoh. Their time amounted to a moment, for when they saw the miracles of Moses, they announced: "We have put our faith in the Lord of the two worlds!" They saw the Way and went along it. Not merely from one hour to another, but in less than an hour they joined the ranks of the gnostics and those who yearn for a glimpse of the Lord. Hence they raised a cry, "We are returning to our God! There is no harm for us! Do whatever you like to us!" The secret of this has been thus expressed:

> Sometimes a dog is shown the way to the threshold;
> Sometimes a cat is granted a royal revelation!

It is written in the story of Khwaja Ibrahim Adham, a man engaged in the affairs of the world, that when he turned his back on them and began to follow the Way, it happened that in the measure of one prostration he reached Merv from Balkh! He was like the man falling off a bridge into water: The Almighty made a sign with His hand that the man should be made upright in the air and thus he was saved from destruction. Then there was Rabia of Basra. She was a slave girl being sold in the market. No one wanted her, for she was no longer young. One of the merchants purchased her for a hundred silver pieces and then freed her. Rabia chose to follow this Way; she took to worship of God. One whole year had not lapsed when the devotees and scholars of Basra came to pay their respects to her on account of the eminence of the stage she had attained. On the other hand, consider the situation of some unfortunate one who has not been blessed by the divine favor, for it has simply passed by his soul. How can it be that one branch of a tree remains with its fresh green leaves for seventy years, during which time it experiences no change and is forever crying out and saying: "How narrow is this road and how difficult this enterprise!"

Know that all kinds of work originate from a single root. "That is the ordinance of the Wise and Great God" (Q36:38). If you ask, "How is it that this one is selected for special grace, while that other one is deprived of the same special grace, even though each of them has a common devotion?" O brother, it was a long time ago that this was heard in the world: "He cannot be questioned about what He does!" (Q21:23). Intellect and knowledge are of no avail here, as has been said:

Thousands became mere polo-balls along this Way;
This is the reason why the gutters ran with blood!
A hundred thousand prostrated their intellects here,
While he who did not ran headlong to perdition!

Hence it is that a renowned Sufi has said: "It was the question of fate and predestination that killed us!" We can take the bridge over hell as an example of this Way in the next life. A person can cross the bridge over hell like a flash of lightning, or like the wind, or he can fly across it like a bird, or gallop across it like a horse. On the other hand, there are some who, on hearing the cries of hell, will fall head-long into it, while still others are destined to be seized by the hounds of hell and dragged downward.

Actually, there are two bridges, the bridge of this world and that of the next. The bridge of the next world is for souls, and those endowed with perception see its terrors. The bridge of this world is for hearts, and people of perception understand its trials. The difference in the states of the travelers in the next world reflects their different states in the present one. Ponder this carefully! Understand it according to the mystical knowledge you have been granted, that you might reach the degree you are capable of attaining! The one who is unaware arrives nowhere, as has been said:

The real work is given to someone who knows what is going on:
What do ignorant people know about present sorrow?

Realize that the real state of affairs is that this Way, with respect to its length or shortness, is not like an ordinary road that one can travel on foot. No, one travels this road with one's heart, on the foundation of one's basic religious tenets and insights. It is rooted in the light of heaven, and the glance of God falls upon the heart of a servant, enabling him to see that the work of angels, as well as the angelic state, is fixed by that glance. This light is such that a servant could seek it for a hundred years but not find it; or he could search for ten years before finding it; or for only one day, or even a mere hour, or a fleeting moment. It is given through the graciousness of the Lord of the worlds and it is incumbent upon the servant to fulfill whatever is commanded. His work is fixed and settled. The decree concerning His justice is: "Whatever He wants, He commands; whatever He intends, He accomplishes!"

And if you say, "What is the use of all this striving and effort since the work is already fixed and determined," then such speech would be proof of your foolishness. It would be as if you said, "Of what significance is all this striving and effort in comparison to that which the weak servant seeks?" Do you actually know what the weak servant is seeking? He seeks at least two things: One is peace in both resting places; and the other is possessions and honor in each of them. Peace in the world, however, has to be gained despite temptations that are such that even the angels, as close as they are to God and bedecked in purity, cannot keep from succumbing to them!

This is what is highlighted by the story of the angels Harut and Marut. It is related that when the soul of a servant was taken aloft into heaven, the angels of the seven heavens said in surprise. "How did he manage to be saved? The very best of us had perished there!" In addition, the terrors and hardships of Judgment Day know no limit, so that the early prophets and even the Apostle himself cried out, "Look to your soul!" He also said, "We do not want our souls separated from You!" How could you say that rest from all this trouble is of no great consequence? But possessions, dignity, and that country itself are under the sway of annihilation and the will of God. The verification of this in the world is seen in the example of the saints, for whom earth and sea are but one step, and, as a result, men, fairies, wild beasts, animals, and birds become subject to them. Whatever they wish comes to pass, but they do not desire anything except what God Himself wants—and everything that God wants must certainly come to pass!

What can you say about such a king? Of what account are two prostrations, or two silver pieces given as alms, or two nights spent in vigil? By God, if a man had thousands of souls, or thousands of spirits, or thousands of lives equivalent to the life of the world itself, and all of these were to be bestowed in place of this dear Beloved, it would be but a trifle! O brother, although it is beyond the limited power of man to intend to arrive at the place glimpsed by you and me, still the treasure and the secrets that are made easy in Him have been evidenced in the world. The stars in this world are very high. The moon has the face of the king. The sun, which is the king of all and the light of the world, comes from Him. Whoever receives light does so from the heart of a believer, while the illuminated heart of a believer gets its light from God, the Praised and Exalted One! He created the divine throne and gave it to those near Him. He created paradise and gave it into the charge of an angel, Rizwan. He created hell and entrusted it to Malik. But when He created the heart of a believer, He said: "The heart of a believer is between two of God's fingers." The meaning of these fingers is the bounty and justice of God. Sometimes, when the gentle breeze of the divine bounty blows, they experience the delight of lovers; at other times the hot wind of the divine wrath blows, and they melt. Astounded by both these qualities, all they can do in either state is to remain lost to themselves!

> Sometimes I am intoxicated by the sweetness of union with
>   You;
> Sometimes I am crushed by the blow of Your departure!
> As soon as I put aside the grief of separation from You,
> Immediately I feel the urge to continue loving You!

*Peace!*


## LETTER 44: HIDDEN POLYTHEISM

*In the name of God, the Merciful, the Compassionate!*

Brother Shamsuddin, the Messenger of God has said: "Among my people polytheism is more hidden than the movement of an ant on a black stone in the dark of night!" Know that this polytheism, even though it does not detract from the principle of faith, nevertheless damages its reality and benefits. Faith can be compared to gold, which can either be pure or impure. In the latter case, it is still gold, but the value of gold that contains impurities is not the same as that of pure gold. Real faith is belief in divine Unity and is the opposite of polytheism. Do you not see that until the root of polytheism has been removed, the unity of faith cannot be acquired? When polytheism has been uprooted, however, the shoot of belief in divine Unity appears. Faith and its unity becomes real for the person who really strives for it. He purifies himself from every defiling impurity that arises from hidden polytheism. The meaning of hidden polytheism is to see either loss or profit coming from anything besides God, or to be afraid or hopeful on account of anything other than God. The subtle ties of hypocrisy, the secrets of hidden affection, delight in marvels, pleasure derived from the praise of people, and dismay caused by their reproaches—all of these originate from hidden polytheism. The command of the Law is to worship God alone, and not place even a particle beside Him! (Cf. Q4:36.)

> You agree it has been well said, "In the Essence
> Unity expels all attributions!"
> Why should we join anything to Your Unity?
> You are both the Sought and the Seeker: what more can we
>     say?

The wise have said that polytheism can be either visible or hidden. Hidden polytheism exists in the community of the Prophet, as we have seen in the above-mentioned tradition, which is said to have several interpretations. One of them is that the crawling of an ant is bereft of beauty; no one recognizes its footsteps; nor does anyone hear the sound of its pitter-patter. In the very same way, hidden polytheism can be creeping along in a servant, and he does not have even the faintest idea that it is there!

Again, the movement was described as being on a stone, not on dust, because the crawling movement on the dust leaves behind a trail, from which one can infer that an ant has passed that way. But its movement on the stone leaves no trace; there is no hint that anything has passed over it. This is a proof that hidden polytheism could gain ground in a servant while he is unaware even of its existence!

The tradition goes on to say that all this transpired in a dark, black night. Black upon black, in utter blackness, simply cannot be seen! In the same way, when hidden polytheism makes continuous progress and darkness closes in on anyone, then something trifling ends up having a great effect. In the entire ambit of faith one should see only God; there should be none but God! Whoever sees anything else besides Him in either world is guilty of polytheism. One beloved of God has hinted at this mystery.

> Since you know and speak only of One,
> Why do you ask about two, three, and four?
> The letters *b* and *t* are on the same line as *a*
> Yet they combine to form "but" [idol], while *a* forms "Allah"!

The proof of this tradition is Haris who, when he made a claim to the reality of faith, argued for the correctness of his claim by declaring that he had ceased to derive profit or loss as from any source other than God. He said: "As far as we are concerned, all gold, silver, and jewels are equivalent to pieces of broken earthenware." The foundation of all commercial profits is gold and silver, since all profits in the world stem from them; and yet for Haris, their status had become equal to that of stone and dust. One's sensual soul gains strength in eating and sleeping. Haris removed both from his life and said: "I keep a vigil by night and fast by day." The gain from that was especially beneficial to him because he cut himself off from what is profitable in the present world. This world became, for him, the hidden world, for he had become firmly established in proofs of the reality of his own faith. The Prophet said to him: "Stand firm in what you have found!"

> As long as people remain in the world of goods,
> They are enveloped in darkness, and dream.
> Abandoning arrangements is the commencement of Unity:
> By ceasing to make plans, one attains genuine solitude!

The Messenger also said: "There is no rest for the believer, except in the vision of God. Deprived of this, he will die!" God becomes the contentment of the believer the moment his faith acquires reality. In verifying his faith, he becomes separated from all worldly connections. If, while still in the world, his behavior becomes like that, then the world assumes for him the quality of Judgment Day as happened to Haris!

> Everyone who seeks the realm of solitude,
> And he who desires the abode of Unity,
> Should not find repose within himself,

Nor should he acquire embellishment without!
If revelation, for you, becomes confined to the body,
Then make of such revelation a shoe, and beat yourself on the
    head!
A cringing dog goes in search of bones,
While the tiger cub seeks living prey!

This cannot happen except by abandoning polytheism, that is, by separating oneself from all worldly attachment. Whoever is afraid of anything except God, or places his expectations anywhere but in Him—even though there is no question at all of the fundamentals of the faith—such a person really espouses polytheism. Similarly, for other qualities, make a suitable analogy. Realize from all this that whoever fixes attention upon himself while he is engaged in any form of divine worship, or thinks there is separation as a result of sin, is seeing union and separation from "what is not God." This is equivalent to polytheism! In sum, the servant has not become so firmly grounded in the reality of his faith nor have his qualities become such that one could say, "All this is from God, just as it is with God, for God, and directed toward God!" In other words, the origin of all things is God; all things exist in Him; all possessions and authority are His; while all things will return to Him. When his qualities become like this, it means that a person's faith has become a firmly established reality for him. The Messenger has also said: "Those who are slaves to the world, to money, to their own bellies, to lust and to fine raiment, have all been destroyed!" And again the Messenger said: "The soul should be for the sake of prayer, or be destroyed, since it will have become the slave of these things. If it is for prayer, then its prayer is accepted." If this is a tradition, it is correct. All of us unfortunate ones perished long ago, but we had no idea of this fact on account of our own blindness and ignorance. Rather, we esteemed ourselves as genuine Muslims!

The idea of the Way before my eyes comes from You:
A whole lifetime transpires in trying to grasp that idea!
When the sun's form is glimpsed, our minds are blanked.
What remains in our eyes is false, in our heads, mere thought!

Another poet spoke aright when he said:

Whatever we have written is fit only to be wiped away;
Whatever we have raised on high is fit only to be thrown
    down.

Everything we have thought has proved to be useless;
What a pity we have passed our lives in such foolishness!

If he is called the slave of such things, then it must be true that his devotion to the Lord has evaporated. Only thus could he become enslaved by things, for as long as a slave of Zaid is not liberated by Zaid, he cannot become the slave of Umru! As long as all his qualities of service are devoted to the Lord, he cannot become the slave of anyone or anything but the Lord! There is an example of this in the Law. Anyone who has one foot inside an inn, and the other outside, cannot be said to have entered the building, nor to be outside it. There is no coming out for him, neither is there any going in. If anyone speaks of entering or leaving, then the person would be a liar in both instances, as he would be also if he turned himself into the slave of someone other than God by any wishing, fearing, fleeing, or seeking. If he completely accepts this explanation, then at one stroke he would place himself beyond the pale of faith. If he shows hesitation between two qualities, then know that whoever is between two inns can be driven out of both! This polytheism about which you have heard, and this service of another about which we spoke, come to us entirely from seeing something other than God. This happens if, when we see Him, we see another as well. Every mirror that we worship is tantamount to worshiping another. The same is the case if we are afraid of Him while remaining afraid of someone else. Or if we place our trust in Him, and yet continue to rely on others. One beloved of God has said:

Since there is only one God in both worlds,
Why be occupied with four pillars?
Pronounce One, desire One, and seek only One!
See One, and speak of One and One alone!

O brother, when the Apostle gave the invitation to men, he transmitted the deposit of faith, girded up his loins for service, and said: "O God, I have carried Your command to the people!" The divine oracle came: "Why did you pay attention to your role of conveying the message? Keep your gaze fixed on Our commission!" The secret of this has been put thus:

As long as even a single hair stays neatly in place,
Then that single hair acts as a shackle on your feet.
If but one hair on your body remains polluted,
You cannot be considered purified for prayer!

One day a poor devotee was saying his prayers. Upon completing them, he exclaimed: "Praise and honor be to God for having bestowed His grace upon me! And I pray for the forgiveness of my shortcomings!" His guide chided him, saying: "I thought you believed in only one God; now you are a polytheist!" "O sheikh," he replied, "why do you say that?" "As long as you did not pay attention to your prayer," answered the sheikh, "you did not perceive any fault. Now your prayer has become your own attribute. I thought you saw only God, but you have proven that you also see yourself! Anyone who sees himself does not see God!" This teaching is for high-minded people! All that you and I can do is talk about such worship! How could we unfortunate ones ever obtain such wealth? Accept your state and say:

> O Lord of the worlds, what can I say?
> I am drowning in blood, yet sail my boat on dry land!
> Take my hand and listen to my cry!
> How long shall I have to beat my head as though a fly were on
>     it?
> O King, look upon me, poor wretch that I am!
> If You see any fault in me, let your gaze wipe it away!
> My grief has grown too great: Send relief!
> Emit a ray of light into the encircling gloom!
> O God, You are aware of all my lamentation;
> You are present in the grief of my nights.
> What should I become, that I might mean something to You?
> If only You take account of me, I will become something for
>     You!
> I am both afflicted by You and astonished at You:
> Yet whether I am good or bad, I am always yours!

*Peace!*


## LETTER 45: MYSTICAL KNOWLEDGE OF THE TRANSCENDENT CREATOR

*In the name of God, the Merciful, the Compassionate!*

Brother Shamsuddin, may God enhance you with His knowledge! Mystical knowledge is the very essence of the souls of believers. Whoever is not destined for this knowledge does not really exist. Knowledge of the Artisan is born through knowledge of His artifacts. From knowledge of the Creator, the knower gains salvation and everlasting life. The first knowledge is that everything He has created is seen to be ill at ease, helpless, and imprisoned. A person should sever all his relationships with creation. He should realize that the Lord is only One, eternal in both His essence and His attributes. "There is none other like Him! He it is Who sees and hears" (Q42:11).

The other way to knowledge of the Creator is through the soul, as has been said: "Whoever knows himself knows his Lord." The Lord first showed forth His power in the entire ambit of the heavens by calling into existence and reducing to nothingness; by varying the states of creatures to include night and day, abundance and scarcity, expansion and contraction; by bestowing kingdoms and taking them back again; and by establishing various states in the world. He is revealed by all things under the heavens, in order that believers in His unity might behold their fellow creatures and gain knowledge of Him. As the Quran attests, "We will show you Our signs in the world . . . !" (Q41:53). This process takes a long time for the knower! God placed the secrets of all creatures within man, for He added: "And within yourselves! Do you not see this?" (Q41:53, 51:21). The spirit of man has been made the exemplar of all creatures. It serves as a ladder leading to knowledge of oneself, that everyone who knows himself might also gain some insight into his Lord. This saying alludes to the alternating states of one's soul, for example, sickness and health, sleeping and waking, death and life, joy and sadness, together with other states and explanations. "Lord" is the macrocosm of which "self" is the microcosm. Clearly, alteration in nature and in creatures is not within human control. This is proof for both the poor and the powerful that everything is under His sway! Whether one is vexed or joyous, it is the result of His disposing. Note carefully the signs along the Way: Sufis of distinction journey on the path of mystical knowledge within themselves and gain awareness from their own nature. All things, whether gross or refined, can be sought within oneself, and the wise find signs and proofs of the knowledge of the Lord within themselves: "Certainly there is a reminder in this for men of insight" (Q39:21). The Lord even casts some of them out of His sight so that, after reflecting, they might be able to recognize Him in all creatures, as has been said: "Look, what do you find in heaven and earth?"

Another group might attain knowledge as a result of persistent struggle. "Those who struggle earnestly for Our sake We will certainly guide them in Our ways" (Q29:69). There are others who, without any discernible rhyme or reason, are granted in a moment the light of divine guidance, and the door to knowledge is opened wide for them. "He follows a light from his Lord" (Q39:22). For others, a veil remains concerning knowledge: "They did not honor God with the honor due Him" (Q6:92). Some are completely hindered from attaining any knowledge of the Almighty. "God sealed their hearts" (Q2:7).

> His beauty has been manifested in a hundred thousand faces;
> In each and every particle, something different can be seen.
> Inevitably every particle points to the Friend, for
> In its beauty can be discerned the face of Another.
> Since He is One, the whole series begins with Him:
> As long as you exist, you are the captive of Another!

Due to these differences it becomes clear that mystical knowledge cannot be gained through the exercise of one's intellect, unless it is granted by the Lord; the uninitiated may be highly intelligent and yet devoid of mystical knowledge. Nor can knowledge be obtained by hearing, unless the Lord grants it, for most unbelievers receive an invitation from the prophets and hear a description of this knowledge without ever acquiring it. It has been established that knowledge of the Lord is granted only through His guidance. Hence it is that Abu Bakr, the Righteous, said: "We recognized God by means of God, and other than God by the light of God." Someone asked Hazrat Nuri for a proof of God's existence. "The proof of God," he replied, "is the Great Lord Who is beyond all!" Again he was asked about the role of the intellect. "As far as this work is concerned," he answered, "the intellect is helpless. It cannot show the way, but only indicate where the way lies, for by itself, it is ineffectual!"

> At the display of Your beauty, love of idols becomes but vain
>     desire:
> Your sole task is to flee from those who seek to captivate Your
>     heart.
> Face to face with Your face, what can the mind of man do?
> Face to face with Your lips, any other life is but vain desire!

The work of the intellect is nothing more than to see the bodies, essences, or occurrences of all things in the context of space and time, and a similar thing could be said for the other qualities of creatures.

There is nothing that is outside these two dimensions. Yet neither of them is lawful for a seeker, since to put faith in them would make an unbeliever of him; or, since nothing bears a likeness or resemblance to Him, the mind of the seeker would become perplexed. He would say: "I do not find any existing being except with this type of quality, but He has no connection at all with such qualities. Perhaps He doesn't exist!" Such reasoning leads to unbelief, for the seeker errs either by anthropomorphizing God or by voiding Him of all connectedness to this world. Hence it is evident that unless and until He grants knowledge, no one can perceive Him! The long and the short of all this is that finding God is not the result of looking for Him—it is a gift! Not everyone who seeks God finds Him, but only he to whom is given the gift of perceiving Him. Nor does everyone who gazes intently see Him; only he sees Him to whom He has shown Himself. Showing is the cause of seeing, not looking! Giving is the cause of finding, not seeking! Many seekers have not become finders, while many who have found were not seeking! As far as seeking is concerned, all are equal. In finding, however, there are differences. An idol worshiper finds Him in an idol; Christians call upon Him in Jesus; while Jews attest to Him through Esdras.

> The tendency of all creatures in this world,
> Whether knowingly or not, is always toward You!
> How can I have anyone besides You as my friend?
> Any friendship with others derives from the fragrance of Your
>     friendship.

The world, too, is in quest of Him, and it is in the very act of seeking that people lose the way. Something is placed in front of each person that becomes a veil for him, but there is one group for whom the veil has been lifted and they are able to find the Way to Him.

> There is a city in which the praise of that good Face resounds:
> The hearts of all peoples of the world have been veiled from
>     Him.
> We desire Him, along with others, each of whom
> Eagerly waits to see who's favored, who will gain the Friend!

True knowledge consists in finding the way to perceive the Adorable One just as He is, in His essence, His attributes, and His action, without fault, shortcoming, or imperfection. The Sufi should know God as the Lord completely true to Himself and revealed

through His own Word. There are two opinions concerning the perfection of mystical knowledge. Some theologians hold that a servant
of the Lord ought to try to know in the same way as God knows Himself, even though this can never be fully accomplished. To some extent, such knowledge is possible, but never completely. They disallow
any analysis of the Lord, averring that the mystics are all equal in
their knowledge of the Known One and also know Him as He knows
Himself. The claim of this group is to the perfection of knowledge!

The second school of opinion, including many intelligent men,
along with a whole body of theologians and Sufis, says that no one
can know the Lord perfectly. All know that He exists while a number
also know that they have found salvation, but make no claim to perfect knowledge, such as Abu Bakr, the Righteous, who said: "To realize that one's intellect is of no avail in perceiving God is itself a form
of knowledge." He also said: "Some of the attributes of God Almighty are such that no one can perceive them!" Members of this
group know and admit what was said about the means of acquiring
knowledge. "Because He commanded, we know," they declare, "and
yet He Himself remains far greater than whatever degree of knowledge we reach."

> Where is the intellect that can attain to Your perfection?
> Where is that spirit which can aspire to Your majesty?
> We want You to raise the beauty-concealing veil,
> But where is the eye that can see Your beauty?

In short, since divine knowledge is the reason for the salvation of
God's servants, if there is anything missing in the conditions required
for it, then the command concerning salvation will turn out to be ineffective. They have said that a Sufi has a clean mirror, his heart,
which has been placed before him. Looking into it, he perceives the
limits of creatures and the rights of the Creator. He pursues the Way
of mystical knowledge just as it is.

> The more I keep gazing at the radiant face of the Friend,
> The more the world becomes for me a depiction of Him!
> Whoever looks at the purity of his heart
> Sees there the resplendent beauty of the Ravisher of his heart!

A man of heart who became a knower contained in his eyes the
argument and proof of God's creation. "I am a sign of all that is His,
proof that that essence and unity has no association whatsoever."

Come, open your eyes, and see that each particle of dust,
If you look carefully into it, contains a world-revealing cup.

Several writers have stated that "I have never seen anything in which God could not be perceived!" "Seeing God in things" is a Way, a proof, going from the artefact to the Artisan, for everything that has been made bears witness to its Maker, and all activities prove that there is an Agent.

Whoever arrives at this stage, it is said,
Cannot distinguish God's splendor from His immanence.

The knowledge of renowned men of the Way consists of a state; it is the soundness of their state with the Lord that they call "mystical knowledge," while others, from among religious scholars and jurists, also call their knowledge about the Lord "mystical knowledge." Those well versed in the principles of the faith make no distinction between acquired knowledge and mystical knowledge, except to say that it is possible to speak of God as a knower without having mystical or intuitive knowledge. It is by reason of their lack of grace that they speak thus! On the other hand, famous masters of the Way call that knowledge mystical which is linked to actions and a state; while a mystic is one who can explain things on the basis of his own experience of various states. Only someone with that sort of knowledge do they call a mystic or a Sufi. Such a person, in their view, must also know the inner reality of a thing, for anyone who is merely concerned with the explanation of something and its preservation, without at the same time stressing the preservation of its meaning and proper utilization, is a knower but not a gnostic. Hence it is that when this group wants to belittle someone before his relatives and friends they call him "a scholar." The externalists deny the application of this label to themselves, maintaining that their sole objective is to gain knowledge, but they gain knowledge without utilizing it.

The Sufis have more knowledge of God than the externalists, and yet they consider themselves to be more in need, mere beginners, and very ordinary people. Their divine knowledge is free of claims and bragging. They are not inflated by an increase of knowledge. They do not pride themselves on their exercise of supernatural powers. The soul of such a gnostic is filled with an abundance of uninterrupted favor and divine grace; his astonishment at the greatness and beauty of the One Known, in the secrecy of intimate knowledge, cannot be expressed in writing!

How can mystical meaning be restricted to appearances?
Is a king concerned with the huts of beggars?

The condition imposed on the traveler is that he should not rest content till he attains the One Known. Nor should he rest content in such knowledge! Though he might know much, he should seek after more. Having drunk deeply of the wine of knowledge from the cup of love, he still wants more: His drinking merely whets his thirst.

If I saw You a thousand times a day,
I would still want yet another glimpse!

Consider Abu Bakr, the Righteous, whose wealth was such that were his faith to be weighed against that of the entire Muslim community, it would be the greater! "O Messenger," he asked Muhammad, "is faith also a form of thirst?" And have you not heard about Mu'az Jabal? He had drunk from this wine and, in an intoxicated state, was going to the door of the courtyards of his friends saying: "Come, let us have faith for an hour!" When the friends heard what he was saying, they hurried off to Muhammad and said: "O Messenger of God, Mu'az spoke to us in such and such a way. Haven't we already accepted the faith?" Muhammad replied: "O Mu'az, you drank wine from the tavern of love and now have become quarrelsome with your friends." This is thirst!

You became intoxicated, and forgot everything:
Who were your friends? And where did you drink your wine?

It has also been said:

Before us is the dazzling beauty of the city.
When you have observed it, go! Burn some wild rue!
What is that beauty before you? It is your intoxication!
And what is that wild rue? It is your very being!

Whenever it happens, as it does so many times a day, that the divine footstool says to the throne, "What news do you have?" and the throne asks the footstool, "Do you have any news?" and heaven asks the earth, "Has any seeker passed by in your direction?" and earth asks heaven, "Has any lover journeyed in your direction?" the cry is always due to the excess of thirst!

O brother, there are thousands upon thousands who have been

180

martyred and killed on this Way for His sake! Many other thousands are wounded and thrown prostrate. Those renowned for their intellect have been utterly perplexed in their search for Him, and those famous for their religious knowledge are annihilated by the Lord at the very outskirts of His glory. All their discernment and insight became submerged like a drop in the ocean of His majesty or singed like sparks from the fire of His glory!

> Reaching out to those consumed hearts, say,
> It is a torch that lovers bear in their hands!

They make the whole world happy with their fragrance and conversation, yet do not drink even a drop from the vessel of the honor of this world!

> I said: "For whom are you so beautifully adorned?"
> He replied: "For myself, since I am the One!
> I am Lover, Beloved and Love.
> I am the mirror, beauty and seeing!"

An imbiber of wine came to the door of the tavern and asked for a little wine. He was told that the tavern was out of wine. "Take my hand and place it upon the mouth of the vessel," he replied, "so that I might smell its aroma. This will make me as intoxicated as others become after drinking a hundred glasses of wine!"

> So intoxicated am I with the heady wine of His love that,
> If I take one more gulp of it, I shall expire straightaway!

One should not be astonished that a beggar became so intoxicated by the fragrance of his Lord that the holy and exalted angelic beings were unable to bear the burden. There was such a breeze of divine favor blowing within his inflamed breast that angels fell senseless. When they came to their senses again, Gabriel said: "In seven hundred thousand years we had never experienced such fragrance as emanated from the age of the one closest to God!" Gabriel asked him [Muhammad] about it. He said: "Surely I smell the fragrance of Yemen! It is the gentle breeze wafting from the inflamed heart of a camel driver that has produced intoxication from the direction of Yemen."

> That idolater, thread in hand, put the city in an uproar
> When he staggered from the tavern in drunken delirium.

*Peace!*

## LETTER 46: THE LOVE OF SAINTS AND THEIR OBEDIENCE[62]

*In the name of God, the Merciful, the Compassionate!*

Brother Shamsuddin, may God grant you the life of one of His friends and intimates! Creatures other than man have no truck with love, for they have no great aspirations. Those activities of the angels that you see going on correctly do so because the tradition concerning love was not applied to them, whereas the ups and downs you see in the affairs of men are because this was promulgated among them: "He loves them, and they love Him" (Q5:54). Everyone who has breathed even a particle of love says: "Remove your heart from safety and bid farewell to yourself, for love keeps nothing in reserve, nor does it leave anything aside!"

It was love for You that made me a frequenter of taverns!
Otherwise, I would be confident and secure in my possessions!

There was an uproar in the kingdom when the turn of the richly endowed Adam came. The angels said: "What has happened, that so many thousands of years of our praising and glorifying God have been thrown to the wind, whereas this creature of clay has been exalted and raised above us?" A voice said: "Do not look at his form of clay! Look rather at the sacred trust given to him! 'He loves them, and they love Him'" (Q5:54). The fire of love has been enkindled within their hearts and a voice came, saying, "Might and victory belong to God!" Thereupon all hearts were consumed by fire; everyone melted in the intensity of love. What is this? Just as He is not restricted, neither is His work!

The kings of this world, when they want to honor their servants, confer a turban and a robe of honor upon them, as well as territories. When God honors anyone, He begins by removing his turban and robe of honor! Then He makes him hungry and strips him naked. This is to reveal the meaning of the tradition that "there is no return for anyone who has turned toward Him till he is slain!"

If you seek Me, you will have to surrender your body to
    sorrow;
Like lovers, you must lose your heart in the world.
Fill your heart with grief; place it before your eyes,
And then watch while you make of your very life a sacrifice!

A certain hapless dervish had traversed the Way, spending his entire life in grief and wandering hither and thither. Right up till his last day he lived in this fashion. Then he died. People saw, written in his heart, these words: "Here is one slain out of love of God!"

> The heart I had snatched from the ravishers of hearts
> I shall never give to anyone, nor even show to another.
> O Lord of my life, when with one glance You bear away my
>     heart,
> Tell me, have I been without a heart for a thousand years?

Divers who plunge deep into the ocean play with their lives, for they do not seek fish that can be sold for silver coins. No, they are after pearls that can light up a dark night. This work requires great skill and much courage. It is no joke. Those pure ones knew that one of them was going to be given a task to perform. Gabriel kept coming to Satan and saying: "If such a state appears for me, then choose me!" Satan kept on saying: "This is my work! Write it down for me!" All the angels kept on coming, making the very same request. Satan said to each and every one of them: "This is my work. Write it down for me!" Hence there are those among the wise who have said that a novice should have some of the qualities of Satan, that he might persist till some work proceeds from him.

O brother, whoever is incapable of placing his head in his hands cannot set his feet in this lane! He should be a man who, when the saying of love comes upon the scene and swords from the hidden world become clearly visible, welcomes them with heart and soul!

> Why should I bear upon my body the robe of loyalty to You?
> Or make porters of my eyes, to carry the burden of Your
>     cruelty?
> Yet if You grant me peace in body, mind, and soul,
> Then, dancing with love, I shall place all three before You!

If a weak, insignificant ant decides to ascend to the heavens, it would be an impossibility! Yet the helplessness of every creature in front of the glory and honor of the Beloved is even greater than that of the ant! When confronted with the great serpent, in all his glory and strength, one people turns toward a lump of dried clay; another, toward the east; another, toward the west; another, to wandering; and yet another, to searching. "God is great and powerful; the way is long and difficult; His nearness is far off; while union with Him is but separation, and still men keep on chattering!"

If, out of love for You, I simply cease to be, it is no cause for
shame!
A hundred souls, placed in Your scales, weigh very little.
I am in quest of You; I cannot be made to blush by You!
How can an ant reach up to heaven? It has no claw!

Many are prattling away, but no one has anything more certain than opinion; many seek a sign, but none is granted; many are searching but find no path; many are making an earnest endeavor, but no effective helper is at hand; many are secretly inflamed, but gain nothing more than waiting and frustration; many have worn themselves out in mosques and churches, but have found only pain and misfortune.

Alas! all my efforts and strivings have produced nothing
Except dust upon my head, and wind within my grasp!

Khwaja Bayazid Bistami said: "It reached my hearing that the Merciful One sits upon the divine throne (Q20:5). I vaulted to it so that I could see its state for myself. I found it more greatly athirst than I myself!" He used to say:

I am exhausted by the mere suspicion of Your love:
Do not talk to me about union with You!
Men reproach me; I am ridiculous, they say,
Like a wolf smacking his lips on an empty belly!

When you glance at His Majesty, you will see livers swimming in blood. When you look at His Beauty, you will see why the consolation of hearts is in Him! Gnostics, confronted with His Majesty, simply melt away, while lovers rejoice at the disclosure of His Beauty. They say: "Mystical knowledge is a fire, while love is a fire within that fire setting the world aflame and filling it with noise and tumult."

In my lane look at the noise and uproar that result from love!
In Your lane note the effort spurred by Your beauty!

There was a beautiful woman peerless in her loveliness. One day she appeared like the sun in the bazaar of Baghdad. A great cry and tumult arose among the people. Everyone was running after her. Entering a house, she shut the door. "If you did not want to be praised," they asked, "then why did you show yourself?" "I like the cry and uproar of the world!" replied she. The heavenly ones have had their heads turned, while creatures of earth are perplexed and astonished. Without Him, no one can experience tranquility! And yet no one has ready access to Him. Every day, the divine footstool says to the divine throne, "Do you have any sign of Him?" Heaven says to earth: "Has any seeker passed by in your direction?" And earth says to heaven: "Has any lover journeyed in your direction?"

O brother, in every corner you will find someone killed by Him, and in every hermitage some whose hearts are aflame with Him. What soul is there that has not melted at His wrath? Or where is the heart that has not been soothed by His graciousness? In the dwellings of the dervishes you will find much enthusiasm for Him; and if you go into the alley of the tavern, there you will encounter the pain of those who have not found Him! If you go to the churches of the Christians, you will find everyone searching for Him with joy. If you go to the synagogues of the Jews, you will find all in eagerness for His beauty.

> A thousand lovers came in quest of My company;
> They offered up their eyes and hearts as My servants.
> All were consumed with grief at the prospect of My departure:
> For none saw or perceived that he himself was but a sign of
> Me!

The divine throne, tarnished by the suspicion that arose from "God Almighty is confined to the throne," cried out like some unfortunate one in pain:

> I am suspected of being in love with a moon-faced one:
> I have no other recourse except remaining silent!

God be praised, seven hundred thousand years have passed by. Every day the flame of this fire becomes more intense, and in every direction thousands and thousands more are consumed by it. There is a fear that both worlds might be consumed by it and be reduced to nothingness. Since this fire has been burning from the very beginning, this is hardly surprising!

O brother, the wealth of water and dust is no small matter! The labors of Adam and mankind are not without significance. Footstool and throne, tablet and pen, heaven and hearth—all are at his service!

Khwaja Abu Ali said: "Since Adam was appointed God's viceregent (Q2:30), and Abraham was called 'the Friend of God' (Q4:125), and Moses was told 'I chose you for Myself' (Q20:40), people have said that if this saying, 'He loves them and they love Him' (Q5:54), did not make a fitting impression on someone's heart, it would be a sign that that person had no heart!" If the sun of love had not shone upon Adam and mankind, then man's activities would have been merely of the same value as those of other creatures. In the beginning, there was this saying concerning love; in the middle, this saying; and at the end, the same saying! It applied today as well as tomorrow.

The verifiers of truth have said: "Both this world and the one to come are simply for seeking Him!" Anyone who says that the next world is not also one of seeking is totally wrong! There is not merely one type of prayer and fasting: both are forms of seeking. Tomorrow, all the prescriptions of the Law will be canceled, but these two things remain forever—the love of God and the praise of God. It has been said that the commands regarding the pilgrimage, the holy war, prayer, and fasting are meant to be observed until they are abrogated, but it can never be proper to untie the knot of love. As you stroll around heaven, each day's perception of God Almighty will reveal a whole new world to you, so new that you will not have even thought it existed up till then! This is such a work that there is no question of its ever being brought to a conclusion. Indeed, perish the thought!

> As long as I live, my trade and my task is this:
> It is my rest, composure, and companion.
> This is how I busy myself each day:
> I am on a chase and this is my prey!

*Peace!*

LETTER 47: THE SIGNS OF LOVE

*In the name of God, the Merciful, the Compassionate!*

Brother Shamsuddin, the friendship of the Lord Most High for a servant is something hidden. When a servant wants to know whether he is one of God's friends or not, let him seek the confirmation of some signs of this love. The Prophet has said: "When God Almighty befriends someone, He rains calamities upon him, and when someone displays diligence in his love for Him, He puts him to the test." The Prophet, when asked what this testing might be, replied: "He does not spare a man's property, wife, or children." A sign of God's love for His servant is that He makes him shy away from anything other than God. The Prophet Jesus was asked: "Why do you not buy an ass for your journeys?" He replied: "I am more precious to God Almighty than to vex my soul over an ass!"

If you say that the Prophet had no cell, while many prophets and saints did have families and possessions without being cut off from the divine love, then it should be known that here it is a question of some but not all objects being desirable, as has been said: "In truth, My saints are under My domes, and only I know them." This description applies to all the saints, while there are some who have been more intently desired, as this tradition attests: "When God Almighty loves someone in a special way, He rains calamities upon his head. If the person bears this patiently, then God grants him the grace of 'selection.' If he pleases God, then he is raised to purity." The meaning of "selection" is that God Almighty makes His servant specially favored so that he acquires many kinds of qualities effortlessly. His purity would mean that he is cleansed of his faults. A religious scholar has said: "When you yourself observe that you love and see Him, and note that He has ordered calamities for you, then know that He desires your purification." That very process of purification is a form of mutual friendship, as has been said:

> Night and day I am engaged in Your work,
> No matter what You do, I remain a wrinkle on your beauty!

A disciple said to his spiritual guide: "He gave me an indication of His love." "Son," he replied, "for you the Friend is to be found in calamities, and yet you prefer love to the Beloved!" The disciple denied this charge. "Do not desire friendship," replied the guide, "for He does not confer His friendship on a servant until such time as He also ordains calamities for him!"

It is related that the Prophet said: "When God Almighty takes a servant as His special friend, He makes him preach to himself and gives him divine knowledge from his own heart so that he might give himself orders with regard to what is commanded and prohibited." He also said: "When God Almighty wants to grant goodness to a servant, He grants him an insight into the faults of his own soul." And also: "Would not the very special nature of the signs of the servant's love for God be an indication of God's friendship toward him, just as the fruit signifies the tree, and smoke indicates that there must be fire?" The Messenger said: "When God loves one of His servants in a special way, his sins do no real damage." That is to say, when God loves His servant, He grants him the gift of repentance before he dies. His past sin holds no dangers for him, just as past infidelity, before embracing Islam, does no damage.

Zayd Aslam said: "Whenever God Almighty loves a servant, He loves him to the utmost, till His friendship attains the degree at which He says to him: 'Do whatever you want! I have forgiven you!' " If you ask, "Is not sin opposed to the very root of love?" the answer would be that it is against the perfection of love, but it is not opposed to its very foundation! Do you not see that there are many men who love their own lives and yet, when they fall sick and want to get better again, still eat things that are harmful to them? They know that something is harmful, and even though their knowledge may be defective and sensuality gets the better of them, that still does not mean that they do not love their own lives: They simply cannot stand firmly rooted in the love of God! A Sufi has said: "As long as one's faith does not penetrate the heart, one's love for God remains middling; but when it penetrates to the deepest recesses of the heart, then he does receive perfect love! He also abandons sin."

It is a risky business to claim that one loves God! The reason for this has been well put by Khwaja Fuzail: "If someone asks, 'Do you love God?' remain silent. For if you reply in the negative, that would be infidelity; while if you reply that you do, you would be lacking a quality of lovers, and your love would be in danger!" Understand that anyone who claims that he loves does about the easiest thing in the world, but actual loving, ah! that is extremely difficult!

A man should be careful not to be deceived by the trickery of Satan or the duplicity of his own soul. We are entitled to our reservations every time someone claims to love God, until such time as he has been tested by signs and confirmed by indications and proofs. One of the signs of perfect love is intimacy in prayer with the Beloved and perfect happiness when alone with Him. In the story of Baruch it is related that Moses, with all his glory, requested Baruch to pray for rain. God Almighty said to Moses: "Baruch is a good servant, but he has one fault." Moses answered, "My Lord, what is his fault?" "He enjoys the gentle morning breeze," came the reply, "and rests while it is blowing. Anyone who loves Me cannot be at peace with any other!"

It is also related that a devoted person was engaged in devotion toward God in a forest for an extended period. He saw a bird that had made a nest. It had a very pleasant voice. He thought that he would make his cell under that tree so that he might be cheered by its singing. He put his plan into execution. In the meantime, a revelation came to the Prophet: "Tell that dervish: You have affection for a particular creature. Hence I shall cast you down from the rank you have acquired, and by no means will you be able to reach it again, no matter how much you try!"

O brother, the delight of the intimacy experienced by some during invocatory prayer reaches such an intensity that even if their house were to burn down they would have no knowledge of it! Others at prayer can have their foot operated on, as did Ali, and be oblivious of it! Wherever love and affection gain the ascendency, then in the privacy of invocatory prayer a person finds refreshment of soul. He ceases thinking about things and sets a limit to the intrusions of worldly affairs, for he does not want things repeated over and over again. Whenever one who loves God engages in conversation with men, it is with his tongue only; his affection has been inwardly given over to remembering his Friend! Love for Him should be such that a person never rests except in his Beloved. It is also said that whoever does not possess three special qualities is not a friend of God: (1) He prefers to converse with God rather than with men; (2) he prefers the sight of God to that of men; (3) he prefers to devote himself to God rather than to be engaged in serving men. From all this it can be surmised that he shows no distress of mind at the loss of anything—except God Almighty!

> Even if I were to have nothing in this world or the next,
> By having You, I do have everything! There is no need for
> anything else!

Khwaja Junaid says that one of the signs of love is that a person derives satisfaction from his devotion to God and that such devotion is in no way burdensome, while any pain that might accrue from it is assuaged, as has been said: "Any labor undertaken for the sake of love has no trace of laziness about it: Although a person's body might grow tired, still his heart never flags." Religious scholars say that anyone in love with God is never sated with worshiping Him, even if he enjoys great favors, since the lover, in worshiping the Beloved, remains submissive, without being obsequious! There is an example of this in contemplating carefully what lies before our eyes. Where is the lover who counts any effort made on behalf of his own beloved as burdensome? Or who considers service to the beloved anything but delightful, even though it be troublesome for his body? And if he is privileged to be near God, then he would be contemplating the very states of the angels and would know that even they show no slackening in their praise of God, nor do they give any hint of committing sins. Every lover who, like a mirror, considers his own love will feel ashamed; He will consider himself as one cut off and the meanest of lovers.

"For thirty years I worshiped the Lord in heart and limb, so thinking I had gained some influence with Him," remarked a lover. "In my ecstatic contemplation I reached the rank of the angels. I asked them who they were. They replied: 'We are lovers of God and have been engaged in worshiping Him for three hundred thousand years. Never have our minds failed to be preoccupied with Him. Except for Him, we have remembered nothing at all.' I became ashamed of my own efforts and presented them to an assembly of those for whom expiatory pain was required." From this it is clear that everyone who knows himself not only knows his Provider, but also to a fitting degree feels a certain sense of shame in relation to God. He becomes tongue-tied because he has taken steps to push his claims; he himself has come forward to reveal them. Rather, the way he carries himself, the moral tone of his actions, and his various qualities should all bear witness to his friendship and love, just as Khwaja Junaid said: "My master, Khwaja Sari Saqati, fell sick. We had no remedy to treat the cause of the ailment. We sought the services of a very famous physician. We showed him the bottle with a urine specimen. He looked at it for a while and finally said: 'This indicates that he is a lover of God!' " Khwaja Junaid continues: "I fell unconscious! The bottle dropped from my hands. When I returned to consciousness, I hurried back to be of service to Khwaja Sari. I told him about the diagnosis and he smiled. 'O Master,' I exclaimed, 'can signs of love be discerned from such a specimen?' 'Yes!' "

> The tale of the scorched breast refers to me, O heavenly
> creature!

Do not ask questions, lest the fire of hell erupt from my
   mouth!


Know now that there could be someone who, out of his own ignorance and self-seeking, might really love the enemy of God, and yet
be proud of himself, thinking that it is God Whom he loves! None of
the signs of genuine love would be found in such a person.

Khwaja Suhail, when engaged in conversation with anybody,
used to say, "O friend!" People said it is possible that the man might
not be his friend. How then could he address him as friend? He spoke
softly into the ear of the questioner: "There are only two possibilities:
Either he is a believer or a hypocrite. If he is a believer, he is a friend
of God. If he is a hypocrite, he is a friend of Satan."

O brother, in friendship things occur that, outside its bonds,
would be impossible but that, under the protection of love, become
supportable. The difficulties and insults of love, by the command of
love, are lifted up and borne away.

A novice was speaking with Khwaja Ibrahim Adham. When the
time came for him to go, he began to excuse himself. The Khwaja cut
him off, saying: "Put your heart at ease! We were having a conversation inspired by love, and a friend sees no badness in a friend." "The
love of anything renders a man both blind and dumb!" The secret
meaning of this dictum is given by Khwaja Bayazid Bistami: "It is no
matter for surprise that I love You, for there is no shortage of lovers
of One so beautiful and perfect in every way! The astonishing thing is
that You love me, full of helplessness and defects from head to toe, a
mere child of dust! Hence you should know how it is that the tree of
love could sprout from your dust, and that the cup-bearer of the delight of this wine could be so generous with His gift of 'He loves
them and they love Him!' " (Q5:54).


Who am I along Your Way that in my abode
Flowers should sprout in my soil from Your glance?
And beyond even this, I have received, from Your bounty,
The adornment of Your love upon my heart!


*Peace!*

# MANERI

## LETTER 48: THE COMMAND CONCERNING AFFECTIONATE LOVE AND PASSIONATE LOVE

*In the name of God, the Merciful, the Compassionate!*

Brother Shamsuddin, may God grant you perfect love! The affectionate love of the Lord for His servant, and the affectionate love of the servant for the Lord, is the correct type of love. Both the Quran and the Traditions concur in this. Within the community of believers there is a consensus that God has a quality or attribute by which His friends love Him and He loves them. Affectionate love, as far as the dictionary meaning of the word goes, is derived from the root that means "affection" or "friendship." It can also mean "seeds" which are sown in the soil of one's heart. This second root meaning can be considered insofar as the germ of life is contained in the seed in the same way that the life of a plant is contained in its seed. That seed, when it is sown in the soil, lies concealed; rain comes and waters it; the sun warms it; cold and heat pass over it, but it does not alter. When its proper time arrives, however, it germinates and produces flowers and fruits. Likewise, when affectionate love dwells in someone's heart, it is not altered by what is in front of it, or by what is hidden; or by any calamity, effort, comfort, delight, absence, or even by union itself.

With regard to its method of operation, however, there is a difference of opinion among religious scholars. A group of theologians contends that affectionate love of the Lord is the sum total of attributes, since if the Quran and the Traditions had not been in agreement, its very existence with respect to God would be an impossible idea for the human intellect to grasp. We confirm that position and put our faith in it, but we hesitate to state that any sort of control can be exercised over it.

Another group of religious scholars says that love is the inclination of the soul, the desire and wish of the heart, and affection, all of which are bodily qualities. It is not fitting to attribute such qualities to God. In fact, they all pertain to creatures in their dealings with one another, according to their nature. This group explains the love of a servant as worship, while the love of the Lord is said to be grace and guidance. The Lord's love for a servant, in their opinion, means that He bestows many favors upon him and grants him merit both in this life and in the next, and keeps him safe from the punishments to come. He also keeps him opposed to sin. In his spiritual life God bestows upon him exalted states and high stages, causing his head to break from respect for any rival and making him adhere to the eternal divine favor, with the result that he becomes separated from all creatures and seeks the good pleasure of Him alone.

A servant's love for the Lord is a quality found in the heart of the believer, meaning that he should honor and revere the Lord, seeking His good pleasure and showing impatience in his quest for His face. Without Him, he cannot rest content with anyone! He makes a habit of remembering Him. He shuns the remembrance of anything else. He becomes cut off from all forms of desire and affection and accepts the King of love; he submits totally to the requirements of love. It would not be seemly that the love of God, for him, should be like the affectionate love shown by one creature toward another, namely a kind of possessing and apprehending of the beloved, for taking pleasure in one's friend is a bodily trait. But the Eternal Reality is all holy! He is exempt from all restriction and comprehension, touching and pleasure. Everyone who thoroughly investigates the reality of love will discover that no doubt at all remains in his mind; all his uncertainty will be removed.

Love can be considered to be of two types. One is the love of kind for kind. It is an inclination of the soul and consists in taking pleasure in a friend. The essence of the beloved is sought by way of bodily union. The second type of love is not between kind and kind. This seeking acquires a certain permanence through one of the qualities of the Beloved, and he finds rest in Him. He feels affection when he hears the speech of the Beloved, or when he sees Him in himself.

There are many sayings of the sheikhs concerning love. They can be discovered by perusing their writings. God willing, you will learn much about love from the sheikhs. One group of them holds that it is fitting to have love for God, but not that God should love a servant. "Passionate love," they say, "is a delimiting quality on the part of the Beloved himself; the servant is restrained by God, not God by a servant! Passionate love on the part of a servant for God would be fitting, but not on the part of God for a servant!"

Another group maintains that it is not fitting even for a servant to have passionate love for God, since it exceeds limits. God, however, is in no way limited. They also say that passionate love can never arise without actually seeing the person loved, while affectionate love can also arise from hearing. But when it is a question of seeing, then it cannot be applied to God Almighty. No one has seen Him in this world! When there is talk of affectionate love, everyone lays claim to it since, as far as the appellation is concerned, all are the same (i.e., all are lovers). Some, however, hold it lawful to have passionate love for the Lord. They declare that there is a limit for everything, and when it attains that limit, it finds a new name that it did not have previously. Beyond that point, its perfection cannot rise any higher. There is a turning back from perfection toward what is harmful. Consider, for example, a plant. In the initial stages of its growth, it is geared to a process of increase, seeking its own perfection. This perfection consists in producing fruit. When it has done so, it begins to decline and dry up. Consider also the state of childhood in a man. From childhood a man is oriented toward growing. When he reaches the prime of life and achieves his own perfection, however, he begins to tread the path of decline leading to old age. The life cycle of affectionate love is similar. There is that first glance which results in a person's falling in love. This love increases hourly, seeking its own perfection. When it reaches its very limit, it becomes incapable of receiving any further increase. Then it becomes free of all the impurities of passion, and becomes separated from the attachments of the soul and, at the outermost limit of friendship, becomes free from union or departure, grief or comfort, nearness or distance. It turns its attention to the destruction of self, talks about the abandonment of all decrees, and remains firm and stable in the desire of passionate love. At this stage the name "passionate love" is acquired, and when it has received this name, it is beyond the domain of imagination and conjectures! It is by accepting the divine illuminations that one receives this name. The name passionate love indicates the outermost limit of friendship and the perfection of the affectionate love of the pilgrim.

As long as a person worships, he is called a "devotee";[63] as long as he knows God, he is called a "wise man"; as long as he perceives God, he is called a "gnostic"; as long as he turns away from all that is not God, he is called an "ascetic"; as long as he lives righteously, he is called a "sincere one"; as long as he treads the path of friendship, he is called an "eager one"; and when he throws away all created beings in order to accept Him, he is called a "friend"; and as long as he makes a gift of himself while witnessing Him, he is called a "lover"; and when he becomes such that both his annihilation and his permanence perish in His existence once and for all, he is called a "passionate lover."

# THE HUNDRED LETTERS

It is said that passionate love comes through divine illumination. The Eternal Friend generates it. It is somewhat like lightning, which comes flashing into our eyes and thundering upon our ears. Its rapidity of movement separates it from other accidental events of the world. A person does things because he is a lover that he would not do if he were a stranger, not even for his own well-being; but out of love for his friend, he simply cannot help himself!

This whole explanation pertains to passionate love, but it is not susceptible of being known merely because it has been described or even proven, for it is higher than words. It is not possible to move around the courtyard of His hidden glory by means of the power of one's intellect, or through a simple description! Nor can anyone glance at the revealed beauty of His Truth and contemplate it with the human eye, for it has been said:

> I am love, which appeared in neither world;
> I am the Phoenix of the West, whose trace was nowhere found!
> My eyebrow and amorous glances have ensnared both worlds:
> Don't look for my bow and arrow—they will not be found!
> I am as manifest as sunlight on the face of every particle,
> Yet from the very intensity of my splendor, I cannot be seen!
> I speak with every tongue and hear with every ear
> But, being too swift for eye or ear, I do not appear!
> Since I am every single thing that exists,
> My equal cannot be found in either world!

As long as you live, be joyous and shout out! Do not tear your garments or throw dust upon your head, for from the time of the Prophet until now it has been said: "In time of trouble, do not rend your garments!" Still, the pain of those afflicted by passionate love is such that it cannot be understood and described by interpreters of the Law!

> My heart said, "It would be better to repent of love!"
> It spoke out of turn, for my soul rejoices in love!
> "Then let this heart of mine no more exist between You and
>   me!"
> Wrong again: 'twere better to be beyond the gaze of both
>   worlds!

*Peace!*

195

## LETTER 49: THE SEEKER OF GOD ALMIGHTY

*In the name of God, the Merciful, the Compassionate!*

Brother Shamsuddin, may you have a long life and gain victory over your lower soul! A seeker has no fixed place in any stage, nor does he rest anywhere along the Way. In fact, he is forbidden to rest contentedly anywhere, in either this world or the next as it has been said: "Rest is forbidden for the hearts of God's friends!" For themselves, where indeed would the necessity of resting arise? O brother, know that if there was a question of anyone's heart being at peace in His presence, then please indicate where, in either world, that place might be, for this world is a mansion where He remains hidden, while the next is a mansion where He reveals Himself. While He is still hidden, it is not proper for the hearts of seekers to be at rest, nor can there be rest in the mansion where He discloses Himself! Contentment in the heart of a seeker arises from one of two causes: Either he finds relief in his quest for the Desired One, because he actually finds Him; or else he becomes negligent with respect to the Beloved.

It is not possible to find the Desired One in this world or the next in such a way that the heart is freed from the pain of seeking Him. Nor should one condone negligence with regard to the Lord, allowing the heart to be relieved of the task of running and searching after Him. This is the meaning of what has been described by the author of the *Kashf ul-Mahjub* [The disclosure of what is hidden] and pointed out in the *Sharh-i Ta'arruf* [The commentary on mystical knowledge], namely, that the Beloved does not enter a house, while the lover is, as it were, confined to a house. He cannot pass beyond it. The pain in the hearts of lovers and seekers lasts forever, and the grief experienced by their souls is eternal.

O brother, the litter of the Desired One is raised high upon a camel, while the existence of the stage of the seekers is very lowly indeed! It is not fitting for the Desired One to descend from His lofty universe, nor is it possible for seekers to rise up and make progress from their abject state of servitude. The sheikhs of the Way have said that seeking does not abate in either world but, in the next, there would be neither good fortune nor hardship, simply seeking itself, since the beauty as well as the perfection of the Desired One is infinite. Seeking is unceasing; it is forbidden for a seeker to rest in his heart.

How can there appear a limit for our love,
Since the Beauty of both worlds has no bounds.

A seeker advances by four stages to that of very great revelation. The first is dread; the second, fear; the third, apprehension; and the fourth, fearing. These fears are inspired, in their respective order, by the punishments to come, by separation from creatures, by seeing some deficiency while contemplating God, and by fearing that union with God might come to an end. The various fruits of these fears are, in order: keeping one's hands off the world, which is the stage of a devotee; cutting oneself off from all except the Friend, the stage of righteous ones; the ability to pass beyond what is not God, the stage of lovers; and, finally, being united to the Lord, the stage of perfected Sufis.

All the sheikhs of the Way are unanimous in affirming that when a servant is delivered from the bonds of stages, has become praised and celebrated for all his spiritual states, and has passed beyond seeing what is not God, his state then becomes hidden from the comprehension of human intellect. His life, freed from opinions and conjectures, becomes hidden from the eyes of strangers behind the curtain of "My saints are under My dome." This tradition comes from those whose hearts were aflame. It is not some fable they concocted. This is a road for men to travel; it is not a game for children!

Go play, since a lover's tasks are not for you!

You need the quality of a Zulaikha or the praise of a Majnun in order to listen to the story of Joseph or that of Laila. "Certainly in their stories there are lessons for men of insight" (Q12:111). It is all an explanation and description of this group who are men of the Way. Every difficulty that is encountered on the Way of the Lord can be solved by referring to the story of Joseph. "It is not a tale that one could forge but a confirmation of previous scriptures, an explanation of all things" (Q12:111). When it says "all things," do you know what is meant? If a thousand volumes were written concerning the wonders of that story, it would be but a drop in the ocean or a ray of the sun! One beloved of God said:

Until you become the laughingstock of people and taste
    derision,
And are slandered like the Jew and Christian,

And still resolve *not* to detest your own religion,
How can you be born into the assembly of lovers?

Those lovers who tread the path of reprobation, and the seekers who suffer for their unconventional behavior, say to those who follow the safe path:

We are not fellow travelers! Take your own road and go!
May your way be full of peace and ours full of shame!

If Zulaikha had grown frightened at hearing the women say "The Wife of Pharaoh wants to seduce her own slave" (Q12:30) she would certainly not have dared even to take the name of Joseph.

O brother, God is infinitely greater than Joseph and Zulaikha! Nor can He be counted along with Majnun and Laila, and yet neither you nor I have the "inner eye" that is required to see this. "First construct the wall, and then decorate it!" The firm conviction of the orthodox Sunnis is that lovers have existed, do exist, and will exist: but what profit is there for those unfortunate ones who are not destined for this bliss? Realize that it has been attested in the Quran: "That it [the Quran] should be a healing and mercy for believers!" (Q17:82). What do infidels have to do with such things? What is the benefit of the sun's shining brightly on an unfortunate bat who has no eyes? Since we have come luckless from the very loins of our father and the womb of our mother, because everything and each person that exists is such as it is, then what adjustment can be expected? "The unfortunate one is branded as such from his mother's womb!" He has been nailed up by the Quranic dictum: "You wish nothing at all: whatever God wishes comes to pass" (Q81:29). This dictum has been stamped on mankind and its secret meaning has been thus expressed:

Look at the one who, even out of fear of You,
Cannot move his tongue except to bless You.

O brother, every lament is because of our ill fortune, and every complaint springs from our own ill luck. If it were not so, the door of mercy would remain open. The sun of fortune shines equally on a rubbish heap and on a rose garden; from the rose garden a very pleasant odor arises, whereas a foul smell issues forth from the rubbish heap. The difference arises here: It has nothing to do with the sun! To speak at any greater length about this would be to enter the domain of fate and predestination, and knowing that is neither your task nor mine. It simply perplexes the mind!

> One people reaches the empyrean; another is plunged into hell:
> This is the cry, out of fear of You, arising from a handful of
> dust!

With every quality, and for every possible cause, give praise, whether you be a man or a woman! Never cease to hope, for He turns a robber into a pilgrim, a fire worshiper into a leader, a Brahmin into a Muslim, and an idol worshiper into a friend. Man, though mere water and dust, has a noble task to perform. He has a great calling. He is poor and indigent in his origins; still, when the sun of the divine trust began to shine in the sky, the angels in the angelic kingdom, who for seven hundred thousand years had been engaged in the difficult task of sanctifying themselves and who had shouted out, "We proclaim Your praise" (Q2:30), fled from the portal of divine effulgence and admitted their own inability. "They refused to bear the divine trust" (Q24:72). In the same way the sky said: "I have the quality of exaltation." The earth said: "I am clothed with a vast expanse." The mountains said: "Stability is our hallmark!" Mines of precious stones said: "It is not fitting that we be destroyed!"

Yet the particle of dust stretched forth his hands in supplication from the sleeves of wretchedness and, taking the burden of seeking upon his soul, gave no thought to either world. He said: "What is it to me that I am afflicted? Everything that is eaten turns into dust. What can dust be rubbed into? Place manliness before you and take upon your shoulders the burden that could not be borne by the seven heavens or the earth, and say: 'Are there any more?' " (Q50:30).

*Peace!*

LETTER 50: IN QUEST OF GOD

*In the name of God, the Merciful, the Compassionate!*

Brother Shamsuddin, God's blessing be upon you! There is no other duty more binding on you than the quest of the Real One. If you go to the bazaar, seek Him! If you enter your house, seek Him! If you go to a tavern, seek Him!

I was in a tavern and so too was my Friend:
He came to me in private prayer, bearing a goblet of wine!

If the angel of death, Azrael, comes to you, be careful not to desist from seeking Him! Say to Azrael: "You do your work and I'll do mine."

One day I will have to go and leave this burden behind;
Except for Your name, nothing will be found in my record.
If my head is not in Your hands, O Ravisher of my heart,
At least the dust from under Your foot will form a crown upon
    my head.

It is related that the Prophet was standing with a toothbrush in his mouth when Azrael arrived. He said: "What do you say? Shall I return, or should I bring forward the one commanded?" The Prophet, not bothering to remove the brush from his mouth, said: "You do your work and I'll do mine." If he bears you off to hell, you ought not to desist from seeking Him. Say to Malik (the keeper of hell): "Rain the blows of torture upon my head, while I pursue the path of seeking Him. The work must go on!" And if he takes you to paradise, then pay no attention to the damsels or the palaces. Run along the lane of seeking, saying as you go:

If both worlds were to be bestowed upon me,
I would remain poor unless united to You!

The first resting place along the Way of seeking is supplication. The sages have said: "The Prophet intercedes with the Lord on behalf of the servant." When this is firmly fixed in his breast, then his reins are pulled in the direction of the Presence. For beginners, supplication is really their first lesson. When a novice has been engaged for some time in supplication, then this turns into magnanimity. Those well versed in the Way agree that love does not begin to dwell anywhere except in the cell of magnanimity.

When a novice has traveled for some time along the road of magnanimity, the road develops into seeking. This seeking is conveyed along the royal road paved by the realities of "There is no god but God." The royal kettledrum is played at the King's threshold: "He who seeks Me, finds Me!" A cry is heard: "O heights and depths, heaven and hell, footstool and throne, get out of the way of those who seek Me! They are in quest of Me, and I am the aim and object of their desires!" Creatures are told, "Nothing will remain of any of you!"

The steps here described form the ascent of the servant along this Way. No one can take even a single step along this Way without considering that merely intending to reach Him would be, for the person involved, an ascent. For the prophets, there is both a visible and a hidden ascent. For the saints, there is only a hidden ascent. There is an ascent for all who set out in imitation of the pride of the world. It depends on their testing and on their strength. This is what genuine strength is!

O brother, a little cunning is needed. The head of useless things should be cut off with the sword of austerity, and the worship of one's own lower soul should be resisted by continuous struggle against its promptings. Passing beyond both worlds, one must place a foot squarely on top of one's lower soul. If even a particle from the entire universe were to intrude into someone's resolution, he would not be fit for this Way. It has been said: "No one can attain to the All until he has been separated from all." The wise have said: "If, on the night of his ascent, the pride of the worlds [Muhammad] had looked back at anything at all, he would have been transfixed there, and would not have been taken up to the distance of two bow lengths from God himself."

How can a base person, by mere talk, reach this Way?
One has to suffer, even be consumed, and stride forth
   manfully!
If there are two directions along the path to Unity, one loses
   the Way:
You must decide either to please the Friend or to indulge
   yourself!

It has been mentioned that, when Adam arrived in paradise, the Law said: "Do not approach this tree!" (Q2:35). The Way said: "Set fire to the whole lot!" Once in heaven, Adam observed: "This is a well-adorned world! Here there is lordship, too, but it occurs to my heart that one day I should like to go to my own grief-filled corner, for the tradition about me is not joined to lordship." Suddenly a voice spoke, "Adam, do you really want to go into exile?" He replied, "Why not? for my work lies along the Way!" He was told: "Do your work!" He said, "There is another work that should be done in preference to this!" Heaven is under the divine command, and Rizwan and the angels form a group of servants. They said: "It will be necessary to change your abode from one of peace to one of trials. It will also be necessary to remove the turban from your head and place a crown of dust and penury upon it. In addition, your good name will be spoiled, and you will have to bear the reproach of 'Adam disobeyed his Lord!' " (Q20:121). Adam replied: "Consider it done! I have already raised this cry in the world, 'I don't care!' I have lifted my hand in plunder and in opposition to the house of wealth!"

> What better work could I do than this?
> I dare to call myself "Your servant!"
> I care not about the reproach of men:
> Whenever I see You, I shall greet You!

I do not want you to say that paradise was snatched away from Adam. You should say this: Adam was snatched away from paradise! A roasted heart is not content with a grilled chicken! An inflamed soul and a wounded liver will not be looking at the damsels or castles of paradise. Do not consider water and dust to be of little significance! Whatever has water also has dust. Whatever has come into existence has come through water and dust. Everything else is like the decoration on a wall—it has been added for the sake of the wall! When the royal falcon of love took flight from the nest of honor, it reached the divine throne. It saw its sublimity. It went inside. It reached the divine resting place. It saw its amplitude. It went inside. It reached heaven. It saw its expanse. It went inside. It reached dust. It saw love. It alighted there. It said: "How strange! What is this?" The reply came: "I am love, and that is toil. Between us there is only a fine distinction. In the world of appearance and the world of meaning, those who understand know the difference."

O brother, be full of hope! Persevere, for this Wealth is a grace, not the end product of an investigation! By God most High, if it were by investigation, not even a particle would be decreed for you or me. But the cause is removed, so that just as the pure ones are full of hope, so too the impure, thousands of them, now have some hope. A rubbish dump frequented by dogs might one day become the seat of kings. But there is a hindrance. If you desire to reach your destination or become somebody, undoubtedly you will have to advance beyond the confines of your confused, tainted nature. One has to step forth with the provisions of the Law to sustain him, and the escort of Truth to protect him. Other traditions and stories at hand can give us heart for today as well as tomorrow. Today it is a matter of passionate love and longing; tomorrow it is peace and enjoyment! It has been said: "If those who are well acquainted with grief were to be raised up tomorrow and were to look at their own breasts, and if they were to find that their grief had diminished, even by the smallest fraction, then they would cry out that the one adornment that the eight heavens did not encompass was grief!

*Peace!*

## LETTER 51: THE WAY TO GOD

*In the name of God, the Merciful, the Compassionate!*

Brother Shamsuddin, may God disclose His way to you! Khwaja Bayazid was once asked: "What is the way by which one can reach God?" Realize from this that just as one who sees the Way does not see the Truth, how can one who sees himself become one who sees God? Your preoccupation and mine is with our beards and hair, for we see nothing except ourselves. Inevitably we worship nothing except ourselves! If your glance and mine were to fall upon the desert of ignorance and to see the grip that our own lower soul has upon us, we would certainly not claim to be Muslims. You would be able to see that when a drop from the goblet of the Law falls into your fortunate mouth and the eyes of your heart are opened, this couplet becomes applicable:

From all that I knew I turned away:
How could I take another name when I call upon Yours?

It is said that when the self-sufficient sun shines upon the seas of knowledge of the learned, not a drop of moisture will be left in all these seas. Someone has also asked: "O lords whose keys open all knots, why has your door been closed?" Do you know what has happened? The firmament and the stars have a claim to existence and activity only until such time as the royal sun rises. When it does, no other can make any claim to existence, speaking, hearing, or any other activity. In what way can mere particles of existence contest with the lightning of divine Unity? When the sun warms the knowledge of a scholar, verily it all turns to ignorance. When longing for Him warms someone's heart, all other desires take to flight. When His power is experienced, all other powers become helpless. When His glory and honor are revealed, all other manifestations of glory and honor slide down into the dust. When the majestic curtain is lifted from the beauty of His Unity, all creatures are plunged into the wilderness of absolute nothingness.

As far as you can, claim no rights! Your inventory will not be required, nor is there any altercation with you over your capital. Rather, you should forget yourself. Do not insert your own name in the Friday congregational prayer! Do not say "I am like this!" or "I am like that!" If you make any claim you will be doing the sort of thing Pharaoh did, for he said: "I am your Lord, the Almighty" (Q79:24). Your lower soul, covered with robe and turban, will say: "I am your lesser provider!" Thus your lower soul begins to act as Pharaoh's did, but Pharaoh's soul displayed itself as it was, whereas your lower soul tries to sell itself to you in the garb of a Muslim, and you drink the sherbet of its pride!

The same claim is made for it as was made for the Pharaoh's soul. Still, it fears for its life. If it shows itself in the desert, then the sword of the Law will lop off its head. Do not try to be an overlord! Be a servant! In this way, the sword will be diverted from you. Everyone who puts himself forward has his head cut off, just as happened to Satan. A slave has no rights, nor can he arrogate a kingdom to himself. Whatever he does has to be according to the orders of his lord, not in accordance with his own desire or authority. The Quran says: "God gave the example of a slave who was the property of another and had no power over anything!" (Q16:75). For him, both ordinary and mystical knowledge are necessary, and also the shade of the wealth of a guide, because a novice cannot reach this stage unless he finds it in the monastery of some experienced guides who have been thoroughly prepared for this task by the vicissitudes of the Way. "He who has no guide along the Way is led by Satan."

Religious scholars have spoken in this fashion: "Knowledge is obtained from the conversation of people." Anyone who carries on his affairs according to his own desire and inclination would be like someone who acquires his knowledge from a book. Of him it would be said: "Though he is a learned man, yet because he had no master, he will not be correct!" Know that when you change, so too does your food and also your work, but if you change only your clothes and food, even though you change them a thousand times, make arrangements for yourself among this people; still, until you yourself are changed, all this is worthless![65]

Hence it is that among this group genuine conversion is considered very important. In the forty-day retreat, in austerities and in solitude, the whole purpose of the exercise is conversion, for without it no one acquires the correct way of behaving. Realize that everyone you see who has remained, as it were, outside himself, and is caught up with his turban, clothes, shoes, how long or how short his robe should be, how white or blue it ought to be, and so on, is still enslaved to himself. He is really worshiping himself. You can be a slave either to yourself or to religion. "Contraries cannot be reconciled to one another." As long as you see that you seek in yourself even a particle of the acceptance of people, or the desire for a place in society, you are still caught! And if anyone makes you suffer an indignity, and you ascribe your disgrace to him and get angry with him, then know that you simply belong to the category of learned men, but your religion has not been accepted by the Esteemed Lord. You will have to return to yourself. You are simply changing your clothes! What profit is there in that? If you are so strong that you can pass a thousand years in one patched garment and spend your whole life eating a little grass, and you kill yourself with austerities in some hermitage where no one will see you, and if birds provide you with shade during the summer months, then be on the alert lest you be deceived, for all of this is the trickery, guile, and deception of your ego! For as long as every hair on your body bears witness to your infidelity and proclaims you to be an idol, the door of wealth will not be opened to you, nor will the King of Religion take you under His patronage! To sum up, everyone who stands by virtue of his own strength will, of himself, tumble down headlong!

The real power and dignity of spiritual guides can be gleaned from what has just been said. It is observable that snakes and scorpions remain quiet during wintertime. This is not the result of their prudence, strength, or self-control. It simply means that the season does not give them an opportunity to act. When the weather warms up and hot winds begin to blow, the environment becomes favorable to them. That is when you can enjoy the fun, for then they will bite and sting! Man's ego is like snakes and scorpions. The venomous sting of a man is his tongue. Sometime or other, when he is sitting at home and displaying his real disposition, you will understand what he is.

Some work may not have gone according to his fancy; or something may happen to mar his exercise of authority and he wishes that the defect that arose in his authority might be hidden by this concealment. Many people are seen engaged in occupations and work who, when they are removed from office and no longer enjoy power and authority, sit down upon a prayer carpet, place a Quaran stand in front of them, and take to reading the Quran. They also take upon themselves extra fasts and extra prayers and are forever reciting short, ejaculatory prayers. To everyone who comes to visit them they say: "This is the real work! All that other activity is nothing! The Lord has granted me a blessing!" This saying is perfectly true when correctly applied to one's soul, but such men as these are not speaking from their hearts. Do you not see that if their position were once again given to them and they were to be restored to the same rank as before, their joy would know no bounds? Such men make impositions on the souls of guides and elders.[66]

In the same say also a man can be sitting at home for some time. He adorns his tongue, whetting this sword of his with poison with which to strike at people. Out of ignorance, he gives the name of "mystery of religion" to what is really poison for a soul. In addition, out of foolishness and ignorance, he claims as an example of the strictness of the Law what is really his own pride of soul. Be watchful that you do not make the mistake of accepting the latter for the former! This would be a fault on your part.

Hence it has been known that none should attempt to traverse this Way without a guide, as the wise have said: A soul, when totally absorbed, remains confined to the world. It is like a bird that has fallen into a snare. No matter how much it flutters about with its wings and legs, it succeeds only in making itself more firmly entangled. It needs someone who will release it from its bondage. That would be a guide sent by the Prophet. There is another secret, namely that in the beginning the novice is not capable of the state in which he could bear divine illumination because he is like a bat whose eyes do not have enough strength to bear the light of the sun. Nevertheless, proceeding in complete darkness would be dangerous, even destructive. Some light is necessary for the Way, but it should be less than that of the sun. That light comes from the hearts of guides who, like the celestial body, the moon, have become capable of receiving hidden light. From his inner vision he will then provide other disciples with a remedy for the pain that arises when they begin to seek God. He then looks for something to assuage that pain. The disciple, however, has no idea as to what should be done but, through the divine mercy, he is led to the guide who will help him. The sweet odor of the Real One reaches his sense of smell through the heart of the guide. He submits himself to him and finds peace. This is discipleship.

O brother, mysterious indeed are His dealings with men of clay, and yet how bountiful! It is related that when Azrael, the angel of death, makes a sortie upon the life of someone, he is instructed by God in this fashion: "First convey My greetings and compliments to him: Only then may you stretch out your hand to take his life!" In the Quran one reads that tomorrow, on the Day of Resurrection, God will greet the faithful without any intermediary and say: "Peace! A word from a merciful Lord" (Q36:58). If it had not been His intention from of old to be gracious with this handful of dust, He would not have greeted man in the very beginning! One beloved of God has given us a hint about all this:

> He who is greeted by the Beloved,
> And receives news from His presence,
> Shines like the sun in the circle of His servants:
> What can I relate? It is but a tale of slavery!

On the night of nearness and bounty, God Almighty said to the Prophet: "O Prophet, peace be upon you!" One beloved of God says about this: "When two friends, after a long separation, come together again, the one whose eagerness is greater will be the first to greet the other: 'I long greatly for him!' is the secret meaning of this." It also explains traditions concerning the Prophet: he was always the first to greet anyone. Your behavior should be in accordance with his!

*Peace!*


LETTER 52: SPEECH AND BEHAVIOR

*In the name of God, the Merciful, the Compassionate!*

Brother Shamsuddin, may God bless you with both learning and mystical knowledge! All religious scholars give precedence to speech and build behavior on the foundation of speech. They say: "The first thing is speech. Behavior is the child of speech. Without speech, there can be no correct behavior." The learning they acquire comes from listening and talking. On the other hand, the seekers of Truth gain their knowledge by means of a divine command. Khwaja Junaid said: "It is my heart that has told me of the Lord!" This happens when a person follows the Law completely and the wealth he obtains is as a result of the blessing conferred upon his behavior.

The seekers of Truth speak in this fashion: "Knowledge is not talking! Knowledge is one thing; speech is something else!" There is no affinity between speech and knowledge. Knowledge means anything that helps a man along the road of religion, whereas speech is simply a path to knowledge. There is righteousness in knowledge but, except in the world of Truth, there is no real knowledge. The tongue has dominion over words, but words are limited. Knowledge, on the other hand, proceeds from the heart, and there is no death for the heart. The world, in fact, exists through its agency. The Lord Almighty does not grant knowledge to all, but He does not withhold speech from anyone. No, even birds have tongues but not hearts. Since they have no heart, they have no knowledge. If a bird learns the name of anybody, he utters it, but he does not know the difference. If a bird were to expend the effort to learn the names of Moses and Jesus, he would utter them too! Hence it is that Khwaja Wasiti said: "In all the heavenly creatures there is a tongue that praises and worships God, but no heart!" He means that except for Adam and his offspring, no one else has been granted a heart. Knowledge is anything that binds up all your evil desires, compulsions, or craving for power, and shows you the way to God. That is the path you should tread!

On the other hand, any knowledge that panders to your inclinations and makes you long for what your ego desires is but a stepping-stone leading you to the courts of oppressors and tyrants. That should not be called "knowledge"! It should be called "the net of deserters." Knowledge will drag you from positions of eminence down to menial ones, and from speaking to being dumbstruck! It will free you from quarrels and contentions, but it will not cause you to have a crown of lordship placed on your head, nor make it possible to bind up your waist with the girdle of pride.

Knowledge, like a mirror, places before you whatever can harm or injure you. Whenever a Muslim approaches you, pull up your skirt to avoid him and say: "It is not proper that any of my clothes should touch him and pollute his garments!" A guide was once walking along with some of his disciples. A dog appeared in front of them.

The disciples drew up their skirts to avoid it. The guide did likewise. He asked his disciples: "What was your reason for pulling up your skirts?" They replied, "We did not want our garments to get polluted for prayer." The guide said: "My purpose was this: I did not want that dog to be polluted by me!" That is the way these people consider themselves! Whenever you see a Muslim on the road, you should give way to him and walk on the other side, just as the protected people (i.e., Jews, Christians, and others) do for the Muslims. It is only when you see yourself as contemptible that a crown of honor may be placed upon your head.

Khwaja Zu'l-Nun Misri, together with his disciples, went to a gathering of wise men. They asked him who the wisest of men was. He replied, "I am!" Then they asked him who was the most ignorant person alive. He replied, "I am he also!" They asked for an explanation. He said: "Because of my faults, [which I know about], I am the wisest of men; but because of the faults of people [i.e., which I don't know about], I am the most ignorant of men." Travelers along the Path to God wield a sword to attack their own defects. Nowadays, however, people wield their sword to attack the defects of others, and all the while claim to be travelers and to possess learning. Inevitably, they produce no fruit.

Any learning that resulted in the fear of God would be another matter, for "only those servants of God who are knowledgeable fear Him" (Q35:28). Hence it is that learning is the oyster that contains the pearl of the fear of God. If you do not see this pearl in the oyster, then know that there is no pearl of knowledge in the sea of your breast. Fear would also mean that you do not travel according to your desires. If you encounter an ant along the way, you should yield to it. You should not argue or contend with it on the road!

If some noble person reads a few words about all this, or gains a little knowledge in such matters, or advances a few steps along the path of religion, he deceives himself into thinking that there is no one else in the city who has attained his spiritual eminence and with whom he can converse. He does not even know how to sit in the assembly, nor does he know how to travel along the road. Placing his bundle of learning on his head and flinging his prayer mat over his shoulder, he cannot be contained by the whole wide world. The wise have said that the limit of the learning of the scholars is the starting point of the discipleship of a novice of the Way. For discipleship to begin a person must first don the garment of a novice. That means that he is brought out of himself. The garment signifies that every-thing he had previously seen in the garb of the divine beauty is now perceived to be but a tether and ignorance. He then proceeds step by step. A long description of what happens can be boiled down to this: The fire of discipleship consumes everything within him! After this, he falls into the world of pride. This happens because he begins to see lights, and speech begins to slip from his tongue, and people are as-tonished at his words, for they are no longer like those of others. He thinks that he has reached a stage of eminence never before achieved by other men. There he establishes himself. He speaks in a flattering manner and beguiles men's hearts. All this, however, is but a net and a deception to the soul.

It is at this point that a guide is necessary to help him advance be-yond this stage and get him on the move again after he has become stalled, for in divine light there is a more profound concealment than occurs in ordinary darkness. Hence it is that a Sufi is lost for words; nor is a pen of any avail to him; nor do his eyes help him out; nothing enables him to translate his experience into human speech! His imita-tion would consist in this, that the prophet of the worlds could nei-ther read nor write. What happened? "He did not speak out of desire; he only revealed what God had revealed to him" (Q53:3, 4). Hence it is that the difficulties of the disciple will not be solved by what schol-ars have to say, for the latter are masters of doctrine, but the ques-tions of disciples are concerned with behavior, not doctrine. The imi-tation of the disciple will not be acceptable to some scholars, because their own decisions are concerned with external matters, while the disciple is concerned about internal ones. The disciple must be care-ful not to get caught in the middle, lest he be destroyed. A scholar seeks salvation by means of what he knows. He is all for picking up whatever learning he can. He knows everything that others have left behind. All of it has been collected within his breast. He knows the accumulated learning of the past. A disciple, on the other hand, opts to throw away all past learning and press on. He desires to unlearn whatever he has learned. He wishes he did not have what, in fact, he does have. He discards whatever is his, that he might become liberat-ed. These two positions are completely contradictory. There can be no agreement between them.

This letter should be studied carefully many times. It will be found to contain many helpful things. O brother, how can a little dirty water [man] enter a portion of the shell of Life? Especially if he says "I am!" or "These things belong to me!" We, born of Adam, were born on a day of trial. The first sound that reaches the ears of a child born on such a day is that of lamentation. Inevitably, everyone who becomes acquainted with this situation simply melts away. He wants to pass away into nothingness in order that the record of existence might be cleansed of him completely. All those who come into existence fall! Even if they attain eternal bliss, still they take along with them a hankering after sanctity, prophethood, righteousness, and love for some who have not yet passed from nothingness into existence. Finally, have you not heard what the king of the prophets, who had the crown of "If it were not for you, I would not have created the heavens" placed upon his head, said? "O that the God of Muhammad had not created Muhammad!" He also said: "If there were to be another prophet after me, it would be Umar!" Once Umar was walking along the road. He stretched out his hand and plucked a blade of grass and said: "O that Umar were this blade of grass!" Umran ibn Husain was traveling in a desert place. He noticed the wind descending on him, bearing innumerable particles of dust. He said: "O that I were even less than this dust!"

*Peace!*

## LETTER 53: SPIRITUAL RESOLVE

*In the name of God, the Merciful, the Compassionate!*

Dear Brother Shamsuddin, may God grant you greatness of soul! Any disciple lacking in spiritual resolve will get nowhere! Until a disciple mounts the steed of resolution concerning Him, and arrives before the portals of heaven, he cannot be considered as a man of this field! It is a saying of the Sufis that wanting to have everything in accordance with your own fancy is a task fit only for women, not for men! The intention of this saying has been explained by Imam Shibli: "The person who is preoccupied with this world and the next has not been sufficiently purified to be able to enter Our assembly!" As the poet has attested:

O son, justice would mean that you bear yourself
Beyond the boundaries of whatever is created:

Then it might be that, aided by your Lord,
You would be borne to the Seat of Righteousness itself!

Everyone is concealed beneath his own spiritual resolve, and the measure of each person can be gauged from the aspirations of his soul, since the true worth of a man can be estimated by seeing what he prizes. Even today everyone is able to approximate his own worth. The person whose aspirations are linked to what he puts into his stomach can have his value gauged by what comes out of it. You and I are in that category! How can it be said that either of us is of any value?

O brother, if tomorrow we were to enjoy the fullness of peace so that "nothing has a claim on us, nor do we have a claim on anything," then you might say that we were departing from the field of frivolity and play! A Sufi was asked, as he lay dying: "Is there anything you would like us to bring you?" "Yes," he replied, "there is!" "What is it?" they enquired. "Nothingness, for it has no existence!" They were astonished! It has been said:

You know my condition to be that of a broken-hearted one;
You can read, on any page of my life, what is my desire!
I am astonished at my good fortune! Take me by the hand,
O You who grasp the hand of all astonished by You!

In a word, the very first step that a resolute disciple takes is to trample underfoot his own soul, and the first sword that he wields in anger is upon himself, not an infidel. Any wound that is inflicted on an infidel is only a bodily one and is made only for the sake of looting a person's goods, but the wound inflicted on the ego goes to the very foundation of faith, and its only intention is to plunder the faith! Hence, any blow you strike should be directed toward your ego. If you connive at its activities, do not be lulled into thinking it will behave kindly toward you. Those well acquainted with this saying heap piles of thorns upon themselves for this purpose. They rain all sorts of anger upon themselves for the purpose of containing this unfortunate dog. In this way they aspire to great wealth. Khwaja Sanai has said:

You are the hidden treasure of the nine heavens;
Come out of the four walls of time!
Break even the binding spell of salvation!
Tear down the door and vestibule of created beings!

You, the treasure contained in an enchanted palace,
You are Life, though imprisoned in a body!
If You show Your face from behind the curtain,
You will consume the seven ancient heavens!
One who, for God's sake, does not leave this prison,
Why should he be astonished that he does not find Him?

These people are men noted for their spiritual resolve. Whatever falls under the sway of "Be!" and comes into existence, they do not look at it, even out of the corner of their eye, nor do they submit to either paradise or hell at the threshold of their resolution! One of noble ambition has said:

O son, separate yourself from yourself!
Put on the garb of patience!
Once and for all, make the capital of both worlds
A present to the very World of Love!
Resolve to ascend to the heights of heaven,
And praise Him without hope of gain—and without tongue!

Do you know what the secret of this is? It is this: Out of 18,000 worlds God Almighty has not created any other group endowed with nobler ambitions than those of mankind! The reason is that to no other group has it been said: "I breathed into him of my Spirit" (Q38:72). Only man heard this! Neither has He sent prophets and books to any other group except mankind. Nor has He greeted, from the very beginning, any other group except mankind. Nor did He give the sight of Himself to any other group except mankind. Also, it was only human beings who, out of the force of their love and their lofty aspirations, did not have the strength to bear separation from God. The curtain of this world has been removed from their hearts, and the curtain of the world to come will also be removed from their inner eyes, for they seek none but Him in this world, and in the next they will gaze upon nothing other than Him. "The eye neither blinked nor exceeded the limit" (Q53:17) is a lesson learnt in primary school!

Take care, O wise bird, to read the signs of the times!
For do you imagine you can find a better nest than This?
Open up your wings for a flight into Meaning!
Open the Inn containing seven doors!
When you alight upon the celestial lote-tree,
You will become All, but you will lose sight of yourself!

Be careful not to amble into foolishness, for fortune does not favor the foolish! It has been said: When anyone wishes to pass through the lane of manliness the leader of the reprobate, Satan, grabs the skirt of his garment and says: "The reason why I have wrapped the accursed thread around my waist is to ensure that no unworthy person turns aside into this lane of manly endeavor. If anyone tries to enter without the crown of Unity and Sincerity, I will cut off his feet!" The poet was hinting at this possibility when he said:

The Beloved instructed me: Sit at My door!
Do not let anyone in till he has grasped My secret!

And that accursed one does not budge from his position for any mean-spirited fellow, for he is arrogant and terrifying, his head full of self-conceit. Do you not see that he had to give way to Adam, but when that righteous one made his appearance in the kingdom, and the rays of his righteousness shone on the supports of the divine throne, Satan protested aloud, "The time for action has arrived! What trick should I employ in order to cut off his feet?" Even if he could have done so, he would only have succeeded in binding himself to his saddle straps and muttering: "O unfortunate one, make do with me!" Otherwise, Satan will appear as a slave and say: "O righteous one! May you enjoy success every moment along the road of religion!" Be careful! I do not say "Pray for me!" or, "Intercede for me!" for my work has gone beyond all this! What I need is to have you apply a soothing dressing to the jealousy inflicted on me by the curse, so that this cursed robe might become fresh in the time of the divine covenant, just as prophets rejoice when they receive the robe of prophecy.

That chief of all wretches boasts that the collar of imprecation has been placed around his neck without any intermediary. There is a tradition that, on the Day of Resurrection, a command will reach the angels: "Take the leader of the wretches to hell!" Ten thousand angels will set upon him. They will not be able to contain him. Another ten thousand will come to their assistance. They, too, will fail to subdue him. A second command will reach the angels: "The neck that bears the collar of My curse cannot be broken by any intermediary except My own wrath!" When the Eternal Strength loosens that collar of reprobation from around his neck, that accursed one will be worse off. A dog from hell will attack him and seize him with its fangs and bear him off in rage to the depths of hell. All this indicates the extent of the curse that, without intermediary, was placed around

the neck of Satan. If mystical union and consolation without intermediary should appear to God's dear ones, then similarly the heavens
will not be able to bear that weight nor the earth, nor will paradise
have the strength for that, nor hell—only the world of the essence of
the Venerable King can bear the righteousness of men!

It is related about Sheikh Luqman Sarkhasi that once, while listening to music, one of the dervishes began to fly like a bird and
alighted on a tree. He said: "O Luqman, come here so that we may fly
off together!" "O man of peace," replied Luqman, "How can our
hearts be contained by any world, for when we take to flight, we head
beyond both worlds!" Any mean denier will not be able to hear this
Tradition. Or if he does hear it, he will not believe it. O helpless one,
listen with faith so that foolishness may not gain ascendancy over
you. One day He may take your hand. If no one comes to your help in
the world, then perhaps someone will do so in the grave. If none
comes even there, then at least on the Day of Resurrection a helper
will come.

Be on the alert, helpless one, lest you try to act with authority
like those self-righteous ones with their paltry intellects, for these
sayings cannot be grasped by a small-minded person. The speech of
the just can be understood only with the aid of faith. Listen, then,
with faith, so that some help might appear and the speech of these
dear ones not go to waste.

If you wish to see a Bayazid on the morn,
You need the service of a hundred Bayazids today!

Look at the King of the Prophets. He is the choicest of both
worlds. Every time that a certain slave of Mughira appeared on the
scene, the Prophet would approach him and bow to him and ask for
his prayers. Muhammad's eyes used to fill with tears at his prayers.
He would say: "If you belong to His community, may His community be such as you have heard! but if—God forbid!—you do not belong
to His community, then remove the cap of claim from your head, and
give back the key of the promise!" Now know in truth that the field
of the seeking of the disciples is not the divine footstool or throne, nor
heaven or earth. If you say, "Where is it?"—it is where He said it was:
"I am in the heart of my servant, the pious believer."

What is this divine throne? Compared to the lofty resolve of these
men, it is no higher than the earth itself! Do you not see that concerning Sa'id ibn Mu'az it was said: "The divine throne was shaken by the

death of Sa'id ibn Mu'az!" He had been given some influence over it, with the result that when he left the world, a trembling seized it.

O brother, the stock of Adam, in the world of Truth, lives on in such people. The highway of righteousness is filled with the constancy of their blessed steps and, in the world of Truth, they are called the outsiders of their respective tribes, just as Bilal came from Abyssinia, Shuaib from Byzantium, Salman from Persia, and Khwaja Uways from Qaran. If the purity of their faith were to fall on brambles that are trampled underfoot they would turn into lilies. The sun of their high resolve makes acceptable every obedient one it shines upon. If it shines upon some sinner, he becomes an intimate friend. [A long poem from Sanai follows.]

Finally, you must have heard of the proof of a righteous man. It was discovered in a urinal flask placed before a stranger. The latter was urged to have a look at its contents. "I was not at all aware," he observed, "among Muslims there were such men whose livers have turned to blood on account of their longing on the road to God." It is not fitting to expound on what happened except to say that he immediately snapped his thread and began to tread the path of Islam.

What can you say, O miserable denier? Is his urine better than your speech and mine? If you have anything Islamic about you, then judge for yourself and say, "Better than a thousand pretenders to knowledge is the one who, at the hour for prayer, can bring over one person from a shop to the mosque." This is the sort of knowledge of which we are speaking! But the scholars of today are not like those of yesteryear. Then they used to be constantly busy; they were not gossipers. Nowadays they are only good for talking and making claims, but there is no steady dedication to work. Speaking about such righteous ones of those bygone days, and raising objections and difficulties concerning them, stems from blindness and ignorance. Someone has said:

> Nothing comes from the light of the eyes of the head:
> It is the light of the eye of the heart that is needed!
> Both Jesus and the donkey had eyes in their head,
> But Oh, the difference in the eye of the heart of Jesus!

O brother, former ages were such that the odor of a heart emanated even from a stone. Nowadays, in these bad times, the odor of a stone emanates from our hearts! "The heavens have been consumed" is one saying, and "the earth has dried up" is another. In the temple of fire worshipers while in a state of ecstasy, you may hear a voice from the fire telling you: "Even though we ourselves are being consumed, still we have the quality that we care not for this handful of graceless people!" And if you go to a temple where idols are worshiped, you will hear the same news. When the Prophet arrived in the world, the first to do him reverence were the idols in the Kaaba—all 360 of them! They fell down in worship.

> I went to the churches of the Christians and the Jews
> And found every Christian and Jew facing toward You:
> In the hope of being united to You, I went to an idol temple,
> And there the idols, too, were murmuring their love for You!

[A poem from 'Attar follows.]

Heaven and earth, footstool and throne, angels and firmament, from the very heights above to the depths below, anything at all that can be named, falls on its face while searching and running hither and thither! Man is cruel, for he has fallen in with the enemy, having strayed far from the Friend. If anyone asks you, "Who are you?" be careful not to say, "I am a Muslim!" Three times on Friday—once in the morning, then between the sermon and the prayer, and again between the afternoon and evening prayer—a disciple should be present to God and remember himself and the writer of this letter in his prayers. After every obligatory prayer the one hundred and twelfth chapter of the Quran on Purity should be recited ten times and he should say ten times: "If they do not take heed, say, God suffices for me! There is no God but Him. In Him have I put my trust! He is the Lord of the glorious throne!" (Q9:129). Let him persevere in reciting this prayer and know for sure that one accepted by Him does not become rejected, while one rejected by Him never becomes acceptable. For the one who has been received with honor, he is "the man of good fortune who has arrived at that stage after which there is no ill fortune," while everyone who has to taste ill fortune becomes "the hapless one who has arrived at that stage where no good fortune can be found."

The seeker of favors is happier to experience His wrath than to bask in the shadow of His mercy, for the shadow may pass away and lose its value, as has been said: "In separation there is the hope of union, while in union there is a fear of separation along with the pleasure experienced."

217

There is pleasure in separation from You, and tyranny in Your
  presence:
That pleasure is better, for we have no strength to bear Your
  tyranny!

A spiritual guide used to say: "For lovers, it is more enjoyable to
be in the company of separated ones than in the company of the joyful." O brother, for one seeking Him, what place is there for rejection
or acceptance? To want the honor of being accepted is to consider
yourself worthy of it, and in the religion of love this is a fault, as an
inflamed one has said:

If you welcome me, then I am Your accepted one:
If You do not, I am still Your rejected servant!
I should not be worried whether You accept or reject me:
My task, in either state, is to remain preoccupied with You!

O brother, if a seeker is accepted, then his blessing and reward is
ordinary. And if he is not accepted—well, a king is free to act as he
chooses! That is the fruit of our misfortune, just as a hapless one has
said:

Since the Beloved is a king, whatever He says, goes!
Concerning His actions, who will be so bold as to ask why?
If He accepts, it is because of His mercy:
If He spurns us, that is our misfortune!

*Peace!*


## LETTER 54: ENCOURAGING THE DISCIPLE

*In the name of God, the Merciful, the Compassionate!*

Brother Shamsuddin, may you be adorned with the ornament of
devoted service! Persist in salutation and intercessory prayer!
It is fitting that when a disciple declares himself publicly to be a
disciple and has clothed himself in the garb of a disciple, it should
be incumbent on him to go to the utmost limits in his quest
for Truth, and set his feet on the way of the straight bridge. He
should constantly apply the collyrium of repentance and sorrow to
his eyes. He should don the robe of separation and solitude and drink

the wine of seeking from the hands of a righteous cup-bearer. He should draw the sword of resolution from the scabbard of the Law and remove from his path the multitude of base desires in his infidel soul. He should make progress in experiencing drunkenness and sobriety, stability and self-effacement. This world and the next become reduced to the same level. When he finds the desired Truth and the sought-after pleasure, and acquires the fruit of struggle with self and austerities, he proceeds to the stage of change and movement, placing his feet in the stages and ranks of the travelers, until he arrives at the head of the lane of manly people.

If asked whether he is a disciple, he ought to say: "God willing, I might become one!" In other words, he gives the meaning of discipleship: He backtracks from the lane of claiming anything. The masters of perfection and the giants of Sufism act in such a way that at no stage do they pay attention to themselves, nor do they give heed to anything they might possess. Many a guide has been esteemed for his self-control, having passed seventy years in devotion and worship as he scaled the stages of the Law and reached exalted mystical states only to come to grief in the end at the hands of divine wrath for no apparent cause: "What they never thought of, God shall make clear to them" (Q39:47).

O brother, anyone who fell into the hands of a tyrant and avenger would discover that if the eight heavens were to become hell itself, and hell were to become paradise; and if a church were to be brought forth from the Kaaba and the Kaaba were to be reverted to an idol temple; and if the angels of the celestial climes were to doff their angelic garb; and if devils were to don angelic garb and place the crown of holiness upon their head; and if Muhammad, the seal of the prophets, and Jesus, the crowning perfection of purity, and John, a sinless being who never even thought of sinning—if they all were to be found together and held in hell forever, still He would not take into consideration anyone's opinion or fear anyone! Not a single particle of the dust of cruelty rests on the skirt of His justice. Can there then be place for rest and contentment? What scope is there for boasting and self-esteem? The one who had amassed the capital of seven hundred thousand years of worship and praise, and who was the teacher of the angels and their master, spoke only once, but what he saw, he saw; and what he found, he got.

One day Gabriel came to the Prophet. He asked him: "What is your state in the chamber of holiness?" Muhammad replied: "Since that one was removed from our midst, no angel rests contentedly in his own abode." Many thousands of disciples with hearts aflame have sunk in the sea of irresponsibility. Many thousands of livers have been roasted by tyranny. From the divine Presence a voice came: "Your existence is as nothing, and your nonexistence is as good as existence." One beloved of God has explained the paradox thus:

> I have slain thousands of lovers like you with grief,
> Yet my fingers have not been stained by the blood of any!

O brother, if the purity and holiness of all the angels were to become the virtue of a single disciple; and if the devotion and worship of all mankind were his alone, and he then considered himself better than a dog or as even somewhat virtuous, it would be a sign of impending calamity, for he would still be proud! It is not proper that they should drink the same sherbet that has already been offered to another! Nor that he should make on another the same scar that has been made on him. He should be restrained in this matter, considering his own faith as a denial of faith and himself as an infidel. He should view his own devotion as sin, his purity as impurity, his own essence as a church and idol temple, his turban and robe as a sacred thread and an idol, his prayer carpet and dervish's robe as idolatrous trinkets and signs of heresy. All this belongs to a disciple as the wages of discipleship. It is for one who has fulfilled all the required conditions and has attained to the realities of discipleship. It is a sign of his safety and an indication that he has arrived, thanks to his spiritual resolve.

But if some hapless one, who has remained bound up in pride and bad habits and who has not read a word of these writings, arrives at this stage, then all you will see is boasting and nonsensical talk— nothing more. Hence it becomes apparent how to distinguish behavior of the wise from that of the ignorant, meaning from appearance, truth from conjecture, mystical insight from error, perception from deception, beginning from end. All concur that: "In the beginning it is all talk; but at the end, all is quietness!" The beginner has a tongue and he speaks; the proficient one has no tongue and simply remains quiet. It is just like a nightingale that has a thousand songs and sings all night long. It is purchased for a silver piece. But a falcon, though it never sings throughout its life, costs a thousand gold coins!

> No one knows how much a falcon will fetch,
> While a nightingale will bring in but a few copper coins.

Do you know the reason for this difference in price?
The former works, while the latter only talks!

Though a beginner might affirm existence, a proficient one has become extinct. Though an ignorant one might have some ideas, for a wise one, all thoughts have become an idol and a sacred thread. God Almighty accepts that brother as a disciple, giving him perception and knowledge so that he might distinguish the investigator of Truth from the suitor of vanity, gnosis from error, the behavior of scholars from that of the ignorant, traditional religion from heretical innovations. In short, it is his ability to recognize everything related to knowledge of God that will set a traveler on the right path. Though he be of little consequence, he may still acquire much. By the favor and grace of the Prophet and his descendants, he will place his trust in God in all circumstances. He should keep his heart free with respect to either separation or attachment. Someone approached Hatim and said: "What is the secret of your good fortune, for you have no income or expenditure?" "From the divine treasury!" he replied. "Does bread come to you from heaven?" asked the man. "If it is not available from the earth," replied the saint, "it is sent from heaven." "Do you bind men up with speech?" he asked. "Only what comes from above can reach every mirror," declared the saint. "I cannot defeat you with proofs," conceded the man. "No mirror can remain empty in front of God!" concluded Hatim.

A man approached Shibli and said: "I am distressed because of the paucity of my means and the affluence of my relatives." "Return home!" declared Shibli. "Everyone who does not trust in God—throw him out of your house!"

*Peace!*

LETTER 55: THE CONVERSATION OF QAZI SADRUDDIN, AND ENCOURAGEMENT TO ACQUIRE KNOWLEDGE

*In the name of God, the Merciful, the Compassionate!*

Brother Shamsuddin, may God grant you a long life of devotion! Accept the greetings of this writer! Brother, the conversation of Qazi Sadruddin should be viewed as something precious. It should be deemed a providential sign. You should display great zeal, both night and day, in acquiring knowledge. You should set to one side all tranquility, resting, sleeping, and eating, for knowledge is to activity—that is to say, struggle with self and austerities—as purification is to prayer. No affair can transpire without knowledge. If, for example, someone were to spend his entire life in struggle and austerities but lacked knowledge, in each of his qualities there would be something missing. It would be like a man who prayed for many years without performing ablutions, or who read the Quran without faith. It should be known, however, that knowledge is of two kinds. One type of knowledge is gained from teachers, or through the study of books. The other kind of knowledge is that which wells up within the breast of a man, and that also is of two types. One is infused into the hearts of prophets from the divine bounty. That is called "revelation." Or it may be infused into the heart of a saint, in which case it is called "inspiration."

The second kind of inner knowledge reaches the heart of a righteous one through the agency of a prophet or the breast of a disciple, or through the agency of a spiritual master. This is the meaning of the Tradition: "The Sheikh in his group is like the prophet in his community." This means that just as righteous men see God in the mirror of the souls of the prophets, so too disciples see God in the mirror of the hearts of their spiritual master. In other words, they recognize and know; that is what "seeing" means! And those things found in the writings of the sheikhs are in the same tenor, namely, that the disciple sees God in the heart of his spiritual master. Of course, that seeing is of the type already mentioned; it does not refer to seeing with one's bodily eyes!

O brother, knowledge is the fountainhead of all happiness, just as ignorance is the starting point of all wretchedness. Salvation comes from knowledge, destruction from ignorance. Heavenly ranks and wonderful powers are acquired through knowledge, but one falls into the very depths of hell and the greatest of tortures and punishments due to ignorance. No one except a believer places his feet in the court of knowledge, for "God is the friend and helper of those who have faith; He removed them from darkness and directs them to the light, that is, he leads them from ignorance to knowledge"; while in the court of ignorance none except infidels have gained admission. "And those who chose infidelity have for their friends and companions the devils, who snatch them out of the light and plunge them into darkness, that is, lead them from the light of knowledge to the darkness of ignorance." Just as a believer should be far from wretchedness and infidelity, so also he should be far from ignorance and the ignorant, for "the wise man is My friend, while the foolish person is My enemy." This is the decree of the Law: it is necessary to keep oneself apart from ignorance and the ignorant, while at the same time seeking knowledge and the company of the learned. One should, however, mix with scholars concerned with the last things rather than those concerned with this world. It is knowledge of what is to come that counts, not of what already is. In this way a person will not fall into error.

It would require much struggle and many austerities to reach that level which can be attained by enjoying the company of this group for but a day! Do you not see that the nature of wood and grass is to remain quietly in one place? When, however, they become associated with water, then they, too, are swept along by the water's current. In the same way, an ant has no power to fly, but by associating with a pigeon, it will necessarily fly when the pigeon flies. The coursing quality of the water and the aerial ability of the pigeon were shared with the straw and the ant by virtue of association. On the other hand, the nature of iron is such that it cannot float on water, even if it is only a tiny particle. When, however, it becomes associated with a wooden ship, then even if it weigh forty or eighty kilograms, it can float and move across the surface of the water. From all this, the excellence and effect of association can be recognized, and one can discern how to obtain this advantage.

For the moment, God has given you the opportunity of associating with Qazi Sadruddin. This should be counted a great blessing. May God Almighty lead you out of the darkness of ignorance and change you into someone illuminated by the light of knowledge! One's poverty and indigence should be admitted, but one should remain far from any claim to lordship. Suhail Abdullah Tustari said: "I glanced at this Way and took note of what I saw. I perceived no other way that led closer to the Lord than that of indigence, nor did I find any curtain more impenetrable than that of self-reliance!"

O brother, look at the path of Satan and see his boasting, and then look at the path of Adam and note his indigence. What did Satan say? "I am better than he is!" (Q7:12). He was made worse than all others! What did Adam say? "Our Lord, we have wronged ourselves" (Q7:23). He then became the object of angelic prostrations, and was seated on the throne of His vicegerency. Look! There was no decrease at all in his poverty, yet the eight heavens were bestowed upon him as his estate! You say, "I am going to make a vicegerent for myself upon the earth" (Q2:30). This is good and proper. And it reflects Your graciousness! But all I can claim is "Our Lord, we have wronged ourselves" (Q7:23). In all ways vicegerency is something bestowed by You! The only claim that arises from me is "we have wronged ourselves."

If tomorrow you go to paradise and look back through the corner of the eye of your heart, then you will sink again into the lazy, irresolute state of mankind. Who will reckon that what your father sold in exchange for a grain of wheat was so precious to you that you might settle down there [i.e., in paradise]?

*Peace!*

### LETTER 56: THE FIRST STEP IN DISCIPLESHIP

*In the name of God, the Merciful, the Compassionate!*

Brother Shamsuddin, may God's peace be with you! The first task of a disciple is to follow the path of the Law. When he shows himself faithful in carrying out the conditions of the Law, to its minutest prescriptions, and with utter fidelity, and also has spiritual resolve, then by virtue of his observance of the Law, and as a fruit of his high aspirations, the Way presents itself to him. That is the Way of the heart. When one shows fidelity to the conditions and demands of this Way and succeeds in emerging from it as one who has fulfilled completely all that was expected of him, then let him be of very high aspiration, for it has been said that a disciple devoid of intense spiritual resolve will get nowhere. Through the blessings of God Almighty, the curtains will be lifted from in front of his heart, and the Inner Meaning of the reality of the Object of the travelers—indeed, the Object of the seekers and the righteous ones—will show its face to him.

> Some there are who think that, without the Law or the Way,
> The whole path to Truth will be revealed to them.
> But, except through the Law, one cannot join the Way;
> Nor can Truth be attained apart from the Way.
> All three are intimately bound to each other:
> No one can separate any from the others!

When this inner meaning discloses itself to the disciple, he turns his face from all creatures and, in quest of Him, girds up his loins and commits himself to a veritable Holy War against his soul. If this world and the next were themselves to be brought before him, he would not even glance at them out of the corner of his eye! Everything bearing the name "not" [i.e., other than God] that falls across his path would be viewed as a veritable idol and sacred thread. Difficult tasks would become easy for him, and what is arduous for human nature, such as being without relationships or news, and being alone—which, after all, describes the state of a dead man—becomes the very object of his desire. If he takes notice of anyone, it means that he has not attained this object, and you can be sure that the inner meaning has not disclosed its features to him, and his gaze has not been drawn toward the Way, nor has he been given the "magic bowl of gathering together."

The sign of a noble disciple would be that he chooses what is not easy, what is little known, the life of solitude, the occupation of a dervish, and takes pride in these things! The lord of the worlds, even though he attained an exalted rank and degree, did not boast or become proud on that account; instead, as an expression of loss, with a hundred cries and lamentations, he besought the Lord of Glory saying: "O God, grant us poverty in both life and death and, on the Day of Resurrection, raise us up in the condition of the poor." Who are those people in this world who beseech the Lord to make them His associates, both in life and in death? If He were to say: "Put them with Me in both life and death!" then there would be no room for wealth. So much the more does He say, "Place Me in life and death with them!" But they have said: "They trek over the whole world in order to find a single disciple," just as Sheikh Abdul Qasim Gurgani used to say: "For so many years I have tried to find a disciple. A disciple should have the qualities of Satan, in order that something might come of him. It is one thing to play according to the rules, and another to be engrossed with the desire of playing! A command is external, while an intention is internal. If Sultan Mahmud had said to Ayaz, "Go! enter the service of another!" and he had gone, it would have been a fault! The person who, at this stage, takes notice of a command would be immature. God Almighty said: "Hasten to forgiveness from your Lord!" (Q3:132). The inexperienced and avaricious run wherever they are commanded to go, while the lovers and mature ones say: "Where shall we go?"

You said, "Seek another!" I shall, O Peerless One—
If You show me another like Yourself!
O God, how can those who seek You be content with heaven;
How can Your lovers descend to anyone else?
You told me to go away and take no notice of what You say!
O Friend, where might I go? How would I know the way?

When the prophet Jacob was coming from the land of Canaan to that of Egypt, he was searching for Joseph. If this were not so, then the bread, meat, and sweets of Canaan would have been enough for him. They say that while there is eating and drinking in this world, beware of both in the world to come!

In the world of souls, the wine of divine gnosis forms our
    nourishment;
For unlike you, we are not enamored of bread in either world!

Heaven is a table laden with victuals and laid out on the way of seekers. Who indeed are the lovers of paradise, and who are those who are lovers of the Lord? No matter how hungry a falcon might be, he would never want things like mosquitoes and ants to enter his gullet! "Each group knows what to drink" (Q2:60). A disciple traveling along the path, however, has to face fear and hope many thousands of times, and thousands of descents and ascents, torments and griefs, and many suchlike things have to be undergone. If a spiritual master comes upon the scene, an experienced man who has himself traveled the Way, and has become the embodiment of a perfect physician, then he will have a particular remedy at hand for all the various causes of trouble; he will know the serum for every sickness. His arrival makes the Way easy. If, on the other hand, the disciple were to go it alone, he would be in the greatest of danger. "Whoever has no spiritual guide has no religion," is a saying of the sheikhs. They note that, in the beginning, when the intention of treading this path appears, it is like an ant, for instance, that wants to approach the Kaaba either from the east or the west. If it ambles along under its own power, then even in a thousand years it would be impossible for it to reach its destination. Moreover, it would be in great danger of losing its life along the way. If it were to attach itself to a pigeon's feather or a falcon's, however, it would easily traverse the distance. All the ant has to do is to affix itself to the feather of the pigeon. By abandoning its own means of traveling, and using that of the pigeon, the ant would be brought to the Kaaba in a short time. For a disciple, the spiritual master acts exactly like the pigeon. When the weak disciple binds himself to a master, he then travels along the path of the master, not his own. It is said that a disciple should see God in the life of his spiritual master. The master is, for the disciple, a mirror in which he sees God; that is, through him he gains some understanding and perception of God. (Nor is it a question of ocular vision!) In this way, he will not make a mistake. Everyone who travels along the way and path of some master is the disciple of that master. But everyone who travels according to his own wish and desire is a follower of his own desire; he cannot be called the disciple of a spiritual master. They say that a disciple should be a worhsiper of his spiritual master. "Whoever obeys the Prophet, obeys God" (Q4:80).

That would be when all objection evaporates from within him and, no matter what the master says or does, or how he acts, he offers no criticism. He should be fully submissive to the sway of his master, both externally and internally. He should restrain his love for himself. He should not open the door of necessity, nor should he take any step that flows from his own initiative. It is possible that, by virtue of the power and spiritual resolve of his master, a disciple could attain a resting place and be lifted up to a position of honor and, from discipleship, be elevated to the throne of becoming a master himself.

O brother, anyone who is so elevated has accomplished all these things about which you have heard. They exist without any hindrance or grief. On the other hand, for us hapless, miserable ones, because such is not our lot, all is difficulty and failure. One is crowned with favor in the garden of grace, while another, caught in the prison of justice, has the mark of wrath imprinted on his heart. Or again, one melts in the oven of glory, while another is soothed by the light of beauty. From contemptible dust, a man was brought into existence and clothed with the garments of grief and penury. The name of this cruel, ignorant fellow spread throughout the world. Masters of seven hundred thousands years of submission received the order to accept him as worthy of worship because of the sincerity of his actions; since he had progressed to the highest states, they were to scatter praise before him!

O brother, when waves of forgiveness and favor from the very sea of divine mercy begin to beat upon the shore, all faults and sins are reduced to nothing. They are simply obliterated! All faults become virtues, because faults and sins "will not remain," whereas mercy "remains forever." These two can never come together. This whole world, with this dust [i.e., man], is one of mercy. Otherwise, how could this black carpet of my existence, this particle of unholy dust, have the power to place its foot on the edge of the carpet of the Master of the angels?

Many a wine imbiber has rubbed the pain of the saying of Satan upon his face, but the tree of his good fortune, planted in the dunghill of his evil inclinations, suddenly sprouted to the dizzy heights of an apostle and, as he approached union with God, the Beloved proclaimed: "Welcome; I have a few things to tell you!"

*Peace!*

## LETTER 57: CONCERNING THE FIRST STEP OF A DISCIPLE—A FURTHER EXPLANATION

*In the name of God, the Merciful, the Compassionate!*

Brother Shamsuddin, may the peace of God be with you! The first step of a disciple is to observe the Law, with all his strength and energy. Then he can be very confident that the Way will show its face to him. This is the way to the heart. When he has observed all the demands of the Way, as far as it is possible for him to do so, then he can again be confident that the veil covering his heart will be removed and the meaning of Truth, which is the way to life, will be shown to him.[67] The sheikhs of the Path commonly talk about four stages on the Way to God for the disciples and the travelers. They say that until a disciple and a traveler has passed through them, he cannot attain the Object of his desire.

The first stage is the world of humanity; the second, the world of sovereignty; the third, that of power; and the fourth, the world of divinity. Until he has passed through the world of humanity, he cannot reach the one of sovereignty; nor can he arrive at the world of power until he has passed through that of sovereignty. Finally, only after having traversed the world of power, can he reach that of divinity. There are no signs associated with this last world: The disciple reaches it of his own accord.

The world of humanity pertains to animals. In this world are preoccupied the five senses, such as eating, drinking, smelling, seeing, hearing, and other similar things. When, as a result of austerities and struggle with self, a disciple passes beyond this world, he passes beyond these qualities as well and, of necessity, reaches the world of sovereignty. It pertains to angels. The tasks allotted to this world are: reciting the rosary, praising God, bowing and prostrating, standing up and sitting down. When he traverses this stage, by not seeing his own virtues and qualities, he arrives at the world of power. It pertains to souls. Nobody can recognize the soul unless God grants him a special grace. The reality of what is experienced here can neither be described nor suggested in a hint. Since the work of this stage is love, longing, enjoyment, further seeking, ecstasy, and divine intoxication, when a traveler is stripped of even these qualities, then by virtue of the passing away of everything that can be called "his," he enters the world of the divine. "Undoubtedly your limit extends up to your Lord" (Q53:42). This is a world utterly devoid of limitation. Here there is no talking or describing. A poet alluded to its secret:

> Perception has been placed in the pupil of the eye;
> And food has been prepared for it along the way of seeing.
> Suddenly they fall headlong at the head of Beauty's lane,
> Freed, now, both from seeing and from things seen!

The secret is that, along the path there are three steps: the Law, the Way, and the Truth. Man is said to be composed of three elements: ego, heart, and soul. There is a path corresponding to each of them: The Law is for the ego, the Way is for the heart, and Truth is for the soul. Through the Law, the ego passes from the world of humanity to that of sovereignty. There it acquires the qualities of the heart. The heart, by means of the Way, passes from the world of sovereignty to that of power. Here it obtains the qualities of the soul. The soul, through a great longing for the divinity, proceeds along the way of Truth to the very summit of the Divine Being. Thus it happens that the ego becomes a heart, while the heart, in turn, becomes a soul. All three heed the one order, as has been said:

> Lover, beloved and love, all three have but one meaning.

This meaning is called "Unconditioned Unity." It is also said that the traveler has three states. The first, that of a traveler; then, awareness; and, finally, return. These three states cannot occur without the intention and will of the Lord. The slave, however, should busy himself with his tasks and wait expectantly. The one who gave the orders will see to his increase. He has no regard for the destruction of anyone or the salvation of anyone. Someone was in a wilderness, perishing from thirst and saying: "There are so many oceans of water, and here am I perishing with thirst!" A voice from the Unknown was heard to say: "I have thrown so many prophets and saints into a destructive wilderness and, at My own good pleasure, have destroyed them, showing My power by having some crows pick their eyes out of their sockets! If anyone wishes to raise his voice to object, then I shall place this seal of punishment on his tongue: 'He cannot be questioned about what He does' (Q21:23). 'All crows belong to Me! All righteous men are Mine too! Who can interfere with Us?' "

Someone who wishes to arrive at the threshold of this Reality does so by engaging in the humble service of men. It is in this way that He gains access into someone's heart. Nobody can pass beyond the clutches of base inclinations and oppression of the ego unless He wills it. Nor will this happen until a disciple is under the protection of a mature and experienced spiritual master. The master will give some particular order to the disciple, which will be based on his own experiential knowledge. After considering the cause and the sickness, he makes use of a variety of remedies and medicines in order that, God willing, he may channel all he has acquired into the very nature of the disciple, and the comings and goings of Satan be uprooted from his heart.

The quest of all the worlds is to have the way to God revealed to them. Each one, however, receives knowledge in proportion to the purity of his heart, and in proportion to this knowledge, he will then begin searching and intending and, if the strength of his quest and intention is sufficient, he becomes a traveler. Disciples who have high spiritual resolve become mature spiritual masters, well versed in the Way and in the heart of man. Hapless ones, however, on account of their bad luck, do not find the Way. They are dogged by misfortune, happenstance, and imprisonment in their ego. Thus they remain constricted to themselves. It has been said: When a master sees the warmth of the intention lodged in the hearts of his disciples, he says:

If some night I find myself granted union with You,
I could not count the kisses I would rain upon your lips!

And when noble-minded disciples discover for themselves some master of the human heart, they all say this:

Due to this good fortune, I have stumbled across You!
God knows, I am bursting with joy on account of You!

But now, on account of our misfortune and bad luck, none of this is for us. Because of our sins and defections, we are excluded, but we hold fast to this: "The intention of the believer is much better than his action." Someone's intention and purpose might be correct, but he does not attain the object of his desire because of some hindrance, just as someone may have to turn back from the pilgrimage or the holy war on account of sickness; or, on account of poverty since he himself has so little, have to abandon all thought of almsgiving. This would be perfectly in order. Necessarily, his recompense will be the same as one who goes on the pilgrimage, or takes part in the holy war, or who gives alms. This is mentioned frequently in the Quran and Traditions. Day and night one should have a heart that is consumed with fire, eyes that shed copious tears, and at the same time burn with deep regret on account of this saying. Thus, God willing, such a person's purpose and intention will become correct. Trust is not only joined to activity: It essentially flows from the heart. There are many people asleep in their homes whose names have been inscribed on the merit-list of those fighting a Holy War. Many others have been killed in the ranks of the infidels but have no good fortune in store for them on that account. There is a saying of the Law: "Usually My martyrs are on horseback, and it is possible that they may be cut down between the two ranks, but God alone knows their intentions." There is nothing more profitable along this way than grief, as has been said: "God loves grief-filled hearts." We have heard in a story that when a pulpit was erected, the tree against which Muhammad used to lean while preaching began to cry out due to the pain of its separation from the Prophet. A command came: "Take this tree to one side, for the weeping of the grief-stricken and exiles has great power in this Way." A grace that had no previous cause comforts one, while justice without any previous reason melts another. Umar was acceptable in an idol-temple, while Abdullah Abi was rejected in a mosque. May God have mercy on the soul of him who said:

You know the construction of everything You consume;
You also know how to destroy everything You have made!

O brother, your work and mine is directed to a cruel and wrathful One, for even the eight heavens can be changed into a hell, and hell can become a paradise. A church can be educed from a Kaaba, and a Kaaba made out of an idol-temple. In His power, both are the same. There remains no power that is not turned to water. The fear is

231

that you might pass your life, breath by breath, and moment by moment, and still be afraid lest a hand of rejection emerge, without reason, from the Hidden World. His rage needs no cause. His favor is also without cause. His favor seeks someone polluted in order to wash him with the water of forgiveness, and thus the purity of His favor might come to birth in his heart. On the other hand, His wrath seeks someone pure in order to blacken his face with the smoke of separation, so that the purity of the King of wrath might be made manifest apart from causes. On one occasion, He will bring forth a prophet from beneath the skirt of a wicked man. On another occasion, He draws forth a wicked man from beneath the skirt of a prophet. Or He might indicate a dog in the ranks of the saints or a saint among a pack of dogs. Whenever He rejects anything, He never accepts it. And when He accepts anything, He never rejects it.

Before you hear the voice of the angel of death, you should make a beginning and, before you are forced by necessity, you should, by your own choice, resolve to act, for if you go out of necessity, of what account would that be? When the prophet Joseph was thrown into the well, he did not say "Kill me!" and when he was imprisoned he did not say "Kill me!" When he became pure, however, and the whole of the revenues of Egypt came under his control, he said, "Make me die a Muslim!" (Q12:101).

*Peace!*


LETTER 58: THE STATES OF A MUSLIM

*In the name of God, the Merciful, the Compassionate!*

Brother Shamsuddin, may God adorn you with fitting states! The states of a Muslim are one thing, and the qualities of human nature, something quite different. Until human qualities are brought under control by sincerity, the states of a Muslim cannot become rooted in a person's heart. The collection of these qualities is called the "ego" by people who investigate reality. It is the "selfish soul" about which you have heard. The form and mold that you see with limbs and joints contains no dangers. It is a mount that bears the burden of the commands of religion. I have sent you a mount from the threshold of my own power. Jump on its back, and proceed along the path of religion. As long as it is going straight ahead, you have nothing to worry about. It is a mount, and it bears the burden of commands. Do not trouble it. If, however, it decides to wander off the road of religion, then rain the whip of self-struggle upon it, that it might return to the road. The limit of the form is this: If someone pricks himself in one of his bodily members with the point of a needle and says, "I am punishing my carnal soul," it would be a sin in the eyes of God Almighty.[68] This fault is a result of great ignorance but, in his foolishness, the ascetic thinks it is a wonderful work. One should be careful not to go beyond the limits prescribed by sound knowledge, for your mount is precious. It is capable of bearing the burden of the trust of God. You cannot bear the burden of your covenant with God except through it, nor can you gird your loins with the belt of devotion except by means of it. It should not be put to grief.

It is the selfishness of one's ego that has to be uprooted and destroyed. It desires to launch an attack on your faith from the stronghold of the qualities of human nature through the torments of rebellious behavior. It wants to upset completely the storehouse of your security and draw you to the threshold of calamity. That desire of the ego should be opposed, and one's inner self should be alert to its snares, and one's outer being alert to its destructive nature. This indeed is one's duty! Anyone who derives any pleasure from his lower soul, by following his own desires, should be told: "Do not say you are a follower of Islam! Do not claim for yourself membership in the community of the Prophet!" The Lord Almighty is percipient. He can tell the difference between a friend and an enemy. "God can distinguish the mischief-maker from the reformer" (Q2:220). Our leader, the Prophet, is completely sinless. He clearly recognizes the members of his own community. "Whoever has washed himself of us is not one of us, nor does he belong to our religion."

> Be careful, O man with head bowed in foolishness,
> For the sake of the world, you abandoned your faith.
> How long will you worry about what you eat or wear?
> How long will you be concerned with name and fame?
> Why are you proud of commanding the respect of a demon?
> You have gone mad! You yourself have become a demon!
> When from this furnace you reach that rose garden,
> It will seem that you had never seen this furnace.

The armies of the entire world are drawn up in two lines: one, the forces of God, and the other, the forces of Satan. Look carefully to yourself to see which is your cavalry unit.

The starting point of both roads is in this world. People are slow to travel, but as the Quran has prescribed: "One group will be in paradise, another in hell!" (Q42:5). On the Day of Resurrection their condition will become clearly visible. The roads to heaven and hell have been open a long time. Many have already trodden these roads, and many are doing so at the moment. The Day of Resurrection is the promised time of arrival in paradise or hell, although we actually travel along the road in this world itself. Anyone who travels along the road to hell in this world will not be allowed to change over to the road to paradise on the Day of Resurrection; even if he wants to change, he will be thrown into the eternal prison. His heart and eyes will be afflicted for all eternity with strokes of grief and regret. The secret meaning of this is:

> The one thing you want is not to be left on the way.
> Keep your gaze fixed toward heaven, less you get stuck in a
> well.
> Real men are not in search of either this world or the next:
> They are only in quest of the One, regarding both worlds as
> dust.
> Adam gave up paradise for a couple of grains of wheat:
> If this work has fallen to your lot, you too will have to sell it.

O brother, it has been said by the investigators of Truth that people of today are too foolish to recognize that Inn for if, some day, the dust of this Inn were to reveal itself intimately to you, and elicit friendship from you, then you would experience even more intimacy and friendship than if the eight heavens were to appear before you, their loins girt for service. Only at the very end will scatter-brained and foolish people know the power of this Inn. By then, however, the opportunity will have been lost; only grief and difficulties will remain.

> A captive, with a hundred pains and professions of repentance,
> Was being borne off to hell on the Day of Resurrection.
> Stabbing his eye with his finger, he plucked it out,
> And flung it angrily by the side of the road.
> "What purpose does this eye now serve?" he declared;
> "I have no desire to see at all, if I cannot see my Beloved!"

From the divine threshold came this address: "Do not bind your heart here. Otherwise you will certainly not find this wealth again. You are simply squandering your time. Five times a day you are summoned to Our threshold with these soothing words: 'Come to prayer! Come to prosperity!' And yet you paid no attention to this call. Nor did you take advantage of this wealth. Hence I have closed the doors of devotion to you. If the master of the seven heavens and the seven earths were to shed tears of blood on that day, pleading that you might once be granted permission to perform one inclination of prayer, or one prostration, you would still not be allowed this privilege. For all eternity you would not see it. 'The world has passed away; only the work you did in the world remains upon your neck!' "

A Sufi has said: "If there is anyone who does not worship the Lord unless you bribe him with the promise of heaven, or who does not keep his skirt free from the stain of sin unless you frighten him with the punishments of hell, then this is a sign that the King of Unity has not yet bound part of his heart with the knot of love." If, for example, Rizwan were sent to you along with the eight paradises, and were to praise you, and say: "Either perform two prostrations of prayer with all the prescribed conditions and with due reverence, or go to paradise and enjoy yourself without any limit," the reality of unity would demand that you opt for the performance of prayer rather than a thousand favors in paradise. A soul of lofty aspirations had this to say:

> When the jewel of Your love is buried in my mine,
> The burden of Your afflictions weighs heavily upon my soul.
> Mere mention of Your name refreshes me, heart and soul;
> Remembrance of You is the comfort that supports me.
> When my intellect has become a slave at Your threshold,
> Then the king of this world is *my* servant and doorkeeper!

This is a great wealth that "has been divided into prayer and union—half for me and half for my slave." Where can you find this in heaven? It cannot be found anywhere else except in prayer. Indeed, what great wealth derives from water and dust! "Half belongs to Me and half to My slave." What more could you want? All praise and glory belongs to Me, while your portion is indigence, need, and petition. This is your duty. When you have fulfilled all that is due Me from the very bottom of your heart, then I shall bestow upon you the Object of your prayer and supplication.

If you understood the great power of prayer you would not hanker after paradise. If you were to choose your mount from the various mounts of prayer and spring upon it you would not even reflect upon the torments of hell. What room is there in the sea of this saying of the Prophet concerning the need of paradise or the fear of hell? "When anyone of you enters into prayer, then his Lord grants him salvation. His Lord is, in fact, between him and the direction of prayer." The self-asserting pride of all intellects should be humbled, and the qualities and desires of human nature should be brought low, in order to be able to arrive at the very Source of the meaning of this saying, namely "His Lord is between him and the direction of prayer." This Tradition is from the collection made by Bukhari, known as *Al-Jami al-Sahih* [Genuine traditions]—and it has been confirmed by a further Tradition: "The person who enters a mosque is paying God a visit, and it is the duty of the One visited to bestow His favor upon the person who visits Him." Certainly no one can take a few steps along My road in righteousness without My showering him with favors. It is impossible, however, for anyone to strike a bargain with Me. If you see somebody in the bazaar at the time for prayer, console him on account of the distress he experiences, for he has not been granted admission; he has been cut off from the threshold of prayer.

O brother, such was the life of those who have gone before us, while our own lives are passed in play and foolishness. Tomorrow, on the Day of Resurrection, every hair from the heads of those just ones will be equal to a thousand worlds, while a hundred thousand like us are not equal to a single blade of grass. All those who are alert to what goes on are grieving over our religion, while we are preoccupied with what we should eat and what we should wear. You go through this vain world in that foolish manner, and you will rise on the morn of the Day of Resurrection full of grief:

> Because of the infidel within our very nature,
> True Muslims in this world will certainly decrease.

On a big feast day Shibli was seen wearing black clothes. The people were astonished. "Today is a feast day. What sort of a garment is this? Why are you getting around like this?" they asked. "I look at the world today," he replied, "and I see people wearing new clothes and celebrating the feast, but not one of them pays any attention to God. Today I am lamenting and grieving over them. They have become accustomed to being heedless. They are consumed with self-concern, bound up with pampering to their base desires and living as creatures of habit. They throw their precious lives to the wind. On no day of your life will you experience good fortune. You will continually be occupied with breaking promises and compromising with all sorts of sin." Hold this to be true: As long as you do not fling from your back the fine garments of your demonic ego, you will not be clothed with the jewel of religion. Nor will the religion of friendship reveal its visage to you until you consider this pleasure-prone self as your enemy. To see the beauty of "There is no god but God!" you must break away from coming to terms with Satan. One who finds the road to the source of all righteousness must first turn away from the allurements of the world.

> When Abraham flung the idol to the ground,
> He shunned all that was doomed to perish.
> On this way there are thousands of heads like polo balls:
> What place is there here for trading and talking?
> You have set out along the road of lovers:
> Can you be less vigilant than a dog on that road?

O brother, the One who has made you the object of the worship of the angels and turned you into the envy of the heavens has done a great work. Every mirror in the presence of this muddy soil becomes illuminated and sanctified, for the secrets of angels and the conjectures of men are of no use in discovering this meaning. When its flames begin to arise, the angels are astonished and the heavens find their head in a spin. The former humble themselves, while the latter are humbled by necessity. Of this Khwaja Attar has given us a hint:

> Were the angels to see your nature,
> They would come to worship you in a different fashion.
> Is not your nature worshiped by the angels?
> Has not the crown of viceregency been placed upon your head?
> You are born of a viceregent. Reject this rubbish heap!
> Go to the rose garden! Abandon the manner of a beggar!
> Since kingship awaits you in Egypt
> Why, like Joseph, do you remain in a well?

"He is the Beginning; He is the End." The secret of this is known to anyone acquainted with Meaning. If you take your beginning from Him, you do not really "come." And since your end is in

237

Him, you will not really "go" anywhere. "There is no god but God" is from the divine world, and nothing at all can become separated from it and joined to what is not God. Since all beginnings are from Him, then certainly all return is also toward Him.

The description of separation and union, coming and going, is really only metaphorical. All such talk is but a story, indeed, a long one, and one should exercise caution here. Khwaja Attar has said:

For many a year it was my impression that
I had passed through several different states:
All those going backward, or all those coming forward,
Show themselves equal in their astonishment.
No one is aware of the secret of the Infinite.
We are all prisoners, from the moon above to the fish in the
    ocean.
We have searched much to gain acquaintance with this secret
But we have not seen, even after a lifetime of searching.
Here it is not proper to speak of this mystery;
Here the door to these secrets cannot be pierced.

*Peace!*


## LETTER 59: PRAISEWORTHY VIRTUES

*In the name of God, the Merciful, the Compassionate!*

Brother Shamsuddin, may God grant you the grace of praiseworthy conduct! Virtuous habits were granted to Adam along with his nature, and they have been transmitted to the prophets and messengers as an inheritance. Thus they reached the Lord of the prophets and the king of the saints. From him, they reached his community. In a similar way, evil qualities were given to Satan at the appointed time and, through him, have been passed down to the proud and disobedient—the people who form his community.

Everyone who is scrupulous in following the Law will develop a better dispostion, and whoever has a better disposition arrives at the threshold of the Lord himself. Such people form the inheritance of Adam, and are a gift to the Master of the world, through whom the gift is bestowed. Of course, no embellishment or decoration would be necessary. A believer should certainly be better than virtuous people, and should stimulate people by his good example. This is the command of God Almighty and the injunction of the Law of His prophet, for all the actions of the lord of both worlds have been pleasing, and everyone who aspires to follow him should lead the sort of life he led. He should be affable in all his own affairs and in his dealings with others, both those who are close to him and those who are not. He should not get angry. Thus his behavior will be constantly polite, and he will not act in an unbecoming way that might change someone's happy state to sadness. He should always be cheerful and somewhat reticent. Whenever he meets anyone, he should be the first to proffer greetings, just as the pride of the world used to do with his companions, even if they chanced to meet one another a hundred times a day.

He should be liberal with whatever he has, for the Prophet used not to harbor any gold or silver coins with him overnight. If anything remained, and he could not find anybody to whom to give it, he would not enter his blessed chamber until the money was expended. A seeker should not indulge in backbiting, telling lies, or immodest talk. He should refrain from acting pompously in his work, since goodness springs from simplicity. In whatever state he finds himself, his attention, in all his activities and words, should be fixed on God, and he should reduce his eating, sleeping, attention to clothes, and talking.

He should aspire to follow the Law faithfully, and be generous in whatever state he happens to be. He should not stain himself with avarice, scorn or base desires. He should keep himself far from faults and his own destruction. He should be attentive to see that he behaves in all the states he experiences as the chosen one did, as much as he can, lest he take to associating with Satan. If he were to do that, he would become like the followers of Satan, stained in speech and impure in action.

It is related that the Prophet said: "Associate with one who shuns you. Forgive the one who oppresses you. Give to the person who gives you nothing." He was commanded to invite people to the divine path by means of wisdom, sound advice, talking, and listening, always urging them toward what was better. When Moses and Aaron were sent to the court of Pharaoh, He said to them: "Speak a kind word to him!" (Q20:44). Anas Malik used to relate: "I have served the Prophet for ten years. In no work at all did he ever say, 'You have done wrong!' or, 'Why did you do that?' When I did something well, he used to bless me. Whenever I did anything that displeased him, he would say: 'The command of God is an absolute decree' (Q33:38). He himself used to arrange the fodder for his own mount. He used to go home and light the lamp himself. When the strap of his sandal broke, he himself repaired it. He used to mend his torn garments with his very own hand. He helped the servants in the house. If anyone asked him to do some foolish thing, he never declined. If a stranger was aggrieved with him, he did not punish him. Never at all were such things as cursing, imprecation, abuse, or vile language found upon his tongue. He was always smiling, but with no laughter or frivolity. Whenever he met a Muslim, he was always the first to wish the other peace. He used to sit with his companions as one of them, and he addressed them all in a respectful manner. In this way, he honored them. If any of the companions or other people called him, he would reply, 'At your service!' If he was passing by some children, he would wish them peace. He always hid the faults of Muslims, such as when he advised a certain thief, 'Did you steal? Say, "No"!'

"He was careful to observe the rights of his wife, children, and friends according to the Law. For the sake of propagating the message of Islam, he would put up with afflictions and recrimination. He would not brush aside questions that might be put to him. If he knew the answer, he answered immediately. If not, he used to say, 'God willing, I shall find it!' Never did he show anger toward anyone. He did not dissimulate, connive at evil, grow tepid in his religious observance, or keep quiet in matters concerning the divine religion. Whenever his friends fell sick, he would help them. If for an hour he did not see them, he would seek them out. Should a servant fall ill in his own house, he would take his place and bring things from the bazaar. He accepted the invitations of free men and slaves. He accepted gifts, even if it were only a drop of water or a mouthful of milk. Anything lawful that was brought to him, such as a hare, he would eat. He never criticized whatever he was offered to eat. He wore such lawful dress as was available. At one time a blanket would cover him, at another time striped cloth from Yemen, at another time a woolen garment or white clothes. He used to ride on whatever happened to be at hand, either a horse, camel, or ass, or he would even go on foot. Sometimes he went barefooted without a cloak, at other times without a turban or cap, according to what he happened to have at hand.

"He would sleep on a bare mat, using no mattress or covers. Whoever turned to him in time of need—whether a servant, a free man, a slave, or a slave girl—he would heed that person's request. If anybody came to him in distress and it happened to be the time of prayer, he would quickly finish his prayer and then attend to his visitor and carry out the latter's request. After, he would return to his prayers. Whenever anyone called upon him, if he gave an order it would be to spread out his blessed cloak, saying, 'Sit here!' He would even have them sit right next to him, on the very cushion he himself was occupying, saying, 'Sit here!' If the person showed any reluctance, he would politely insist, 'Kindly be seated!' And if Hasan and Husain climbed onto his back, using him as a horse to ride upon, saying to him, 'O mount, go this way!' or 'Go like this!' then he would do as he was bidden." All of these anecdotes have been related by Abu Sa'id Khizri. They are all found in the collections of genuine Traditions. They are all examples of the Prophet's considerate behavior.

These are the ones that have been related, but there are one hundred thousand others like them that have not been recorded. If there were no other miracle, his virtues and pleasing manners would be a sufficient witness of his genuineness. Among the false claimants and people who rejected him, there were those who, when they saw him alone, said: "This is not the face of a liar!" Immediately they placed their faith in him and accepted Islam, without miracles or arguments. Such pleasing behavior has also become the Way of the masters of knowledge. In all matters they follow the injunctions of the Law, and they test their own behavior against the touchstone of canonical tradition.

Anyone who travels along the Way but is not an investigator of Truth will not gain any benefit from the Way. The foundations of virtue depend on insight and mystical knowledge, but anyone who becomes imprisoned in pride will never acquire these virtues. By insight, the traveler should strive to seek this rank and be adorned with the virtues of prophecy. He should note carefully whatever he has acquired by the grace of the Lord, and he should also call to mind what still remains to be acquired, that he may obtain virtues, too, by means of struggle, asceticism, the service of this order, and association with members of this group, for most of the states and virtues can be acquired, and man is commanded to dwell in the mansion of striving.

O brother, the soul of a man is a mirror. When it undergoes training and attains its own perfection and becomes purified of the rusty qualities of human nature, then the appearance of the encompassing glory and beauty of the Lord Most High is manifested within it. A person recognizes himself for what he is, and understands the purpose for which he has been created, just as a Sufi has hinted:

O you who are a copy of the divine book!
O you who are a mirror of the beauty of the King!
Apart from you, everything that exists in the world is nothing.
Everything you desire—seek it within yourself, for you are it![69]

This gift is only bestowed on one who has traveled along the road of the Law, the Way, and the Truth. One has to go on trying, for he cannot know beforehand which key will be the one to open the lock of this wealth, nor can he know who will be favored with this wealth. Not every king is granted an everlasting kingdom, nor is the cap of honor placed on every head!

The domain of seeking Him is not granted to every Solomon:
The promulgation of His sorrow is not made to every heart
    and soul!

God Almighty has eighty thousand worlds, but they are all ignorant of this Tradition. They have no knowledge of it nor are they destined to attain it. It is only for man. To no other created being has it been granted. Hence someone said:

You are both the world above and the world below,
All things lack existence; whatever exists—it is You!

*Peace!*

## LETTER 60: MEDITATION

*In the name of God, the Merciful, the Compassionate!*

Dear Brother Shamsuddin, may God's favor be with you! Meditation has been termed a divine work by the Prophet. He used to say: "Meditate on created beings, not on the divine Essence," for whoever thinks about the Lord Himself will soon fall into infidelity, since the object of thought should be limited and focused if thinking is to be of some use, while the divine essence and attributes, on the other hand, are free from limitation that applies to the boundary of scientific knowledge and to other matters cognizable by the human mind. One should meditate on His creation in order to recognize the various manifestations of change and stability, transience and permanence, in creatures of the various ranks of existence. A person can pass on from these to acquire a knowledge of the Creator of everything. It is fitting that when a seeker emerges from the grip of external activity he should immediately focus on reciting short ejaculatory prayers at the same time that he gives full justice to the canonical prescriptions and carries out whatever is obligatory. From time to time he should also engage in reflecting on the conditions of God's creation and the world, and yet keep in mind that the Creator must infinitely transcend the work He produced.

In reflecting on the world as divinely created, he examines his own soul, heart, and body, and his various degrees from the time of his birth until his death.[70] He also contemplates his own ways. At the same time, he should reflect on the road of the Law and construct his assets out of knowledge and activity in order that, along the way, he may not be cut off by either emptiness of praise, delay or hesitation, or similar things.

The capital of disciples should not consist in seeking profit or loss. On the contrary, through the process of reflection, they will gain the treasure of insight. The profit of mystical knowledge will accrue to them. What it would take worldly people many long years to acquire as a result of good works and worship will be reaped by them in a very short period of proper meditation. The Prophet has given us a hint of this outcome when he says that an hour of meditation is worth sixty years of worship. This reflection should be on matters of religion, the conditions of His creation, and the benefit of seeking wisely, which is itself a virtue. Such meditation is equivalent to sixty years of good works. It is said by the Lord Most High: "Wherever one's eye falls in the Quran and finds a command, the purpose of the order is revealed to him who meditates." He profits from it, and, in understanding it, learns lessons and gains insight, since the eye of man cannot completely perceive the perfections of earth and heaven. What profit is there in investigating something that can never be fully grasped? God Almighty gives us no command to waste our time in what is useless!

It should also be noted that the truths concerning created beings can be perceived only by people endowed with keen insight. Such a gifted person will be able to see everything in such a way that the door of ostentation remains closed for him. Just as there are differences in the understanding of externalist scholars, so there are also differences of inner perception. Some are weak, others, strong; some are quick to perceive, others, slow. Similarly, the masters of hearts differ with regard to their insight. Some see as far as heaven; others as far as the divine throne. Some reach the tablet and pen; some gain a perfect, genuine insight, passing beyond all creatures, and see just the Creator Himself. The difference of peoples, manners, religions, and beliefs has only one root, and it is to be found in Him! Certainly the benefit derived from reflection is a profusion of knowledge. It is a means of acquiring mystical knowledge, which could not take place unless learning and interior knowledge had been acquired in the heart due to a change in the state of the heart. If this takes place, then one's deeds and actions are also changed. A person has fallen into "change." From there, he falls into "travelling." After this happens, he falls into "attraction." When this occurs, then he arrives—through a veritable craving for God—at a place that no jinn or man has reached either by struggle or good works. The fruit of consideration is all sorts of knowledge, and states without limit. It is beyond all reckoning and estimation, for even if a disciple desired to gauge all kinds of things and occurrences, and to know all about thought and reflection in the world, he would not be able to do so, since occurrences of reflection are innumerable, just as the fruit of reflection is without limit: It is simply beyond reckoning or description.

The sheikhs have said that many things are contained in reflection. Abdullah Mubarak saw Suhail ibn Ali quietly meditating one day. He said: "How far have you reached?" He replied: "As far as the bridge across hell!" Khwaja Sharih was traveling along a road. After a while he sat down, drew his blanket over his head, and began to cry. People asked him what had happened. He replied: "I was thinking of how my life is passing away, and how little I have done." Khwaja Da'ud Taiy, while sitting on his rooftop one moonlit night, was reflecting on the angels of heaven. He cried much and fell into the courtyard of his neighbor. The master of the house sprang up naked from his bed. He thought it must be a thief. When he saw it was Da'ud Taiy, he said: "Who threw you down?" He replied, "I know nothing about my fall!" Muhammad Wasi reported: There was a man from Basra who, upon the death of Abu Zar, went to his mother and enquired about his devotion. She said: "Every day he passed his time in a corner of the house, engaged in meditation." Khwaja Fuzail Iyaz said: "Reflection is a mirror that reveals to you your good points and your bad ones." The disciples of Jesus asked him: "Is there anyone else like you upon the face of the earth today?" He replied: "Yes! Those whose speech is a remembrance, and whose silence is meditation, and whose glance is a warning—such a person is like me!" Ibn Abbas said: "If you perform two prostrations of prayer while fully applying your mind, it is better than a whole night spent in distracted vigil!"

In reality, meditation is the best form of speech. Such instruction should be sufficient for this letter. May God Almighty grant us assistance to reflect on these facts as is fitting, and make the way of correct thinking easy for us! "He is our helper, and makes everything easy by His grace." If you seek but do not find, do not become downcast! The Lord has said: "Call upon Me and I will answer your prayer!" (Q40:60). His prayer is not that of Moses; neither is His purity that of Moses; nor is His longing that of Moses. "Can you not see us? The anger of friends is like that!"

O brother, a certain people was in search of Him day and night. The reply they received was this: "Your seeking has been rejected; the road has been closed!" Another group turned their face away from the path and walked heedlessly, according to their own desires. A voice came from the Unseen: "God invites them to the abode of peace!" (Q10:25).

> One brought forth from a Christian hermitage was called
>     stranger:
> But to another brought out of an idol-temple He said: "My
>     friend!"

Someone was seen wandering around in the wilderness without provisions or mount. People told him he was not bound to perform the pilgrimage. "For a long time I have known this," he replied, "but I simply cannot stay cooped up in my own house!"

A small boy played truant from school. The teacher sent some other children to bring him by force. A spiritual guide arrived on the scene. He was very happy. "The boy is being conveyed by His wrath!" he noted. "In this way he is learning a lesson about a divine quality!"

The hearts of dear ones have been torn to shreds! Their minds and eyes have been thrown into astonishment. They are on the verge of death. All previous connections have been wiped away like a mere wish. The seal has been stamped on them, as on a person's will!

Today all has been deemed an empty display;
Tomorrow they will do what has already been prepared!

*Peace!*

## LETTER 61: SEPARATION AND DETACHMENT[71]

*In the name of God, the Merciful, the Compassionate!*

Brother Shamsuddin, may God be generous to you! In the beginning of this work are found separation, which is like the bazaar day of seekers, and detachment, which is like the New Year of righteous disciples. What is meant by this separation? It means that you should come freely out of everything you find today. What is this detachment? It means you should not be enslaved by what is to come, as has been said:

Today, the day before yesterday, yesterday, tomorrow,
All four will be one in the life to come!

Second, there is external and internal seclusion. What does external seclusion consist of? It means that you pass beyond all creatures and turn your face to the wall, that you might be enabled to offer up your soul upon His threshold. What does inner seclusion entail? It means cleansing your heart of thinking about any things except God. Third, consider as unlawful for yourself any other name or thinking about anything other than God. Fourth, one should speak, eat, and sleep little, for such restraint is extremely beneficial in controlling one's selfish soul. Much talk prevents us from being preoccupied with the remembrance of God. Too much sleep deprives us of the opportunity for reflection. Too much eating makes us feel heavy, and prevents us from working well.

You should be continually engaged in ablutions, for external cleanliness is an indication of internal purity. When, for instance, a dervish was asked: "Tell us the secret of purity," he replied: "It is a secret: just as one must always be meticulous about external purity, so too should one be fastidious about inner purity," for what sort of separation can be achieved merely by external purity? By itself it cannot sustain a strong yearning for God. "A strong yearning for God is equivalent to the good works of both worlds!" It will lift you up and take you to a place to which all the struggles and activities of jinn and men would not be able to take you, if you were to rely only on them. This task is extremely easy to talk about, but frightfully difficult to accomplish. Traveling along this road is not a matter of hands and feet, but requires one's heart and soul, and these do not obey orders. For those endowed with spiritual resolve as well as for righteous lovers, however, it is as easy as eating and drinking are for you and me. The doorway leading to this form of travel consists of learning and mystical knowledge. Anyone who does not enter by that door will wander around aimlessly in a desert and fall into the clutches of a fearsome demon, a demon who will snatch away both life and faith, as has been said:

> These false claims are the demons of the Way:
> Be careful lest their sudden attack detour you from your path!

If the pain of this endeavor has taken hold of anyone, then realize that it is a pain without remedy. One has to live with oneself, and with one's own pain. A person should not attempt to find a remedy, because he could pass his whole life fruitlessly in such a search. Some of the Sufis have said: "All these seekers to whom You manifest Yourself remain in pain, and do not obtain any remedy." Hence it is that they have become engrossed in searching for a remedy, and the capital of disappointment is absorbed in this way. Prepare yourself for whatever you want! "I swear that, until you abandon your relation to all things, you cannot attain to the All!" This is a confirmatory hint. One beloved of God has said:

> If you want to hold the heavens within your grasp, then arise,
> Lift up your foot, and ascend above the earth.
> Move forward, but never let your gaze wander backwards,
> Lest, from your heavenly perch, your eye rest upon earth.
> Look at the conflict experienced by a dying man:
> His thoughts are turned toward his bodily form,
> And yet one who knows what is the root of his work
> Understands that his soul can exist without a body!

Eternal life is lived through the soul, not the body. This is the work of love rather than injunction. Because it is incumbent upon servants to obey orders, they run after a remedy for every pain. Lovers, on the other hand, heed only the call of love. They want pain without remedy! All the time the Beloved says, "Stay away, lest you be destroyed," but they say, "We made an offering of our lives on the very first day. We have destroyed ourselves with our own hand. It would be better to die than to have to live without You. If we had to live without You, we would turn our faces toward nothingness!"

Better to be dead in Your lane than alive and far from Your face!

O brother, we should not trust our head on this road. Those famous for learning know nothing of this secret. If someone does not have the strength and does not believe, then he will turn toward a desert where he will see a hundred thousand heads rolling around in the base dust. Nobody, however, either outwardly or inwardly, has seen the countenance of his Recompense. Love calls you in order to raise you up from the secret of a head that is really nothing but dust, that He might place you upon the throne of honor and union. The choice now lies with you!

> Love is the new wine of the garden of youth,
> Love it is which can purchase an everlasting domain.
> If, like Khizr, you seek living water,
> Look to love, the source of living water!

Even though there is no head completely devoid of this benefit, still this esteemed wealth and refined rank is not granted to every greedy person, for by prayer and fasting such people think they have become worthy, but they remain deprived of the Perfection of all ranks and the Honor of all stages.

> Union with Your face is a treasure sought by all creation.
> Yet it is the task of Wealth alone: who can attain it now?

Be of good cheer and remain constant in hope, for the door of favor is open. Abu Sulaiman Darani wrote Khwaja Bayazid: "If there is a foolish fellow who sleeps all night long, can he reach the mansion?" The answer came: "If the wind of divine favor blows!" It has been remarked that "if all the possessions of man were put into a sieve, then not even one particle of Truth would descend upon his head!" The dwellings of men were searched again and again, but no one was found who could display a face that contained purity equal to the point of a needle!

Doubts have been created to act as irritants upon the visage of faith. Habit and metaphor have been brought forth and are in conflict with Unity. Hypocrisy has been nurtured along with sincerity, staking its own claim. For every friend, there are thousands of enemies, and along with every righteous man, thousands of heretics have been created. Wherever there is a place of worship, a tavern has been built facing it. Wherever one finds a cape, there will be a sacred thread as well. Acceptance has been marked by rejection. From east to west ornaments and blessings have been bestowed, and yet beneath every blessing has been arranged some affliction or sore trial. The unfortunate one throws dust on his head and says:

> God does all this and yet, out of dread,
> Man has no power to utter even a sigh!

*Peace!*

### LETTER 62: SEPARATION AND DETACHMENT—A FURTHER EXPLANATION

*In the name of God, the Merciful, the Compassionate!*

Brother Shamsuddin, may God grant you the adornment of His own devotion and greatness! May you ever remain in His grace! Receive the greetings of the writer of this letter! For a disciple, separation and detachment are the conditions of the Way. Separation is from all relationships and from all creatures, while detachment is from oneself: no "other than God" in the heart, no burden on the back, no association with anyone, no getting engrossed in the bazaar or in work with any creature. A disciple's aspirations soar above the pinnacle of the divine throne. He shuns the universe, and finds rest in the Object of his desire. In spite of having both worlds he would not be happy without his Friend, while if he did not have them, but had his Friend, he would experience no unhappiness at all. One beloved of God has said: "If you are with God, there is no anxiety or difficulty, but with anything other than God, there is no peace and quiet." Similarly, it has been said: "Whoever is veiled from God would experience, by that very fact, calamity and grief, even though he had in his hands the key to the treasures of the two kingdoms!" A person who wears a patched garment and begs will have a chance to interact with his own Lord. He will be king of both worlds, though he may have no bread on a particular evening. Hence Khwaja Sari Saqati has said: "O God, if You want to punish me, do as You will, but do not punish me by hiding Yourself from me!"

O brother, this is the very reality of hell itself, as the Quran has suggested, with reference to the punishment of the infidels: "On that day they will be hidden from their Lord" (Q83:15). There is a corroborative point hidden in this punishment. The saying of the wise is that if tomorrow the tent of union were to be pitched in hell, then His seekers and disciples would apply the collyrium of its fire to their own eyes. And if in paradise, for only a moment, they were to be afflicted by His concealment from them, then they would raise such a cry that those in hell would take pity on them!

> With You, my heart is a mosque: without You, it is but a fire-
>     temple:
> Without You, my heart is hell itself: with You, it becomes
>     paradise!

In other words, when the glory and greatness of God become known to a disciple, and the pain of seeking has taken hold of the border of his garment, and he realizes that "all things belong to Him who is designated Lord," he then sees that he has to flee from everything except God, whereas there is no escape whatsoever from God Himself, just as He filled Moses with life, declaring "I am necessary for you! There can be an escape from all things, but for you there is no escape from Me!" Certainly the tablet of claim will be broken. The eyes of "by me" and "for me" will be opened. Life and death, in the sight of such a person, come to mean the same thing. Rejection or acceptance, praise or blame, all are of equal weight in his scale. Paradise and hell do not even pass by the perimeter of his soul. There is no place in his breast for this world or the next. He does not seek apparel or nourishment from creatures. How can a stout-hearted diver, who plays with his life in the depths of the ocean, and brings up a night-illuminating pearl, look at the smoke of the tiny lamp of some old woman? His aim is the Exalted Court. His hand has been withdrawn from us and stretched out toward God. The feet of his seeking always urge on the mount of rank and favor. The tablet of name and fame and safety is washed clean. His way of acting is such that "if the divine footstool were to come before me, I would turn away from it! And if this world and the next were to display themselves to me, I would reduce them to nothing!" Comfort would be this: to be always seeking on Mount

Sinai, like Moses, asking, "Show me," even though the reply from the Lord is, "You cannot see Me!" (Q7:143). Behold the work, and behold the profit to dust and water!

> There is for us another world beyond this one:
> There is another dwelling besides hell and paradise.
> Revelry and recklessness flow from the capital of love:
> Denying self and reciting the Quran belong to yet another
>     world!

When an honest disciple has acquired this separation and detachment, his revelation in the world occurs in this fashion: "O David, when you see anyone in search of Me, become his servant!" A prophet like David is to be his servant! Just imagine! It can be understood now what others should be like. This Meaning is acquired in stages by the disciple, and only gradually becomes apparent. To whom can it be revealed all at once—unless God so wills? Anyone who wants to learn the Quran by heart or become a Quranic reciter must necessarily begin with the A, B, C and work through all the chapters until he reaches the final one. Gradually he will become a reciter or a memorizer of the Quran. The way of the Lord is similar to this! What should be done? A poet has expressed what is intended when he said:

> You can become an angel, if you set out manfully and struggle,
> Just as the leaves of the mulberry tree can be turned into silk!

A disciple should not be downcast on account of his penury, lack of merit, disloyalty, or pollution. His gaze should be fixed on the power and grace of God. If He so wishes, thousands of churches and idol-temples can become Kaabas or Domes of the Rock. Thousands of sinners and scoundrels can become friends and acquaintances of the Almighty. An address can come, even with no intervening cause, if He so wishes, and in a moment a thousand infidels will become believers, and many thousands of polytheists and idol worshipers, professors of the divine Unity, without delay. Many thousands of reprobates are granted mercy, while thousands who used to frequent taverns become people given over to fervent prayer. There is no room for anyone to ask "How" or "Why."

> Many devoted to prayer fall from their mount and remain by
>     the wayside:
> Others, habitués of the tavern, reach home safely on the back
>     of a lion!

The letters already written should be read, time and again, in a reflective and systematic manner. They should be studied carefully. God willing, you will be blessed with the ability to investigate reality and confirm it. What is meant will be understood due to a common conscience. Fruits and impressions of the Truth, which appear in a person's limbs, will become clearly manifested to him, through the grace and favor of the Prophet and his descendants.

O brother, we ourselves remain caught up in misfortune, and the world also suffers our misfortune. It was said to the Chosen One, "Muhammad, I have sent you in order to test you with calamities and, through you, I will also involve other people in calamities. Draw your sword and strike manfully, wreaking destruction on all sides." One day it will be a Badr [i.e., a victory], another an Uhud [i.e., a defeat]; on one occasion thousands of robes of honor will be bestowed on him while, at another, all that is left behind for Muhammad will be camel tripe! You say, "I like a pleasant odor"—but what is camel tripe in comparison to That? You say, "I like women"—but what is the diversion of Aisha in comparison to That? Here minds are perplexed, while thoughts and opinions whirl in astonishment—what can His majesty and beauty have to do with this handful of dust and water?

> O you who have been imprisoned by calamity,
> Did you not once aspire to a kingdom?
> Except for soul and heart and liver, I see
> Nothing else in the revolving or the celestial millstone!
> The lovers of this world become awestruck
> In the world of Your honor and greatness!

*Peace!*


## LETTER 63: KEEPING PURE THE PATH OF FAITH

*In the name of God, the Merciful, the Compassionate!*

Dear Brother Shamsuddin, one should keep the path of faith free from any disgrace on one's own part. The thorns of human nature should be cut out, and one's own anger should be snatched from the way. Also, the miseries of human nature should be internally expunged for, as the wise have said, "Everyone who strides forth ac-

252

cording to his own desire and considers his own ego as more important for him than God cannot become a believer!" In this context,
how could the question of love even arise?

> My ego, without my consent, swept me along.
> I had thought it was my friend, but it was my deadly foe.
> Up till now, I have befriended rank and honor,
> Like a moth that mistakes fire for light!

It is the teaching of the wise that if, even for a moment, the ego is
given free rein, it will entwine you with a thousand sacred threads
and will place a thousand idols before you. It behooves one never to
consider it friendly to you for any reason at all. If you contain your
ego for a hundred thousand years, but then make even a single move
according to its dictates, it will fling your Islam upon the ground.

> The grief-filled repentance of a hundred years deceived the
>     monk:
> Caught by a single hair, he was drawn to the door of a tavern!

Thus it has been said: If you pay attention to your ego, you will
never see God. All the trials of Satan came upon him because he took
notice of his own soul. Those who make a claim on God do so as a result of paying attention to their own carnal soul. The audience hall of
repentance is for the sake of this work, namely, that a person might
advance and be released from the miseries of his own soul. O brother,
realize that it is an extremely important duty to preserve one's faith
from the misfortunes that arise from one's selfish soul. Except
through repentance, this misery is easily aroused. The wealth of repentance has made its appearance from the time of Adam. The garment of Adam was the victory of the door of the court of repentance.
Some beloved of God have said: "If a hundred thousand treasurers of
wealth and eternal bliss had been bestowed upon the descendants of
Adam, it would not have been as beneficial as drawing Adam into the
royal court of the wrath of God, for 'Adam disobeyed his Lord!' "
(Q.20:121).

If he had placed the foot of refraining from sin in this royal court
of destiny, then certainly the door of repentance would not have been
opened up for his descendants. This was the arranging of the power
and seclusion of the threshold of "There is no god but God," for the
reason that a pearl of this quality should be inscribed in the register
of honor, for "I created him with My own hand!" (Q38:75). For such

honor there should be no robe or cap less than this, that "Adam disobeyed." A poet hinted at what was meant here:

Heaven does not strike those who have no resources:
It strikes at the foolishness of those richly endowed.
Except for you and me, there was no one else in this garden.
It was you and I who formed the new shoots of this garden.

Everything in paradise and in the abode of peace that had the power to comfort and delight fell in love with Adam, for the simple reason that, since he had not seen such wonderful things, all the hands of love took hold of his skirt. Adam, with great spiritual resolve, snatched his heart away from them all. It was preferable for him to come to the inn of commands and bear the burden of commands. Paradise, however, is the abode of display, and he could not discover the burden of obedience there. He said: "The burden of God is to provide a pretext for me to escape from the clutches of the damsels of paradise! I found liberation in the wheat that was produced as a pretext." A voice was heard in the world: "Adam disobeyed his Lord!" (Q20:121). All hands were withdrawn from his skirt. Be careful, lest you call the very foundation of 124,000 prophets a sinner, otherwise, on the Day of Resurrection, your tongue will be cut out! And if you say, "It is found in the Quran, 'Adam disobeyed his Lord' "—I answer, "Yes, so it is!" It is also related that Adam's head was raised and that the crown of avoidance of sin was placed upon his head. But as for you and me, and others like us, we can make no such boast. Muhammad Shah [Tughluq] can say whatever he likes to Khwaja Jahan [his prime minister], but if you or I were to say what he says, our heads would not remain attached to our bodies!

O brother, you have not trodden the path of Adam, and so you cannot carry out what is related about Adam. It was grief lodged in the faith that caught hold of his skirt. An abode of peace was exchanged for one of trials. A voice came, "Are you able to fight with Satan? How can you descend by choice? How can you stain a fair name by calling him a sinner? Can you make the sandal of seeking from the very crown of vicegerency?" "We gird ourselves for all this!" he replied; "do not on our account cause the grief of this saying to fall into oblivion!" Thus did a disobedient one act: He rejected paradise and all its display!

Paradise with its milk and honey, damsels and castles,
If bestowed on me without You, would be of no avail.

You and I have only reached the stage of feathering our own nests! We are good at serving our own needs, but that is all. We have preached no other sermon than ourselves. It is cupidity that prompts us to find from Adam an inheritance, and yet, unless there is some relationship, there can be no inheritance. It is a long time since we have been ruined, and had the dust of hopelessness and suffering loss poured upon us in bad days. Lift up your hands and say, from an inflamed heart:

> Everyone has reached the Kaaba of union with You,
> But I have remained among the unsuccessful ones.
> I am like some who, though unworthy of mercy,
> Can still hope to have the divine curse sent upon them!

Everyone who remains a stranger to the threshold of repentance has no share in all the states that constitute the inheritance of Adam. Take care lest you say that one should repent whenever a sin has been committed. O brother, since we ourselves are sin, it is now necessary to become something else! Have you not heard this?

> When I asked what sin I had committed, Love replied:
> "Your very existence is a sin! No other could be greater than
>     that!"

What question of sin was there for Moses, who said, "I turn in repentance toward You!" The Chosen One said: "Every day I beg forgiveness of God!" O brother, just as you and I ought to repent of our wickedness and sins, so do the righteous have to repent of their righteousness! While unfaithful ones have to repent of oppressing others, all faithful and sincere people have to repent of their fidelity and sincerity. We worship ourselves, and have to repent of the way we pander to our own inclinations, while those who are masters of their own hearts have to repent of contemplating their own states. It is the saying of Sufi masters that, just as one should not commit sin, so one should be obedient to prescriptions of the Law and repent of everything. If you say, "Sins should be committed first," then the wise say that all the righteousness, redemption, and devotion of the world should be brought forward and, when this is done, be handed over in order to destroy any semblance of independence. The secret is this:

> You wish, by reciting the rosary and praying,
> To make happy Him who has no needs!
> Prayer is nourishment for the long road ahead,
> Yet of your prayer He has no need at all!

If tomorrow all kingdoms were to be handed over to a beggar, it would be no cause for astonishment. Tomorrow, the beggars of this community will be brought forward and seated on the divine throne. They will be asked: "O man of dust and water! How did you recognize the Lord of the world?" They will reply: "O God, the entire earth and heaven belongs to You!" A word came: "I have given everything in heaven and upon the earth to a beggar!" They will say: "O God, know that Your possession is the divine throne." A word came: "I have made the throne as a cushion upon which members of the community of Muhammad may recline, that they may realize that my kingship does not rest upon that! It cannot be contained either in your imaginations or understanding. All those graced by a mystic state wish to repent of their knowledge, unity, and mystical knowledge, and even be "bound up" in repentance, as it were. They repent, with shame, of their own mystical knowledge, but they remain bound to their own insights, and just as those in hell have to bear the distress of fetters and handcuffs, so they too will face shame on account of their restricted understanding of divine unity and gnosis.

> When ascetics take Your eyebrow as the direction of their
>     prayer,
> Look at all the prayers they neglect, lost, as they are, in
>     astonishment!

If they are asked on the Day of Resurrection how they have discharged their duty of proclaiming "There is no god but God," they will say: "We were created slaves of religion. We have been tied in the knot of religion. For us the special quality of the Lord is 'There is no god but God!' " They were asked: "Whom have We deputized to praise Us, since no one can recognize Him except Him!" O brother, it is not a work that can be fathomed by any intellect! All intellects and imaginations are useless at this threshold!

> Imagination comes back destitute and barefooted,
> Just as the hand returns empty from His door!

The wise say that, if all the prophets and righteous men upon the face of the earth, as well as the close ones and the sinless ones of heaven, were to exercise their chaste tongues for all eternity in describing His unity, they would end up saying, "We repent of whatever we have said!"

O brother, if the dress of your nature has been sewn from the chastity of all the pure ones, and the sincerity of all the sinless ones, be careful lest you become enamored of it! And if a thousand swords are sharpened with the destructive poison of the divine wrath and you are struck on the head, be careful lest by fleeing you become like that speaker about whom it was said by an inflamed one:

> Would to God that my heart were separated from You,
> Or were acquainted with someone else!
> Yet if it abandoned its love for You, whom would it love?
> And if it were to abandon Your lane, where would it go?

Anyone in this abode who has not been inflamed with the fire of repentance will certainly have to endure the fire of hell. Everything you know about yourself, whether fault or virtues, should be burnt today in the fire of repentance, so that you might become receptive to this judgment: "The person who has repented of his sins becomes like one who has not sinned!" Then, from an inflamed heart offer this prayer:

> O God, have mercy, for we are polluted,
> Stained by the blood of our hearts and livers.
> We have no power to purchase You with our coins,
> For we are but an alloy of lead and brass.
> Be gracious toward us, at least this once,
> For we are unable to bestow anything upon ourselves.

Every thorn that ought to be removed from the path of religion, if it is not removed today, will some day become an arrow piercing your heart and liver! Do you not see what happened to Moses when he was blessed? "God spoke with Moses" (Q4:164), and 120,014 words were bestowed upon him without any intermediary, and from the tip of his head to his toenails, all his members became "ear," with the result that they heard Him in such a way that, by listening to every word spoken, Moses himself ceased to exist, absorbed as he was with such a total listening. Every time that he became "clever," then this wound was inflicted on his heart: "O Moses, you killed an Egyptian" (Q20:40). "Without My revelation you were doomed." If the punishments of the seven divisions of hell had been unfolded before his vision at that moment, they would not have flashed into his mind like that deed of his! It was in such "comfort," and after having passed along the way in such a robe of thorns, that Moses resolved to see the divine wealth.

You must also have heard the story of Umar. He drew his sword, came forward, and said: "As long as I live, who is there who would dare insult Lat or Uzza? I myself have prayed to Lat and Uzza and have vowed to them that I would go and bring back the head of Muhammad!" In a word, from the day he drew his sword, and as good as did the deed, whenever he displayed his fighting prowess on the battlefield in a superior way, a voice used to come to him: "Are you not that Umar who came forward with drawn sword to remove the head of the Messenger of God and destroy the kingdom of 'There is no god but God?' " When he was thus addressed, he used to feel brokenhearted and wish that the earth would split open and swallow him up! His discomfort arose on account of this saying. Every time it was repeated to him, he could do nothing for a whole week. He would go out to the pebble-strewn water courses of Mecca and rub his face in the dust and say: "O Lord, take away the life of Umar, that he might not have to stare into the mirror of his own oppression! O dust, be upon my head and yours, that Umar was in a church engaged in idol worship, and woe upon this prayer and fast, and upon all work not permitted by God! If it were placed in front of a dog, he would not accept it!"

> Our days have been marked by depravity and wickedness,
> And our cup and jug filled with forbidden things.
> Fortune laughs at our devotion, prayer, and fasting,
> While we ourselves shed tears!

*Peace!*

LETTER 64: THE FEAR OF GOD

*In the name of God, the Merciful, the Compassionate!*

Dear Brother Shamsuddin, fear of God is the gateway to bliss and the door to wealth. All the dwelling places that have been prepared in the world of "There is no god but God" have been prepared for those who fear God, and all the abodes constructed in paradise are reserved for those who fear God. It should be known that anyone who fears God has been delivered from the miseries of self and has escaped from the knot of self, for a man cannot be purified until he escapes from himself as well as from all traffic with his own self; otherwise, hell lies in wait for him. "There is not one among you who will not pass this way" (Q19:71). All creatures should be placed within the circle of hell, so that their own destiny may be removed from that of the rebellious. At that moment, those who fear God will be brought forward, and those who worship themselves will, out of fear of hell, pass on in a fitting manner. "This decree has been promulgated."

O brother, those who fear God will pass beyond the seven stages of hell like fish in water. Hell itself does not possess the strength to give them proper respect. For they are kings, and their royal signet is this: "God loves those who fear Him!" Just as those who fear God cannot be enclosed in hell, neither can they be contained in the eight heavens. And if you say, "Well, where can they be contained?" then the answer is that their realm is that of divinity itself! The last judgment of those who fear God will take place before God Himself and nowhere else. The secret is contained in this:

> Tomorrow we shall reign over all of Egypt,
> So why be upset if we are in prison today?
> Do you know what kind of birds we are?
> Or do you know what each recites to himself?
> If we seem to be beggars in this lane,
> Look at our true condition: We are kings!
> Even though, outwardly, we may appear indigent,
> Glance inward, and behold the mines of precious stones!

Have you not read this verse from the Quran: "Those who fear God will be gathered to Him as regal emissaries" (Q19:85)? Be careful lest you think that there is no other place for such emissaries than heaven! Have you not heard what the lord of the prophets gave his friends to drink? This is a saying that has come to us from God through Gabriel: "I have prepared for those faithful to me such favors as no eye has seen, nor ear heard, nor has it entered into the heart of man to conceive." This serves as a reminder that, if I remove the mercy of heaven and the misfortunes of hell, there would be no loss for God or damage to His commands.

> Behold the vast Tract that, if the world were not to exist,
> Would suffer no loss, no, not even by a hair's breadth.
> There is no beginning at all to His greatness,
> Nor limit nor boundary to His possessions.

You cannot possibly fathom the secrets of the Quran by means of your puny intellect. If you want to enjoy the slightest trace of its perfume, you should know that it is only through the aid of the Quran that you can recognize the truth of the Quran. "No soul knows what refreshment of the eyes is hidden for them" (Q32:17). You should realize that there is no more precious flight in religion than that a person should flee from himself in order to be liberated from all praise of self, for such praise causes a man to remain content with himself. When, by the favor of divine grace, he finds help, let his hand be removed from self-praise, so that he goes and grabs his own head, as has been said: "If you have any connection with even a particle, or a particle has any with you, it is as though you were mortgaged to it." As long as any of your qualities has a hold over you, you are enslaved to it. The fear of God will not disclose its visage to you until you are freed from even the most minute particle of any quality. Have you not heard the Tradition concerning Him? He wants you in your entirety!

> If the Ravisher of your heart stretches out His hand,
> Passing beyond self is not a long or difficult road!

But it is not like that, perhaps you would say, adding that there should be the rank and magnificence of the world, ostentation and munificence, and, along with all these, fear of God as well! The answer to this demurral is "By no means! Do you not see what was said—'I am utterly beyond all association with partners.' In no way can He accept any partnership with himself!"

> Say to the person who looked at My friend in this fashion,
> "Do not look in such a way," for love does not tolerate any
>     other!

Fear of God is a great possession. It does not allow contention and strife. Religion removes the self-respect of partnership. Though it is natural for an important person to have a great reputation, it becomes an obstruction on the road to fear of God. Until you overcome this unfortunate obstacle, whatever you say about the piety of those who fear God will not be free of self. Insofar as you take notice of yourself, that ill-fated and unfortunate obstacle becomes more firmly rooted so that, as you grow in acquaintance with yourself, you become more of a stranger to Him. Become a stranger to yourself, that you might become acquainted with Him! It is all the same for anyone who remains behind the obstacle of self, whether he wears tattered clothes and carries his prayer mat, or whether he is attired in a fine robe and has a sword buckled to his side! Yet this baneful obstacle cannot be overcome, except with the help of an experienced spiritual guide. Nor can this destructive wilderness be traversed except in the company of a God-endowed escort. Thus it has been said:

Take care that you do not enter this Way without high resolve,
For it will prove to be a bloodthirsty wilderness!
Unless you be a man of the Way, how can you smell the
fragrance of roses?
Go, turn back, for this Way has shown itself to be full of
thorns!

Fear of God means that you do not look down on any creature with a contemptuous eye. If an ant has pursued your path, you should not have the gall to stomp on it. It is related that the Commander of the Faithful, Ali, was one day passing along a road. The edge of one of his sandals landed on an ant, injuring it. The distress of that ant had an effect on the heart of Ali. He saw the ant writhing on the ground. Ali sat down in front of it, his heart filled with grief. A fit of trembling seized his limbs. He suddenly felt very weak. Somehow or other that wounded ant managed to retreat to its nest. Ali returned home with a grief-stricken heart. When night came, he saw Muhammad in a dream, crying out to him and saying, "O Ali, why do you not pay attention to what you are doing? Today the seven heavens were taken aback at your cruelty. That ant upon whom you trod was one of the righteous ones of the Lord. It experienced various kinds of joy in itself. From the very day it had been created the recitation of the rosary and praise of the Lord had never been omitted from its life, even for the twinkling of an eye, except at that moment when you placed your foot on it!" Ali related: "My heart was overcome by fear and trembling before the pride of the world! I said: 'O Prophet, what should I do? How should I go about this matter?' " He replied: "O Ali, remain where you are! Calm down, for that very ant besought the Lord to pardon your fault, saying: 'O God, You have placed great emphasis on a person's intention in his actions, and Ali did not intend to hurt me as he strode along. Grant him peace!' "

The Prophet continued: "That ant interceded for you because you are an intrepid member of Our court. You were tied to the saddle straps of its innate courtesy and thus were forgiven. O Ali, if the ant had not interceded on your behalf, then your self-respect, as far as this court is concerned, would have been lost. Do you know what this means? You can waive your own rights, but not those of your friends! Be on the alert, for there is no particle in creation upon which the pain of this saying has not alighted:

Everything you see, whether black or white,
Is busily at work in this great workshop.
Just look at these particles, all astir,
Praising Him by proclaiming His unity!

All this occurred in order that you might understand that the Lord has many secrets hidden in His creation and works. There is no way for our intellects to discern them. "There is nothing at all which does not sing His praise" (Q17:44). As the poet has attested:

Thousands of particles arise from this valley,
To this door where indigence finds an entry.
From their own helplessness they cry, "O Pure One,
You are both known and knower: *We* did not recognize You!"

Never, indeed, have your blessed eyes fallen on this paper. "No one knows the hosts of Your Lord except He" (Q74:31). If the veil of ignorance were to be lifted from your eyes, you would see the whole world adorned with slavery and beholden to Him, and if you came out of the quality of tyranny, you would see all creation running hither and thither in search of Him. Hence it is that Khwaja Nizami has said:

Knowledge of God has been taken away from men:
The manly themselves have been removed from their midst!

When the Prophet was informed of these secrets, he immediately made this request of the Almighty: "O God, grant me the ability to perceive things as they are that it might not happen to me that I am always in pursuit of the jewel of my sinlessness." Sadiq Akbar used to be forever saying: "O God, show me clearly each obligation and then give me the grace to discharge it. Show me also those which are useless and, then, give me the grace to avoid them!" A hint lies in this: "When God wishes to bestow some favor upon a servant of His, He reveals his faults to him." He says: "Did you see the idol-temple? Enter in! At last you will see what used to be the site of a tavern, and, after a while, was replaced by a mosque. This is the real thing!" What is meant is that his heart was changed, as has been said: "One heart, which was that of an idol-temple, has become a mosque." Even more magnificent than that is the fact that from east to west all became painted with the color of the Kaaba!

O brother, if you are told, on one occasion, that your prayer has been answered, say: "O Lord, remove from my mind this preoccupation with myself!" Know for certain that you can only hope for untold good when this preoccupation with self is removed: As long as your attention is fixed on yourself, you cannot help but be a worshiper of self. That was exactly what Satan was—one who worshiped himself. Whatever form you wish to take, be it of an angel or of Adam, and whether it be in the heavens or upon the earth or in paradise, one can still find ways to worship self. A worshiper of self is one who has not gone beyond himself. The poet gave us a hint of this meaning when he wrote:

> Though countless veils do hide You,
> None can compare to self-conceit!
> Burn the veil of self-conceit! Then will you know:
> There is no nobler work than this in either world!

O brother, realize that the love of water and clay bears away both worlds. In the world of devotion, both paradise and hell carry some weight, while in the world of love, neither of them has the slightest influence. The eight paradises were lined up for Adam, yet he sold them for a little wheat and turned his courageous face toward this abode of grief.

> We want no other chains except Your tresses:
> Just see what intelligent madcaps we are!

A revelation came to the prophet David: "O David, I remember those who remember Me! My paradise is for those who obey Me. I visit those who long for Me and My special favor is for those who love Me." O brother, the Traditions about forgiveness and punishment and the names of paradise and hell are left so far behind in the Tradition concerning love that no concern for today or tomorrow arises—but this Tradition cannot be digested by one and all. Nor does this sherbet suit every person's taste.

> Not everyone has a gullet like a falcon's,
> Nor is every belly capable of bearing the secret!

*Peace!*

# MANERI

*In the name of God, the Merciful, the Compassionate!*

Brother Shamsuddin, may God bless you! Khwaja Zu'l Nun Misri has said: "Righteousness is God's sword upon the earth: Whatever it touches it cuts to pieces." Seeing the truth requires "one who causes," not affirmation of the thing caused. When the cause is firmly established, then the command to be righteous lags far behind, for the reality of faith means seeking absolutely nothing except God, as has been said: "Worship God, and associate nothing with Him!" (Q4:36). Everyone who claims that he has the righteousness of faith really claims to have no use for anything except God. The proof of the truth of his claim would be that, if he finds anything other than God, he does not accept it; but if he does accept it, he will be proved to be an imposter.

> The heart desiring union with Him is shielded against
>     adversity.
> Agitated is the soul ensnared by fear of separation from Him.
> Yet beyond union and separation there is still another work:
> For one whose aspirations are lofty, both become a mere
>     headache!

Once Zu'l Nun Misri was coming from Jerusalem. He saw a person afar off. He found a compulsion arising in his heart to question the person. As he came nearer, he saw that it was an old woman, staff in hand and clad in a woolen robe. "Where are you going?" he asked. "To God!" came the reply. He took out a gold dinar to give to her. "O Zu'l Nun!" she exclaimed, waving her hands in front of him: "What are you doing? What are you after? I do everything for the sake of God and I take nothing from anyone besides Him. Just as I worship none other than God, neither do I take from anyone except Him." Saying this, she disappeared. A disciple of the Way should be just like that! The secret lies in this:

> Lofty aspiration—no matter to what it aspires—
> Do not despise it; it will accomplish its purpose.

If anyone says that he works for the sake of God, then here is a test of the genuineness of his love, for people can be divided into two groups according to how they act. One group thinks that whatever it does, it does for Him, but its members actually are acting in their own interests, even though they may have succeeded in bringing their natural desires under control. Yet they will be granted their reward in the world beyond. The second group is that for whom all concern of reward or punishment of the next world has no place at all in their affairs. Whatever they do is in obedience to the exalted command of, and under the compulsion of love for, Almighty God. This outlook has been thus expressed:

> The present world is the abode of calamity; the next, of
> pleasure.
> I would not expend a grain of barley to acquire either!
> Mischief is for this world, honor for the next:
> I am free of both, belonging to neither!

It has been said that more good things lie in store as a reward for the obedience of the submissive ones than benefits that accrue to a sinner on account of his sins. Sin brings its momentary comfort, while obedience results in eternal bliss. What benefit accrues to God from the mortification of people? What loss is it to Him if anyone abandons Him? If all were to live with the righteousness of Abu Bakr, the benefit would be theirs! And if all were to act in the haughty fashion of Pharaoh, the loss would be theirs! When righteousness alone is seated at this banquet, then "the people of the Quran are God's people and His elect," for their nourishment derives from the feast of the Quran! The people of heaven form one group, the elect another. The holy souls of "There is no god but God" have come into existence from this root: "I breathed into him of My Spirit" (Q38:72). This group finds no nourishment except in the Quran! Anyone who sits down to the feast of the Quran cannot tolerate the impurities of his own nature, which is the center of all calamity. He yearns for death and for the time when the blessed messenger of death will come and remove his impurities, that by means of the purgative power of grief and the pain of seeking he himself will come to his Friend and sit down at the feast of the gracious manifestation of the Beloved. The very first of the signs that indicate this group of people has been given by the masters of the Way: "The lover experiences death!" He passes his days in that pain, awaiting the coming of death by looking for the direction from which the blessed brow of Azrael [the angel of death] might appear, that he may go out to welcome him. Azrael comes to such a person in order to remove from before him the unfortunate obstacle of his self. It is not, however, the task of Azrael to take away his life. He bears this wealth, "God takes men's soul at the time of death!" (Q39:42). The Prophet said: My bones melted away from the pain of love, and my desire reached such a point that I thought I could no longer remain in my body, until Gabriel came and said: "O prophet of God, moderate your eagerness! Be patient for a while longer! I have been ordered to do my work in the first month of Rabi. The time cannot be foreshortened simply to alleviate the pain of your heart!"

> Strange is the work that at the Beloved's behest
> Cannot be endured, nor can it be hurried up!

O brother, there is no pain more refined than that of the desire for God, as one who yearns for Him has said:

> I experience a thousand frustrations in my desire for Your face.
> My whole life has passed in grief over You: I have done
> nothing!
> Yet if I am helped and directed by You, this is wealth enough
> for me:
> Otherwise, I shall make an uproar like that of Judgment Day!

Such is this pain that if a particle of it were to shine upon the world, no sickness at all would remain in any kingdom. Master Abu Ali Daqqaq said: "During the early days of my discipleship, I was wandering in a deserted city, as is the habit of beginners and novices. I entered a dilapidated mosque. I saw an old man. When he wept, the floor of the mosque became covered with blood. His eyes were drenched. 'O Sheikh,' I protested, 'be more lenient towards yourself! What has happened to you?' 'Young man,' he replied, 'my life and my strength have ebbed away in my desire for the Lord. I have reached the end of my days.' "

> Those desirous of Your face do not achieve their object in a
> day:
> A pilgrim may set out on the road but remain far from the
> Kaaba.

At the time of his death the Prophet prayed: "O God, come to my aid during the trials of death! It is not the task of Azrael to remove my soul. O Lord, come to my rescue, for I am being separated from my soul!"

# THE HUNDRED LETTERS

I sacrifice my soul out of friendship for You, O Beloved.
The lover lives through his Friend; of what use is a soul?

O brother, long ago it was said that, for a hungry person, listening to the stories of others produces nothing but a headache! What other effect can the detailed description of a banquet have on such a person except grief and pain? If you can, stride forth, offer up your life and risk your head!

It is impossible, by mere talking, to attain union with Him:
In no way can the expanse of the ocean be controlled by a
  dam!

Every heart that experiences death has breached the gates of eternal bliss. One cannot remove the obstacle of a claim to fame, which is the obstruction and knot of this Way, except by reflection on death. There was a spiritual master who was called Sayyid ul-Autad [The Chief Axis]. His real name was *Kalib*, which in Arabic means "a small dog." He was close to death. Despite this he experienced a great deprivation; indeed, ten days and nights passed during which not a morsel of bread reached him. Khair Nisaj said that he was walking by the saint's hermitage one day. He heard Kalib say to God in the midst of all his mortifications: "O God, my name means 'small dog.' Is it for this reason that I am inflicted with leprosy and undergo all the privations of poverty and destitution? With such great adversity to endure, where is Gabriel? He should see me sally forth to battle!"

Those who, delivered from their bodies, travel toward the
  Throne
Experience the protection of Gabriel's royal wings enfolding
  them.

O brother, there is but one God. There is also but one believer. Since the divine essence is unique, it is fitting that a believer be nothing except one. The proof of this saying is shown in the profession of faith: Half is "separation" and half is "making friends." "There is no god" is separation, and "but God" is making friends. To the extent that you drive out "not-God," you will be chosen by God as His friend. Hence arises the lament of all who say:

Where is that fire in which I may burn this cloak?
For upon my back it shows itself to be but a sacred thread!

Everyone who claims to be a believer has to look deeply into himself. If anything besides God is found there, and he flees from it, then know that his claim is genuine. But if he sees himself seeking the secret of anything that is not God, and fleeing from everything that leads toward God, then he should weep over his faith, for either he has already lost it or is in imminent danger of doing so. The secret of this has been thus expressed:

> Up till now you have been totally ignorant of your infidelity!
> How then can you possibly know about the realities of faith?

Hence a wise one has said: "The whole world claims to be a lover and to love, but when you examine this claim, all play the role of the beloved, not that of a lover. When a lover claims to love, the genuineness of his claim becomes clear the moment that he emerges purified from all selfish desire. As long as he seeks his own desire, he is really seeking to be the beloved of all, not the lover of all. His affairs put the lie to his claim! Hence you can understand that his claim to be a lover is false so long as he desires even the smallest particle besides the Beloved! A hint has been given to us in this verse: "O you who believe, believe [again] in God and His messenger and the book etc." (Q4:136). The believers are commanded to believe again, even though they are already believers, for they have been led to realize through this "second" faith what was intended by the "first" faith. The initial faith is a testifying and establishing. It is a verification of the truth, and the establishing that there is nothing to see except Him. Whenever man looks at anything besides God, he becomes like it. You would say that he has returned to the first level of faith and is not yet completely freed of the grip of looking at "other than God." "Review your faith!" is the universal command. "Do not look, as it were, inside your own gullet! Look rather into the Artisan of the gullet, so that the slave may flee from every danger and difficulty that comes to him, and return to God. His faith should be constantly scrutinized."

O brother, the eternal bliss awaiting you has been thus described: "O handful of dust, be for Me with a pure heart! O drop of thin water, look nowhere except toward Me! O fragment of clay, place your foot in the garden of union! What wealth will be yours! Beyond that, each day, five times, the beast that bears the burden of union by virtue of the divine command is sent to the door of your lowly cottage and makes this announcement throughout the world: 'Prayer has been apportioned between Me and My slave!' "

It is not enough for me to be called a slave:
Let me be known as the dust at the head of Your lane!

Moses, the man who spoke with God, waited forty days and nights in expectation of Him. When it became Muhammad's turn this waiting was removed and exchanged for a vessel filled to the brim with union, which he enjoyed, from time to time, at the hand of the gracious cupbearer! "Prayer is the ascent of hearts." This is not to exalt believers over the prophets, but "those who are more indigent and needy enjoy a greater measure of God's kindness."

Your revolution is beyond the confines of the revolving
    heavens:
Your magnificence far exceeds that of both worlds!

*Peace!*


## LETTER 66: LINEAGE

*In the name of God, the Merciful, the Compassionate!*

Dear Brother Shamsuddin, descent from Adam becomes legitimate for a traveler when it pervades the realm of his heart; then the complete revolution of the world has taken place! This is where one's mode of behavior should originate. Whatever he comes in contact with also gets changed, just as he himself has been changed. Whatever you heard that has appeared by the hand of his authority, namely that a certain dervish was able to turn wine into sherbet, or a bitter plant into a sweet fig—at this stage, all this would be proper. If he wanted, such a traveler could extend his hand toward the wealth of kings, and obtain it. It has been related by certain sheikhs, and it is also the injunction of the Law, that if there is blood from east to west, then a believer would not taste of it. He would eat only what was lawful. The reality of faith cannot be realized until it reaches the realm of the heart. But first there must be a good understanding of the Law, and it is this point that is conveyed in a story about a young man who came to the Prophet and asked if it was permissible to kiss in the month of Ramazan. He was told that it would not be lawful. Afterwards, an old man came to Muhammad. He asked the very same question. He was told it was lawful for him. The companions were astonished when they heard this. "O messenger of God," they protested, "you allowed to one what you forbade to another!" "The first one was young," he replied, "and there was danger of misfortune resulting from the fire of his youth, while the latter was an old man; he could be trusted." Hence it became known that the Law changes from man to man.[72] This is the reason why someone enjoys miraculous power and walks on water, while another, if he were to attempt to do the same, would only sink! Whoever imitates the former in this stage and claims authority over the wealth of kings, even though he really should not be stepping in this direction, will discover that he is simply trying to destroy himself!

This step should be taken only with the permission of the Lord, and when a traveler's heart has been blessed. All the parts of the Sufi master become "heart." It is not fitting that anything belonging to him, from his toenails to the hair on his head, should go to waste, for they too partake of the world of the heart. Hence it used to happen that when the Prophet combed out his hair, the companions used to distribute among themselves the hairs that fell. Every garment that he wore was endowed with a special power because it was his. Hence it was that the Prophet gave a shirt of his to a hypocrite in order to console the man's son, who was a Muslim. That very same shirt was placed on the grave of the hypocrite when he died. Some companions asked the Prophet if it would be of any benefit to him. "As long as even a thread of it remains," replied he, "that man will not have to undergo any torments." Hence it is that young men treat the patched robe of their spiritual master as a blessed thing and distribute it. Everyone receives a portion of it. What is the purpose of such distribution unless it be the garment of a genuine master whose heart has been touched? Anyone whose conversion has been complete and who has reached the world of heart[73] becomes a man of prayer and a religious leader. It would be proper for such a person to make claims, but someone who has not yet reached this stage should not attempt such a thing.

Hence it was that Ali, the Commander of the Faithful, came to Basra and spoke to Khwaja Hasan of Basra, a saint unique in his age, making him understand that whatever comes from a man's heart is that to which he ought to submit.

O brother, if it was said concerning the Prophet himself, "Undoubtedly you can show the straight way!" then this royal proclamation also was made to the spiritual masters: "Among those whom We created is a community guided by truth and dispensing justice" (Q7:181). If you say, "How shall we know that someone is a pretender, or has been genuinely authorized by God?" the answer is: "If the seeker is genuine in his search, he will be granted an inner eye, which will enable him to see the authorization of the King. He will not be misled by the claims of pretenders!" Do you not see that if thousands of kinds of animals are gathered together, and thousands of varieties of food are placed before them, the palate of each will tell it which is the food suitable for it? No animal will desire the food of another. The Quran itself gives us a hint in this matter in the verse where it is written: "Each group knew what to drink" (Q2:60). Seek the humble service of the manly ones! If you seek service among the false claimants, there will be no profit. A pretender is not fit for this work! Who is a pretender? One who has neither seen the Way to God, nor traveled it, nor acquired it. All he does is make claims! The Quran gives us a hint of this: "If you obey most of those in the earth, they will lead you astray from the path of God!" (Q6:117).

When most people have lost the way, then there will certainly be fewer guides! When a genuine seeker is given a glimpse of the eternal sign of approval he recognizes it and focuses his attention on that one point. There his palate finds its proper food and nourishment. The spiritual master will take charge of him. He will become like a dead man, and his master like the washer, cleansing him of all that is not fitting till he has been fully purified. When this takes place, his conversion will have become complete; he will have become a real traveler on the Way to the Lord! This is called his "manner of acting." "God is pure, and He does not accept any except the pure."

This is genuine devotion, O brother, not the sort of thing you consider to be devotion! Whenever you pray, observe the fast, or give alms, you should realize that this is devotion to your mother, father, fellow-citizens, and to your own habits, but the command is this: "If you serve the Lord, you will find guidance." It is not said: "If you are devoted to your own habits you will receive guidance." Whatever you do at the command of a master of the heart is genuine worship, and its fruit is divine guidance. "Whoever obeys the Prophet, obeys God" (Q4:80). Nothing more need be said.

If you reflect a little, one prostration of prayer, performed at the command of a master of the heart, is better than a thousand whose basis is one's own desire and habit. Similarly, one day spent in fasting at his behest is better than a thousand days of fasting according to one's own inclination. And if you give one silver piece at the command of a master of the heart, it is better than giving a thousand according to your own custom and preference.

O brother, strive to discern how you can extricate yourself from habit and how you can seek after true religion! It is not possible to rise above habit, or actions that are superficially sincere, except through submission to men of the Way. From his store of knowledge the spiritual master, at the opportune moment, breaks the snare; gradually each day he leads a disciple out of the bonds of Satan and clothes his nature with the robe of "There is no god but God!" This is because the master is acquainted with the condition into which a person is born, as well as his inner disposition. Whatever someone has imbibed from his parents is firmly established within him. Twenty years later, he is the same. Similarly, thirty, forty, fifty—and even till the very end of his life he remains the same person, with the same face and beard he had at the outset.

Men of God are different from men of habit and men of the world. How could anyone who does nothing, night or day, except worship his own habits, and knows no other work except foolishness and pandering to his own desires, be equal to someone who has shouldered the burden of the first steps of the Way to God? This requires the cutting of the idolatrous thread of habit, and the cessation of dalliance with this world and the next. In an ecstatic state, a Sufi proclaimed:

> I saw the basis of this world and its foundation;
> Easily did I pass beyond the trap of habit!
> I realized that a black light is better than "There is no god";
> And yet I passed beyond that too: neither now remains!

As far as possible, be always in quest of Him! It might happen that, while you are seeking, He will reveal His own beauty to you. If one day He removes the veil that conceals His beauty, a great change will occur in you.[74] There will not remain enough of you to be able to discern whether you are a seeker or not! Hence it is that a wise one has said: "Every form of seeking in which you see yourself is far from real seeking." Do you not see that if a man is completely intoxicated he has no idea that he is drunk! Alas, as long as even a fraction of his awareness remains, and he has enough power to discern that he is drunk and others are sober, he is not yet utterly inebriated! What is the perfection of intoxication? It occurs when the existence of man is given over to plunder! If it is said to him, "Are you part of the human race or not?" he makes no reply. If he says anything, he is still possessed of the power to discriminate. Hence something remains. Have you not heard what was said?

> So dumbstruck have I been with love for You
> That only the shell of my existence remains!

When the reality of seeking shows its face, then no element remains in the seeker. When this takes place, "Whoever seeks, finds" turns out to be true. At this stage there is nothing left for the disciple to do. The searching itself becomes pure. Hence an inflamed soul has said:

> Love does all that is necessary: be patient!
> Simply be a disciple! Let love be your master—that is all!

"Whoever desires anything else cannot find Me" is a saying that should never be forgotten. As long as there is even a tiny part of you that seeks anything except God, you are not a genuine seeker. In the end it becomes apparent what exactly your nature is. How can you possibly attain your Object, in view of this constricted nature of yours? "You love Him" (Q5:54) becomes correct the moment you are completely turned toward Him! The one referred to in "He loves you" (Q5:54) has thousands of loved ones. There is no difficulty for Him: He can reach all, but your nature is extremely limited!

The sun can have an effect everywhere because its visage is so broad. It reaches India and Turkey, yet is not restricted to them. Until your nature is completely exposed to the sun, however, it cannot receive any share of its rays. It has to be completely exposed to the sun in order to derive influence from it. Many thousands of worlds can derive a share from its rays. It is in no way diminished as a result of this. "Among His signs is the sun." This should be studied carefully, and one further point should be noted: Loving something partial and dependent in no way detracts from the perfection of love,[75] as has been said:

> My love for Laila makes me love the countryside of Nejd.
> Apart from my love for her, I would have no interest in it!
> One reaches the stage of loving one's enemies
> Because they are closely united to God!

Welcome to me are the reproaches of men due to my love for
  You!
For those who rebuke me also bring Your love to mind!

This is not associating others in one's love; instead, it constitutes
some intimations of one's love for one's Friend! It was because of his
love that Majnun considered black to be the very best color, as has
been said:

It is for Laila's sake that black is so pleasing to me:
In my love for her, how precious indeed is her black hue!

O brother, the world of love is indeed an incredible place! Where
else, except in the world of love, could you find love for one's very enemies? A group was heading off to do battle with some infidels. Abul
Abbas Qassab said to them: "Take my beard as an offering for the
dust beneath the feet of that infidel whom you will kill for the sake of
God!" The Prophet said about himself: "If I were to make friends
with anyone, then it certainly would be with Abu Bakr, but I have already made friends with God!" It is not fitting for anyone to ask:
"Why did the Prophet get entangled with his wives and children?" It
is known that when he was asked who his favorite wife was, he replied, "Aisha." When asked who his favorite friend was, he said,
"Abu Bakr." To this extent had human love found a place in him.
"But Muhammad had already made God his Friend." In a similar
way, the Prophet was attached to his son Abraham, and wept when
the child died. Concerning Hasan and Husain he said: "Our offspring
are as close to us as our own livers." What does this mean? Perplexity
occurs at the beginning, but for those endowed with insight there is
no such ambiguity!

O brother, consider a person who is utterly in love with study.
He has no other task, day or night, except to pursue his quest for
knowledge. Now if he loves his pen, paper, and ink, you cannot say
that he is not completely devoted to study! Without doubt a beloved
should in essence be only one, but if other things are loved because of
their dependence on the real Beloved, then no harm arises; for a man
who loves Almighty God will inevitably also love the prophets as
well as his spiritual masters and teachers. It is also entirely reasonable
that he will love all things associated with Him. The whole world is
His masterpiece, His structure, and His writing. He Himself is neces-

sarily all of it—if one insists on making a measurement.[76] A poet noted for insight has said:

> In Your presence there is no room for duality:
> All the worlds are but You and Your power!
> The whole created order is but a shadow in Your presence:
> All things are the result of Your majestic handicraft!

But if it is the good pleasure of the Friend that a certain letter written by His own hand should be burned, then the lover must certainly burn it. Let no one say that he has shown disrespect to the letter of his Friend, for the seeker has carried out His will. "This is a very high stage for you." If the Chosen One and his companions removed infidels from His way, they did so at His bidding. Should not the seeker's good pleasure be whatever He intends? What does a lover have to do with authority in the kingdom of the Beloved?

*Peace!*

## LETTER 67: A GOOD MENTAL ATTITUDE

*In the name of God, the Merciful, the Compassionate!*

Dear Brother Shamsuddin, this group has a better attitude toward God than all others. Khwaja Yahya Mu'az said: "Everyone who does not have a good attitude toward God Almighty cannot have his face illumined by Him!" This accords with what the Prophet recorded: "God Almighty says: 'I am close to the mental outlook of My slave, namely, to what he thinks of Me and desires. I know what My slave thinks about Me, and I deal with him according to what I know.'" It is related in the story of Joseph that he said to Zulaikha: "Your husband has a good opinion of me. He says of me: 'Perhaps he will be of some use to us' (Q21:21). I will not do anything against him."

When a creature does not oppose the good opinion of an infidel, then how much the more will God Almighty not oppose the good attitude of believers? The secret of this has been put thus:

> O Generous One Who, out of Your hidden treasure,
> Give sustenance to Zoroastrians and Christians,
> How could You possibly disappoint Your friends,
> You, a King, with eyes even for me?

Having a good opinion of somebody results from an experience of his generosity, while a suspicious attitude toward a person would indicate the opposite experience. Everyone who has an actual experience of the generosity of somebody becomes an even firmer friend of his. Khwaja Yahya Mu'az said: "Everyone who does not have a good opinion of God does not have his inner eye illuminated by Him." It is because of this tradition that he says that God's attitude toward you will accord with your opinion of Him.[77] If you have a suspicious attitude toward Him, then He too is suspicious. No one who experiences bad things from God will ever have his eye illuminated by Him. Another meaning is that one is very suspicious of one's enemy but trusts one's friends. One's heart is lit up by one's friends, not by one's enemies. Suspicion signifies the onset of enmity, while a good opinion points to incipient love. Here is something of fundamental importance and constituting a very delicate point in which the majority of men are deceived: it is necessary to distinguish between simply desiring something on the one hand and being really hopeful and having a proper attitude on the other.[78] Hope and a proper attitude have some basis, whereas vain desire is without root or justification. As an example of both of these, consider a person who does some cultivating. He prepares the land, ploughs the soil, casts the seed, and, in general, does all that is required in order to secure a good crop. Then he says that he hopes, with the blessing of Almighty God, that he will obtain such and such as a result of his labors. This desire is genuine hope and shows a proper attitude. Another fellow does no work, leaves the land as it is, passes his time in sleeping and idles away the whole year. When the time of harvest arrives he says that he hopes, with God's blessing, to obtain some grain from his field. Every intelligent person who hears such nonsense will get very annoyed and say: "How can you possibly get anything?" This is simply vain desire! Well-founded desire is like a slave who struggles to be devoted to God, and carries out to the letter whatever He has commanded. He keeps away from sin. He says: "I hope that God Himself will accept this little I have to offer. He is the one who can make up for my shortcomings. He is the One Who rewards and He is the One Who forgives." Now, such a desire shows a good outlook and firm hope having a solid basis; but when someone remains foolish, abandons submission, gives himself up to sin, has no fear of God in his heart, and pays no attention either to ritual or legal obligations, but says instead: "I hope that God will grant me heaven, and save me from hell!"—clearly this is but vain desire! It has no basis, for nothing can be obtained by it. Yet he has the audacity to call it a good attitude. This is a great fault, about which the Prophet commented: "A wise man is he who supervises his soul and acts with a view to his death, but a fool is he who thinks only of himself and still expects God to forgive him."

Having grasped this, you must realize that these people exalt themselves above the rest of creation: "They consider themselves to be beyond advice, whether in temporal or religious matters!" They say that they took note of what Joseph said, even though he was a prophet: "I do not call myself sinless, for myself still urges me to sin!" (Q12:53). If this is the description of the state of soul of the prophets, then what must that of others be like? The secret of this condition has been thus expressed:

> As long as you are enmeshed by self and Satan,
> You will act like Pharaoh or Haman!
> If you accede to the inclinations of your soul, beware!
> All your members, from head to toe, will weep over you!

Know that the association of this group with their souls should be as though they were already beyond this world. They do not grant their souls anything they desire. Whatever the soul commands, even if it be full of devotion, would not be for his peace.[79] Everyone who entrusts himself to his enemy will soon be destroyed. For the believer, self is the real enemy, while God is his friend. For an enemy, there is nothing but suspicion, whereas for a friend, there is nothing except a good opinion! Everyone whose friend can be of assistance to him will certainly not associate with his enemy! The reason is that, by associating with his enemy, he cuts himself off from his friend. Some great men have said:

> If two friends are completely devoted to each other,
> Then a single hair between them would act like a curtain!

It would be a sin for a mystic to think about anything else except God! The desire of anything except God would be polytheism. Associating with anything other than God would be infidelity. An adulterer does not flee from his adultery the way these people flee from such things! This is their oppression and sin—not the sort of thing you and I are guilty of! Majnun was asked: "What is your relationship to God?" He replied: "When I recognized Him, I ceased all oppressive behavior!" "When did this occur?" He replied: "From the time people began calling me 'Majnun' [a madman]." Actually, the truth is the very opposite of this! A madman is one who brings anything other than God into his heart, not the one who brings God into his heart in place of the world!

> I desire no chains other than Your tresses.
> See what a wise madman I am!

This path is called the path of blame. Those who follow it are called the blameworthy ones, because they have seen that good fortune and rank in the eyes of the people are more dangerous for a slave than a thousand idols. An idol cannot cut off a unitarian in the way that rank and position can! There is a story in this vein concerning Bayazid, the prince of mystic knowers. He entered a certain city. The people received him very well. He perceived that his attachment to the people was resulting in his becoming distant from God. His strength no longer remained. He left the city. The people accompanied him out of the city. He said to his servant, Abdullah Duvaili: "Watch how I worship my own soul!" The servant said: I was watching to see what he would do. He performed two ceremonial prayers. He stood up and turned toward the people. The people thought he was about to pray. Instead, he said: "Surely I am God. There is no god but Me, so worship Me!" (Q20:14). Everyone said: "Bayazid has become an infidel! He has claimed to be God!" Everyone got up and left him alone. But he had not claimed to be God. He had simply recited a verse from the Quran. The servant said: He turned to me and said: "My son, you saw that I recited a verse from the Quran and what misfortune befell me!" The secret is contained in this:

> Beware, for by being flayed, I shall be purified!
> All for Your sake, O dear, knowing Friend!
> If I love another, why should I fear the people?
> If I have my Beloved, I shall throw dust upon the whole world!

Associating with anything other than God is polytheism. Looking at anything except God is a veil. A unitarian is single. Everyone looks at him. He does not look at anything except God. His fear overcomes all other fears. His hope overcomes all other hopes. His glory overshadows all other glory. His kingdom vanquishes all other kingdoms. His power subdues all other powers. The same could be said for His other qualities. The Messenger has given us a hint of this when he said: "In my union with God there comes a time when no angel near to God or prophet could draw breath." The secret of this was revealed by God alone. Nothing remained as a blockage between him and God! He experienced the perfection of singularity. That stage is not for everybody, and yet each could have some experience of it, in accordance with his capacity. When a slave's capacity for perception is perfected, he has nothing to fear from this world or from a thousand similar ones. [A poem follows.]

Hence realize that no matter what claim creatures make to manifestations of divine unity, they are still really veiled. They have not had any experience. Whoever has a truly divine experience, in which a taste of the divine unity is granted, has no fear of anything but God, nor does he hope for anything from any source other than God. In fact, he sees nothing but God! He associates with none other than God. Of this secret the poet said:

Apart from You and me, it seems nothing else exists:
What is there that can mediate between us?
I do not want even the sun to rise together with You.
And when You Yourself come, I want no shadow to come with
  You!

The swooning Majnun said, "When I recognized Him, I stopped my oppressive behavior. Namely, when I saw that He had graciously granted me mystical insight into Himself, I recognized that being immersed in anything other than Him was intolerable behavior, as was paying attention to anything but Him. Such is the iniquity of preoccupation with other than God; it is no mere sin. When God showers His favors upon me by removing the veil upon my head so that I can see Him, then if I look at anything besides Him, I again place a veil between Him and me. Being well known among the people means that when someone is talking to another person, if the latter does not pay attention to what the former is saying, he exclaims, "Don't ignore me like this!" Also, if a friend has eyes only for his friend, but then begins to glance elsewhere, his friend will say: "Such behavior is intolerable!" Ismi has something to say about this in a story he relates. I saw a really beautiful girl. My heart went out to her. I said to her: "My whole being is completely taken up with you!" She said: "If this is true, I too will lavish myself entirely upon you! Yet I must tell you that I have a sister. Once you see her face you will become oblivious to my beauty!" "Where is she?" I asked. "Right behind you!" I turned and looked behind me. She jumped up and hit me on the back, saying:

"O deceiver! If your being was completely engrossed in mine, how could you possibly look at another?"

As far as Sufis are concerned, this is the sort of thing they call "iniquity"! Majnun said, "When I recognized Him, people called me mad," by which he meant that to the extent that mystical knowledge is granted to a person there is a corresponding turning away from what is not God. Whoever turns away from creatures, however, becomes, in the eyes of people, a madman. A Sufi has the quality of turning away from whatever people put before him. The very thing ordinary people are partial to is that from which he flees. His qualities, actions, deeds, and states are exactly opposite to those of most people. This is why he is called mad. As someone has explained: "Heavenly minded people are usually considered to be rather foolish." Certainly those who flee from people and from the world are labeled as foolish. There is nothing strange about this, for the simple reason that just as the mad are adjudged mad by intelligent folk, so the mad deem the intelligent to be mad! One beloved of God has put it thus:

> Those who are forever occupied with prayer
> Should be considered as initiates into the Mystery.
> They do depend on no one at all,
> Except for the One without need Whom they continually
>     remember.
> They are forever burning in the oven of poverty
> And being consumed with their own grief.
> At one stroke they are cut off from both worlds,
> And are separated from whatever is less than God!

A number of books have related the saying of the Almighty: "I have created the whole world for your sake, and you for My sake." One day, a religious-minded man was looking at himself in a mirror. He was dumbstruck realizing what wisdom God had displayed in creating him. He heard a voice from the mirror saying: "My real wisdom in creating you is that love which has been implanted in your heart." This remains a hidden secret to prevent jealous eyes from falling on it.

O brother, if He had not granted you kingship, you could not possibly have attained a genuine mystical insight into Him, for only kings can recognize kings! Listen to what the Quran has to say: "I

have made you a caliph and granted you kingship" (Q10:14). Khwaja
Nizami has given us a hint when he says:

> Your dust is intermingled with much grief:
> Many are the treasures hidden in this dust!
> Your dust, on the day of mixing,
> Was stirred by the feet of one familiar with the heart.
> We who have mastered knowledge of the hearts,
> Though we come from a mine of clay, are precious gems.
> Ascend to the sky and scan it with your heart.
> So long as you remain in this dust, what will you gain?

*Peace!*

### LETTER 68: THE WORLD TO COME

*In the name of God, the Merciful, the Compassionate!*

Brother Shamsuddin, may God reveal to you the way to eternal bliss!
There are two groups of travelers along the path leading to the world
to come, namely the blessed and the wicked. Each group travels in its
own particular way. The road along which they travel is this. Everyone who experiences felicity as he travels along arrives at the world to
come. The blessed themselves can be divided into two groups: those
who are privileged, and ordinary people. These ordinary people travel along the path of struggle with their own soul and its unruly desires. They also try to abandon delights and lustful passions. Thus
they travel along the road of submission to the commands of the Law
and of observing the traditions. They thus arrive at the resurrection
of paradise and its various degrees. The privileged ones, on the other
hand, "whom He loves," travel along the road of "and they love
Him" (Q5:54). And in the next life they will sit "in the seat of
strength, with a powerful King" (Q54:55) and reach the stage of favor
where "those who fear God will enjoy the pleasures of gardens and
canals" (Q54:54).

> Why do you reject the state of the dervishes?
> What has been denied you may not have been denied others.

The wicked also fall into two groups. The first comprises ordinary wicked people, the second the incorrigible. Ordinary wicked

ones are the majority of sinners in the Muslim community who act in response to the unruly desires of their souls and persevere in their opposition to the commands of the Lord. They are engrossed in obtaining all the pleasure they can by fulfilling all the desires of their lower soul and animal nature. Running headlong down the road of sin, they end up in the lowest pits of hell. The very wicked have the bad qualities of infidels; they are entirely devoted to seeking and enjoying whatever this world has to offer. They are intent on deriving maximum pleasure out of what they do, and they try to indulge all the cravings of their souls and bodies. They turn their backs on the work of religion and on the world to come. They exchange eternal bliss for temporary comfort. They do not get all they want in this world, while the next world has already slipped from their grasp. "Whoever desires the produce of this world, We will comply with his wish and he will have no share in the blessings that are to come" (Q42:20). Ordinary wicked people derive their fate from their faith, on the basis of the wealth that is on their tongues, even though they do not implement the pillars of Islam in their affairs and actions. It is certain that, according to the threat of the Lord, they will go to hell and will have to undergo the punishments of that world, but, at the last, because of what was at least upon their tongues, they will find liberation from their torments.

It is related in a genuine Prophetic tradition that one group will be led out of hell. It will only burn like coal in a small stove. This group will be taken to the canal of life. New flesh and skin will appear. When they are taken from there they will become radiant like the moon. These words will be written on their foreheads: "Here are those liberated from hell by God Almighty." The very wicked, however, will be confirmed in their sentence of everlasting torment. Why? Because they derived no benefit from the light of "There is no god but God," which was the cause of the liberation of the former group. Hence hell is, for them, eternal. For the various groups in hell and its nethermost regions, there are different stages in relation to others, as was said about the hypocrites: "The hypocrites will be in the lowest reaches of hell!" (Q4:145). Even in hypocrisy itself there will be degrees. The reward of each person will be proportionate to his conduct. Among the infidels there are imitators of good example and investigators of the Truth. Just as the belief of an investigator or an apt imitator has its appropriate reward, so the punishment of an infidel in search of truth will be greater than that of a blind imitator.

The infidelity of imitating others relates to what has been acquired from one's parents. "Surely we found our fathers practicing a religion, and we merely walk in their footsteps" (Q43:23). Such people will be cast into the first stage of hell. The infidelity of investigators of the Truth refers to those who have seen what their parents do and not been content with what was acquired from them. They make an effort and even suffer in their search for proofs, passing their lives in the acquisition of knowlege about their infidel doctrines; through the study of books and also austerities as well as self-struggle, they become totally absorbed in their search for that knowledge. They make great efforts to purify their souls for the sake of reflecting on reasons and arguments, that they might investigate intricate points and thus deny the Creator. Or they might find defects in confirming the existence of the Creator. They might say: "The Creator is not supreme!" or "He is not a knower of particulars!"

There are many other infidel sayings similar to these to which all wayward groups subscribe. Satan has been enhanced in their hearts and opinions. They make claims, saying: "Whoever is not endowed with this knowledge, and is not of this faith, is defective in knowledge and mystic intuition." They go so far as to say that the prophets were philosophers and whatever they said was the result of their own wisdom. They also adduce many other invalid opinions and suspicions and continue to be immersed in the search for this temptingly provocative yet destructive knowledge. They call it the "knowledge of the principles of religion," that nobody might detect the impurity of their faith. Those devoid of insight, out of mere imitation, accept those expressions of infidelity and completely pass beyond the pale of Islam. Many calamities occur for them.[80] May God protect us from such things!

O brother, if sinners do not submit, then they quite naturally continue to sin. There is a secret hidden here about which Khwaja Mu'az has spoken: "If it were not known that the quality most prized by God is His forgiveness, then Adam, by eating the wheat, would not have sorely tried Him!" The favorite slave of the sultan stands at the very edge of the carpet, while the courtiers and the great nobles are seated around the throne itself. In spite of his distance, however, the slave has a hundred thousand jokes up his sleeve of which the courtiers and nobles, despite their proximity to the sultan, are ignorant. His distance is not that of reproach for error; it is the distance of an amorous glance! A hundred thousand closely kept secrets are progressively revealed to one at a distance, and a hundred thousand remote secrets are revealed in intimacy, till astonishment knows no bounds! You see the branch in a mosque, yet the root is in a church. Umar was on his way, with drawn sword, when a voice came from the hidden world: "Let the slave of the Lord of both worlds have free passage!" Does astonishment know any limits? A Sufi has said:

> A fire was enkindled on the water of life,
> Which consumed both the faith and infidelity of lovers.
> Sometimes your rage raises swords from dark fortune;
> At other times your mercy lights candles as bright as ruby lips!
> In one hour Joseph experienced Your love in the well,
> Though intellects had missed it for a hundred years!

*Peace!*

## LETTER 69: RETAINING OR ABANDONING POSSESSIONS

*In the name of God, the Merciful, the Compassionate!*

Dear Brother Shamsuddin, may God bless you! As far as this group is concerned, there are different states in which a person should retain possessions or abandon them. There might be someone who depends on gifts but pays no attention to where they came from, nor does he think about working or begging. This sort of person would be one who, at the proper time, receives a command to abandon all concern about ways and means. He will be someone who has experienced a manifestation of the divine. It implies that he has had a genuine, indubitable experience of the divine Unity. He is looked after perfectly by the Lord Himself. Any inner anxiety springing from different ways and means is destroyed. Whoever finds himself in this state would actually be relying wholly upon the Lord. Khwaja Bayazid Bistami was told: "We do not see you engaged in any preoccupation. Where does your sustenance come from?" He said: "My Lord provides dogs and pigs with their daily needs, so why will He not feed Abu Yazid as well?"

One of the wise said: "A truly poor man is the one who does not even depend on the Lord!" This means he has so much righteousness and trust that he knows that God will give him his daily needs even if he does not ask for it.

The gifts God provides for your needs will not be lost.
Do God's work! Do not worry about daily needs!

There might be another who will have to work for his livelihood. This goes back to Adam himself, who was a farmer and taught his sons how to cultivate the soil. Do you not see that Shu'aib [Jethro] was a trader and the shepherd of many flocks? Moses, too, looked after his flocks. David was a maker of coats of mail. Solomon used to make sacks out of leaves of date palm and sell them for two pieces of barley bread. One he would give to the dervishes, the other he would keep for his own daily sustenance. Abraham was the shepherd of many flocks. In fact, he had to spend four thousand pieces of silver purchasing slaves to look after them all. Even some of the companions of the Prophet engaged in trade, such as Usman and Abdul Rahman ibn Auf. If it were true that such activities were an impediment to perfect trust in God, then the prophets would have remained at a distance from them, for prophets are more filled with trust than others. The Prophet used to admonish his close friends lest their trust lead to harm. It is obligatory for a person to work in order to provide for those who are dependent on him. Indeed, it is a serious duty![81] It has been reported that the Prophet used to put aside a year's provisions for his dependents. And yet it has also been said that one's livelihood should not drive the slave away from God. If anyone understands his own condition so well that he can say: "If I don't work, my soul will turn away from God and run after creatures," then work is as obligatory for him as are the prescribed prayers. Again, if when he works he puts his confidence in the work itself, it would be better not to work. In short, he should look at his own condition, examining both his internal and external circumstances, considering both work, and abandoning work. If he considers that abandoning work will drive him away from God, then it would be better for him to work. If, however, work takes him away from God, but abandoning work drives him toward God, then it would be better for him to lay aside his work.

It is related that Khwaja Junaid said: "Earning wages is making use of the relaxation of the Law, as can be done in all instances of works of supererogation." It does not mean that one sees one's daily sustenance as coming from one's labors, or that one seeks to derive advantage for oneself from it. The meaning of the saying has been put thus: "It is quite lawful to earn one's own livelihood, just as it is lawful to fast and to pray." The more you do these the better it is, but you should not regard your actions as a basis for your own advantage. Nor should you consider that your own salvation is found in the actions you perform, for if a slave thinks that his salvation comes from anything besides God, he commits polytheism. One should do one's best, and give the glory to God. You yourself can verify your own love, as has been said:

When your love proves to be true, then you will obey it,
For the one who loves is obedient to the One Whom he loves!

In all circumstances, however, salvation should be seen as deriving from the grace of God, not from one's own service. Work is also like this. Engage in work, but do not see your daily sustenance as coming from your efforts. You should see it as deriving from the grace of God. This door, like the door of service, has been opened for you. Among dervishes there might be somebody who, at the time of necessity, is reduced to the begging of the indigent. As has been said, if a dervish struggles hard with all his strength and yet it happens that, for a while, his needs are not fulfilled, and if he beseeches the Lord but nothing is revealed to him, nor is the divine decree with regard to him made known, and out of concern for his own condition he devotes himself to work while his circumstances are straightened, it might happen that he says something about the reason and begs from respectable people. This is because the pious, in time of necessity, used to beg from good people, just as has been related about Khwaja Abu Sa'id Kharraz. He used to stretch out his hand in the time of necessity and say, "A little something, for the sake of God!" And Khwaja Abu Hafs Haddad, who was the master of Khwaja Junaid, used to come outside between the evening and night prayer and beg from one or two people according to his needs. He would repeat this after a day or two. His actions were known, and the reason became clear.

It is related about Khwaja Ibrahim Adham that he had been in seclusion in the principal mosque of Basra for some time. After three days and nights, he would take a slight repast. The night he ate something, he would go begging from door to door. It is also related about

Khwaja Sufyan that while he was making a journey from the Hijaz to
San'a in Yemen, he would beg on the way.

This was the sort of behavior of all the people whom we have
called to mind. One should always keep in view the limits of good behavior, however, and never go beyond them. When an indigent person has knowingly brought his soul under strict control, then God
Almighty will grant him a knowledge and an insight according to
which he will come to perceive the proper circumstances in which he
should beg, and also those in which he should not.[82] As far as possible, it is best for a dervish not to beg, because many allurements and
dangers can find their way into this practice.

According to the sheikhs there are three reasons for resorting to
begging. One is to obtain freedom of heart, which is very desirable indeed! They say: "We do not hold those in esteem who claim: Night
and day we pass our time waiting for Him and, but for Him, we experience no need. God has endowed us with the state of restraint from
becoming engrossed with anything, since being engrossed is not very
laudable." Hence it is that Khwaja Bayazid asked a disciple of Khwaja
Shafiq, who had come to visit him, how his spiritual guide was. The
disciple said: "He has been freed from all created concerns. He is
wholly given over to trusting to God." "When you return," instructed Bayazid, "tell him to be careful not to put God to the test for the
sake of a couple of pieces of bread! At the time he is hungry, he
should beg a little bread from his fellowmen. The command to trust
should be tempered, lest that city and province be brought low as a
result of the stinginess displayed in this one matter."

The second reason is that begging is a good form of asceticism
for one's soul, for it kills the self-esteem of a person, and the grief experienced can effect a change of heart, and those practicing it might
thus know their own value by discovering their worth in the eyes of
others. Have you not heard what Shibli was told by Junaid: "Your
head is filled with haughtiness and ideas of your own importance,
thinking to yourself: 'I am the son of the chief chamberlain of the Caliph; I am the son of a man of consequence'? You will not be able to
make any progress until you go to the bazaar and beg from every
shop and every door and so discover your real worth." This is exactly
what he did, for he was a genuine seeker. Day by day he received less
and less in the bazaar until, by the end of a year, he was reduced to
such a state that, even though he went through the whole bazaar, he

did not receive even the smallest coin. He returned and explained his situation to Khwaja Junaid, who said: "Now you know your worth in the eyes of people. You are not worth even the smallest coin!" This is a very beneficial sort of discipline for one's self-esteem!

The third is that begging helps people realize that everything belongs to Him. They see all creatures as His representatives. They ask One of His representatives for whatever is needed for the good of their own souls. They tell him what they have to say about themselves. It is up to the discernment and witnessing of the slave to know when he should petition a representative for the fulfillment of his needs. This is a better form of service and submission than to approach his Lord directly.[83] Their begging is a sign of His presence, and an acknowledgement of God, not of His absence, or of a turning away from Him.

Khwaja Yahya Mu'az had a daughter. One day she said to her mother that she needed something or other. Her mother told her to ask God for it. She replied that she was ashamed to beg for the needs of her soul from God himself. Even the fact of a person's asking is a gift of God! The proper way to beg would be by not being happier at having your request heeded than you would be if it were *not* granted. You should not see creatures as being interposed between yourself and God.

Nor should you reveal your plight to anyone except a person whose property has been clearly obtained by legitimate means. What is obtained by begging is not meant for any sort of display, nor should it be turned into one's own property. One should observe carefully the exigencies of the situation. Do not let the saying about tomorrow pass by your soul! And do not be content to beg all the time. And, above all, do not display your own piety in order to acquire things by means of it!

A famous Sufi came in from the wilderness. He was penniless and suffering from the privations he had endured. He entered the bazaar of Kufa. He had a sparrow sitting on his hand and went about saying: "Give me something for the sake of this sparrow!" They said: "What is this you are saying?" He said: "It is impossible for me to ask for anything for the sake of God!" For this insignificant world there should be no other intercessor except contemptibleness itself! Be careful to retain or abandon things according to the measure of the instructions contained in this letter.

*Peace!*

# THE HUNDRED LETTERS

LETTER 70: COMPANIONSHIP OF THE GROUP

*In the name of God, the Merciful, the Compassionate!*

Brother Shamsuddin, may God grant you the grace of good company! A very important need of the disciple is to associate with these people. Such association makes a deep impression. It is a total attack on a person's temperament and habits, to such an extent that a falcon, by associating with men, becomes wise, and a parrot learns to speak, while a horse, because it associates with men in its training, loses its animal traits and takes on those of men! There are many examples of this sort of thing. Everybody has seen and witnessed the effect of association. The phenomenon can be described under the rubric of "the influence derived from associating with others!"

Association overcomes not only innate habits but also one's created temperament. To begin with, the sheikhs seek the benefits of associating together and command their disciples to do the same: For them, association becomes an obligatory duty. The intent of all this is to provide rest for a person's soul in whatever group he happens to be. Association relates to the ways of behavior that characterize the group, since all the group's affairs and influence develop in the context of mutual interaction.[84] The Prophet is reported to have said: "A man chooses the religion and path of his friend. Take note of who his associates are!" If his companions are good, then he himself, even though he is bad, will become good, because their magnanimity will effect a change in him. On the other hand, if he associates with bad companions, he, too, will become bad, because his situation encourages him to be satisfied with what is bad, and even though he was good, he will end up by becoming bad.

There is the story of a man who was making his way around the Kaaba and praying, "O God, make my brothers good!" People said: "You have finally reached this holy place; why do you not pray for yourself? Why are all your prayers for your brothers?" He replied: "I have several brothers to whom I shall be returning. If I find them acting virtuously, then I too will become good on account of their virtue; but if I find them steeped in wickedness, then I too will become perverted by their wickedness. Since my goodness will result from associating with good people, I therefore pray for my brothers, that I might achieve my aim through their help."

Malik ibn Dinar once said: "Do not associate with any brother or

289

friend if you derive no benefit therefrom for your faith or for the world to come. Such company should be considered as forbidden for you." The proper way of associating with others has been thus expressed: "Your associates will either be senior to you or junior to you. If you associate with your elders, you should be the one to derive some profit from their company. If, on the other hand, you associate with people younger than yourself, then they should profit from the contact and learn something from you that will deepen their faith. If you also learn something from them, then your faith, too, will be deepened." The Prophet has said: "Make many men your brothers for the sake of their good behavior and upright dealings, for your God is full of life and bounty." It is for this reason that the Lord does not like to see His slave tormented in front of his brothers. As for the Day of Judgment, however, a person should prepare himself by associating with others for the sake of God, not for the sake of his own personal desires, no matter what they be.

It has been said that being alone would be destructive for a disciple, as the Prophet noted: "Satan dwells with the man who is by himself, but he remains at a distance if there are two together." The Lord has said: "Where three of you are gathered together in an attempt to fathom the divine mystery, God himself makes the fourth." In fact, there is no greater misfortune for a disciple, and nothing more dangerous, than living by himself. There was a disciple of Junaid who said: "I have attained perfection. There will be no harm if I abandon the company of men." He retired to a place by himself and lived in privacy. When night came, he saw a whole troop of people approaching him: "Be seated on this horse and come to paradise!" they beckoned. He mounted the horse and went off. He saw a place where all was joy and pleasure, filled with handsome youths, delicious food, and running streams. He passed his time there until dawn when he fell asleep. On waking up, he found himself at the door of his hermitage. The pride of youth manifested its influence in his heart. He began to boast, saying that he had attained such and such a state, and was doing such and such. News of this reached the ears of Khwaja Junaid. He set out and came to the door of the hermitage. He enquired about his disciple's spiritual condition. He related everything that had occurred. Junaid said to him: "When you go to that place tonight, then repeat three times: 'There is no power or strength except in God Most High!' " That night he went off as usual with the group. After quite some time, he thought of what Khwaja Junaid had told him to do. As an experiment he repeated three times, "There is no power or strength except in God!" They all cried out and disappeared. He found himself on a rubbish dump with bones scattered all around him. He realized his fault and, having repented of it, returned to the company of his fellow disciples. Now you can understand what a misfortune it is for a disciple to be alone!

The etiquette of associating with others is to treat everyone in a manner that befits his position. A person should be respectful toward his elders, affable with his peers, and kindly disposed toward those who are younger than he is. He should consider his elders as his father, his peers as his brothers, and those junior to him as his children. It is not proper for a young person to speak in the presence of his elders, unless it is absolutely necessary. Even then, he should pause for a while before speaking to enable his elder to finish what he has been saying. Then he should ask permission to speak, and, sitting down respectfully, say what has to be said. A young person should by no means contradict his elders, or argue with them, or interrogate them, for the one upon whom the benevolence of the elder radiates experiences the fulfillment of his wishes both in religion and in the world. It is considered proper to make some request of him, but a disciple should not come and sit at the head of the carpet in the presence of his elders. He should be engaged in serving them. The precondition for association and brotherhood is communal living. Each should hold it as lawful for another to have authority over his goods. This group gives nothing on loan, nor does it ask others for loans. Whatever they give to another is never asked again, as the sheikhs have said: "A Sufi neither borrows nor lends!" No one should give orders but, if someone does give them an order, they should execute it wholeheartedly. Although they do not give others work to do, nevertheless they unhesitatingly carry out whatever work is enjoined upon them. They live congenially with everybody else in a lighthearted fashion. An individual member does nothing against the group, unless it is a question of some infringement of the Law, and he should not associate with anyone who is against religion, or who holds different views about religion, even though the person be close to him in any way. On the other hand, let him associate with those who confirm him, both outwardly and inwardly, in his faith, piety, religion, and spiritual outlook.

It is entirely improper to associate with beardless youths, for many calamities result from this practice. Some venerable Sufis have

observed that, for young people, the desire of associating with revered elders can be a grace and lead to an increase in knowledge and a
stimulation of their mental development, but it would be shameful
and foolish for elders to seek to associate with youths.

In its practice, this group calls the initial association "knowledge," after which comes "good behavior," and then "inclination";
followed by "well-being," "association" and finally "brotherhood."
When association becomes perfect it provides the best preconditions
for mystical states. Do you not see that the most important group of
all was constituted by the companions of the Prophet? Their knowledge, grasp of judicial matters, worship, devotion, and trust in God
knew no equal. Their contentment had no connection with any single
thing except their association with the Prophet, which was the best of
all possible states. One of the practices of this group was to avoid saying: "This is mine and that is yours! If things had been like that, this
would not have happened! O that this might have happened! O that
this might not have happened! If only you had done so! Why did you
not do so?" All this is the way ordinary people talk.

Ibrahim ibn Shaibani says: "We do not keep company with anybody who says: 'These are my sandals!' " The learned have said: "God
does not consider anyone acceptable who says: "We, I, undoubtedly I,
for me, I have." Do you not see that when Satan said, "We praise
You," he heard a voice saying that his praise was not necessary, but
that Adam should be worshiped! (See Q38:75.) Satan retorted that he
had been created out of fire (Q38:76). How could such a retort be tol-
erated? The command descended, "My curse is upon you till Judgment Day" (Q38:78). Similarly, Pharaoh declared: "Does not the kingdom of Egypt belong to me?" (Q43:51). And again, "I am your exalted
lord!" These words were unlawful! Calamity descended upon him
and he sank into the sea. Qarun said: "I am a very learned man"
(Q28:78). This was not acceptable either! A command was given to
the earth and it swallowed him up (Q28:81).

When the turn of the Prophet came, He said: "O Muhammad,
you are not like them. 'And say: "I am the fearsome warner" (Q15:89)
just as I say, "I am God! there is no god but Me!" ' "

O brother, if you want to sit in the tree of the hidden garden and
enjoy the life-giving water of its running streams, as well as trample
underfoot the seven heavens, you can pass in a moment from what is
transient to what is eternal by closing the five doors of your desires
and changing the clothes of this world of calamity and this house of

rebellion, just as an oyster in the sea, through the compulsion of long-ing for you, becomes deaf and blind to all that is not God!

Shibli was asked: "Who are the Sufis? By what signs can they be recognized?" He replied: "They are deaf, dumb, and blind!" (Q2:18). They said: "These are the qualities of infidels." He replied: "Infidels are deaf to the word of God, incapable of uttering it, and blind with regard to His face." Here is needed a falcon, which, after escaping the snares laid by Satan in this world, can set out toward the world of purity, just as a bird would fly when released from the snare, its heart in tune with its flight, its flight with its thinking, its thinking with the divine secret, and the divine secret will attune it to God Himself. This happened to the Chosen One, who in a single stride was in the mosque of Aqsa, and in another traversed all the heavenly stations, arriving at the highest degree of nearness to God. The wine of union was bestowed upon him. He obtained marvelous revelations. Passing beyond the pale of both worlds, he found repose with his Friend.

*Peace!*

## LETTER 71: SERVICE[85]

*In the name of God, the Merciful, the Compassionate!*

Brother Shamsuddin, may God grant you a noble rank in the service of the saints! An important task of the disciple is rendering service. In service one acquires many benefits and special favors that are not found in any other form of devotion or submission. One is that a person's selfish soul perishes. Pride and haughtiness are removed from his countenance and, in their place, humility and submission appear. A person becomes well mannered, and his behavior improves considerably. He learns both the theory and the practice of the group. Gloom and heaviness are removed from his soul. He becomes gentle, lighthearted, and radiant, both internally and externally.

Numerous are the benefits that accrue to the person engaged in service. A wise man was asked how many paths there were that led to God. He replied that every particle of existence was a path that led to God, but there was no other path that could lead a person in a better fashion, or closer to God, than that of bringing comfort to hearts.

"This is the way I found what I was seeking, and this is what I have bequeathed to my disciples!" The saying of the wise is that a disciple stands to gain more by submitting to the group than could ever be described. Even if an exhaustive description were attempted, its sole purpose would be to state clearly that there is no prayer or submission more excellent or more beneficial than that of serving one another!

It is related that when the Prophet was asked, "What is the most excellent offering of all?" he replied: "The service of a slave in the way of the Lord, or providing the shade of a tent on the way of the Lord, or providing transport for someone on the way of the Lord." In another place he said: "Being quick to assist widows or the poverty-stricken is like fighting a holy war on the Way to the Lord, or like observing the fast by day and keeping vigil by night."

A precondition of service, however, is to abandon entirely one's own wishes, desires and control over one's affairs, and to live according to the desires of the group. Disciples should serve each traveler and sojourner according to the nature of his visitor's needs. In this way will the disciples acquire the contented heart and peaceful mind of these men, being liberated by means of the latters' prayers and spiritual merits and, freed from all anxiety concerning their own spiritual condition, they can devote themselves to service.[86] In this way, through this service, they obtain all that others in the group obtain by means of austerities and struggle with themselves. "Anyone who has helped in a good work has a reward equal to that of the doer of the work." All these Sufi centers, hospices, and endowments have been established precisely for this enterprise!

A second precondition of service is not to consider one as important or favored. Whatever belongs to the disciple should be viewed by him as the common property of all. To the extent that he is able, he spends himself, his goods, and even his own desires and inclinations for the sake of others. In all circumstances he gives preference to the group over himself. He does not refuse any of its members in any matter, unless it be something forbidden by God. He accomplishes without delay whatever they ask of him, even though it be the work of a laborer, until such time as their request is fully complied with.

A disciple should behave toward all as a slave does toward his master. He has to put up with whatever harsh treatment his master metes out to him. He has no alternative, for he is a slave! It is necessary for him to preserve, at all times, the secrets and hints contained in the speech of the group. He tries to help anyone in the group whom he sees is in a confused condition, even though the person makes no request for help.

A final precondition is that the disciple considers it incumbent upon himself to be grateful for whatever service he performs on behalf of anybody, or whatever favor he enjoys. He does whatever he can for the group, utilizing every opportunity for advancing their good. If he wastes even a moment, he considers himself bound to be sorry for it. There are innumerable ways of rendering service. The purpose of saying this is to indicate that there should be no young person who can not find some appropriate work to do for others!

Sheikh Abul Abbas Qassab has said: "Every disciple who shows himself constant in any form of service derives more from it than from a hundred supererogatory ritual prayers!" This group considers that each one's rank depends on his service; the abundance of his association with, close connection to, and training given by, the sheikhs; and on their instruction, as well as on the progress they make on the way, and on the length of their life, not on their lineage. They place no confidence in genealogy, except for the descendants of the Prophet and the sons of the sheikhs, whom they honor on account of their lineage. What have they said? "Genealogy is a man's religion and his drink is chastity." Just as it is necessary for a wealthy man to part with a portion of his wealth as alms for the dervishes, and a learned man has to give instruction to others, giving part of his knowledge "in alms" as it were, so it is with this group that, in the beginning, it is necessary for a novice to devote all his actions to service, and thus be of assistance to strangers and make friends of his brother Muslims. He should be of service to those who are senior to him. The rank of service and the benefits derived from it become evident when the disciple becomes a person who craves for nothing, reproaches none, and is devoid of all guile.

Any disciple who does not devote himself to service, but is greedy for others to serve him, will not become perfect. Instead, he becomes heavy at heart. Heaviness of heart is a fever in one's soul, abhorrent to one's basic nature. The disciple considers all of this as being somehow deficient, and has little faith in it. The Chosen One acted in this gentle way in order to instruct and correct the companions and the community. When a large pot of milk was brought to him, he got up, picked it up, and, with his own blessed hand, distributed it to the indigent and then to the companions. He himself drank only what was left over. The people said, "O Messenger, why did you not drink first?" He replied: "Is it not fitting that the one who provides drink for others should himself be the last to drink?"

It is well known among the people of this group that, whoever is more devoted to service is held to be dearer and more tenderhearted, and a person is more inclined to pay attention to such people.[87] "The leader of a people is the one who serves them!" A famous Arab was asked: "How did you become a leader?" He replied that he served the people and thus became a leader! It is said that Abu Bakr, who received the honor of viceregency from the Apostle, was granted this wealth on account of his assiduity in service. All great men began their careers in this fashion. They girded up their loins for service at the outset, and ended up by becoming leaders. The benefits derived from service are greater than can be described. As far as possible, disciples should count their blessings and be full of hope for the future.

O brother, the commands of God are beyond the power of the human mind to comprehend! Canaan was a son of Noah. He was not allowed to proceed into the ark, yet there was a passage for the accursed one, Satan. This saying should be uttered not to the King, but to the guard. Do you not see that it was not Pharaoh but an old woman in his palace who was told: "The One who looks at you looks at the command of His own pure knowledge, not at the value of your stained works."

The religion of the orthodox is that there is no limit to the gentleness of God. It reaches the whole world, but nobody can penetrate to the heart of the divine bounty, which is found expressed in this handful of dust. On the Day of Resurrection there will be a voice saying: "You have all become dust." The angels will be told, "You are not gathered around the divine throne. You have no business with the robe of the keeper of heaven, nor with the group of your leader, Satan. From the station of knowledge do you not see what for Me are the works of this handful of dust?" Hence it has been said that if there had been no dust, this saying could not have existed, nor would all this tumult and pain have existed. Paradise, with all its blessings and holy favors, is the consolation of dust. Rizwan and all the youths of paradise are attendants at the joy and union of dust. No dust existed, nor had there taken place what you have heard happened to this handful of dust, at the time that the work of dust, by a pure divine desire, had already been brought into existence. There was as yet no palate, but the wine was prepared! No head, but the cap of honor was already stitched! No feet, yet the way was laid out! No heart, yet perception existed! No sin, yet the treasury of mercy was filled to the brim! No devotion, but heaven was already adorned for the devotee! "Favor was bestowed before the creation of water and mud!"

*Peace!*

### LETTER 72: PURIFICATION OF BAD HABITS

*In the name of God, the Merciful, the Compassionate!*

Dear Brother Shamsuddin, may you be always devoted to the service of God! Peace and prayers from the author of these words! A brother should study carefully how to purify his behavior and change his base qualities into praiseworthy ones by striving, day by day, as much as possible, toward this goal. It is important that he realize that terrible calamities—may God preserve us from them!—can result from carelessness and negligence in this task.

There are, in man, animal-like qualities that correspond to the various beasts of prey, wild animals, and brute beasts. Whatever quality becomes predominant in this life will be the one in accordance with which the order will be given tomorrow that he be raised in that form, rather than in his present human form. For example, the person who is overcome by rage in this life will be raised on the Day of Resurrection in the form of a dog. The man who succumbs to lustful desires will be raised as a pig. Whoever is overcome by pride will be raised as a leopard. If anyone indulges in sly behavior now, he will be raised as a fox, and so on for other similar qualities.

It is related in a Prophetic tradition that the Friend of God [Abraham] will see Azar [his father] on the Day of Resurrection, as he is being carried off to hell. He will say: "O Lord, could there be any greater disgrace than this, that I am standing here in this open space and Azar is being borne off to hell? In the world I had declared, 'Do not disgrace me on the Day of Resurrection!' " (Q26:87). Meanwhile, Azar had changed in form from a man to a hyena, for this was in keeping with his disposition while on earth. Abraham was told: "What relationship do you have with this hyena? How can you have any affinity with him?"

By contrast, the dog of the Companions of the Cave, on account

297

of its good qualities, had its form changed and was brought forward as a man for, although it had the form of a dog, it had the qualities of a man; while Azar had the appearance of a man, but the qualities of a hyena. In the same way, O brother, there are many today with the appearance of men whom you will see tomorrow raised up in the form of beasts of prey and wild animals, while at the same time, many beasts of prey and wild animals of today will be brought forward as men of the Day of Resurrection. The wise have said that the stony garb of Mount Uhud, concerning which the Prophet had said, "Uhud is the mountain which loves me, and of which I am fond" will, on the Day of Resurrection, be brought into the row of the righteous, for the virtue of the righteous has predominated in it! Of a certainty, everything will be changed into its correct form. At this point, someone might object: "Mount Uhud is an inert mass. How can you talk about love or hatred with regard to something inorganic? Both love and hatred necessarily presuppose life." The answer to this is, "Uhud is the mountain which loves me, and of which I am fond!" Moreover, it has been related by that master of the human heart, the Prophet, that those united in heart receive some knowledge even from solid things, and also hear something concerning which another person might not have any knowledge whatsoever.

Eyes that are veiled derive no benefit at all from a lamp!

It has also been related that those favored with revelations are aware of the praise of all things, even if it be an inert mass of rock, and they realize the truth of the Quranic declaration that "all things in heaven and on earth are engaged in praising God" (Q59:24). They have voices, as the poet said:

It appears to you that these stones are motionless:
But for us, they are superbly eloquent in their speech!

In *Ismat-i-Anbiya* [The sinlessness of the prophets], it is related that the notable prophet Solomon said: "The entire world, along with all its parts, is enamored of its Creator, and is in quest of Him." In this vein someone said:

A hundred thousand secrets are inbedded in an ant,
And in its heart an agitation arises out of love for Him!
Every particle is a lover filled with desire;
It is filled with a ray of the love of God!

All particles, whether visible or hidden,
Of both worlds, are really centers of love!

We are confronted with this difficult and frightening task in which none except those endowed with insight succeed. One should not be imprudent. One should develop, ever so slowly, the habit by which, little by little, these qualities might decrease and, if the Lord provides assistance and they are entirely pushed aside, then this itself would appear as a great work. Whoever wishes to know which quality will be his on the Day of Resurrection should look into himself here and now in order to discover which quality predominates in him. Tomorrow he will rise with that very same quality. This much should be easily understandable; is it not that difficult to grasp!

If anyone wishes to know whether the Lord is pleased with him or not, let him look at his own actions! If they are all full of devotion, he will know that God is pleased with them, for devotion is a sign of God's good pleasure. If, on the other hand, his actions are all sinful, he will know that God is displeased with them, for sin is a sign of His displeasure. If both are found, then the dominant one will determine his fate. Your fortune is not set before you today! When a work is not done here, then it will not be possible there either. And if these wicked qualities were to remain in him and not be transformed, then even if he goes to paradise and all its blessings are showered upon him, still his bad qualities will not change. There will be no turning back then. Such a man would remain separated from himself, and he would not attain his true Wealth.

It is necessary to make the change here. If no change is effected here, then none will be possible there either. A person will simply go to heaven! Moreover, for all eternity, he will not change; he will remain within himself. All the blessings of heaven will be lawful for him, but he will not be able to be satisfied with the delights that are in store for man tomorrow—such as the damsels, comfortable dwelling places, roasted chicken, and flowing waters—for what are all these when compared to the Object of souls, the Desire of hearts, the Direction of all righteous ones, and the Kaaba of all travelers?[88] If anyone loves this Wealth, then of what value is anything else that he gains? For someone who has attained that Blessing, what could be counted as loss?

There is a need for the fast of the full moon and Ramazan, so that there is no loss in journeys or at home due to lethargy or drowsiness.

By taking many baths and by performing many ablutions, the seeker finds a remedy for all these drawbacks.

O brother, the angels received this command: "Turn your face toward the dust!" and men this one: "Turn your face toward a stone!" Do you know what this means? This is to show clearly the value and refinement of works. Moses was told: "Look toward the mountain!" because, "Sinai is stone, and you are a clod of earth." Now, there undoubtedly is an affinity between stone and earth. On the other hand, He who will grant the vision tomorrow does not do so because of any affinity. Man is not worthy of such vision. There is no eye that has been fashioned to contemplate Him, nor ear shaped to hear Him, nor intellect capable of comprehending Him, nor foot capable of finding its way to Him!

> My eye desires only the sight of You:
> My ear longs to hear nothing but Your speech!
> Look upon the high aspirations of both,
> Even though they be not worthy of Your splendor!

No one can claim to be seeking Him wholeheartedly until he has weighed himself in the scales of complete powerlessness, and looked at himself with the eyes of unworthiness. Shibli said: "My baseness has not retreated from that of the Jews." Bu Sulaiman Darani said: "Whoever looks at his soul, or gives the slightest value to all his actions, states, and words, will certainly never arrive at a taste of the sweetness of this saying!" A wise man said: "I was performing the circumambulation of the Kaaba. Someone came up behind me and pulled me backwards. When I looked to see who it was I saw it was Khwaja Fuzail Iyaz. He said to me: 'If you think that at this time and in this place there is any holiness originating from you or me, then beware of destruction!'"

*Peace!*

## LETTER 73: GREED AND PETITIONARY PRAYERS

*In the name of God, the Merciful, the Compassionate!*

Dear Brother Shamsuddin, any work or action performed hypocritically, or out of a desire to attain the rank of a righteous man, cannot be considered as emanating from a master of the faith. Whatever you did would not be free from greed. The secret is this: The manifestation of devotion is sincerity, not avarice. Greed is one thing, the manifestation of devotion, something quite different. The fine distinction between them can be grasped by attentive observation. Yet you and I are such that we need to be bribed to serve God.

What sort of love is this, that would love souls for a bribe?

O brother, remove greed from your path, for it is not necessary for God to do anything for anyone. Whatever is given to men today in this world is given freely, and what will be given to us tomorrow, on the Day of Resurrection, will be given freely. The wise have said: The sermon that He has commanded to be preached to you tomorrow is: "This is a reward for what they did" (Q56:24). Such an order was given to relieve your heart of sadness tomorrow, for a man finds food he himself has earned is more enjoyable than what is given to him by someone else.

Whatever the King of Glory bestows upon you from His abundant self-sufficiency He bestows without cause. Your task is to pay attention to your own unfortunate state first and foremost, striving to do everything as a manifestation of your devotion, not out of avarice. You should seek whatever has been commanded of you in any circumstance, not your private gain. Whatever you do should be done first and foremost for His sake, not out of the hope of heaven, nor the fear of hell!

I experience neither aversion to hell nor desire for heaven:
Remove the veil from Your countenance, for it is You I long to see!

Such an outlook is a sign of the prophets, and an embellishment of the saints. Our share in all this is simply our faith, nothing more, until such time as the dust and dirt kicked up by the hooves of their blessed mounts settles on the heads of us wretched ones and becomes a crown of eternal bliss for us, unfortunate though we be! Whoever sets foot on the carpet of the Law of the Chosen One, and desires the religion of God Almighty, and takes pride in it, is really proud of this desire, and is boasting of being in this particular stage. But when one steps onto the carpet of the Law, the real struggle is precisely in becoming purified, and in standing firm in compliance with all that God has commanded and prohibited. The true seeker should weigh himself on the scale of religion to see how far he has abandoned prohibited things. Then will it be fitting to repeat this saying of the father of the community, Abraham, the Friend of God. I desire "the One Who, I hope, will forgive my sins on Judgment Day" (Q26:82). In the beginning of his period of trial Abraham said: "Save me and my children from idol worship!" (Q14:35). At the end of this period of trial he said "[I desire] the One Who, I hope, will forgive my sins on Judgment Day!" (Q26:82). It might happen that a person, in the days of his youth, does not know anything else except playing and amusing himself, and does not observe the demands of the Islamic community without, however, intending to differ from the father of that community, that is, Muhammad. If anyone has the desire of weighing his actions against the measure of service, then say: "Give the reins of your heart into the hands of right intention!" Hence religious scholars in Islam have noted: "Intention is the activity of the heart." An action that does not fulfill the expectations of intention does not pass beyond the world of habit, nor is the treasury of divine service attained. Moreover, every action that is cut off from right intention is bound to the threshold of one's habit, and will not find its way to the row of manly actions.

The intention of serving God forms the pillar of faith for those blessed with inner peace. It is the safe-conduct pass of the Lord for His own servants. The secret of this is that, by means of intention, you cleanse the skirt of your heart of everything except what pertains strictly to religion. Thus you will be able to gird up your loins for service without the bother of habit and calamity and, without apprehension about enemies, you will be able to implement faithfully the covenant of unity that was made at the outset.[89]

> If you are aware of the primeval covenant,
> Why separate yourself from that Presence?
> Return your soul to awareness of its meaning!
> Make yourself worthy of proximity to the King!

There may be someone who forever repeats the words of his rosary and sings the divine praises, who considers that he has already placed his foot in the row of those remembering God, and thinks that he is now on the path of those going straight toward Him. This is a great mistake for a man of devotion, for the tongue is only like a branch. If it is lopped off, there is no harm done to the trunk of faith! The remembrance of those who act merely out of habit does not go any deeper than the tip of their tongue. The rosaries and praises of the tearful are nothing but the practice of hypocrisy and the production of sound—and yet they desire to be equal in perfection to the masters of sincerity!

O brother, whatever you send without the help of purification is, for all eternity, nothing but loss. "He was given no other command than to serve God with a sincere heart" (Q98:5). Habit, of itself, cannot be raised to the heights of sincerity. We know nothing but the path of habit and custom, yet, in our blindness and inability to see ourselves, are convinced that with such capital we can serve God faithfully. All this is a sign of our lack of wealth.

> If you wander for a thousand years proclaiming His praises,
> I know not that you will enjoy a scent of His fragrance.
> Consider that your fortune depends on Him!
> From the viewpoint of faith, who are you? What can you offer?
> What does a beggar know beyond this wealth,
> That he can offer up his soul for the sake of the King?

The secret of the heart is required to enable you to perform divine service; then will you be engaged in genuine service. But when you are neglectful and act out of habit, then whatever you do will remain incomplete. It will be a remembrance on your tongue, but not from an inflamed heart. May that sort of remembrance not be allowed to bring disgrace upon the threshold of the Law! How can it even be called remembrance? If anyone should say, "There is no god but God," which is the kernel of the way of Unity, as though it were a matter of, say, buying and selling, or like the speech of careless people, then this word could be raised up from his lips to the realm of divine Unity.

Whoever, by means of his action alone, without a covenant or internal agreement, does something and claims that he is serving God will, on the Day of Judgment, be thrown into the row of the enemies of religion and will descend, along with them, to the depths of hell. The secret of this has been expressed by the poet:

> For the noble, rosary and sacred thread are the same:
> You are free to be whatever you like, either master or slave!

Woe to you who lay claim to service, for you have bound the turban of knowledge upon the head of your own excellence and have refused to be contained in this world! Look carefully to see whether you are in the row of friends or in the midst of enemies! Woe to you, O creature of habit, who tie upon your head the turban of assumption that you serve God and draw up the skirt of your own purity away from men that it may not be contaminated! Be careful, lest the dress of defection bear you off to the grave! Busy yourself in looking after others' shoes, that the sacred thread of habit and the pride of custom may perhaps be removed from your neck!

> As long as you remain like a crow on a stinking corpse,
> How can you come like a white falcon to the presence of the
>   King?
> If, like a sparrow, you become food for a falcon,
> Merging into the falcon, you will become fit for the hand of
>   the King!

When the inner heart of someone is touched by respect for this word, he is more eager to trample the eight heavens under foot, like dust, than is a thirsty person to find pure water for the relief of his thirst. This is because of the claim of Islam upon you: if, throughout your whole life, you were but to utter this word from the secret of your heart, all would be well! Be careful lest you sell It for heaven, as though the latter were of more value! If you sell It, you will incur a loss. Be careful, too, lest you sell the Lord of the inn merely for the sake of the inn!

> When the Beloved comes, at least we can offer our souls to
>   Him.
> You seek so many things: does He not suffice for you?
> Seek only One, lest you find yourself left by the wayside.
> Travel toward the sky, lest you get stuck in some well.
> When You support me, so does everything else.
> Everything comes to my aid, when You stretch out Your hand
>   to help.

If you say this word except for His sake, then you are not speaking with sincerity, whether you be in heaven or in hell. If you speak for the sake of heaven, it is yourself you are worshiping. Correct worship of God occurs when a person desires to find himself for God's sake, not God for his own sake. "[These are real] men who, even when engaged in business, do not forget God" (Q24:37). God Almighty says: "My threshold is not a place for buying and selling." When you go to the bazaar, your intention is to acquire something you do not have. But when you come to His threshold, your intention is to give Him everything you have, and return a penniless pauper. One renowned for his insight has said:

> There is no other way for a lover but to become nothing,
> That his very existence might come from the divine court.
> Can you not see that, in the profession of faith,
> The "not" precedes the affirmation "but God!"

Khwaja Ahmad Khazru saw the Lord in a dream. He said: "O Ahmad, everyone asks Me for something, but Bayazid asks Me for Myself!" There are many disciples who say, with regard to this matter, that it is not permissible to speak about seeing Him in a dream. But the issue there concerns the states of the righteous, not of you and me. The dreams of the righteous are quite a different matter; they are not like your dreams and mine. Ours do not go beyond this sensible world, while the states of the righteous do not descend—either to this world or the next! As long as a person remains in this world, such an explanation is unacceptable, either in a dream or when one is awake. But when someone becomes cut off from the qualities of human nature, he passes out of this world and reaches the next. Whoever reaches God realizes that there is no room within him for opposition to God. It is proper, however, that the Almighty should make use of dreams for showing His friendship or that He should, in that very dream, snatch a person away, taking him out of this world and the next in order to manifest to him this wealth, about which I have spoken. In this way does He remove your rational doubts about the state of real men, and also lead you to believe in Him.

> If a man is remembered for the quality of his love,
> And is famous because of his steadfastness,
> Then the mind must grant his pure existence
> To have a rank far beyond this world of ours!

[Details of prayers to be recited are then set forth.]

*Peace!*

## LETTER 74: AN EXPLANATION OF THE WORLD AND PETITIONARY PRAYERS FOR THE EXPIATION OF SINS

*In the name of God, the Merciful, the Compassionate!*

Dear Brother Shamsuddin, the Prophet has said that the world and everything in it is accursed, except for whatever of it is for the sake of God. Know that whatever is in the world can be divided into three categories. The first is whatever, in both appearance and reality, relates solely to the world. In no way at all can it be for the sake of God! This covers every kind of sin, which neither in intention nor in purpose can be for His sake. Next, an overabundance of lawful things must be considered. Sin originates from such overabundance, for that is precisely what is meant by "the world." Herein lies the seed of negligence, and the origin of all sins. The next category is whatever, in both appearance and reality, is directed toward God, but in intention and purpose, is for the sake of the world. Three kinds of activity must be considered here: meditation, remembering God, and checking one's passions. All three, even though they occur in the world, are for the sake of the world to come, and are pleasing to God. But if the purpose of all that meditation is a quest for knowledge in order that, by means of it, the person might acquire acceptance and rank; or if the purpose of remembering God is to have men look upon the rememberer as a pious person; or if the intention behind his struggle to control himself in all things is that people might think of him as an ascetic, then he will be condemned and accursed, even though what he does may outwardly appear to be for God. The third category is that which, as far as appearances are concerned, is directed toward this world but, in purpose and intention, is for the sake of God and is, in consequence, not really restricted to this world. In this category are such things as eating for the purpose of divine service, and marrying with the intention of having a son who might say, "There is no god but God, and Muhammad is the messenger of God!" and seeking a modest quantity of the goods of this world in order to be able to submit to God, for by having some goods, a man becomes independent of other people. There is a saying of the Law that says that whoever seeks any goods for the sake of pomp and glory thinks he sees God at his side with his own eyes. If, on the other hand, he seeks some resources in order to be independent of people, then on the Day of

Judgment he will come forward, his face as resplendent as the full moon. In short, we can say that, by "the world" is meant whatever brings pleasure to the human soul, both in the present and in the future. There is no need for it. Nevertheless, whatever is found in it that helps toward the world to come is necessary; since it is consecrated to the world to come, it is not really for this world! Consider, for example, fodder and beasts. They are required for the pilgrimage and, therefore, are necessary provisions for the journey.

Understand that there are three degrees in the world. First, there is the measure of necessity in food, clothing, and dwelling. More than that is the measure of felt need or of what is convenient. After that is the measure of adornment and articles of luxury. This knows no limit. There are those who have reduced their needs to the bare minimum and seek only that; and those who fall into luxurious living, and end up by falling headlong into the nethermost hell, which has no end.

> You cannot have the goods of both this world and religion!
> When deprived of the former, you can acquire the latter!

Whoever retrenches to what is convenient is still not entirely free from danger, for he is still close to living in ease and comfort. It is for this reason that the masters of religion cut down to the bare necessities of life. The leader and initiator in this is Uways Qarani, who so restricted his necessities of life and his involvement in the world that he appeared to have gone mad. For one, and even two years, it happened that he was not seen. His nourishment consisted of dates picked up along the way. He wore sacks he picked up and sewed into a garment for himself. Wherever he went, the children hurled stones at him as though he were a madman.

> Those who shine like the moon above the eight heavens
> Are, on the chessboard, those who checkmate the King!
> They are aware of the secret of this saying:
> Those considered mad by the people are actually treading the
>     Path!

The conduct of anyone who has recognized the calamities of the world would be like this. It is the path trodden by prophets and saints alike. If you have not attained this rank, then the burden still rests on you to reduce to what is minimally necessary. In no way should you take up a life of ease, lest you fall into great danger! Turn in tearful supplication to the Lord and say:

> O God, Your mercy is a boundless ocean:
> A mere drop suffices for me!
> Even if the filth of all the sins of mankind
> Were to be thrown into that ocean all at once,
> it would still not be darkened for a moment;
> Rather, all earthly labor is transformed into light!

The wise have said that the very lowest rank that appears in anyone who treads the path of the righteous is that he is made mad for the next life. Hope is inscribed in his heart, that he might remain forever a stranger to this world and become acquainted with the next.

There is a tradition that the Prophet had built a bower out of pulped reeds because when it rained he had no place to go to protect himself from the rain. Abu Bakr said: "O Messenger of God, there is a command that we should build you a mud dwelling!" He replied: "O Abu Bakr, do not sadden me with such talk! When Jesus came into the world and went where he went, he had no more than I have. If Jesus, who is the forerunner of my community, had no place of refuge in the world, then how should not I, who am Lord of both worlds, do greater works than he, and more easily? You should understand that my delight consists in this sorrow and grief!"

> May the dust of the whole world be upon the head
> Which does not rejoice in grief over You!
> Any grief that comes from You is a mountain of rejoicing;
> Even death, if it comes from You, is really life!

[Another tradition about poverty follows. Its meaning is summarized in this poem:]

> When the dear ones who did the work of men
> Became disgusted with their souls,
> They gave no bread to their longing souls,
> Nor did they eat a morsel for their own well-being!

[Certain petitionary prayers are enumerated.]

*Peace!*

# THE HUNDRED LETTERS

*In the name of God, the Merciful, the Compassionate!*

Dear Brother Shamsuddin, may God grant you the grace of self-denial! Worship does not become correct until the world is abandoned, because while you might outwardly appear to be totally engrossed in the search for God, inwardly you may be desirous of that worship itself. How can this be, since we have but one heart? When the heart has become engrossed in one thing, it cannot concern itself with something else, for example, it cannot be entirely taken up with both this world and the next, any more than it could turn to both east and west simultaneously. To the extent that it becomes closer to one of them, it will be estranged from the other.

It is related that Abu Darda said: "I wished to bring together this world and the next, as well as worship and trade, but it was utterly impossible. When I turned my face toward the next world, I abandoned this one; and when I engaged in prayer, I abandoned trading." [Two further examples are quoted.]

When worship reaches such a stage, the devotee has to embrace this abandonment. He should recognize what abstention in the world actually entails. Know that abstention, according to the religious scholars, is of two kinds: There is an abstention that is within the power of the slave, and there is another that is not within his power. The former type consists of three things: (1) abandoning the quest for things he does not have in the world; (2) keeping at a distance whatever he has acquired from the world; and (3) the internal abandonment of desire for the world. On the other hand, the abstention that is not within one's power means that the world seems utterly cold to the heart of the ascetic. When, however, a slave carries out whatever form of abstention he is capable of achieving, he does not seek after what he does not have; he keeps his possessions "at a distance," as it were; and he removes all desire of them from his heart. Only then is he granted, by the grace and bounty of God, that type of detachment which is not within his own power! In other words, his heart grows cold toward the world. This, according to a number of the wise, is genuine detachment. The most difficult task in this whole matter is to expel the very desire of the world from one's heart. There are many who outwardly appear to have grown completely detached from the world but inwardly are enamored of it. What is really important is that the desire of the world should go out of one's heart. This is the task at hand! It has been said: "When a slave becomes assiduous in those two things, namely, not seeking after what he does not have, and keeping those which he has at a distance, then God Almighty will also enable him, by His favor, to expel all desire of the world from his heart. If someone empties his hands of the possession of both worlds, still he has not acquired detachment until his heart is emptied of all hankering after them. The reason is that a seeker is inclined toward something, and inclination is the opposite of detachment, and two opposites cannot coexist with one another!"

Moreover, the leaders in the matter of detachment are the prophets. The king of the whole world, Solomon, was without doubt detached from the world. It was good for him to empty his heart of all seeking, even though he possessed dominion and wealth, for this is better than emptying one's hands but retaining a hankering in the heart. And if you ask, "Is this detachment in the world something obligatory or supererogatory?" then know that detachment refers only to lawful things. Where forbidden things are concerned, there is not detachment but rather obligation. Works of supererogation are in the category of lawful things, yet even these are forbidden for certain people who have attained stability in submission, which is the stage of those men who eat only when necessary and according to the measure of the materials at hand. Detachment in lawful matters for the proficient, however, would mean that, as far as they are concerned, even lawful things are like carrion![90] But such strength has not been granted you: without doubt, you will have to go on seeking.

It is necessary that your intention should be to seek after those things by means of which sincere service might be strengthened and you might act as a true servant should, and not indulge your passions in pleasure, luxury, and comfort. You should not grasp at the world with the intention of acquiring things that are for your comfort. Whatever is helpful to worship is already included in divine service. There is a famous saying: In the practice of asceticism no one can accuse you or deter you from its pursuit.

The wise have said: "Asceticism or detachment is the foundation of all riches and the root of all pleasing states and of favored stages." It is the very first stage for the disciple, since the foundation should be firm and stable. All other stages can be built in a proper fashion upon it. Whatever is not built solidly at the ground level, however, cannot be corrected by other builders later on, because "any building erected on a defective foundation will itself be faulty." One group of venerable Sufis has said: "Whoever has acquired a name for detachment in the world will gain a thousand worlds of praise; whereas everyone who has earned a reputation for hankering after things in this world will have to bear a thousand unpleasant names." Hence it is that Imam Nasirabad has said: "An ascetic yearns while he is in the world, while a mystic is longing while in the next!"

It is related that Khwaja Junaid said: "There are three types of asceticism. One is the abandonment of what is forbidden; it is the asceticism of ordinary people. The next is the abandonment of an overabundance of what is lawful; it is the asceticism of the elect. The third type is the abandonment of anything that might draw the attention of the servant away from God; it is the asceticism of the Sufis." From this division there should arise a good understanding of the verses of poets and the sayings of the sheikhs in praise or disparagement of asceticism, while ascetics too should understand the matter well and not fall into error. Khwaja Fuzail Ibn Iyaz has said: "God has placed all forms of wickedness in one house, and the key to it is love of the world; whereas He has placed all goodness in one house, and its key is abandonment of the world."

Take note, O brother; if you coil up your body that is filled with jealousy, and your own foundationless nature, you will be like a silkworm that, when it coils itself up, remains confined in the prison of its own soul, and there gives up its life! Come out of that black house of your soul, walk around the Kaaba of hope and fear of God, and dwell in the sanctuary of asceticism and renunciation, that tomorrow, when you appear filled with the light of knowledge of God on the plain of the Resurrection, hell will have no hold over you! This is the slogan of hell: "O believer, pass on quickly, for your light extinguishes the power of my flames!" In other words, "O believer, pass on in safety, for my fear is that the light of your faith might destroy my very nature, and no trace of burning or utterance might remain in me!"

Why do you fix your attention on your own sin? Why do you look at what is but water and dust? Look at the One who is with you! You want to refrain from sinning, but are unable to refrain because you are someone who sins, while He is One who forgives. Each acts according to his own particular disposition. You will say that He says: "My servant has a tendency to sin, but it is My nature to forgive! Since you do not desist from your inclination to sin, why should I desist from displaying My special attribute? Tell My servants that I am forgiving and merciful (Q15:49). Even if you are a sinner, you still belong to Me. But if you are submissive, then I already belong to you!"

Do you know why it is that, when you sin, it is called your ignorance? It is in order to forgive you! It was said of Adam: "Surely he is cruel and ignorant" (Q32:72). When you bear witness to God, and are called wise, do you know why it is so? It is because you acknowledge that "God bears witness that there is no god but He, as do the angels and those possessed of knowledge" (Q3:17). Do you know why it is that you are weak? "Man has been created weak" (Q4:28). It is in order that He might forgive your trespasses!

*Peace!*

LETTER 76: BLISS AND MISERY

*In the name of God, the Merciful, the Compassionate!*

Dear Brother Shamsuddin, may God keep you in safety! Bliss and misery are two treasures as far as the Lord is concerned. The key to the former is submission, while the key to the latter is sin. The one who, from the beginning, "is fortunate, has been blessed from his mother's womb." Such a person is given the key to bliss, whereas the one who, from the beginning, "is unfortunate, has been born accursed." Sin is the key to misery. It is placed in his hand today. Everybody should look at his own hand to see which key is in it. That will indicate the divine ordinance with respect to him. Hence it is said that bliss and misery are not born today—at least this is what those learned in matters of the next world say, not those well versed in worldly learning! There is a hint of this mystery in the following verse:

We know both brocade and the striped cloth of Razi:
We can distinguish genuine love from what is feigned.

All the honor and wealth of a servant lies in submission, while all his baseness derives from sin. All nearness depends on submission, all punishment, on sin. All those who are thrown down are thrown off the path of sin; while all those who are raised aloft are raised up from the path of submission. One who for seven hundred thousand years

312

was devoted to religious exercises in a holy place, his rosary constantly in his hand, forever purifying himself, was thrown down simply because he abandoned prostration, with the result that he was never able to rise up again. But the dog of the Companions of the Cave, originally endowed with dirty and unclean qualities, simply by associating, for some time, with righteous men, was so lifted up as to be incapable of falling. What is all this? "This is the decree of the great, wise God" (Q41:12).

> One nation reaches the firmament, another descends to hell:
> A cry, due to terror of You, comes from this handful of dust!

God be praised, what could be more astonishing than that the knowledge of all the learned should be turned upside down? No one has become acquainted with the full meaning of this mystery! The intellects of the intelligent have gone astray. No one knows the way to this saying. Peace be upon the pure soul who said:

> I am love, but My dwelling is invisible in either world:
> I am the traceless Phoenix of the West.
> With My eyebrow and coquetry I have ensnared both worlds:
> Do not take heed of the absence of bow and arrow!
> I am visible, like the sun, on the face of every atom:
> My manifestation is so dazzling that I am imperceptible.
> It is I who speak through every tongue, and hear by every ear:
> Astonishing, though it be, that neither ear nor tongue is
>     visible.
> Since I am everything that exists in all the worlds,
> There is nothing in either world that is the life of Me!

How astonishing and mysterious that Adam was told, "Do not eat wheat!" and yet another command came that he should eat. Satan was told, "You have to worship Adam!" and another command came that he should not. Men of the West were thrown into the East, while those of the East were thrown to the West. Wherever they arrived or went, they heard this very same thing: "There is no way out for you—you simply have to go on seeking! But, of yourself, you have no way of finding!"

O brother, not more than one secret from the world of God has been made manifest. Those who are treading the Path as well as those who dwell at the divine threshold have said: "We know nothing except what You have taught us" (Q2:32). What can mere dust and water say? All steps have become blameworthy! All minds have become stupified! All imaginations boggle! No more of the secret concerning Him is known than this: "I know what you know not" (Q2:30). And it was said: "O Muhammad, your prophethood is a holy one, your covenant is pure, your glory is exalted, and your address is favored. Yet I am the Lord who does whatever He wishes. It is a long time since I put a seal on tongues, saying: 'He cannot be questioned as to what He does' " (Q21:23). The Lord of Glory is utterly free of faith and submission! His pure abode has no trace of disbelief or sin. There all is holy, its hue one and the same. Sanai has said:

> In His utter self-sufficiency, what is disbelief and what is faith?
> In His perfection, where is there room for doubt or certainty?
> The wolf and Joseph, the small and the great, are both from
>     You.
> Indeed, for that Exalted One Joseph and the wolf are the same!

Knowledge is the basis of obedience, while ignorance lays the foundation for sin. Faith and obedience are the offspring of knowledge, while disbelief and sin are the offspring of ignorance. By no means can disbelief and sin proceed from ignorance! Obedience, therefore, is the key to bliss, sin to misery.

You should not overlook any point of obedience, no matter how minute it might be. Nor should you commit any sin, no matter how small it is. The wise have said: "Three things are hidden in three other things: pleasing God, in obedience, displeasing Him, in sin, and friendship with Him, in believers." No act of obedience should be overlooked, even though it be small, because it be the cause for incurring God's displeasure. Also, you should esteem every believer you meet as being better than yourself and consider him as one of God's friends. It is possible that your own friendship with God rests there! This is the labor of true servanthood.

It is not possible, however, to remove the dress that was sewn on somebody from the beginning. "The words of God cannot be changed" (Q10:64). A certain people passed its time, night and day, in struggles and asceticism, and their food was extremely meager. Yet they heard the pronouncement: "Their seeking was useless and the road was closed." Another people were engaged in worship in an idol-temple. They were worshiping Lat and Uzza, prostrating themselves before them. An address from the Lord came: "I am for you, whether you like it or not! And you are for Me, whether you like it or not!"

314

O brother, if there is sin but no obedience, then His forgiveness and pardon come to the fore. When the angels said, "Are You going to make the one who will spread mischief Your viceregent?" (Q2:30). God Almighty did not deny that Adam would do wrong. Instead He said: "I know what you know not (Q2:30). If men are not worthy, I shall make them worthy. If they are far off, I shall bring them near. If they are disgraced, I shall make them dear. If they are preoccupied with their own greatness, I will make them realize that they must trust in My mercy. Of what value is your greatness if it is not accepted by Me? And what harm can arise from your sin, once you experience My forgiveness? I know what you do not know." Such persons are the bearers of the divine good pleasure for eternity. Some damage done from time to time cannot act as an obstruction to what has, from the very beginning, been ordered for life everlasting. Do you know what sin is? It is a mole added to your beauty, so that the gaze of jealous ones might fall on that mole and not on your beauty. Thus you will know that we are those blessed by receiving His favor. We are creatures without an equal, and He is the Incomparable Creator. You can find many like us, but none like Him. With respect to power there are many others like us, but no one at all is like Him with respect to honor and love. From His power He can create a hundred thousand people like us, but out of His sense of honor and love, He has not done so.

There was a man who had a son. He had a great love for his son. People said, "How much do you love this son of yours?" He replied, "Out of the love I bear him I do not want to have any other children, for I do not wish to associate my love for him with love for any other."

*Peace!*

LETTER 77: THE SECRETS OF FATE AND PREDESTINATION[91]

*In the name of God, the Merciful, the Compassionate!*

Brother, "the lords of righteousness will be questioned about their righteousness," and they are all trembling! And "the obedient ones are in great danger!" The devout, the ascetics, the Sufis, and also the scholars—all will fear the sword of His complete self-sufficiency. "Undoubtedly God has no need in either world."

> This work has proved to be very difficult, for
> The Beloved is so rich and we are simply beggars!

We have become the fuel of hell, joining the company of Nimrod and Pharaoh. We have fallen asleep, dreaming foolishly about ourselves. The effect of such foolishness on the hearts of men is greater than that of hell on unbelievers!

O brother, what place is there here for either stability or rest? A creature, made out of water and dust, has been destined to be thrown onto the field of calamity. If he eats his fill, he grows drowsy. If he is hungry, he grows mad. If he is asleep, he is like a dead man. If he gets up, he is perplexed. Indigence and helplessness are his inevitable qualities. If he seeks mystical knowledge of God, the reply comes: "They do not honor God with the honor due Him" (Q6:92). If he becomes immersed in divine service, it is said: "They have been given no other command than to serve God with great sincerity!" (Q98:5). And if a person ceases to pursue either gnosis or service, it is said: "I did not make jinn and men except to worship Me!" (Q51:56). If he becomes foolish and sits down, he is frightened with, "Know that the grip of your Lord is very tight!" (Q13:6). If anyone seeks an intercessor, the order comes: "No one can speak except he whom the Merciful permits to speak, and he will declare what is right" (Q78:38). And if you have looked at yourself or at someone else, it is said: "If you have made anyone an associate with God, all your works will come to nothing" (Q39:65). And if you want to have some small benefit in your heart, it is said: "Undoubtedly these are protectors over you" (Q82:10).

If, on the other hand, you desire any rank in your heart, it is said: "He knows the hidden secrets of the heart!" If someone flees and goes into hiding, it is said: "There is no place to which he can escape!" If he continues to flee, calamity befalls him: "All have to return in His direction!" If a person abandons everything and sits helplessly, he hears: "And those who strive hard for Us, We will certainly guide them in Our Ways" (Q29:69). If he tries to exert himself, he hears: "God distributes His mercy to whomsoever He will!" If anyone despairs, it is said: "Do not despair of God's mercy!" (Q39:53). If, on becoming filled with hope, you grow fearless, it is said: "Are they secure from God's design?" (Q7:99). And if one cries out, it is said: "He cannot be questioned as to what He does!" (Q21:23).

One is accepted, while another is borne away:
The secret of all this has been revealed to no one.
Fate reveals just this much to us:
You are the measure, and You measure out the wine!

The Sufis have said: "We entered this world in a condition of instability. We pass our days here in astonishment and, with a cry, we leave." The Prophet of Islam went to sleep one night. When he got up, seventeen of his hairs had turned white. The companions asked what had happened. He replied that the chapter *Hud* ["Warning," Chapter II of the Quran] had descended upon him. This resulted from the command "Hold firm to whatsoever has been said!"

O brother, the road is not secure. The resting place is a long way off. There is no limit at all in our Beloved and Desired One, whereas we have a weak body, a helpless heart, a lover's soul, and a secret longing.

Except for soul and liver, You have no other hunting or meat:
Hence it is that no head has grasped Your secret!

My harvest is devotion for the heedless, who, at the end of their lives, will be held accountable: "And We shall turn to the work they have done, and We shall render it as scattered dust" (Q25:23). The breasts of many, in the throes of death, will have something they never thought of made manifest to them by God (Q39:47). One can become lost at the very last moment, if his head is not placed in such a way that he is facing Mecca. A friend may be called a stranger on that night. One is told: "Have sweet dreams, like a bride," while another hears, "Sleep like an unhappy man!" One who has not abandoned any devotion may still be rejected. All the courteous behavior of a person who is incapable of divine union is nothing but sin. On the other hand, one who does not even reflect on his sins may be accepted. There is something in his face that intercedes on his behalf and effaces his faults from hearts. Seeking pardon and forgiveness, he makes his way forward. Look at Abraham, the Friend, emerging from the idol-temple of Azar! "He brings forth the living from the dead" (Q6:96). Look at Canaan and Noah: "And He brings forth the dead from the living" (Q6:96). Look at what Adam attained, though he did not desist from his faults. And look at Satan, who was rejected without deriving any benefit from his devotion.

Those who have been called "have received joyful tidings" (Q39:17), but "today there is no good news for the guilty" (Q25:22). "They carry the scar of their prostrations upon their faces" (Q48:29). Hence, "you will be able to recognize the guilty from their foreheads" (Q55:41).

> Do not sit around like a contented fool!
> Gain some benefit from this passing world!
> Dust settles of itself, and doubt arises;
> Am I mounted on a horse, or on a dead ass?

As far as you can, remain brokenhearted and miserable. When Moses spoke with God, he said: "Lord, where should I search for You?" The answer came: "In that heart which has been broken as the result of a wound inflicted by Me!" He said: "O God, there is no heart that is more hopeless or broken than mine is!" He said, "I am where you are!" As long as a man has a shield in his hand, he still wants to remain alive; but if he has flung away his shield, brought his horse to a halt, drawn his sword, and jumped down onto the ground, one can truly say that he has lost the will to live.

One beloved of God said: "I visited a dervish and said: 'Any lover who is unable to bear patiently an oppression inflicted by the Beloved is not a true lover.'" The sheikhs of Iraq said: "No person has attained the epitome of mystical knowledge until rejection and favor become, for him, one and the same."

When Shibli heard this, he said: "This is wrong! A man becomes a Sufi when, for him, rejection becomes preferable to favors, since rejection and difficulty underscore desire for God in a special way, while favors contain some admixture of the servant's desire for himself. A genuine Sufi is he who sacrifices his own desires for those of the Friend."

*Peace!*

# THE HUNDRED LETTERS

*In the name of God, the Merciful, the Compassionate!*

Brother Shamsuddin, may God keep you safe! Hope and fear are like the sun and shade. Any fruit that is always in the shade does not ripen. If, on the other hand, it was always in the sunshine, it would shrivel up. Until such time as it experiences both, the fruit cannot reach the stage of ripening. In the same way a servant, in good time, grows to perfection through the caressing shade of divine favor and the blazing rays of divine wrath. Sometimes, the divine favor solicitously proclaims: "Come here, for here has been prepared from the dust beneath the feet of dogs, a soothing collyrium for the eyes of friends." "Their dog stretched out its paw at the entrance" (Q18:18). In the Word of God they themselves continue to increase until the Day of Judgment. Sometimes, for no apparent reason, "Get away! Get Away!" is heard. Here the teacher of the angels has spent seven hundred thousand years of devotion at the divine threshold. His angelic garb was snatched off his head and this seal was imprinted on his forehead: "Surely My curse is on you till the Day of Judgment!" (Q38:78). Sometimes an Umar, who might have passed his whole life as a stranger, is raised up from before an idol in some temple and told, "I am for you, whether you like it or not: and you are for Me, whether you like it or not." Sometimes it happens as it did to Balaam, who was unique and enjoyed a very exalted estimation, yet was turned out of the mosque and chained to a pack of dogs and heard the indictment: "He is like a dog that, when a load is placed upon it, pants; but even if nothing is placed upon it, still it pants." Sometimes thousands of millstones of calamity, and the fear of affliction, are rained upon the heart and liver of the disciple; or thousands of those dwelling in the sanctuary are sent in to encounter Him and are called to favor; or mountains of favors, as it were, are bestowed; at other times nothing is left. Sometimes he is seated on the very presidential seat of heaven, at other times he is cast completely outside, and is not even allowed to stay at the door. In a similar way, the Almighty sometimes discloses Himself to him, at other times hides Himself from him.

When God displays Himself to him, a person exclaims: "O God and Lord, accept me as Your dog!" When God takes him completely out of himself, he can say nothing except "I am the Truth" and "Praise be to me!" Both of these aspects are correct! Insofar as man is but dust and water, what else is he except a dog? Yet insofar as God has said, "I have breathed My own spirit into him" (Q38:72), he is a spirit. Why should he not utter, "I am the Truth" and "Praise be to me?" Here intellect and knowledge fail! Here spiritual master and disciple are but paintings on a wall! Here "He does whatever He intends to." Here "God does what He wants and gives orders for what He intends" (Q85:16). As a result of all this abandonment and consolation, throwing down and lifting up, driving and coaxing, granting intimate knowledge and also intoxication with the divine favor, a person gradually attains maturity, as does the aforementioned fruit. If the process was all hope, it would lead to indolence and laziness. Immaturity would be engendered. Yet unrelieved fear would cause a person to be consumed by the fire of despair. He could not persevere! There should be a mixture compounded of both fear and hope, in equal portions, that the disease of the disciple might be treated effectively. It has been said that hope and fear are like the two wings of a disciple. A bird is well balanced if its wings are equal. If they are unequal, it can still fly, but in a crooked way. And if it has but one wing, it must surely perish.

It is related in the books of the Sufi sheikhs that hope should be such that if all the sin and opposition of the entire world were his alone, and a voice were to come and say, "There is only one person who will go to heaven," he would know that he was that person! On the other hand, his fear should be such that if all the obedience and devotion of all the worlds belonged to him alone, and a voice were to come and say, "Only one person will go to hell," he would know that he was that person! As far as a disciple is concerned, however, it is fitting that fear should predominate over hope, for the masters of the Path had a fear that knew no limits. If you saw their eye, you would say, "They have become bereft of hope in God's mercy!" Such are the hopeless. For a disciple, progress will be quicker by associating with this group and by serving its members than by mortification and retiring into solitude. The story of the dog and the Companions of the Cave[92] illustrates this point beautifully. It was a mere dog yet, after serving the men of the Way for a short time, it became a man, as is said:

> The dog of the Companions of the Cave, in but a few days,
> Followed the footsteps of good men, and became a man!

In the early years of their lives a number of the Prophet's companions prostrated themselves before idols in churches and temples and abandoned themselves to estrangement from God. Suddenly the wealth of companionship with the Apostle appeared on the scene. For some days they had the honor of serving at his threshold. They became disciples. They attained their desire. Though strangers they developed into exemplar Muslims. Each of them became a vice-regent in Islam. Their imitation of the Prophet began here, and when tomorrow arrives, you will see them as resplendent as the sun or the moon.

It is related that when the blessed ones reached paradise and were completely taken up with damsels, castles, and purified wine, suddenly there was a flash of lightning illuminating the whole of paradise. All fell down in prostration, crying: "God Almighty has manifested Himself among us!" It will be said, "Alas, that is not the case." Usman, the leader of the faithful, had just gone from one room to another. It was the edge of his cloak that had been glowing. Hence you should know and recognize what results from companionship with this group and service devoted to it!

> If you wish for honor, devote yourself to those who have
>     drawn near!
> For from such men as these a man quickly learns to do the
>     same.

Whatever you do, no matter how insignificant it might be, it is necessary that you be sincere and truthful. Sincerity means that you remove all creatures from your path, while truth means that you remove yourself from your path. When you reach this stage and cut across this treacherous wilderness, hypocrisy will have no claim on you, nor will any wonder be able to influence you. When these two veils have been removed, no further veil remains between you and the divine threshold. All will be disclosure and light! One becomes a confidant. The veil is for the person denied entry. When you are welcomed into the arbor of intimacy, the veil is lifted as a matter of course. The confidant is he who cleanses his nature of estrangement from God, but know that your nearness to God lies in your distance from yourself.

The very least of the signs of Nearness is contemplation and persistence. In reality, every wayfarer who claims a position of rank and dignity should realize that he is nurturing the core of self-deception! That is the world of great distance from God, not of nearness to Him! Do you not see that the angels looked upon their works with approval and pleasure, saying: "We sing Your praises" (Q2:30)? The king of all those renowned in the world of intention entered and said: "Prostrate yourselves before this handful of clay" [see Q2:34] that the estimation you have of your praise might be lifted from before your eyes!

*Peace!*

LETTER 79: SPIRIT

*In the name of God, the Merciful, the Compassionate!*

Brother Shamsuddin, there is a difference of opinion among people with regard to the spirit. One group calls it a body; another group, a substance; another, the soul; another, eternal; still another, created. The Christians also call it eternal, and a number of philosophers agree with this opinion. The orthodox view,[93] however, is that we shall call it "spirit," and not say anything about its nature or quality. Hence it is that Khwaja Junaid has said: "The spirit is at the command of my Lord, and of knowledge you were given but a little" (Q17:85). We are not permitted to explain it through any creature, for God has said: "When people ask you about spirit, you are to say that it is at the command of my Lord." Junaid added: "The jurists firmly maintain the same viewpoint, namely that God Almighty has told us just this much about its nature, that 'when people ask you about spirit,' God put an end to the matter by prohibiting any further discussion saying, 'You are to say that it is under the command of God.' " The reason is that beneath this command there is nothing but a creature, something contingent. We should take our stand on what God has said and not ask, "What is it?" and "Where is it?" for its Creator has told us about it, but not about its nature and quality.

Hence the venerable Sufis have spoken in this manner: "Among all the creatures of God Almighty there is one called spirit, but He did not disclose what it is, or where it is. The result is that people are unable to understand it. Hence people should realize that if they cannot understand a creature when God does not tell them about it, how can they hope to know the Creator unless He first makes Himself known to them?" Maulana Rumi has said:

Listen to this address, and prepare to give an answer!
An atom has become a great sign for the sun.
All the kings on the way of religion, all the trustworthy angels
   say,

Bowing in prostration; "I am a tiny basket, ready to receive what God gives."

Another of the beloved has said:

Your body lives by its soul, yet you ignore it:
You live by the soul, without knowing the soul.
Behold, how delicately fashioned is everything, both hidden
and visible.
There is no alternative, O friend, but to keep silent!

Abu Bakr was asked what the soul was. He said that it was not produced under the creative command of God. The meaning of someone who asserts this is that spirit is nothing more than making something alive, or life itself. Yet we know that it is God Almighty who makes alive—"Bestowing life is one of the divine attributes," for creating is proper to the Creator. The proof of this is that God has said, "The spirit is at the command of my Lord" (Q17:85). God's command is His word, and this is hidden from creatures. It is as if you were to say: "This speaker says that the body that came to life did so at the divine command." There is no other meaning in the terms life and spirit.

The wise have said: "This is incorrect! In point of fact, there is meaning in the term, 'spirit.' It is created inside the body, just as the body itself is created." As for the saying: 'It does not come under the divine command,' this is an apt hint that things are of two kinds: Either they are passing, or eternal. All ephemeral beings are under the creative command of God, whereas all eternal beings are not. They are called 'eternal' because every being that does not cease to exist is eternal. It is clear that spirit, from which the body derives the attribute of life, is a quality of the body, for it is unthinkable that an essence be modified by a quality that is completely extrinsic to it. Hence it is correct to say that spirit is a quality of this living creature. Now this essence is transitory, and it is impossible for such an essence to have an eternal quality, just as it is impossible for an eternal essence to have an ephemeral quality. Yet it has been said: "It is nothing but bringing to life, and bringing to life is the quality of one who does just that, in the same way that giving existence is the prerogative of the Creator." This line of argument is false, for the simple reason that, if we admit this for the spirit, we would have to do the same for all qualities. Hence we would say that a being at rest is not at rest because it is resting but because it has been put to rest by a "quieter."

Or, a being in motion is not in motion because of its own motion, but because it was put in motion by a "stirrer." Similarly, sleeping and waking, health and sickness, and all the qualities of beings would have to be restricted to this source, and it would have to be said that all of these did not come within the ambit of the creative command of God.

But this is incorrect. It could not be correct! The person who argues about this revelation of the Lord, namely, "Say: that the spirit is at the command of my Lord" (Q17:85), says that His command is His word, which is not created. This way of arguing is incorrect because God did not command Muhammad: "Say that the spirit is the command of my Lord," as though spirit were a command, and this command was His word! On the contrary, He said: "It is at the command of my Lord." Thus the spirit has been confirmed at the very moment when He said that spirit "is at My command." It is clear that spirit is not a command, but proceeds from a command. If by this description one were compelled to say that spirit was not something created, then one would also have to say that all things are not creatures, because just as spirit is from His command, so, too, all things are from His command, for His command is creative—"Be! and it came to be" (Q2:148). All transient beings, from the divine throne to the nadir of hell, from the beginning till eternity, share in this quality that He said, "Be! and it came to be." All are transient, not eternal. It is impossible that spirit be eternal.

This is why most people say that the members of this group have gone astray in this matter, and give witness to their unbelief on the topic of spirit. They say that these call spirit something eternal, just as the Christians do. The latter have said: "A group that belongs to Islam is our friend, for they say that spirit is eternal." This accusation became abominable for the group in question. If such a charge is correct and Sheikh Abu Bakr of Qahat subscribed to this belief, then a certain group in one of its books has remembered that error and tried to explain his position. It is not known, however, whether this is what that great man said or not. And it turns out that these heretics have not remembered him correctly but have striven to denigrate the real Muslims, and to strengthen their own sect. Even were it true that the firm opinion of Sheikh Abu Bakr of Qahat was this, then just because one member of a group is at fault, we cannot say that the whole group went astray and became unbelievers. We have described this not with the intention of proving that spirit is eternal, but to affirm that it is an order from the Giver of life, not a quality within the living creature. One should not call this spirit "eternal."

There may have been a mistake in the argumentation of that great man. When one whose heart is intoxicated makes a mistake in his chain of reasoning, this does not make him an unbeliever. Since he himself did not become an unbeliever because of his error, it is impossible that all the group should be accused of having gone astray and become unbelievers on his account. Or, even if the entire group of that great man is held to be in error in its argumentation, and if, because of that fact, it is said that all groups have gone astray, then it must necessarily be added that there cannot be found a single correct investigator of reality in the whole world, since there is no group in quest of God that does not include someone who has unintentionally erred. But are they called unbelievers simply because of a single error?

The same applies here. God knows the full truth of what takes place. The author of *Kitab at-Ta'arruf* [The book on seeking knowledge] has spoken about spirit, heart, the lower soul, and the world, and what he said can be taken as a common basis for the first conviction of Muslims. Let us recall something of what he said. In his view, spirit, heart, the lower soul, and the world are the four things that God Almighty has mentioned by name in His own book. The Law also speaks of them. The people, too, acknowledge their existence. Although the Law and people speak about these four, mentioning their features, activities, and outward qualities, nowhere is there a description of their inner qualities and essence! Khwaja Attar said:

> The soul had loftiness, but the earth-formed body, lowliness:
> There occurred a meeting of lowly dust and pure soul.
> When the exalted and the lowly became friends,
> Then man emerged as a secret, filled with wonder.
> But nobody was acquainted with His secret;
> Nor could a single beggar's work be compared to His!
> You are able to say only so much. No path remains but silence,
> Who is there who can even dare to utter a sign?

The wise have said: "If it were permissible to speak about spirit, then the Messenger would have been the first to do so, so that when he was asked about spirit he would have answered, because his intellect surpassed all others! As far as both the orthodox and heretics are concerned, the orthodox acknowledge him as the Apostle and easily admit that Muhammad is the most intelligent of men. The heretics, too, call him Abu Ja'far, the Wise. Certainly a wise person must be highly intelligent! Hence there is concurrence about his intelligence, and it was he who was asked about spirit. Yet he did not reply from his intelligence. Instead, he hesitated, until a reply came in the form of an order that confirmed the existence of the spirit, but said nothing about its nature or quality. It was the perfection of his intellect that made him consider this as the proper response. It was the harm done to our intellects that makes it even more necessary for us to respond in a similar way, for we are but slaves, and must conform to the injunctions of the Law. The Law also corroborates this opinion; we should not enquire into the nature and quality of the spirit, since the Law does not treat them.

> It is lord, yet totally at my service:
> Even if it is not God, still it is my lord!
> Do not say this, for it does not come within your perception!
> Do not waste your breath, for you will not be able to explain
> it!

The sheikhs say: "Some of the venerable Sufis have seen the spirit, each of them in some particular form or another." And this is understandable from what we have just said, for since it exists, it should be visible. Reflect on the way in which it is permissible to see God, Who also exists. Well, then, the spirit, which is His handiwork and exists, should likewise be visible, for the creature cannot be more refined than its Creator. Whenever seeing is possible with Him, it must also be possible here. If God Almighty wishes to disclose Himself to His servant, He shows Himself just as He wants, and no tongue can act as a wedge between Him and His servant. Sa'di has said:

> The keepers of secrets hold their tongues in check,
> In order to conceal the secrets of the king.
> Who, fearing You, has the boldness
> To move his tongue except in praise of You?

O brother, it is all amazement. No knowledge or intellect suffices. When He wishes, the King beyond all needs makes a raid on the souls and the hearts of one hundred thousand upright saints. And when He wishes, He makes one hundred thousand others into lovers with inflamed hearts and roasted livers. The profile of God's will is thus made resplendent! Who is not bound before His glory? And who is not intoxicated by His grandeur? And what heart is not wounded by the sword of His anger?

> You have played with love, so wash your hands of heart and
> eyes!
> This is an event of today, but Oh! that it might last till
> tomorrow!

It is an astonishing world! Moses was told: "You cannot see Me!" (Q7:143). Then he was told: "Look to the mountain!" (Q7:143). Then again: "Go to Pharaoh!" (Q20:24). Just see the way He acts toward souls filled with love in the preceding story! When Moses arrived at that station and these exchanges took place, he wanted to return to his wife and children. An address came: "Since you have fallen into My net, and have put My name on your heart, and have set out on the way to Me, your heart should become acquainted with grief and your soul with danger!"

> Your heart should be acquainted with grief, your soul with
> danger:
> All devoted to idols have their gaze fixed in one direction.
> No longer enamored of their own heart or soul or sight
> Are those whose heart desires the company of a certain face.

*Peace!*


## LETTER 80: THE HEART

*In the name of God, the Merciful, the Compassionate!*

Brother Shamsuddin, may God enlighten your heart! The treasury of the King is found in the heart. Look carefully to see what you have in this treasury! If it is filled with gold and gems, then it is indeed a treasury. But if it is full of straw and refuse, then it is a mere rubbish dump. One treasure is said to be in heaven, and consists of the blessings of paradise. There is also a treasury in the hearts of Sufis. It is known as love. In God's eyes a single gem from the treasury of love is worth thousands upon thousands of paradises. The keeper of the treasury of paradise is an angel called "Rizwan," but the keeper of the treasury of love is the Lord himself.

Your worth can be estimated by what you seek. If you seek a dog, your worth is that of a dog. The same could be said about other things. The dog of the Companions of the Cave also illustrates this point. Because it desired God, its worth was enhanced. God Almighty made it clear in His venerable revelation that "their dog stretched out its paws at the entrance" (Q18:18). Look also at Balaam, the son of Beor. His desires were lustful, and that was all he was worth. Such people are neither heavenly nor earthly, nor of the East or the West, nor of the heights or the depths, nor of Adam or of his sons—they simply seek themselves. The secret of what is meant has been thus expressed: "The poor man is the product of his time."

Now look into the treasury of your own heart, and see what you are worth. Know that every heart that depends on God has a value beyond reckoning. Even if you rub your precious face in the dust, you will not be granted what Pharaoh and Nimrod were granted gratis. This is not due to their worth but to your inestimable value.

A beggar saw a king and asked him for a silver coin. The king replied: "Such a request is not worthy of me." So the beggar said: "Give me a thousand silver coins!" The king replied: "Such a gift is not sufficient for you!"

A man asked God for a son. A hermaphrodite was born to him. He said: "O God, I asked You for a son, but You have given me a hermaphrodite." He heard a voice: "I know how to give, but you do not know how to ask!" Whoever does not know how to ask will acquire nothing but regret. Whoever worships God because he desires heaven is a slave of his own desire. Whoever worships Him out of a fear of hell is a slave of hell, for anyone who is afraid of anything is a slave of that thing. By the same token, whoever puts his hope in anything is a slave of that thing. Your true reality is that which is within your breast. A man is where his heart is! The exterior of a man is like a sword revealing his inner state, for his outward demeanor covers what lies within. If his interior is insincere, so too will his exterior be. If his interior is under God's sway, however, such a person will be called a "man of God."

You have been chained by your own desire. What you choose becomes your prison. The order you have been given is to come down, not to fall upon some dead prey, for it is the vulture that always does that. Though it is stronger in flight than a falcon, it only descends upon a carcass, while a falcon pounces on some living creature. Whatever pertains to the world is merely a carcass, but whatever has to do with the next life is alive. The tradition of this group lies behind these two, as you must have heard:

> For us there is another world besides this one:
> Beyond hell and paradise there is yet another resting place!

Hence it is that many renowned religious men have paid no attention to either hell or paradise, as is evidenced by the story of Abdullah Mubarak. One day he came crying out of his house. He was asked what had happened, since he was the leader of a Sufi order. He replied: "Last night I brazenly committed a sin. Now I am full of repentance for it." He was asked what it was. He replied: "I asked God to forgive my sins. Of what use could such a thing be to me? I am but a slave, and a slave is wholly bound to his master!"

Once Khawaja Junaid had a fever. He prayed: "O God, restore me to health!" A voice was heard: "Why do you impose yourself between you and Me? Do you think I do not know what should be done on your behalf? This worry is for others, not for you!" To people like us, however, devotion means that we fear hell and hope to reach paradise. The Lord of the world said that the prayer of common people is this: "O God, I ask You for paradise and fly to You for protection against hell." If it is not possible to reach the world of Truth, at least we may be saved from hell and acquire paradise. Be careful not to rest on your laurels for even the twinkling of an eye: The heart is such that it must be afflicted either with the pain of not finding or with the joy of finding!

Abul Qasim Nasirabadi was asked if he had any of the qualities that belonged to the Sufi sheikhs of old. He said: "Yes, the fear of not finding Him!" If you say, "I am doing my work well," be careful to see what exactly you are doing: Is it something demonic or something divine? Every morning you go to the bazaar, and return home each evening. If this is all you have to show for yourself, how are you any different from Zoroastrians and Jews who do the same? What is it for which you pray? God's blessings on your activities! If you go on the pilgrimage to Mecca, you do so in order to earn the title "Pilgrim." If you do anything else, it bears the same stamp. You are forever stuck in names and customs, while the real meaning of your activities remains hidden from you.

O soul and world of mine, this tradition is for manly people, not for us defiled hermaphrodites! This is the way of the pure, not of handfuls of feeble dust and iniquity! This wine is for the fortunate, not for luckless paupers like us!

*Peace!*

LETTER 81: THE LOWER SOUL[94]

*In the name of God, the Merciful, the Compassionate!*

Brother Shamsuddin, may God honor you! There is a controversy about what exactly constitutes the lower soul. Whatever somebody says turns out to be the opposite of what others say. The seekers of Truth in this group, however, have two opinions about the matter. One faction says that the lower soul is an essence within the body, similar to the spirit. The other faction maintains that it is a quality of the body, like life. They concur that both bad behavior and displeasing actions stem from it. These are of two kinds. One is sin itself, and the other, blameworthy ways of acting, such as pride, envy, avarice, anger, and similar things. Such defects can be removed from a person by means of asceticism, but repentance is necessary to remove sin, for though external actions lead to sin, such external behavior, in turn, originates from inner qualities. Asceticism deals with outward actions, while repentance is concerned with inner qualities and must purify the sinner inwardly.

It is said that the lower soul and the spirit are very delicate, and are in the body, just as devils and angels are in the world, as well as in heaven and hell, one representing the abode of goodness, the other, the source of evil. There is no escape from evil, except by asceticism.

To find the worth of a person's heart and his life,
One can discover it by no means other than asceticism!
If for an instant you bring your lower soul under control,
Then let no doubt remain: paradise is already yours!

There is even a controversy among the people as to what human nature is. What, in fact, is signified by the word *man*? Knowledge of this is obligatory for every seeker, because anyone who is ignorant of himself would be even more ignorant of what is other than himself! Whoever does not know his own essence will be even more ignorant of the essence of others. The Law has this to say: "Whoever knows his lower soul knows his Lord." In other words, anyone who grasps the nature of his lower soul by virtue of its mortality also perceives God through His attribute of immortality. Some have said: "Whoever understands the baseness of his own lower soul thereby realizes the exalted nature and honor of God." It has also been said: "Whoever becomes aware of his lower soul as an expression of servanthood also perceives the sublime magisterium of his Lord!" In short, everyone who fails to understand himself will also find the Almighty veiled from him.

The purpose of what has been said is to gain a deeper knowledge of human nature. One group says: "Man is nothing but spirit." This is erroneous, for the spirit lies hidden in the body. Spirit itself is not called "man." Another group says that the name "man" is given to the combination of spirit and body, just as a black and white horse is designated by only one word, "piebald." This, too, is erroneous. The proof is that God Almighty called Adam a man when he was still nothing but lifeless dust. "Surely there was a time when man was nothing that could be described" (Q76:1). There is also a group of false Sufis who say that man neither eats nor drinks nor is subject to change. Yet man is a divine secret whose body is his talisman! As the poet has said:

> The treasure is in the hold, the ship is the talisman;
> Finally, the talisman of the body will be destroyed.
> You will find the treasure when the talisman has passed away:
> You will come to life when your body is no more.
> After that, your life will have a different talisman,
> When your life has ceased, you will acquire another body.
> Sew up your lips! Do not inquire about footstool and throne!
> Even if you want to ask but a little about them—do not!
> No one knows completely even a particle of creation:
> A little you ask, a little you say; then your life is over!

There is a group that says that all the natures that are compounded within us are called "man" in the venerable Word itself, and what God says is more truthful than what anyone else can say. Beginning with dust and ending with dust, this special form, with all its manifold arrangement, is man. Know that the perfect man, according to the investigators of Truth, consists of three constituents: One is spirit, another is the lower soul, while the third is the body. Man is a microcosm of the entire world, that is to say, both this world and the next. We get some idea of both from man himself. This world is water, dust, air, and fire, and man is composed of phlegm, blood, bile, and melancholy. At the same time, man is a sign of the next world, of paradise, hell, and the heavenly courts. His spirit anticipates heaven on account of its refinement; his animal soul, hell on account of its baseness; while his body presages the celestial courts. We can say that it is the spirit that draws the believer toward paradise, for in this world it exemplifies paradise; while his animal soul impels him toward hell, of which it is the prototype in this world. [A long poem from Attar follows.]

It is related that Sheikh Abu Ali Siyah said: "I once saw my lower soul in the form of a pig. Someone snatched a hair from it and gave it to me. I bound it to a tree and resolved to destroy it. 'O Abu Ali,' it called out to me, 'do not kill me, for I am a soldier of God. You cannot destroy me.' "

It is related that Khwaja Muhammad Nuri said: "One day I saw my lower soul in the form of a baby fox that came out of my mouth. I understood that this was my lower soul. I flung it beneath my feet and, the more I stomped on it, the bigger and stronger it grew. I said: 'All things are destroyed by wounds and affliction, yet you thrive on them.' It replied: 'This is because I am made differently. What is affliction for another is comfort for me!' "

Sheikh Abu Abbas said: "One day I entered my house and saw a yellow dog. When I tried to chase it out, it ran under my skirt and disappeared." Sheikh Abul Qasim Gurgani said: "I saw it in the form of a serpent." Another dervish said: "I saw my lower soul in the form of a mouse. I asked: 'Who are you?' It replied: 'I am the destruction of the heedless and the salvation of the friends. If I were not with the latter—realize that my existence is a trial for them—they would grow proud of their own purity and boast of their deeds when they see the extent of their sanctity, comprehension of secrets, and stability in devotion! Pride and a spirit of self-sufficiency would begin to appear in them. When, however, they see me at either side, then they are washed clean of all such temptations!' "

All these stories go to prove that the lower soul is an essence, not simply a quality. It does, however, have qualities, and we can see them clearly. When the lower soul is recognized, it can easily be brought under control by austerities, but its essence does not pass away. When it is clearly recognized and the seeker masters it, then its continued existence within him provides no cause for fear. It has been said: "The lower soul is like a dog that barks and bites. When it is subdued by austerity, then it is lawful to keep it." This wilderness is arduous. It cannot be traversed without grace and favor of Almighty God, and the shade of the riches of a compassionate spiritual master.

> The man without a guide will get lost,
> For the way is long, dark and perilous.
> He should hold the lamp of knowledge before him,
> Otherwise he will fall headlong into a pit!

Khwaja Nizami has given us a hint about what is meant:

> Do not turn away from the service of hearts;
> Nor let go of the skirt of the acceptable ones.
> Because the thorn associates with the rose,
> It is like perfume on the skirt of a flower.
> Seek the mark of the exalted, O astute ones,
> And strive to go even beyond the mark.
> From below they rose to the firmament, crown on their head,
> For their whole body, from head to toe, was girded for service!

O brother, do not worry about your own safety, even if poison-stained swords descend upon you! Place your feet on the heads of garbage dogs in order that all might revile you, but remain calm throughout, your head bowed in adoration while secrets are manifested to you.

> When you yourself become the ocean and abandon your boat,
> Then you will become a world, even though you leave this one!

A certain dervish passed a night in prayer. The next day he appeared in front of his sheikh in the hope that the sheikh would praise him. He said: "O sheikh, what form do you see in me today?" He replied: "You look like a Jew!" The dervish rose up and raised a cry, saying:

> Nobody's day was ever made by worshiping idols!
> Where have I, wretch that I am, fallen today?

A man of insight wrote:

> Whoever does not make himself wretched today
> Will tomorrow become as contemptible as Pharaoh.

Whoever has not become intoxicated with love,
Will have to remain perpetually half-asleep!

Have you not heard about the heights to which the Lord of the world was raised on the night of ascent? On the Day of Resurrection, the uproar will not be less than at the battle of Uhud! Nor will the exalted crown of honor be worth less than the broken teeth and the garment soiled with blood from his liver! An inflamed one has said:

Blame is pointless for those slain at the head of Your lane.
How can anyone who has seen that Face remain free from
    trials?
All my life's troubles come from the thought of You:
When the King draws his sword, who is left in the city?

*Peace!*

## LETTER 82: INORDINATE DESIRE

*In the name of God, the Merciful, the Compassionate!*

Brother Shamsuddin, may God be gracious to you! Inordinate desire is explained as springing from the qualities of the lower soul. It is a veil for those in union with God; it is a battleground for disciples; and it is a mansion to be shunned by seekers. All its qualities have been ranged against seekers as obstacles to good works, as has been said: "Everyone who succumbed to his inordinate desires was destroyed, while everyone who opposed them attained what he sought."

Turning away from inordinate desire springs from sovereignty:
Shunning unbridled desire is the very sustenance of a
    messenger.
When the mount of your nature has been broken in,
Then coins will be known as pure because they bear your
    name!

All inordinate desires can be listed under two headings. One is the desire for pleasure and sensuality; the other is the desire for position and dominion. Those given over to pleasure and sensuality frequent taverns, but common people are not bothered by their wickedness. On the other hand, those who hanker after rank and power are

found in places of worship and in religious circles and become a se-
duction for the masses.[95] Falling from the way themselves, they divert others from it as well! Whoever simply accedes to his desires in
all his actions, being content to do whatever is agreeable to him, is far
away from God, even though he be above heaven itself!

> Since you have a hundred idols hidden under your patched
>    garment,
> Why do you parade before people as a Sufi?

On the other hand, the person who is far from his own desires,
and does not heed their promptings, is, in truth, close to God, even
though he be in a fire-temple!

> Whoever succeeds in chaining this dog with heavy fetters
> Has dust worth more than the blood of others!

Khwaja Ibrahim Khass says: "I heard there was a monk among
the Christians who, in accordance with his vocation, had passed seventy years in solitude. I said: 'This is astonishing, for the vow to live
the life of a hermit does not extend beyond forty years. Why did he
spend seventy years as a hermit?' I decided to visit him. When I arrived at his place, he opened a window and said: 'O Ibrahim! I know
why you have come! I am not sitting here simply to play the hermit! I
have a dog maddened with many desires, which I have chained up. I
am keeping guard over this dog in order to prevent its wickedness
from reaching ordinary people. Indeed, I am not what you took me to
be!'"

> This unruly soul is a total infidel:
> It is no easy matter to kill it.

Khwaja Ibrahim said: "When I heard what he had to say, I said:
'O the power of Almighty God who gives His slave the path of merit
and shows him the right way, even though he is totally in error! This
is the kind of favor He bestows!' He said to me: 'O Ibrahim, how long
will you go seeking after men? If you want Him, seek yourself! When
you find yourself, become your own watchman! Every day this inordinate desire dons three hundred and sixty forms of divine garb and
entices the servant of God into error! Have you seen those people
who made idols of their own desires?' " (Q45:43). The hidden meaning here is that the hearts of the dear ones have turned into blood in
this task.

A hundred thousand hearts have all perished with grief,
But this infidel dog does not retreat for a moment!

To sum up: Abandoning one's inordinate desires ennobles a man, but by giving vent to his desires, a noble man becomes a prisoner. Zulaikha, following her unbridled desires, changed from a noble lady to a prisoner, while the renowned Joseph told her to abandon her desires. He, though a captive, became a great man.

Whoever has chained this dog through his bravery
Can catch a lion with his lasso in either world.

Khwaja Junaid was asked: "What is union?" He replied: "The abandonment of following one's own desires." Everyone who is intent on attaining God should be told to abandon his own desires, for a servant can perform no greater act of devotion than to oppose his inordinate desires. It is easier for a man to dig up a mountain with his nails than to oppose his own desires!

Khwaja Zu'l Nun Misri said: "I saw a man flying through the air. I asked him how he had acquired that stage. He told me he had trampled desire underfoot and thus could fly through the air."

It is related that Khwaja Muhammad ibn Balkhi said: "I am astonished that anyone should go to His house in order to practice austerities out of his own unchecked desire. Why does he not tread desire underfoot in order to reach Him and see Him?" "Abandon your own desire and come along!" This is the hidden meaning. You should understand clearly now that Satan does not have the power to arouse sinful or lustful desires in the heart of a servant. It is only when they have originated in confused desire and begun to appear that Satan pounces on them, drawing them out into the full light of a person's heart.[96] This is known as a temptation of the devil. It has to take its origin from a man's inner desire. "The one who makes the beginning is very cruel." This is the meaning of the saying of the Lord concerning Satan for, when he had said "I shall lead all men astray," the Lord rebuked him, saying: "Surely you have no authority over My servants!" (Q17:65). Satan depends on the reality of this lower soul, and the inordinate desire of the servant! This is what the poet meant when he said:

If you are a servant of God, do not look at idols:
If you are a man of the Way, do not become an Azar!

Hence it is that when some sheikhs were asked what Islam was, they replied: "Cutting the throat of the animal soul with the sword of opposition." Khwaja Zu'l-Nun Misri said: "The key to worship is thinking, and the sign of the rectitude of your thinking is your opposition to your lower soul and your inordinate desires." Opposing one's animal soul means abandoning all lustful desires. Hence it is said that opposition to the lower soul is the crowning achievement of worshipers. Khwaja Junaid said: "Living according to the desires of one's soul is the foundation of unbelief." It is necessary for the disciple or the seeker to pass his time, night and day, doing this, his proper work, so that this pull of the animal soul, which takes its birth in the senses, might be entirely excised from his being. With cries and lamentation he should also request God to hear his cry: "When You have placed it here, who can snatch it away?" [A long poem follows.]

It is related that Khwaja Abu Ali Siyah said: "One day, according to the hallowed tradition, I was shaving my pubic hair. I said to myself: 'O Ali, this is the member that is the root of all lust, and has thrown you into so many calamities! Get rid of it, so that you might acquire release from its wickedness!' I heard a voice that said: 'O Ali, you are trespassing on My domain! One member is not of greater dignity than another in My estimation. If you yourself get rid of it, I can place in every hair of your body what I have placed in that one member!' "

> I was suddenly killed by astonishment;
> I knew no way out of my helplessness!
> Both believer and infidel are wading through blood;
> All have either grown bewildered, or retreated!

O brother, a servant has absolutely no power to destroy his lower soul. It is a mount that carries the burden of the commands of the Law. A servant can succeed in transforming a quality only by God's grace, since no quality is associated with him except what God has allowed. Unless and until He so wishes, the servant, by his own effort, cannot bring himself under control in anything!

> How is it that, finally, the way of Khusrau should become
> acceptable to You?
> For he is but a hopeless pauper, while You are joyous and do
> what You like!

Man has nothing to do with dignity in either dwelling. He either strives to divert the divine decree from himself or, in opposition to the divine decree, strives to acquire something for himself. Both are impossible, for God's decree cannot be altered through anyone's efforts. Imam Shibli fell ill. A physician came to him. He said: "You will have to practice abstinence." Shibli said: "Abstinence from what? From something that is allotted to me, or from something that isn't? If you say that the abstinence should be from what is my daily portion, there is nothing I can do about it; while if you say it is from something not included in my daily portion, then it simply won't be given to me. So tell me what I should abstain from?" The physician was left speechless.

> My wailing had reached heaven itself, though I was not yet
>   wounded:
> All the unfortunate physicians remained astounded at my pain.

It is related that Moses said: "O Adam, a cloth filled with delicacies was presented to you. Why did you stretch out your hand to the wheat?" Adam replied: "You must have read in the Torah that before I was created, this had already been written about me. How can you blame me?" Moses replied: "Then why did you explain, 'My lord, I am guilty of oppression?'" "My enemy had routed me," he explained, "and had proofs; my only approach to the threshold was to confess, 'My Lord, I am guilty of oppression,' for nobody can approach Him by means of arguments." Someone said to a beloved one: "First He ordains sin for me and then sends His punishment upon me." "Yes," replied the other, "that's what it's like! One cannot even find time to draw breath!"

> What business do you have with the wisdom of God?
> Do not even breathe—lest you lose what you have!
> Your Way is to remain silent and be patient:
> You will find no better helper than He!

It is related that Sultan Mahmud Ghazni had a very precious jewel in his hand. He gave it to his chief minister and told him to break it. The chief minister replied that it was as valuable as the king's entire treasury: How could it possibly be broken? The king then gave it to Ayaz and told him to break it. He placed it under a stone and promptly broke it. The king asked him why he had broken it. Replied Ayaz: "I have done evil and not good." Sultan Mahmud turned to his chief minister and said: "Learn courtly behavior from Ayaz, for he cannot be faulted either for his deed or for his speech!"

Beg to be excused for whatever fault you commit,
For Adam, by that very repentance, attained his rank!

*Peace!*

## LETTER 83: CURBING THE LOWER SOUL

*In the name of God, the Merciful, the Compassionate!*

Brother Shamsuddin, God grant you a high position among the pious! Man's nature is refractory. It is a mixture of bad qualities and unbecoming behavior. It has come down to us in verses of the Quran and in Tradition that, when the effects of bad behavior, which are the fruit of the domination of the lower soul, gain the ascendance over the states of a man, he falls into much loss and disappointment. He remains far from the light of faith and at a distance from the divine threshold, for the lower soul is the enemy of the heart, and the opponent of the faith. It is always preoccupied with its own advantage. Never is it inclined to follow the Law. The calamity of the lower soul strikes more lethally and swiftly than an infidel, and more frequently than the deception of Satan and his cunning, for a man's soul is inside his own shirt! Hence it has been said that the worst enemies and the most difficult calamities are those of the lower soul. Similarly, it is extremely difficult to treat it. This is all the more true since it is an internal enemy. Look what effort is required to drive out a thief who lives in the house itself. Moreover, this enemy is loved by man, and man has become blind to the faults of his own beloved: He considers anything wicked in his lower soul to be praiseworthy. Since such is the state of affairs, it does not take long for man's lower soul to hurl him into disgrace and destruction, and yet he is completely unaware of what is transpiring.

O brother, if you consider the matter closely, the root of all the discord, infamy, baseness, destruction, sin, and calamity with which mankind is afflicted, from the very origin of creation till the Day of Resurrection, is the lower soul. Whoever falls into calamity does so because of what his animal soul does, either by itself, or in association with others. Until the Day of Resurrection, you will not find among the people any discord, wickedness, infamy, or sin that does not owe its origin to man's lower soul and its inordinate desires. If it were not so, then everybody would be living happily and peacefully. Since it is the enemy of this Path, it is necessary for an intelligent man to rouse himself from its clutches. It is not possible for anyone to do this all of a sudden, as one could deal with other enemies, because it is the very mount and instrument of the seeker. It is difficult to lay it aside suddenly on account of the harm that would result. Here it is necessary for a disciple to follow the middle way. This means that the animal soul should be looked after and nourished as much as is needed to enable it to do its work, while it should be weakened and kept in check to the extent needed to prevent it from transgressing your commands. Whatever does not conform to this rule is wrong.

In a Tradition it is related that the Chosen One saw Masud, who had tormented his lower soul with such excessive austerities that he did not have strength even to move his hands or feet. When the Lord of the world saw his condition, he was displeased and said: "O Abdullah, your animal soul too has some rights over you! If you intend to destroy it, you will be caught and fall into sin." It has been indicated that the subduing of one's lower soul must be undertaken in an intelligent manner, lest it be destroyed or gain ascendancy over a person, or become refractory. To what extent should I keep it under control? One has to adopt a strategy in the matter.[97] First, one has to make it docile enough to bridle it. Those skilled in this matter enumerate three means by which the animal soul can be tamed. One is to keep it away from all lustful desires and pleasures, just as unruly cattle become docile once they are deprived of fodder. A religious scholar has said that the wickedness, ignorance, and rebelliousness of the animal soul is such that when it wishes to sin and gains a free rein then, even if you have the Apostle himself as intercessor before God, together with all the other prophets and sacred books and all former pious people, and remind it of death, the grave, judgment, paradise, and hell, still in no way would it stop, nor would it abandon that sin! When, however, you stop merely lamenting and restrain it, it is checked. The second is to place a heavy load of devotion upon it: Just as an ass, when it has a heavy load upon its back, becomes docile, so too will the lower soul, especially when its fodder has also been reduced. The third is to beg for help from Almighty God, and fly to Him for protection; otherwise, there is no escape from its wickedness.

When you show some accomplishment in using these three approaches, your animal soul will change from revolting against you to being obedient to you. While it is in this state, hurry up and put the bridle of Godly fear upon its head, and you will gain peace from its wickedness. If you say, "What is this 'Godly fear,' so that I might utilize it to curb my lower soul?" realize that it is an immense treasure and a vast grant of land wherein are gathered all the things from this world and the next. Something really special has been put here, and it is Godly fear.

Qatadah said: "In the Torah it has been written: 'O sons of Adam, fear God, and sleep peacefully wherever you wish!' " This quality applies to all good things, and suffices for all matters of importance. It will carry a servant to every possible rank and favor. It is such an indispensable foundation that no one can be a disciple without it. For the present, know that in the Quranic commentary of Imam Zahid it is mentioned that Godly fear is of two kinds: one the root, and the other its branch. The root is abstinence from infidelity by accepting the faith; its branch means abstinence from sin by the practice of submission. The sheikhs have said that there are three stages in Godly fear. The first is a fear of associating anything with God, the next is a fear of heresy, while the third is a fear of sin.

Godly fear implies abstinence from everything that you fear might be harmful to your faith. Do you not see that a sick person who abstains is called "abstemious," for he abstains from all that harms him, whether it be food, drink, or fruits and so on? Two things, as far as faith is concerned, have to be feared, on account of the damage they can do. One is what is simply forbidden and sinful, while the other is an overabundance of lawful things, for it frequently happens that an overabundance of lawful things draws a man to what is forbidden and sinful. Everyone who wants to remain free from any damage to his faith simply abstains from what is unlawful and sinful, and protects himself from an overabundance of lawful things. Mature and complete fear of God implies abstinence from all that would harm the faith—in other words, both sin and an overabundance of lawful things.

There is no room for negligence in this task, for opportunity is itself like gratuitous booty. It is also possible that you may seek but not find! Jesus said: "The world consists of three days. The first is the day that has passed—you can expect nothing from it now! As for tomorrow, you do not even know if you will survive until it comes. You are now in the third day—do not expect anything more than that!"

Abu Zarr said that there are no more than three hours in the world: the one that has passed, from which nothing can be expected; the coming hour—but will you see it? The third hour is the one in which you are living. So your life is but an hour! A renowned investigator of Truth said that the world consists of three breaths: the irredeemable past, the uncertain future, and the one you are now drawing!

You are not the master of a single day, hour, or breath! It is fitting to expend this breath in repentance and submission. Do not be anxious about your support. Perhaps you will be dead and buried by the time real need arises. It would be ruinous if a man were to fret over what was happening any particular day or hour—when he was destined to die at his next breath.

Remember also what the Apostle said concerning Usamah: "Usamah has too much hope, for he delayed for a whole month in buying a slave girl. By God, when I have completed one step, I am uncertain whether I shall take another or not! I do not even know if I shall swallow the morsel I have picked up!" A disciple should show himself to be assiduous in reflecting, night and day, over what has happened. Certainly his hope will become more sober! He will see his own animal soul and swiftly submit, repent, treat the world with indifference, and become wholly occupied with getting ready for death.

*Peace!*

## LETTER 84: STRUGGLING WITH AND CONTROLLING ONE'S LOWER SOUL

*In the name of God, the Merciful, the Compassionate!*

Brother Shamsuddin, may God grant you self-control! Struggling with, and overcoming, one's animal soul is praised in all faiths, in all religions, and among every people, both those on the right path and those in error. All who strive after Truth confirm the need for this struggle. One of the causes of divine manifestation has been cited as self-struggle, with manifestation being its resultant inheritance. This has been built on the foundation of the Lord's pronouncement: "Those who strive for Us We will certainly guide to Our own paths" (Q30:69). He who complies with the divine mandate will indeed be rewarded. Even the coming of the prophets, the establishing of the

Law, the granting of scriptures and every difficult command—each involves struggle with self. The result of this effort shows up as a change in a person's nature and the appearance of wonderful qualities. It is like a guide that leads to contemplation. Rejecting it is tantamount to rejecting contemplation itself, and contending that one already beholds God face to face.

Do you not see that when a horse is broken in, its animal qualities become almost human, being so compeltely altered that it can pick a whip up off the ground and give it to its rider? Or it can place a ball in the hand of its rider. Or it is like some rather slow-witted little Persian boy who, by constant training, learns Arabic, as his way of speaking gradually changes. Or, again, consider some fierce animal that, through training, attains such a degree of ability that when it is let go, it wanders off, but when it is called, it returns. Indeed, it prefers to be at the beck and call of its master rather than to be perfectly free to roam wherever it wishes. By training, even an unclean dog was raised to such a degree that whatever it killed became lawful, just like anything killed by a believer. The whole Law revolves around struggle with self.[98]

Even though the Apostle had been in a state of great nearness to God Almighty, was assured of salvation, and wore the garb of sinlessness, he still practiced so much struggle with self, during long nights and days of union, as well as on vigils, that a command came: "O Muhammad, I did not send the Quran upon you in order that you might destroy yourself!" It is related of Abu Huraira that while the mosque was being constructed, the Apostle was picking up bricks. Abu Huraira saw that he was experiencing some difficulty. "O Apostle of God," he called out, "give me the bricks! Let me do your work!" "O Abu Huraira," rejoined the Prophet, "you can pick up some other bricks. Do not look for rest here! It is meant for the world to come!"

To sum up, we can say that struggle and training are agreeable to people of this persuasion. They concur on this matter. They see only one difficulty, namely, that struggle with self is an activity of the servant, while contemplation is something granted by God. Until the activity of the servant is accepted by God, it has no value. Insofar as possible, say little about your own activities. Nor must you give in to any of the urgings of your animal soul, for your very being is your own veil. If you were veiled by but one activity, you could be aroused by another. When your entire being is a veil, however, until you have entirely passed away, you will not be fit for everlasting life and contemplation. Here you have to take note of one point: "Subduing one's lower soul" refers to the transformation of the qualities of the soul, not to the extinction of the soul itself, for the root of a person's egoism never ceases to exist. When a seeker, by means of struggle with self, masters his carnal soul and makes it submissive, however, then he has no fear if it remains within him.

Know that going hungry is something very honorable. It is praised by one and all because it is quite clear that the mind of a hungry man grows sharper, his understanding clearer, and he himself healthier. It is related that Abul Abbas once said: "My submission and sin are bound up in two situations. When I eat, I receive within myself the core of all sins; when I don't eat, however, I see within myself the source of all submission."

The venerable Sufis have said: "It is an extremely difficult task for the disciple to bring the belly under control. Its damage is greater and its influence stronger insofar as it is the source and mine of each and every sin. All a person's members, strength and weakness, continence and sin, take their origin from the belly. First of all, you have to be on the watch for forbidden or doubtful things. Then you should be careful about an abundance of lawful things. If you want to do any work, you should abstain from eating all forbidden and doubtful things, otherwise your worship will not be favored by God. Yahya Mu'az noted: "Devotion is a treasury of God. Prayer is the key to that treasury. Eating what is lawful is the teeth of the key. When the key has no teeth, it cannot open the door. Until the door to the treasury is opened, how can the submission that is contained therein be obtained?" Moreover, whoever eats forbidden and doubtful things is excluded from good actions. Even if he does something good, it is not acceptable to God. It is useless for him! He derives no benefit from such a work. Also, an abundance of lawful things is a calamity for the devout and a misfortune for those struggling with self, for overindulgence in eating causes hardheartedness and a loss of light, as well as a lessening of understanding and knowledge. Filling up the belly, in truth, ruins a person's constitution.

Khwaja Sulaiman Darani said: "If you want to be completely engrossed in important affairs, either religious or worldly, then you should not eat until you have completed your task, for food clogs the mind." Overindulgence ruins all the faculties of a man and causes both excesses and depravity, for a man whose belly is full wants all sorts of other things. Abu Jafar said: "The belly is such an organ that, if it goes hungry, all the other organs and faculties are content and no longer prone to sin; but if it is full, all the other faculties have their appetites whetted for sin!" From this it must be surmised that the words and deeds of a man depend on how much he eats and drinks! If even a morsel of forbidden or doubtful food enters his belly, all the words and deeds that proceed from him are unlawful and unbecoming. You may say that food and drink are the seeds of words and deeds, for both the latter originate from the former two.

The prophet John the Baptist saw Satan carrying ropes in his hand. He inquired what they were for. Satan replied: "These are various lusts by which I ensnare men!" John retorted: "Make a prisoner of me with this snare." "I can't do that," said Satan, "but the very night you eat your fill and become too bloated to pray you will provide me with an opportunity to catch you." John exclaimed: "After this, I shall certainly never overindulge myself!" "Never again," swore Satan, "shall I give this advice to anyone!"

Now since this is what happens to someone who fills up his belly on only one night during his whole life, what must await us who have never been hungry a single night in our whole lives but have, on the contrary, eaten voraciously and excessively? It is also said that the pangs of death are severe in proportion to the pleasures of life: Whoever indulged in many pleasures during his life will experience very severe pangs at the time of death. In short, the benefits of going hungry are without limit; they cannot be numbered. But the calamities arising from overindulgence are also numberless! Controlling one's appetite is indeed a difficult task. This whole topic of food is challenging and frightening, as I have just explained.

If you say, "Well, now, what are the injunctions concerning gifts and presents? Is it necessary to reject them or investigate where they come from?" It is said: "When a man is manifestly righteous and honest, one should have no fear about accepting his gifts and presents, nor is it necessary to investigate their origin. It needs to be said that the times must be evil if one has to be suspicious of Muslims, for we are ordered to have a good opinion of them! Understand from this that the principal matter of this chapter concerns two things above all. One is the command embodied in the Law; the other is the directive of piety. The claim and command of the Law is that whenever anybody esteemed for his honesty gives you anything, take it and do not ask where it came from. By the same token, whenever you know for certain that a thing is tainted by extortion or is unlawful, it should not be accepted. The directive of piety, however, is that you should not accept anything until you have inquired where it came from and ascertained that there is no doubt about it at all. Otherwise, you should reject it.

If anyone says, "From this explanation it becomes clear that piety is against the Law," the answer is that the force of the Law is to make things easy, while that of piety is to make them difficult! It has been said that the work of the pious is more difficult than unraveling a knot. Despite all this, piety is not contrary to the Law. At root, both are the same. Nevertheless, know that there are two types of command in the Law. One refers to what is permitted; the second, to excellence. The former is called the command of the Law; the latter, the directive of piety. At root, both are the same, however much they appear to differ outwardly.

O brother, this is the Path for those who are prepared to struggle with themselves. This task requires a high spiritual resolve. It is a fearful work, for which a person has to risk his neck. One should recall what Sheikh Abu Sa'id was told: "Such and such a place is the abode of a master." He rose up and, together with his group of disciples, went there. He saw a person sitting in the dust with his mat folded up nearby. He asked him if he were the master. "That is what people call me," was the reply. The sheikh enquired as to how he had acquired the title "Master." "Because of my righteousness and purity," he replied.

> Even though, because of our work, we have reason to be proud,
> And, because of what we know, have grown independent of
>     others,
> We are still no more than dice thrown by gamblers;
> We are mere dust on the soles of the pure players!

O brother, the weaker and more feeble anyone is, the more gracious God is toward him. He works with the weak in such a way that all the holy ones close to God are left astonished. A hundred thousand of the near and holy are continually engaged in genuflecting and prostrating themselves, yet nobody has anything to say about them! But lo, when this resourceless one arises from sleep, He Who is Lord of the heavens and the earth speaks about his rising in the Holy Quran: "They forsake their beds to pray to their Lord in fear and hope" (Q32:16). A dog followed for a while in the footsteps of some friends. From the dust of its paws collyrium was prepared for the eyes of those close to the divine threshold. In the Quran this saying proclaims the praise of that dog until the Day of Resurrection: "And their dog stretched out its paws at the entrance" (Q18:18).

*Peace!*

## LETTER 85: LIBERATION FROM ONE'S LOWER SOUL

*In the name of God, the Merciful, the Compassionate!*

Brother Shamsuddin, the joyous marchers on the Path are unanimous in attesting that "the first stage in Sufism is for the servant to become liberated from his animal soul." Until you become indifferent, you cannot attain the rank of friendship with God. The reason why everyone has his eyes fixed on himself is that human nature itself is an obstacle on the road to friendship. True seekers test their swords on themselves, and vent their anger on themselves, in order to overcome this formidable obstacle and thus enable their hearts to find the Way that leads to the mystical knowledge of God: They seek to become mere dust on the way of seeking.

> Marvel at that Grandeur which is beyond all need,
> And for which so many minds and souls are mere playthings!
> Marvel at that Jealousy which, if it were to fall upon the earth,
> Would destroy both worlds in a single hour!
> Marvel at that Compassion which, if Satan were to receive
> But a particle of it, he would leap ahead of the prophet Enoch!

Mystical knowledge is success in reaching the divine threshold and salvation through intimacy. Such a blessing [i.e., salvation] is not compatible with such an obstacle [i.e., the lower soul] for "two contraries cannot coexist." This is not work for mud and water; nor is it riches from this world or even from the universe. Rather, it is from the eternal threshold—blessings from eternity and qualities for eternity! If all creatures were to revolt against Him, it would not lead to the slightest stain on His threshold. Nor, if all were to bow down in submission, would there be any adornment to that threshold.

> Marvel at that Expanse, for if the world ceased to be,
> It would not be diminished by a hair's breadth!

Marvel at that Unity, which cannot be contained in a single
  hair,
And where the entire world does not equal even a hair!
Marvel at the astonishment the soul experiences in You!
Now it is rendered helpless—its heart has become bound to
  You!

This work of knowing God belongs to a unique Jewel, not mere
dust and water! Nor is it the work of some devout or ascetic person.
Rather, it is suitable for those who suffer, those who go hungry, and
those who are without clothing, for this is the pain they experience:

I walk along Your path. How is it that I do not see You?
Would that I could be liberated from the trials of life!
You have not even sent me a greeting from where You have
  gone!
O that but once I might find some trace of Your whereabouts!

The prince of Sufis said: "I received mystical knowledge when I
was hungry and naked. The first key of the door to friendship with
God is nakedness and hunger. Acquire these, for they are precious
and will unlock the door to Him." He also said: "There are three
groups that are afflicted with being veiled from God: The ascetic is
veiled by his asceticism; the devout, by his devotion; and the scholar,
by his learning." This saying is a veritable ocean, for its wonders never come to an end! As long as one thinks in his heart that there is at
least somebody in the world who is worse than he is, he is still proud!
Be careful not to place the cap of claims upon your head; otherwise
your fall will be very great. You will be enmeshed by your own pride.
Only the proud talk about mystical knowledge. As long as a servant
doubts that there is anyone else worse than he, he is still proud and
caught up in a veil. A wise man has said:

Since you have knowledge, act according to it!
Solve your problems through knowing and doing.
Only a little effort, inspired by religious knowledge, is better
Than a whole ass-load of untried religious theory!
Engage yourself with that work, for this other is immature!
One word of religious knowledge will fill you completely!

Yahya Mu'az says: "I approached Khwaja Abu Yazid. I caught
sight of him. He had a piece of leather bound around his head and

tied with a piece of old, black leather. He was reciting, 'God is great!' I said: 'O proof of those who proclaim the Unity, has something happened to make you sing God's praises?' He replied, 'O Yahya, if you want to know the secret of this, go to Rome.' When I reached Rome, I saw a large fortified town filled with a multitude of the enemies of the faith. They had been burnt to ashes. I said, 'What is this?' I was told: 'The people of this city were fighting against the army of the Muslims. The Muslims were facing defeat. Suddenly, from Bistam came the cry, 'God is Great!' followed by a fire that appeared in the city and all were instantly destroyed.' I returned to Bistam. I saw Bayazid squatting on his big toes, engaged in prayer. He remained thus until the time for night prayer. When he had finished everything, he turned around and saw me. He said: 'O Yahya, I was in the presence of the Lord. I passed through thousands of stages. I prayed to the Honorable Presence at each stage. Finally, He said to me: "O Bayazid, what is it you want?" I replied: "My desire is not to desire anything! My wish is not to want anything!"' "

Your name remains upon my tongue, but still I am not filled:
O the misfortune of a poor lover—he has but one tongue!

Yahya said: "Why did you not desire for yourself the blessing of friendship with God?" He replied: "My sense of honor does not allow me to think about such knowledge of God, for it would be improper for the Eternal Word to be acquainted with transient qualities!" It has been reported that when Bayazid said "My sense of honor" he returned to his grave so that Yahya might not see him! This is the way of those men. They act in such a manner that those traveling along the Way will not experience any pangs of jealousy or uneasiness.

If you spend the night in intimate converse with God,
And speak about it the following day with conceited pride,
Then know: Hypocrisy and haughtiness are a mountain ablaze,
And the pit-fire of Hell consists precisely of that!

A sheikh said: "I cried for ten years. Then I shed tears of blood for ten years, and discharged pus for another ten. For the last ten years I have been laughing." That man had lost the way and was weeping on account of the despair and affliction of his own faith. The ignorant abused him for having fallen in love!

All those who disparage a lover are ignorant:
O Muslims, it is from the ignorant that cries arise!

# MANERI

People are greatly mistaken when it comes to the question of mystical knowledge. For the most part, they do not know that the highest knowledge the wise can attain is to realize that they really know nothing at all! The limit of friendship for all who are intimately acquainted with God is to recognize that they really do not perceive Him in His state of Incomparable Beauty. "We are sorry, for we know so little!"

> The world is filled with You, yet You are not in it:
> All are lost in You, but You are not within them.
> The world is filled with Your name, but of You there is no
>     trace!
> Their minds have been opened, but You they see not!
> The world of the mind and of the soul was astounded,
> For You remained hidden behind such a curtain!
> O Pure One, we speak from our own helplessness:
> You are both Known and Knower: what knowledge do we
>     have?

What a wonder it is! All the brave who reach the lane of mystical knowledge are conquered by love.[99] And all the rivers of insight that join the ocean of Omnipotence become mere trickles. All the honorable ones who resolve to seek Him become like microcosms of defilement. Every boastful person who hears His holy Word is destroyed. If the helplessness of creatures was not for some purpose, how could it be said: "Nobody has earned the right to mystical knowledge of God?"

The whole world recognizes God. That is what makes it precious! Countless thousands were placed on a bier so that at least one might be raised up. The secret of this has been explained by Khwaja Junaid: "The divine Mercy attracts many thousands of genuine disciples to travel with me along the right road, but as they approach mystical knowledge all of them sink into the ocean of His wrath in order to become disciples of the Sun itself!" Khwaja Zu'l-Nun Misri was told: "What would you like before death?" He replied: "My desire is that before I die, I might receive a moment of mystical insight!" An inflamed one has said:

> When You are about to slay me, let me kiss Your feet:
> Yet I wish that even this desire did not remain!

Hence it has been said that most of the travelers along this Way leave the world carrying with them the pain they experienced in their hearts. Those grief-stricken ones are never removed from the carpet of their lamentation. People come and go. Those destined for heaven are borne off there, while those destined for the earth are taken there, but in no way are the mourning clothes of this grief ever removed from the lane of the afflicted!

> Burn every heart that has not been captivated;
> Put fire to the house, for no guest has entered it!
> I died on Your doorstep, without ever entering Your dwelling.
> Now I am but dust, but Oh, that the wind might waft a little inside!

Sufyan said: "If anyone in the community of the Prophet weeps because of an affliction, then God Almighty has mercy on the entire community because of his weeping." Also, "God Almighty bestowed revelations upon Moses so that when any distressed member of Ahmad's community cried out 'O Lord!' then the answer would come, 'Here am I!' " In every age there is always one man noted for his grief and others pass their time in the shade of his protection. Khwaja Waki ibn Jarrah says: "When the excellent one [Ibrahim Adham] died, grieving departed from the world." The sheikhs say: "A master of grief makes more progress in a month than one who does not grieve makes in several years." Others have to undergo years of struggle with themselves in order to advance a little in the faith, or they might not even advance at all, but anyone who advances along the path of grief will find that his very first step is placed on the carpet of righteousness, and the very first drink he quaffs is from the beverage of love!

> Even in the heat of the Day of Judgment, I pine for my
>   Friend!
> Show this canal of milk to the one who longs for that of
>   Paradise!

The secret of what is meant has been revealed by the Chosen One: "God loves every grief-stricken heart!" The Torah says: "When God loves any servant, He pours grief and sorrow into his heart, while if He is displeased with anyone, He makes his heart merry!" In this matter it is God's way not to leave the hearts of His friends free from lamentation, while the hearts of His enemies are never free from mirth. No heart had as much grief to bear as that of the Prince of the prophets: "How can a man be mirthful when he receives fresh trials every moment from the Unseen?"

Young man, as you pass here on your mount,
Kill me, for you are in search of game!
You, drowsy with sleep, how do you know how far you will go
In that heart, whose core you strive to reach in the darkness?

Khwaja Junaid was fanning his spiritual master, Khwaja Sari Saqati, as he lay dying. The latter opened his eyes and said: "My son, you are fanning me, but there is a fire that has been enkindled in my heart and is now raging there. It is such that a spark from it, upon reaching a mountain, would reduce it to dust. Of what benefit could your breeze possibly be for me?"

This thirst of mine is for another water from on high;
Do you not see that in each eye I have another river?
O physicians, do not trouble yourselves: I will not improve,
For I have other fevers inside my disturbed head!

Now be of light heart, even though your sins be many and your submission nonexistent! This saying, "Never abandon hope in God's mercy" (Q39:53), has brought all sinners under its protection. Also, "Do not despair of the spirit of God" (Q12:87) has encompassed all the poverty-stricken within its shade. Since God is compassionate, how can sinners despair of His mercy? O brother, He is all-forgiving; how can sinners be without hope, for He is the One who effects forgiveness out of His own mercy? Since He forgives, it is from the treasury of His mercy that He bestows forgiveness. O brother, do not be brokenhearted, even though you are in a state of penury, for the face of your existence has been adorned with beautiful ornaments. "He created man in His own image" is the very crown adorning your own head! His beauty is yours, as is His perfection!

If you go to a tavern stained with lust, realize that the saints of the heavenly court are seated on the carpet of holiness in order that you might be washed clean as a result of their prayers for forgiveness on your behalf. And if you go to the lust-filled bazaar and become stained with sin, then Eternal Compassion and Everlasting Graciousness causes this saying to be heard in the world: "What is a spot of sin on such a beautiful face? There is no one like you!" The secret of this is that one day, Sultan Mahmud Ghazni, out of the perfection of his justice, had a proclamation made in his camp to the effect that anyone found guilty of disorderly conduct would be punished and feel the effect of his anger. When he felt gracious, he called the herald and told him to announce that this did not apply to Ayaz since he was already protected by his selflessness: He seemed to be a slave, but was actually a king!

> Through Your beneficence, annul sins and make them nothing!
> Be our protection from the fine cutting-edge of Your jealousy!
> Give peace to our souls if they have to face Your justice:
> Let Wisdom plead for us at the appointed rendezvous!

*Peace!*

## LETTER 86: COMING TO TERMS WITH ONESELF

*In the name of God, the Merciful, the Compassionate!*

Brother Shamsuddin, may God honor you by making you an esteemed seeker! Anybody who has come to terms with himself and accepted his self is dead, even though he appears to be alive. Whoever lives in God, however, even though he appears to be dead, is really alive. Death is not the death of the body! Nonexistence is not the nonexistence of the body! Just as there is an apparent death, there is also a real one. Men are sunk in the sea of human nature. The prophets come along and, through their assistance, men are extricated from their plight. They then become submerged in the ocean of Unity, till not a trace from even one of them is left behind!

O brother, when the sun of Unity rises, certainly the lamp of your being, out of modesty, will flicker into nothingness! You will continue to exist since it is only with respect to appearances that you will be nothing. A lamp, face to face with the sun, for instance, would have no brilliance of itself: All brightness would stem from the sun. Since no effect flows from its presence, its existence would be tantamount to nonexistence.[100]

Someone might say that nothingness is the opposite of existence, and existence the opposite of nothingness, and that it is impossible for anything to both exist and not exist in something else. The answer would be that this whole discussion concerns the nonexistence of qualities rather than essence, for it is not the essence that changes but the qualities. It is not the creature that changes but its disposition! If the sun shines on water, it makes it warm. It is a quality of the water that has been altered, not its very substance. The substance of the sun produces a change in the qualities of the water but not in its essence! In this there is no coincidence of opposites. God himself has said about his enemies: "They are dead, not alive, nor do they know when they will be raised up" (Q16:21).

Strangers, with respect to God, appear to be alive, but are really dead, for real life means that a substance should abstain from its own life. That, however, is not within a person's power, just as tomorrow they will be desiring death, but will remain in the calamity of their own existence. Concerning the friends of God, on the other hand, it has been said: "Those who are killed along the Way to God—do not number them among the dead, for they live through their Lord!" (Q3:169). A person should be ready to give his life at the head of the Way and walk along it stripped of his own life, so that this special situation might arise wherein "they live through their Lord." Whoever, on the other hand, sets out on this Path, holding to his life, will be sent to Rizwan, the keeper of paradise. He will be told: "Here is a guest for you!" But whoever sets out along this Way after having sacrificed his life, and continues to walk in love, has to pass by no other intermediary. This group consists of friends who seem to be annihilated but who really live, while the other group is comprised of strangers who are seemingly alive but actually dead.

The condition needed for you to really exist is to pass by the whole world, to remain at a distance from yourself, to remove your heart from yourself, and to wash your hands of yourself, just as the Companions of the Cave did. Make a cave of your heart and, entering therein, pray four times "God is Great!" on your own behalf. Expel the dog of your animal soul from within you so that you might be displayed before the people, as was done to the Companions of the Cave. "If you look at them you would turn back from them in flight, and you would be filled with awe on account of them!" (Q18:18).

A dead man cannot be punished. So much punishment and fear were placed within them that it was revealed to the king of the prophets that if a person were to see Him, he would certainly retreat in flight from the Wealth, having been filled with fear. When the sun passes that way, it shines softly and warms the dog that lies sound asleep at the entrance to the Cave of the Companions. Heavenly and earthly beings, and the angels as well, stand with their loins girt ready for service. They are carried away from themselves, and the whole of creation becomes lost in astonishment.

Whoever passes beyond himself, abandons himself, and takes refuge in God, discovering that God will make his face shine with that very goodness which He has granted the Companions of the Cave. And if you yourself enter the very same court as they did, He will bestow upon you what He bestowed upon them. A disciple who is a seeker along the Way to God should be like Jesus, who never stayed in the same place. When He was traveling around from town to town, people asked him: "What is the reason for all this journeying?" He replied: "It might happen that a righteous man had once set foot in a place before I reached it and the dust of that place might then intercede for me!" Yet if you were to gather all the pain of the righteous in one place, it would not be equal to the pain of Jesus. A supplicant treading the Way should be like this!

O brother, it is a while since this saying was heard: "My treasuries are filled with service; if you can, acquire a particle of supplication!" It has been reported that supplication is a tree that grew up in the garden of Adam and men. The angels were bold to say: "Will You appoint in it [as your viceregent] one who makes mischief and sheds blood, while we are devoted to praising You?" (Q2:30). But Adam in his indigence exclaimed: "O Lord, we have wronged ourselves!" (Q7:23).

It is related that Solomon, the son of David, was walking alone one day. An ant was speaking to its companions. "Go back to your nests," it warned them; "otherwise, the people of Solomon might come and stomp on you and destroy you!" Solomon, upon hearing this, said to the wind: "Place my throne here, for the voice of a supplicant has reached my ears." A sincere follower of the Path has said: "It is related that Solomon sat for forty days at the entrance to that nest and said: 'Let everyone go about his own work, for I wish to be with this ant!'" Both Solomon and the ant were freed from their occupations. Two such people will have many things, both joyous and sorrowful, to talk about. They have taken life's measure, for they are really alive. We, on the contrary, are dead and completely incapable of such activity. If anyone is astonished that an ant could do all this, since it experiences no stress, nor will it have to render any account on the Day of Judgment, nor undergo punishment, then such a person might be asked to explain the purpose of the hoopoe of Solomon, or the dog of the Companions of the Cave! This will throw dust in the eyes of the impertinent!

*Peace!*

LETTER 87: THE DIFFERENCE IN STAGES, AND A PRAYER FOR OVERCOMING DIFFICULTIES

*In the name of God, the Merciful, the Compassionate!*

Dear Brother Shamsuddin, there is a great difference in the way various people tread the path of faith. There is as much difference from one step to another, one breath to another, and one person to another as there is between the earth and the sky, even though they were created the same and appear to be the same. The Law says: "Man is like a gold or silver mine." Outwardly, all mines look the same, but there is a great difference inside them. Do you not see that different mines yield gold, silver, iron, and diamonds? Similarly, all men who exist, have existed, or will exist are mother of pearl, filled with mysteries! In each body there is a mystery: Every form displays the handiwork of God. Similarly, the witness of faith produces a desire for God in every heart, a radiance in every soul: Neither is incomprehensible to angelic or human intellect. Attar has said:

> Vegetation, minerals, animals, and the sky,
> Along with water, wind, fire, and dust,
> All are in motion due to love,
> No matter the time, the month, or the year.
> If the eye of your heart looks back on this,
> Each particle will yield a hundred mysteries.
> Among all the particles of the world, in this lane
> Not a single soul will be perceived to be at rest.
> Who knows all the secrets hidden here?
> This is the source of light for both intellect and life!

Those, however, who are striving after the sun in the firmament, and are favored by the Eternal Lord, and are generals commanding the wealth of Islam make happy all those upon whom the dust, raised by their mounts, happens to fall. Even if such dust falls on a temple, it will become a mosque!

> People say that a venerable Sufi went to a tavern last night.
> During his invocations tears dropped into a bowl of pure wine.
> The wine became honey in his hands; the temple, a mosque:
> O Lord, what miracles were wrought by this favored one!

The Tradition concerning the elect, from the threshold of the Glorious One, attests that there is no difficulty in speaking or hearing for them and, on account of their commitment to the way of faith, the core of their heart manifests the cuts they bear from the sword of divine wrath. Whoever has any relationship with the Path that leads to his Creator sees that nothing raises its head from the treasure house of their faith. The Eternal keeps them protected out of His own sense of honor, that no evil eye might find its way to their beauty. "You see them looking at you, but they see nothing" (Q7:198). This means that in the world of Truth they are called "foreigners to the tribes (of the human race)."

They know the value of the Law of the Lord of the world, and they recognize the worth of his Tradition. They are fit for the stage of the prophets. They shine as pillars of righteousness by the way they expound the commands of the Law, just as if they were giving authoritative decisions. They come so close to both God and His slaves that they could say, "And among those whom We created is a community who give true guidance" (Q7:181). As for their education and permission, "My companions are like stars: If you follow any one of them, you will receive guidance." These are the states of both the spiritual master and the disciple.

> The person whose guide along the Way has no face like the
>    moon
> Will find the Path to his true self is long rather than short!

What can be done? All do not emerge as righteous ones from the hidden curtain, nor are all born kings from Mother Fortune. Many thousands of pure souls, fallen in the region of seeking, have been passed by, so that some other might be raised up as a righteous man, often as he lies prostrate before an idol! Many thousands of those devoted to prayer are removed from their places of worship and consigned to hell in order that the breast of some frequenter of taverns might be illuminated by the profession of faith in the Unity of God.

But what do you and I have to do with such sayings about the pure ones? What share of this Wealth has been apportioned either to you or to me? Your pain and mine is that described by Khusrau:

At night dogs roam Your alley, but there is no access for
  Khusrau.
From time to time allow me entrance along with that pack of
  dogs!

Once Zu'l Nun sent a disciple to Bayazid to find out how he was. When the disciple reached Bistam he entered the convent of Bayazid, and saw the saint sitting in a secluded corner. He did not recognize him and so did not know that this was Bayazid. Bayazid asked him whom he wanted to see. "Bayazid," he replied. The man said: "*Where is Abu Yazid?* I myself have been looking for Abu Yazid for many years, but have not yet found him!" The disciple thought he was a madman who understood nothing of what he said. He returned to Egypt and told Zu'l Nun what had happened. He wept and said: "My brother Bayazid has gone with the caravan of the yearners to the land of 'there is no god but God,' and has left me behind!" Take note of this saying: "Many are the people who have been brought into the world and taken out again, without having any knowledge that they have been brought in or taken out!"

Sheikh Abul Hasan Kharaqani said: "Junaid came to his senses in the world but, on becoming intoxicated, departed from it. Shibli was intoxicated both on entering and on leaving!" What comment could be made about this? He replied: "If they are asked, they themselves will not know!" He said: "If both Junaid and Shibli were to be asked on the Day of Resurrection about how they had come, and in what state they had left, they would not be able to say anything in reply!" While Sheikh Abul Hasan Kharaqani was in a mystic state, an angel spoke to him thus: "O sheikh, you spoke correctly! If they are asked, they themselves will not know! Anyone who is wholly taken up with God has knowledge of nothing else!"

Your lovers have been intoxicated with "Am I not":
They came, their heads swimming with the wine of "Am I
  not."
They drink the wine, disregarding all advice,
"Am I not" has made them into worshipers of wine!

Listen with faith to the words of these righteous ones! Refrain from criticizing them with your puny intellect, for they are dear to

God! The world has been regulated by their footsteps. The faith has been upheld by their vigilance. Both the eastern and western lands are under their command. Do you not see that when the Lord of the universe and ruler of the worlds used to see Hilal, the slave of Mughira, he would say: "Pray for me!" When he prayed, the Prophet himself would answer, "Amen!" Early one morning, the Prophet turned to his companions with whom he was sitting and said: "Get up! At this moment creation has been clothed with the garment of the trial of Hilal!" He arose from the group and headed off for the house of Mughira. Mughira, however, was unaware that Hilal had received the command to leave this world, for there was none more lowly in his entire household than Hilal. The people in the house knew nothing about his life and nothing about his death. Mughira came outside. He saw the Chosen One standing there with his righteous companions. He fell at his blessed feet. The Prophet asked him: "What has taken place in your house today?" He replied, "O Prophet, nothing but good has occurred today!" "O Mughira," rejoined the Prophet, "the soul of the most precious member of your household has been borne aloft, and you have no knowledge at all about it?"

On hearing this, Mughira was dumbstruck! "Never for a moment," he exclaimed, "did I imagine that Hilal had attained such a rank!" How astonishing that there was glory for Hilal in the seven heavens, and yet upon earth—except for the Chosen One—nobody recognized him! This is to bring home the lesson that this Tradition refers to those who have no fame whatsoever on this earth. Whoever becomes famous in any work should wash his hands of its prosperity, for "whoever is esteemed by people is not safe!"[101]

If this Tradition concerning kingship were not necessary for the faith of people, then the Prophet would certainly never have advanced from the stage of "I am the son of a woman who used to eat dried meat" to that of "I am the leader of the sons of men, but I do not brag about it!" Real kingship means that when the carpet of mystery of self is spread within your breast, you cease to be inclined to those who live according to habit and custom. Hence, all of those with unwashed faces are unable to see what they really are. The Chosen One knew who Hilal was, for he had received help from him. Yet he said nothing about his state until he passed away, for it was not his task to tear aside the curtain. There is no resting place that is more decorated or safer than that of the concealed ones!

Hilal passed his life in such concealment that even the master of the house knew nothing about him. The Prophet said: "O Mughira, where did he stay? Take me there!" Mughira took him to the stable. They saw Hilal lying at the feet of the animals. He was dead. The Prophet entered and placed the slave's blessed head in his lap. His eyes filled with tears as he declared: "O Hilal, you seem to be lying upon this dust, but in reality your substance is with the Pure Presence!" The companions had never before seen the Prophet so upset, nor had they themselves ever been as astonished as they were on that day. All the noble and righteous desired to be the dust upon which Hilal had trodden! "O that our lives had been the leather of Hilal's sandals!" they proclaimed. Finally, the Apostle said: "In every age there are seven slaves of God whose prayers provide the people with daily blessings. The Muslims are victorious on account of their magnanimity. Rain descends from heaven on account of their prayer. Hilal was more excellent and dearer to God than were these seven of the age. By God who holds sway over the soul of Muhammad, if this Hilal swore by God that the world would suddenly cease to exist, his oath would turn out to be correct. Not a particle of the world would remain!"

Anyone with the temerity to object to these words should be told that this is the community of the Prophet! If you belong to his community, then accept this faith! If not, then surrender your contract to be a Muslim! If anyone experiences difficulties he is unable to resolve, let him resort to this prayer: "In the name of God, the Merciful, the Compassionate, inspire this seeker with the righteousness of Abu Bakr and his successors, the justice of Umar and his firmness, the modesty of Usman and his generosity, the wisdom of 'Ali and his descendants, the beneficence of Hasan and his affection, the witness of Husain and his self-effacement. That is the sum total of my needs, O You who control all needs!"

*Peace!*

### LETTER 88: HEEDLESSNESS

*In the name of God, the Merciful, the Compassionate!*

Dear Brother Shamsuddin, heedlessness is not praised in any religion or community! Realize also that a slave does not fall into sin and rebellion unless he grows negligent. It is said that Fortune extracts a fine from those who are heedless. It has also been reported that when anyone sets foot upon the earth for some nefarious purpose then all the particles of the various layers of the earth cry out, proclaiming in ecstatic speech, "O faithless and false one, we have been created in order to bear the burden of worship-filled service, not that of sin! We are the ones out of whom Adam, the Pure One of God, came into existence, as well as Noah, the prophet of God; Moses, the Word of God; Jesus, the Spirit of God; Abraham, the Friend of God; and Muhammad, the Beloved of God. All these stars of the seven heavens and the earth were decorated by us. When Almighty God created us, He adorned us with His own precious and revered blessings—"We ourselves spread out the earth! See how well we did it!" (Q51:48). It was with such praise that God Almighty displayed us, and yet you place your renegade foot upon us. Remember, we shall be your resting place after death. Give us only as much now as you can bear from us tomorrow! Whatever lack of consideration you display toward us now will certainly be shown to you when you are placed without our power! If you do not want trouble tomorrow, be careful about what you do today!"

> Since this world is the field where the next is cultivated,
> Sow your seed, for now is the time to labor.
> If you depart from here without sowing anything,
> You will become the laughingstock of the age!

It is said that when a person treads heedlessly in the lane of the faith, the Accursed One says: "Do you not recognize me? The royal patent of my teaching has been affixed to the dome of the seven heavens. The honored congregational sermon of Islam has been read out in my name. I have lost all these riches and possessions, and today stand at the doorway of the Law, as has been destined for me. Either place the crown of sincerity upon your head and proceed, or turn away, for you are not a man of this Way!"

> When you do not even know the secrets of the tip of a hair,
> Why have you come, in total ignorance, to attempt this work?

From the threshold of the Quran this help is available to him: "Excite as many of them as you can with your own voice! Urge toward them your mount and feet! Share with them both wealth and children!" (Q17:64). The explanation of this verse is that every voice that is not of the Law is a shriek from Satan. He is associated with all goods that contain even a single unlawful silver piece, and with every child whose birth is not in complete accordance with the Law. You could say that it has been said: "Sit at the honorable threshold of the Law, and make use of the heedless ones as your mount and feet. And if anyone with an unwashed face places his feet in mirth on this carpet, cut them off!" He makes a hundred boasts:

My beloved said to me: "Sit at my door!
Do not let anyone enter who does not know my secret!"

It is related that one day Adam saw Satan and said: "You did such and such to me!" He replied, "O Adam, I certainly did such and such things to you, but who did such things to me?"

Look, but do not inquire about my condition.
Deal with me as it has been foreordained!

O brother, remaining undefiled by any sin, from creation till dissolution, is the work of angels. Remaining forever steeped in sin and rebellion is the lot of Satan. Turning back from sin to the path of devotion, by means of repentance and sorrow, is the task of Adam and men. Whenever some fault is forgiven through repentance, the relationship between oneself and Adam is cemented, but whoever persists in sin till the end of his life and does not repent links himself to Satan inextricably.

It is said that man of himself does not have the power to pass his whole life in worship-filled devotion for, from the very beginning, he was created defective and devoid of understanding. The first desire that came along conquered him! That is Satan's weapon. Understanding is the enemy of lust and the light of the angelic substances. It was created afterwards. When lust gains the upper hand, the fortress of one's heart falls into its clutches, while the animal soul grows accustomed to it and becomes intimate with it. When understanding is born, however, a person will necessarily experience an impulse toward repentance and mortification, which will lead to victory for the fortress of his heart and its extrication from the clutches of lust and of Satan.

At the moment, you are held captive in the mouth of a lion:
Why do you suppose that you are capturing the lion?!

Hence it is that repentance is necessary for man. It is the place where a novice must begin his journey. This is not possible for him without the assistance of a mature and experienced spiritual master—unless God wishes otherwise. The secret of this is contained in the angels' question: "Do You intend to appoint as Your viceroy upon the earth one who will act wickedly?" (Q2:30). God replied: "Undoubtedly I know what you do not know!" (Q2:30). He did not say that man would not sin! Instead, He said, "I know what you do not know!" When man becomes defiled with sin, the ocean of repentance lies before him, so that he can be washed and made pure. One should also take note of what Umar said: "There is no man who is not a sinner, but the best of sinners are those who repent."

O brother, no other creature in the seven heavens or upon the face of the earth was given a throne like that of the Chosen One, yet every hour in the heart of that exalted one, on account of the justice of the divine tribunal, there was great fear. If even a portion of the fear in his heart were to be distributed over the seven heavens and the entire earth, then not a single particle of joy would remain throughout the universe. "He was always sad and in difficulty." The inner core of his heart experienced fear in all his varying states, and he tasted the grief of the inhabitants of the seven heavens and of the earth in such a way that neither Abu Bakr at his right nor Umar to his left was aware of what was happening. This is something of fundamental importance in his heart, while anyone who is clearly heading for an evil end experiences ever-greater ease.

> Unfit for the King is a self-conceited man:
> It is grief of heart that is pleasing to God.
> Along this way, self-conceit is never laudable:
> One's body should be lean, and one's heart broken!

It is the sinlessness of the Chosen One that adorns earth and heaven; his is the name that is proclaimed as king throughout creation. The beginning and the end were predestined for him. Since forgiveness was inscribed for him, he was rendered secure from the punishments of the next life. Everything was granted him and, yet, not for the twinkling of an eye was fear removed from his heart! Having discharged his apostolic functions, he would step inside the veil of his heart, close the door of existence upon himself, tie the girdle of continence, doff the cap of prophecy, and, loosening the tongue of need and helplessness, exclaim: "O God, my sins are great! Great sinners can only find forgiveness in the Great Lord. O God, number me among the devout who have been redeemed and saved from the fire!"

When he prayed in this fashion, his heart could find no solace for the affliction it experienced, except in repeating "there is no god but God."

It is said that blossoms of grief would sprout from the trees; storms of grief would descend from above; the vegetation of the earth would take pity on him; the divine throne would be astonished at his pain; the hearts of those near God in the heavens and of the righteous upon the earth would be snatched away from their own salvation; they would wash their hands of their own sincerity; and all the particles of the kingdom would don the garb of mourning, crying out: "What has happened?" They would be told: "Muhammad, the Apostle of God, is pleading with his lord for forgiveness for his sins; he is seeking to secure the jewel of his sinlessness from the stain of justice." Someone has given a hint about all this in the following:

> When we think of Him, our hearts begin to bleed:
> Our cries ascend to the utter independence of God!
> If some order were to come from His domain,
> Then all the hopes of sinners would be dashed to pieces!

"Surely God Almighty is completely independent of both worlds" (Q29:6). It is a long time since He visited His punishment on the hearts of sinners and righteous people. It is said that there is not a single saint or prophet who has the strength to bear the load the greatest of men bore. Would that some of the wretchedness that marks the pain of the Chosen One were to appear on the Day of Judgment! If Abraham is called the Friend, and Moses the Word, it is because of their association with him, for without the aid of his sinlessness they could never have reached such positions. Despite all this, he was given over to this prayer: "O God, do not burn up my heart and eyes in the fire of Your justice! Place the halter of freedom upon my neck! No prophet had to bear the affliction placed on me. I have had to endure both calamity and struggle, for I have been set before the inhabitants of the seven heavens and the earth." Muhammad, the Apostle of God, also said: "The sin of the offspring of Adam has been tied to the skirt of my intercession. It has been said: 'God will provide for you, and you will be satisfied' (Q93:5). As for me, I must travel the Way of those who have no Way; and I must beg pardon for all sinners, and do the work of all the lazy ones!" He also said: Sometimes I am raised to the throne of intimacy with God. At other times I am sent to the abode of the violence of Abu Jahl. Sometimes the title of "Witness and Announcer of Good News" is given to me. At other times I am called "madman, sorcerer, or poet"! Sometimes the address of praise, "Except for you, I would not have created the world," is lavished upon me; at other times I hear, "If we wanted, we could have raised a prophet in every nation" (Q25:51). Sometimes they bring the key to the treasures of the Kingdom to the door of my cell; at other times I am simply a barley measure at the door of Abu Shanah, the Jew!

O brother, on the Path of the Chosen One, wrath is mixed with consolation, consolation with wrath. Along this path there are pulpits but there are also gallows. Khwaja Attar has given us a hint about this:

> It is necessary to bow one's neck to the command:
> Except for patience and silence, we have no other recourse!
> We simply must accede to the way of silence!
> For our bodies are not capable of uttering even a sigh!
> Who possesses anything in the valley of greeting?
> Who dares traverse the wilderness to its outer edge?
> Those in search of the secret have become so utterly lost
> That no trace at all remains—not even the tip of a hair!
> I have revealed thousands of meanings, only to discover
> That silence is the path decreed for this Way!

O brother, the speck of dust is a mine of supplication and indigence. The heavenly beings are awestruck, and yet it is not astonishing that Adam played at loving; what is astonishing is that his sons jumped into the boat of distress and sat in the skiff of calamity! The Gracious Tongue answers from the most excellent of pulpits: "Do not be astonished! They are like ducklings that do not have to be taught how to swim!"

> Even if ducklings are but one day old,
> The water comes up only to their breasts!

O brother, know that not everyone is able to drink wine from this cup of water and clay! The goblets of the elect and the ordinary people of the realm have not passed by this door, even though "they are honored servants" (Q21:26). The wine of "He loves them," among the eighteen thousand worlds, was offered to man alone. This Tradition does not refer to a wine that is meant for every palate; nor is it a kingdom meant for every area; nor is it a cap that fits every head; nor

is it a breeze that blows through every garden! A Sufi has given us
this hint:

> O infidelity, for what reason do the Magi boast of you?
> Worshiping your name, they excuse themselves from knowing
>   you.
> Those people in Islam who are veritable hairsplitters,
> Due to pride, will not advance toward You by a hair's breadth.

*Peace!*


## LETTER 89: GRIEF

*In the name of God, the Merciful, the Compassionate!*

Brother Shamsuddin, even if you were to travel fifty times, barefooted and bareheaded, and full of religious fervor, from the East to the
West, from your own homeland of adversity to Mecca and Medina, it
would not be the same as if you were plunged in the grief of "not-
finding God"! Take heed of this saying for a moment. As a matter of
fact, there is no daily practice that is more precious than that of reading one's diary of grief. Who would not benefit from this, even if he
be a traveler in the realm above as well as the present world? Khwaja
Attar has correctly said:

> We have prepared this almanac with much effort
> Yet, because of inexperience, we are still half-baked.
> We have tasted many a variety of grief:
> Often, lying in the dust, we have had to drink blood.
> We have often, like spiders, spun our web,
> Or, like flies, have narrated our stories.
> Sometimes we have donned the girdle of the Christians,
> At other times we have sat in their hermitages.
> Often we have sought the remedy for this pain:
> Now, in our very tears, we have washed our hands of life.
> We have spoken much, but our hearts found no rest;
> Far have we traveled, but never reached the end.

O brother, whoever, in this world, has his diary of grief placed in
his hands has had this said about him: "Here is your book: read it.

Your own soul shall this day call you to account" (Q17:14). In whichever breast the tale of "not-finding" is inscribed, a thousand Judgment Days will be stirred up within him. Whoever has a name for spiritual resolve is afflicted with the torments of death. Whoever is preoccupied with shifting from external impurity to inner purity will be borne from this world to the next! As long as someone remains in time and space he will not see the Wealth that has been vouchsafed to the Chosen One. If the birds of the air were to sit on the heads of those dear ones, they would not know if they were sitting on a living creature or on some piece of inert mineral. Do you know what this is all about? The sons of the world to come have all been killed—they remain bodily in this world, though their hearts are in the next. Here they have been caused to pass their life in pain and affliction to such an extent that even the lord of the world must struggle, while our own thirsting souls have become scattered before the swords of the enemies of the faith: Inwardly we are really already in the world to come, and outwardly we will soon be there too!

Umar used to leave the precincts of Mecca and roll in the dust and yearn to die, saying: "I have been disappointed in what I had expected from the people, while the people are disappointed in what they had expected from me. Therefore, do not keep us bound to each other! Take my life so that I might be released from my prison and contract!"

Ali ibn Abu Talib, in whose intrepidity Islam takes pride, would place his hands upon all his admirable good works and say, with a hundred sighs during the time of private prayer: "Why have You not appointed misfortune for me, that my good works might be colored with my blood, and that I might thus be released from the name and claim to any intrepidity of my own accord?"

> Everyone who, in the world, experiences pain
> Has at hand the remedy for that pain.
> What is this remedy for the pain of the afflicted ones?
> One glance at "There is no god but Him!"

It is related that there was a person who had already given up his soul before Azrael arrived to take it. When the latter arrived, he saw the man lying dead. He was astonished! He heard a voice: "This slave did not have the strength to wait, on account of his great desire for Me!" Listen to what the Holy Book has to say: "O spirit, will you remain with the body? O body, you were made along with the spirit.

Your journey is complete. Everyone returns to his homeland, for the new moon is more beautiful when it rises in one's own sky.

> No matter how happy you were in any other place,
> Come back, for the moon looks best in the sky!

Labor reveals the secret of the Munificent, whereas fortune is the abode of privacy, and time the occasion for peace. How can this be? "I am content with you, and you are content with Me."[102] This has been explained as follows:

> The New Year has come! The plains are carpeted with
>   verdure;
> The nightingale, perched on a blooming rose, is filled with
>   love.
> Now is the time for us to renew all our pledges.
> What was to be has come, O God, and what was to pass has
>   taken place.

For the most part, when young men of this court leave the world, they do take with them the pain of not having found God. The saying of the wise, however, is that the grief of not-finding is, for the disappointed ones, more complete than the joy of finding!

> That one whose visit with Him depends on Him
> Becomes astonished when He visits him!
> Continuously the attention of this broken heart,
> Whether in the Kaaba or temple, is toward Him!

On the day of the victory at Khaybar, the Apostle saw one of his friends dragging a child by its ears toward Abdullah ibn Umar. He said: "O Ibn Umar, do you see this captive child in the clutches of that man?" He replied, "Yes, I see it." "In my community," declared the Apostle, "there will be free men who will come on the Day of Judgment with the seven doors of hell held more securely in their intrepid grasp than the child in the hands of that man!"

Hell is concerned with lustful desire, flesh, and skin, which have come along a forbidden road: It cannot shake the steps of the righteous ones nor the piety of those who fear God. These great men, whose stories you are hearing, were neither prophets nor angels, but were just like you and me—ordinary men. They were caught by the desire of what they had heard about God. They sought with supplication that which they desired, and proved the reality of their claim with signs. You too should do likewise. If you do not have silver for your daily expenses, still you have your life in place of it. Make use of this life of yours so that nothing may be able to cling to your skirt. Place your feet on the Path of loyalty to the covenant of the faith, so that no one may have any claim on you. Remove everything that is a veil for you on this path. Long ago it was said: "This Way is such that you cannot reach your destination unless you first destroy yourself." The resting place, as far as the faith is concerned, is the destruction of one's animal soul. First destroy yourself, then set out along this road! Otherwise, take your troubles and get out of the way of those who are heading toward God, that the manly might enter!

> Abandon yourself; then set out along the Way of faith!
> This infidel soul is an idol; fling it on the ground!
> Set out on the road, if you are a man of the Way!
> Having set out, sacrifice yourself on His Way!
> If you are told, "Risk your head along this Way of Mine!"
> Then rejoice, and fling the sash off your turbaned head!

Now, since you are not a man of such initiative, what should you do? Grab hold of the saddle straps belonging to a man of this Way. Bind yourself to him, for all of us are not born kings. In every age there is only one king, while all others pass their days in the shadow of His good fortune. O brother, the grief of the faith is no small matter. You have heard that all jinn, men, animals, and birds were subject to the prophet Solomon. Nevertheless, he was inflamed with the pursuit of the faith. Whatever he possessed was out of grief born from this faith. Do not say that the world was for the companionship of Solomon; it was for his service! There is a big difference between companionship and service. Many fiery rivers have to be crossed before one can pass from service to friendship. When he heard the cry of an ant, Solomon ordered the wind to bring his throne and place it there and, for forty days, sat down beside the ant in order to hear divine secrets from it, for God has hidden, within His creatures, many secrets of which nobody has any knowledge.

If a person has any misgivings about this, he should pay attention to what the Quran has to say: "All the creatures of earth and heaven praise God!" (Q64:1). Even a boaster must have read, "None knows God's army except He!" (Q74:31). It is related that David was in the sanctuary. An ant passed in front of him. He lifted his hand with the intention of throwing the ant away from the place of prostration. "O

David," the ant protested, "what wantonness is this that you intend to inflict upon me? It is scarcely your task to lay hands upon me in God's own house!" David was grief-stricken and said: "O God, how should I deal with Your creatures?" A voice was heard: "Make it your habit to act out of fear of God so that none has to suffer on your account! Do not locate the true source of creatures in their bodies! Look rather at the mystery of their creation! If We were to order an ant to come out of its black robe, so many indications of the divine Unity would radiate from its breast that the monotheists of the whole world would be put to shame. The secret of this is indicated in the saying of the Apostle, who used to pray: "Show me Your creatures as they really are!"

Moses once enjoyed such a warmth of consolation one night while immersed in prayer that the effect endured till the following day. The thought occurred to him that no other creature could have been vouchsafed an experience similar to what he had enjoyed the previous night. In a moment Gabriel arrived and said: "O Moses, there is a person in this forest who is able to cure whatever ails the hearts of the righteous!" When Moses arrived at the spot, he saw a frog. It was croaking away in the water. On seeing Moses, it said, "O Moses, I have been waiting for you for a long time, in order to uproot the shoot of pride from your heart! You should on no account claim anything unique for yourself, for every gift that was bestowed upon you last night from the divine Presence was first of all granted to me, and only afterwards to you! Be careful not to make such a claim for yourself in the future!" Yes indeed, brother, there is a dignity that is taught to some by hell, to others, by an ant, and to still others, by a frog!

When Moses saw the loving concern of this frog, he understood that it was an agent of God. He flung his turban on the ground and exclaimed: "O agent of God, grant me a share in the fellowship of your largeheartedness, and present the story of my pain and grief to God!"

> Behold His honor, which renders every soul speechless!
> Understanding is left standing, finger in mouth.
> The door that had been closed could not be opened,
> Neither could a person place his finger upon it!
> Not every one who sets out is certain to be made a confidant!
> Not every one who comes seeking finds out about this Way!

Those who discover the secret are so lost to view
That no one sees even the tip of their hair afterwards!

[Advice on what prayers to say for some specific needs follows.]

*Peace!*


LETTER 90: HEALING

*In the name of God, the Merciful, the Compassionate!*

Brother Shamsuddin, every action not permissible according to the
Quran is unacceptable. Every desire, on which prophecy is silent, is
completely vain! Every proof along the path of faith except what
comes from faith itself is purely and simply a deviation! Every plea
for assistance you make along the path of faith that does not itself
originate from faith itself is totally rejected. "Whoever includes anything in the faith that does not bear the stamp of My testimony is rejected." As long as your actions are not sincere, they are not permitted by the Quran, and sincerity resides in a grief-stricken heart.
Wherever the gentle breeze of serenity blows, the glorious Quran is
accepted as the bearer of joyful tidings, whether by jinn or men. The
former said: "Surely we have heard a marvelous Quran, which gives
guidance to the straight path, and so we have put our faith in it!"
(Q72:1, 2). The Quran is also a balm for the pains of seekers, for "in
the Quran, I send down those lights which are a healing and a mercy
for believers!" (Q17:82). It is the orientation for those traveling along
the Way, since "it gives guidance to the straight path!" (Q72:2).

When the Quran provides a guidance for anybody, then his
countenance remains humble even though his breast be raised to
great heights of intimacy. "Had We sent the Quran down on a mountain, you would certainly have seen it fall to pieces out of fear of
God" (Q59:21). Every action that is not permitted by the Quran is a
stumbling block along the way of the faith. It is all blindness. When
the sun of the Quran shines forth from its ancient tower, the sky of
the heart is warmed, for "undoubtedly there is in this [the Quran] a

reminder for those endowed with heart and ears and it bears witness
to Him!" (Q50:37).

> When the guide of the Law arrives at the door,
> The desired Beloved comes out to meet it there.
> Everyone who travels according to the Law receives,
> From the Beloved, the crown of acceptance!

The men of this Way are masters of spirits. Their speech is life.
The life of creatures stems from the purity of their grief, while the
stability of the world depends on the magnanimity of their grief.
What security is enjoyed by the dwellers of this world derives from
their legacy of kindness. Their actions have no blameworthy elements. Their various states are not a turning back. Nor are their
sayings ineffective. There is nothing harmful in their knowledge. Until you ply the sword of the rejection of all names and customs, you
will not reach the stage when you can remove any head! Until you
clean the plain of your heart of whatever knowledge you have acquired, springs of wisdom will not well up from the very depths of
your heart, nor will you find any taste for the knowledge of Truth.
Khwaja Attar says:

> Make the illumined heart a river of faith.
> Let it utter the revelations of the Lord of the worlds!
> Step into the world of holiness for but a moment:
> Catch hold of that circle and throw it at the sanctuary door!
> Be sweet-tongued like Jesus when you speak.
> Smash the oyster and extract the pearl!

Any heart that does not see in this life will not be able to see tomorrow either! Listen to what the Quran has to say: "Anyone who
today has no knowledge of God will tomorrow remain blind to the
face of God."

O brother, on that day, when the testers will strike hearts on the
testing stone, whatever dross is within them will emerge on the plain.
Those who are investigating Truth will be sent to oversee hearts so
that whatever is in the most hidden recess will be brought forth as on
the Day of Judgment. They will say: "O God, nowhere have we
found even a particle of fidelity to the covenant!" A voice came: "Every breast not bound to the covenant of fidelity to My faith remains

far from Me." That judgment will persist, so that such a person will never come near God again! It has been thus explained:

> When you will be aroused for your testing,
> All your deeds will be hung about your neck.
> The crucible itself will tell you, when the smoke arises,
> Whether you are pure gold throughout, or merely on the
> surface!

The food of the believer should be that, at every moment, this rank is imprinted in his heart and on his eyes: "O faithless one, is this the way to act with Me, and is this the way to observe My covenant? Even if you do not belong to Me as you should, for My part I cannot but be devoted to you, for I am God! Even if you repudiate My covenant, still I am bound to the blessings promised of old, because of My own fidelity! Although you are not saddened by your defective devotion, I am bound to make you happy and console you with My favored blessings, by virtue of My very lordship!"

> Those men who are fully content in their unconcern,
> And who, in their hearts, consider oppression as justice,
> Act disobediently before the very eyes of the King!
> They are shameless, for they are mere men!

O brother, get up, for this is no place to tarry! Nor is it an opportunity to develop bad habits. There is no scope for boasting, that you should become caught up in the worship of your own baseness. Along the royal road of the divine decree, there is no other stratagem than the greeting of a profound prostration. Nobody benefits at all by giving rein to his own inordinate desires, but there is no harm at all in following the practice of the Chosen One.

> O God, give me an illuminated heart as my companion;
> Make Muhammad the one who intercedes for me!
> Accept my heart and soul as a sacrifice offered on his way;
> In holy fear turn your face toward his threshold!
> On the brink of the next world, let your breath praise him;
> In this world, place your hand in his saddle strap!

In short, every affair not conducted with knowledge is simply vain. Every austerity and mortification not in accordance with the Law is an error and belongs to the faith of Satan. All the doors of eternal bliss opening onto the truth of gnosis can be recognized only by knowledge. The secrets of those renowned in the faith and the kingdom, the pride of Islam, the dignity of the call of the prophets, the mystical perception of the divine blessings, the various ranks of holiness of those devoid of sin, the distinction of the grades of those near God, the secrets of Adam's descendants, the secrets of those guilty of grave faults, the recompense of those of deep faith, the respect for ordinances, including the observance of what is commanded and the avoidance of what is prohibited—all of these can be recognized only by means of knowledge, and can be found only on its plain! Until a man emerges from the wilderness of his own ignorance and places his footsteps on the open plain of knowledge, these blessings of faith will not become manifest within him.

Concerning this heavenly enterprise, there is nothing more inimical or contemptible than ignorance. Now is there any shorter or more impelling way than that of knowledge. "Knowledge of God is the nearest door to God, while ignorance is the greatest of the veils that separate one from God."

Just as knowledge is the field of all blessings, ignorance is the valley of all errors. The mark of wretchedness appears out of this valley of ignorance. This ignorance is soil in which springs up the vegetation of the domination of infidelity, the undermining of the foundations of faith, the neglect of the commands of the Law, accommodation with Satan, estrangement from the imitation of the prophets and the righteous ones—all of these misfortunes, and a hundred thousand similar things. Khwaja Attar says:

> If you become pure and separated from both worlds,
> You will find but one way: the light of Muhammad!
> And if you become like dust along the path to Muhammad,
> Both worlds will turn to dust on account of your purity!
> Otherwise, like a philosopher, you will remain far from Him;
> It is your very thinking that will cut you off from Him!
> In decorating this wall by means of your understanding,
> You will be tying your girdle as a fire worshiper!

It is related that when the mark of the curse appeared on Satan's forehead, Adam said: "It will not be auspicious to contend with those graced by fortune. Nor will it avail an ignorant person to be envious of the work of a learned man. Grasp the standard of misery in your hands. Wherever you find one of my sons who is not walking in the field of knowledge or traveling along the path of seeking it, bind him to your saddle straps so that the hindrance of his existence might be far removed from my chosen offspring." He also said: There are, in the world, two groups of people devoted to God. Some have already reached their destination, while others are still treading the path in hope of attaining their goal some day. Whoever is not included in either of these two groups belongs to that people of which it is said, "They are Satan's party, and surely Satan's party are the losers" (Q58:19). All of them are Satan's cavalry and foot soldiers.

O brother, the Quran enjoins: "Struggle on the path to God!" (Q22:78). Do not turn your steps toward your own lane. There you would be reckoned a self-conceited person. Enter, instead, into the lane of My covenant, that you might become a beloved of Mine. You may have been thrown down, but now have been raised up by Me. You were pusillanimous, but now you have been comforted by Me. If you step into your own lane, you cannot remain unscathed. If you find it agreeable to remain in your own lane, you will diminish your own worth. You cannot possibly earn any interest. An inflamed one has said:

> If you were utterly in love with My beauty, and
> If you had any standing in this affair, one word would suffice.
> So long as you cling to yourself, it is but you! Me, you cannot reach.
> In order to attain Me, you must abandon self!

O brother, you should place all selfish desires on the carpet of an enlightened struggle with self. Cut off the head of your animal soul, and curb it by means of austerity in accordance with the precepts of the Law. Don the dress of submission. I swear by God that nobody has ever benefited by worshiping himself, nor has anyone suffered any loss by worshiping God. You possess nothing dearer to you than your own life, but if you have appropriated to yourself the gist of this saying, then place your very first step upon this life of yours. Do not be afraid of dying! After death, there is only life filled with Life![103] It has been thus explained:

> If you remain dependent upon your own life, you will remain;
> For, even though you are in the world of Life, you still live!
> If you grasp this point well, you will realize,
> Everything you are seeking, you are that!

The perfection of the seeker consists in holding firmly to the being of the Desired One, and in removing the obstacle of one's own being from the Way. Someone engaged in this work has said:

Do me a kindness—remove my being from the Way,
That this hindrance, which is myself, might disappear!

Tomorrow, lovers of God's beauty will enter paradise uncertainly, fingers in mouth, or will be carried off to hell, clicking their fingers for joy! In paradise, they will remember that God is the "Wrathful" and the "Most Cruel," while in hell, that he is the "Most Compassionate" and the "Benign." In the one place they will see that His wrath is really a veil concealing many blessings; in the other, that His mercy makes a rose garden out of a consuming fire! All this happens when lovers realize that with respect to God, the blessings of this world constitute a veil for the blessed ones, to such an extent that the very abundance of blessings can cause them to be excluded from the Bestower of Blessings himself! Lovers also realize that, in the very heart of the fire, Abraham was granted a vision by the Divine Majesty Himself, so that the fire became, for him, a rose garden. Hence it is known that blessings, without the Friend, are simply destruction and punishment; whereas the fires of hell, together with the Friend, constitute a veritable paradise!

I have not drunk that wine to become sober;
Nor do I drink to revive myself again!
Only one cup, manifesting Your glory, suffices for me;
Oh, that I might be immersed in the pleasure of seeing You!

[Instructions concerning specific prayers and practices follow.]

*Peace!*

LETTER 91: DRESS

*In the name of God, the Merciful, the Compassionate!*

My brother Shamsuddin, may God grant you the robe of friendship with Him! In the matter of dress, the sheikhs insist that their disciples should be adorned with the jewel of being clad in rags. They themselves also dress in this fashion, that they might be a sign among the people, and that the people might become their watchmen. If they make a false move, people will speak out to rebuke them. If they desire to commit sin while wearing that dress, they will be seized with shame. In short, a patched garment is the adornment of God's saints, and it is customary to wear it!

Ibn Abbas says: "The Apostle wore a woolen garment." It is related that it was made up of twelve patches, of which some were bark from the date tree. Similarly, Umar wore a woolen garment. It is related that his had thirteen patches, of which some were bark. Sheikh Abu Ali was asked who should be entrusted with the wearing of this garb. He replied: "That person who is a superintendent in God's kingdom, because nothing in the whole world, regarding states or commands, can occur without being known to him!" They should wear a dress of a light hue and they should take pains to sew it well so that people might think that they are men of means, since it is related that God loves those who practice this pious deception! Among the various colors, blue and khaki are preferred, for they are the colors worn by the afflicted or sorrowful. They are also the darkest colors, signifying that if those who wear them permit even a momentary negligence, then they will become estranged from the divine Presence!

The afflicted wear a blue garment, for it is necessary to wash clothes of other colors after every few days. They do not care to become involved in washing, for it will not leave them time for ejaculatory prayer and their other duties. They choose khaki also for this reason—it does not have to be washed so frequently. Other colors, too, arouse the spirit of self-adornment, but by this color they are held to be grief-stricken and brokenhearted. One of the reasons for wearing coarse grass garments is to hope that the coarseness of the grass might produce a similar effect in the wearer! After wearing it, a person should then proceed to get tough with his animal soul, and put it in its place, as do the ascetics. Excising anger and deceit from their soul, they should be straight and humble before God. They should have eyes for no other person or place. Nor should some disappointment cause anger or envy to appear in them. Another reason for wearing such a garment is to imitate our revered sheikhs.

On the other hand, a white robe is suitable for anyone who holds that the garment of his life has been washed with the soap of austerity and "return to God." Also, the page of his heart should be cleansed of anything written in praise of rivals, and purified of the lusts of his

lower soul. A blue garment is suitable for anyone whose lower soul
has been conquered and its head severed by the sword of inner struggle! Also, mourning and the wearing of a khaki robe are fitting for the
person who is so thoroughly immersed in the presence of God that he
never has time to wash it. An azure dress possesses the quality of the
purity of the sky, and is granted to anyone who has passed from the
world below to paradise above, and been endowed with a heavenly
magninimity! A woolen garment is bestowed upon anyone who is a
Sufi. All seekers, both in the faith and in the world, should turn aside
from themselves and observe all the practices and good manners that
are prescribed. A coarse garment should be worn by anyone who has
emerged from the condition of human nature and is no longer under
the sway of any creature, because the power of the sewer, the weaver,
and the spinner has not reached this garment. This means that the
animal soul should have been trampled underfoot and ground into
the earth. A black robe is fit for the person who has passed beyond all
the stages and stations along the Way to God, and has reached the
Goal of his endeavors—"Undoubtedly your goal extends to your
Lord!" (Q53:42). Having reached the object of his affection, he will
find no veil remaining between him and God, as has been said:

Realize that there is no color beyond black!

"Poverty is blackness of the face." If you have grasped this you
will be able to understand what Khwaja Sanai wrote:

All these colors are filled with variety,
Yet the ring of Unity makes them one!
Choose black, for it will not run,
Nor does it accept any other color.
The sparks of the Fire the heart seeks
Are the object of the seeking of an inspired, black-faced one:
It is the nature of an Abyssinian to court trouble!
In fact, he takes delight in his black face.
If you do not want to disclose the secret of your heart,
Remain with the black-faced one of both worlds!

Trousers are suited for the person who can continuously keep his
inner self before him, and be engaged in the remembrance of God,
just as the person occupied in plaiting and weaving the trouser cloth
needs to be very alert lest his mind get distracted by other matters.
There is also a closely stitched garment called the "mixture of a thou-

sand" that is frequently worn because of its durability. It is also un-
comfortable. Weaving it, one will need no other garment for a long
time. Most of the sheikhs wear such a garment. Its wearing also involves the penance of putting up with the inconvenience of its
weight!

[Many more details of different types of clothes worn by the Sufis are given.]

The sleeves should be wide according to the practice of the companions and the sheikhs. In this way one's ritual ablutions are facili-
tated. Also, if anyone wishes to carry around his prayer carpet or
something else, he can slide it up his sleeve!

[Still more details of dress follow.]

> O Wisdom, in Your path a child is better than a lion!
> The intellect of the guide has become lost in quest of You.
> O Wisdom, all are perplexed along Your path!
> Intellect has been spun around and left dazed by the wayside!

It has also been said:

> The royal throne and this world are naught but talismans;
> He exists! All those others are nothing more than names!
> Look carefully! This world and the next are nothing but Him!
> If there is anything apart from Him, then it too is He!
> Alas, nobody has been illuminated!
> Eyes remain sightless—yet the world is filled with the Sun!

*Peace!*

## LETTER 92: BLAME

*In the name of God, the Merciful, the Compassionate!*

Dear brother Shamsuddin, may God honor you on account of the intercession of His friends! Any group that sets out along the Way will
have blame relegated to it. This applies especially to those dedicated
to God who are showered with blame by people all over the world, especially His chosen ones. It is a tradition concerning God Almighty
that He deals in exactly the same manner with His friends and those
who seek Him. Whoever observes His sayings will soon discover that
the world will turn to finding fault with his behavior.

Blame can be of three kinds. The first is that of compliance. It pertains to anyone who does his work conscientiously, is upright in his practice of the faith, and keeps all his affairs in proper order. People will certainly find fault with him and, in all his states, twist whatever he does to serve their own purpose. Whatever name they are called, however, it is all the same to them. Consider, for example, what happened to the Apostle himself, who was the outstanding lover of God and leader of the entire community. Until revelation came upon him and he made it known, he enjoyed a good reputation among one and all. He was considered a great man. He used to be called "Muhammad the Trustworthy." When the robe of revelation was drawn over his head, people began to loosen their tongues to reproach him. One called him a soothsayer; somebody else, a poet; one group called him a liar; yet another considered him to be a madman, but he paid no attention to any of them.

The second kind of blame is that of intention. This happens when a person is showered with honors and respect by people, and he becomes a celebrity among them. He wants to free his heart from them and remain immersed in God. He deliberately sets out upon a course of action that will lead people to reproach him for doing something that would not, however, infringe the Law. This explains the behavior of the leader of the faithful, Usman. One day, while he was caliph, he was carrying on his head some branches from his date palm grove. At that time he had four hundred slaves. People said: "O leader of the faithful, what is this you are doing? You are the caliph and you possess many slaves." He replied: "I am subduing my soul, for I do not want my position among the people to prove to be a hindrance to it!" There is also the famous story of Bayazid Bistami who, on returning from Mecca and Medina, was entering a certain city. A cry arose within it—"Bayazid is coming!" Everyone hurried outside and began to lead him into the city with great honor. He was disturbed by all this fanfare. When he arrived in the bazaar, he drew a round loaf out of his sleeves and began to eat it. It was the month of Ramzan. Everybody deserted him. He remained there, all alone. He turned to a disciple who was his constant companion and said: "See, I have performed an action pertaining to one tenet of the Law, yet the entire populace has rejected me!"

The third type of blame is that of abandonment. It occurs when infidelity and error catch hold of a person's skirt and he proceeds to abandon the Law, removing his hand from loyalty to the Traditions and saying: "This is what is meant by the 'path of blame,' and I am now a blameworthy one." He commits a manifest error! It is a great calamity, and it has come to birth in this period. The purpose of such men is to utilize rejection by the people as a means of gaining notoriety among them. First of all, however, a person should be accepted by the people before he can resolve to become rejected by them. And if a person has not tried, by his deeds and behavior, to become acceptable, then anything he does in order to become blameworthy is simply pretense!

Concerning their acceptance, the wise say: "Blame is the abandonment of peace and security." When anyone talks about his resolve to abandon his own peace and take calamities upon himself, he then turns away from all ease and comfort, with the hope that the divine glory will be manifested to him; and that he, though himself a creature, might not place any hope in creatures; and also that he, after having been cut off from all human expectations, might become united to God! The eyes of all the creatures of this world are fixed upon peace and security, but the blameworthy ones turn their backs upon it, so that their spiritual resolve might not depend upon any creature. For the masters of love, however, there is more hidden in blame than they realize, so that it can be said: "The path of blame is a veritable garden for lovers, a joy to friends, a solace for those who yearn, and a delight for disciples," since it contains the effects of being accepted. It is at once the beverage of God's saints and a sign of nearness to Him. Just as everybody is pleased and happy to be accepted by people, so too, even though he is poverty-stricken, he should remain expectant, for one might find in a tavern what is not glimpsed in the Kaaba itself!

The incantations of Pharaoh were the very essence of infidelity, yet the magic of divine unity appeared through them. Take a firm hold on abjection and helplessness! Reduce your being and any authority you possess to nothing, for both pride and being are qualities that pertain to God. There is no dress more suited to dust than that of humility and abjection. How can anyone who has passed twice through the human urinary tract have anything to boast about? The foolishness of his being has been confirmed from its inception! No dress is more suitable for the King's servants and slaves, in His presence, than that of humility!

If you wish to preserve your health in the presence of the
King,

It is better for you to stand at a distance and look at him!
Why prolong my story? Brevity is to be preferred.
Before a growling lion in the forest, play the fox!

Dust should bear burdens, not engage in rioting. It is meant to bear the weight of creatures rather than to rebel. Know that when the King raises up a destitute beggar whom He finds along the way, and says to him, "I am yours, and you are mine," the beggar should never forget his real condition. It would be a mercy on the part of God if that beggar were to realize his own condition—a mere man who is nothing but a handful of dust. Whatever else he has, is all by the divine favor. He showed favor to you! Not because of any claim of yours did He give you existence. You could only prostrate yourself, but He exalted you! It was a work of His lordship, not of your beggarly condition. "Grace had already performed its task before the water and clay were mixed." Adam had not yet transgressed when, by the divine mercy, the robe of repentance had already been sewn!

*Peace!*

## LETTER 93: LISTENING TO MUSIC

*In the name of God, the Merciful, the Compassionate!*

Brother Shamsuddin, may God honor you! Hearts and minds are the treasure houses of secrets, and mines filled with precious gems of hidden meaning. The manner of concealment of those secrets and gems is like that of a fire within iron and stone. It is listening to music that brings forth the fire that was previously hidden in stone and iron! It is not possible for listening to educe anything from the heart if it is not already there, just as nothing can exude from a porous pot that is empty to begin with!

Hence it should be known that whoever is overcome in face of the love of the Lord, and who yearns to see Him, finds that listening to music is a stimulant that excites his holy desire and serves to further strengthen his love and ardent yearning by bringing it out into the open. Listening brings forth the fire in his breast from its hiding place, and makes it visible in favored states, by means of clear manifestation and mutual enlightenment. This could not have taken place within the blockaded heart itself. Know that if anyone is destined to experience this grace, and to have these blessings showered upon him, then these exalted states, in the language of the Sufis, are referred to as "ecstatic outpourings." At this stage, listening to music is lawful—even desirable! Some even say it is necessary that this step should be taken, for although something may be playful in this world, yet when it reaches the stage of hearing the Lord himself, it becomes something truly wonderful. How greatly a person is transformed in his very essence! Whatever then comes to him will also be transformed.

Hence it is that spiritual guides have said that, although the verses sung before them might smack of the tavern, yet when they hear the word *union*, they think of the vision of God, just as the word *separation* connotes a veil between them and the Lord and the word *eyes*, the glance of the Lord. Imagine the pleasure of the person who hears: "I have poured out on you a love from Me that you might be brought before My eyes" (Q20:39). The word *tresses* reminds them of nearness to the Lord, "so that they might bring us nearer to God" (Q39:3). It could easily happen that the word tresses might make someone think of the whole chain of attributes of the divinity itself, as the poet has noted:

> I said: I shall count the ring of tresses upon her head,
> In that way I shall remove all ignorance of what concerns her!
> Laughing at me, she twisted sharply her billow of dark tresses,
> And reduced to confusion all my careful calculations!

This means that, if anybody wishes, by means of his own powers, to understand even the tip of the hair of the wonders of God, he will fall into such confusion that all his counting will be incorrect, and all his intellectual efforts utterly confounded! It could be that tresses might be taken for the darkness of infidelity, and light for the brightness of faith, as has been said:

> Your tresses snatched away my heart, which belonged to Your
> face.
> Look at the Hindu! He has grasped what, by right, belongs to
> the Muslims!

Or again,

> The darkness of Your tresses has darkened the face of fortune;

The light of Your face has turned the oppression of night into
day!

By the word *infidelity* Sufis understand the concealing of one's
being and actions, and by the word *apostasy* they understand a turning away from self. When a venerable Sufi heard the following couplet being recited,

Until you become an infidel, love will not purchase you:
Who but an apostate can do the work of a *qalandar*?[105]

He raised a cry and swooned away! When he came to his senses, people asked him what had happened. He replied: "The dictionary meaning of 'infidelity' is 'to cover up,' so an unbeliever is one who 'covers
up.' A farmer, who hides his seeds in the earth, is also called an 'unbeliever.' " The meaning of the verse would be this: "As long as the
righteousness of your very being and actions has not been hidden
from yourself as well as from other people, you cannot genuinely lay
claim to be a lover! Further, until you turn away from yourself and
become freed from your animal soul, you should not say anything
about being a *qalandar*!"

Mention of wine and intoxication also has a different meaning
for Sufis:
If you were to measure out two thousand cups of wine
How could you relish it, unless you first tasted it?

These words are meant to suggest that religious matters cannot
be correctly appreciated by hearing and by knowledge alone, but only
by tasting them! If you speak a great deal about love, ardent desire,
austerity, fear of God, and so on, and even compose books about
them, there will be no profit at all until you yourself are changed by
the particular virtue you extol.

Take note, too, of verses about taverns.
Whoever has never been to a tavern has no faith:
In the tavern is the very foundation of the faith!

The poet is here saying that until those human qualities that predominate within you are destroyed, then those other qualities that lie
hidden within your inner being cannot come to birth and begin to
flourish.

It could happen that because Sufis are in a mystical state they might understand some Arabic verse to mean something other than what the words actually say. Someone said:

Even when I dream, it is all about You!

And a Sufi, on hearing this, was overcome. He was asked, "What is this? You don't even know what he is talking about!" He replied, "What do you mean by saying that I don't know? He is saying that I am rejected, abandoned, and in great danger."

One of the venerable Sufis was walking in the bazaar. He heard a cucumber-seller calling out, "Ten cucumbers for a penny!" He fell into an ecstatic trance. The people asked him about what had happened. He said: "When ten just men are sold for but a penny, what must the wicked be worth?"

It can happen that there is one and the same couplet, but each one who hears it understands it in a different way, according to his own condition and outlook. For example, a slave girl, while filling a pitcher at the river bank in Baghdad, was singing this couplet:

Undoubtedly the Master of the heavens is pure;
But lovers are caught up in grief and difficulties!

One man fell into a trance, exclaiming, "You are right!" Another also fell into an ecstasy, muttering, "You are wrong!" Both of them were correct! The one who said she was correct had his attention fixed on all the grief and effort of a lover; while the one who disagreed with her saw only the spirit, contentment, and union with the Friend that is found in love. Sometimes it happens that the mere sound of the words, without even understanding their meaning, is enough to send them into a trance.

Finally, have you ever heard about Arab camels that get so intoxicated by the singing of their drivers that, even though they are heavily laden, they run so swiftly that, when they arrive at their destination and the singing ceases, they immediately fall down in a heap and die? That is the sort of listening that befits this group! Whoever is overcome by whatever happens to him, no matter what he listens to, is hearing Him. Wherever he looks, he sees Him. If he rejects anything he sees or hears, he rejects a chance to experience Him. Whoever has ever been inflamed by the fire of love of God—or even of some unsubstantial creature—should understand this matter very well!

For the present, it is necessary to pay close attention to one fundamental thing, in order to escape from the possible pitfalls and ca-

lamities involved in listening to music. It is this: You should understand anything that pertains to defective qualities or to change as
referring to yourself; while you should understand whatever is concerned with qualities such as beauty, glory, existence, beneficence,
and anything that evokes similar perfections as referring to God Almighty. If you do not do this, you are in danger of falling into blasphemy! This is the reason why listening to music is a great danger for
one's friendship with God Almighty. If someone, for example, hears
this couplet,

> Where now is that inclination to kindness I used to experience?
> What is the reason for such dejection today?

then, even though he used to be strong in facing up to adversity, he
might suddenly become weak and, on this account, when he hears
this couplet, imagine that God Almighty used to favor him, but now
has changed. Yet to suppose that this change has taken place in God
Almighty himself would be blasphemy. He should understand that
there is no possibility at all of change in God. It is completely out of
the question that any rejection, veil, or vexation should proceed from
that direction. The divine threshold lies open to one and all, just like
the sun, which showers its light upon all; but if anyone remains in the
shade of some wall, then it is he who remains veiled as far as the sun
is concerned. The change is in him, not in the sun, as has been said:

> O beloved, the sun has risen a long time ago:
> If it does not shine on someone, it is his own misfortune!

The responsibility for the veil should be ascribed to a person's
own misfortune, or to some fault that he has committed, but not to
God, for He is completely unstained by all of these things. Those who
are impure, stiff-necked, frustrated, or ill-fortuned are astonished that
anyone could derive pleasure from listening to such music. Listening
with pleasure, ecstatic utterances, an agitated condition, and change
of color—all astonish them. Remember that beasts marvel at the delicious taste of almond syrup, the impotent are surprised at the pleasure of intercourse, and the ignorant stand awestruck at the pleasure
of mystical knowledge of the Lord, His glory, His greatness, and the
wonders He has fashioned. A person greatly blessed by God is beyond the estimation of men! No matter how importunate someone
may be, it is impossible to praise Him adequately in this abode. What
wonder is it if a blind man is not interested in the sight of greenery

and flowing water, for he has no eyes with which to see. Also, if a child rejects the enjoyment of kingship and dominion, what cause for astonishment is that? He is only interested in playing! What use does he have for the satisfaction of ruling a kingdom?

If a person's heart is captivated by the ardent love of somebody upon whom it is unlawful for him to look, then everything that he hears at a musical gathering would turn out to be understood with respect to this forbidden person. Listening to music is strictly prohibited for such a person, since he would be agitated with thoughts about the person, and become concerned with various exciting and dangerous actions. Anyone or anything that incites a person toward what is forbidden is itself forbidden. Nobody disagrees on this point. If the love of God is not uppermost in a person's heart, so that listening to music becomes something commendable for him, and an occasion for overcoming sensual fancies—if it is not this, then listening would be unlawful for him. Others say that listening to music is permissible for him, just as other kinds of actions are permissible for him.

Listening to songs can be divided into three categories: lawful, forbidden, and permissible. Hence it is that a venerable Sufi, when questioned on the matter, said: "Listening to music is desirable for those devoted to God, permissible for those who vacillate, and improper for people given over to sensuality and pleasure!" All the sheikhs agree that, while a person is engaged in reciting the Quran, he should recite it in such a way that no obstruction is placed in the way of understanding it.

One day the Apostle was asked about odes and poetry. He said: "They are merely words. As such, they can be either good or bad." In other words, whatever it is lawful to listen to—whether it be wisdom, advice, rational demonstration of verses concerning the Lord, the remembrance of His blessings and favors, the qualities of the righteous and of those who fear God, in verse or prose—all are lawful. On the other hand, listening to anything that concerns what is forbidden, such as backbiting, shameful things, disparagement, satirizing anybody, or blasphemous talk, in both verse and prose—all are forbidden. The description of cities, houses, past ages, peoples, and so on is permissible, while descriptions of moles, shapely figures, tresses, lips, eyes, and other similar things that pander to the sensual soul are all improper. This censure applies both to verse and prose as well.

As for those who are close to the Lord, who are given over to struggle with self and austerities and who can differentiate between

what originates from human nature and that which is from on high—
as described in the first category—then the listening to any sort of
music becomes permissible for them. The Messenger of God listened
to the recitals of verse, while the companions composed verse and also
listened to recitals.

In this whole matter a number of people are at fault. Some con-
demn the listening to all verse as forbidden by the Law—yet spend
their days and nights backbiting their fellow Muslims! Another
group proclaims that it is lawful for anybody to listen to any music
that strikes his fancy, and act accordingly. They spend their whole
time listening to frivolous songs and arguing with one another about
them. Realize from all this that it would be quite wrong to make any
categorical statement about any matter that is under dispute and of
doubtful value.[106]

The author of the *Kashf ul-Mahjub* [Revelation of secrets], Ali
Hujwiri, who was a radiant luminary of his age, said: "Once when I
was in Merv, one of the leading traditionists said to me. 'I have written a book to demonstrate that listening to music is permissible.' I replied, 'A great difficulty has appeared in the faith. A noted leader has
legitimized that frivolity which is the root of all wickedness.' 'If you
don't consider it lawful,' he retorted, 'then why do you practice it?' I
declared: 'Any instruction concerning it must depend on the circumstances. No blanket statement can be made about it. If listening to
music produces a laudable effect in one's heart, then it is lawful. If its
effects are unlawful, so too is it. Likewise, if the effects of listening
are permissible, so is the listening.' " It is impossible to make an absolute statement about something that, on the surface, seems to be bad,
but that is inwardly illuminated by many compelling reasons.

Consider dancing, too. Imam Ghazzali has cited three reasons for
dancing. He said: "The command about dancing refers to what moves
a person to dance. If something praiseworthy stimulates a person to
dance, and the dancing helps him grow, and strengthens him, then
the dancing is also praiseworthy. If something despicable stimulates
him to dance, then the dance also is despicable. But if it is something
permissible that inspires him, then the dance also is permissible." He
also declared: "It became customary for a group of the companions to
dance for joy when anything wonderful happened."

There are, moreover, some good people who dance with a
swaying motion even though they have not been overcome by the ecstasy of union; they simply move around in imitation of the dervishes.

# THE HUNDRED LETTERS

Many more are moved to perfectly balanced movement in order to show that they are not in any ecstasy or trance, 'to save themselves from any falsehood.' Yet, despite all that has been said, people attest that it is not good to make a habit of dancing. For the most part, the states of people who merely imitate others take their origin from sport and frivolity or from similar activities. Men of spiritual insight should shun their example lest they become of little worth in the eyes of people, who will then cease to follow them. There is something unseemly, as far as the Law and the mind are concerned, in all forms of play. In short, it is impossible for the most excellent of men to engage in such activities.

Nevertheless, when any lightness appears in the heart while listening to songs, and a floating of the heart, occasioned by divine intimations, takes possession of someone and, as time goes by, this gets stronger, a restless condition arises of its own accord, and all order and custom are removed. That agitated state which makes its appearance could not simply be called "dancing." Nor is it a mere movement of one's legs. Nor is it a pandering to nature, since it is a purification of one's soul. Anybody who called that dancing would be very far from the path of truth. This is a state that cannot be described in words. Unless you have tasted it, you do not even know what is meant. All movement of this group would be an inner stirring, not dancing. Anyone who talks about this state by itself proves that he has merely been dancing, and has not had this inner seizure!

There are Traditions that deal with the genuine ecstatic states that can occur while listening to songs. One such genuine Tradition confirms this matter, and I shall bring it to your attention here. Uns has related this incident: "I was near the Apostle when the great Gabriel appeared to him. He said: 'O Apostle of God, here is some good news for you! The dervishes of your community will enter paradise five hundred years before the rich.' The Apostle was filled with joy upon hearing this news and said, 'Is there anyone present who can recite a poem for the occasion?' A man said, 'Yes, I can, O Apostle!' He replied, 'Then recite!' This was the poem that all heard:

> The serpent of love has stung my heart:
> There is no physician, and none to administer a charm,
> Except that Beloved with whom I am enthralled.
> With Him is the charm and the antidote as well!

The Prophet and also the companions were so enraptured that the Prophet's cloak slipped off his shoulders. When this condition subsided, Mu'awiyya ibn Abu Sufyan exclaimed: "What a good game you are playing, O Apostle!" "Get far away, O Mu'awiyya!" retorted the Apostle. "No one who fails to rejoice when he hears the description of the Friend can possibly be favored!" The Prophet's cloak was divided into four hundred pieces and distributed among those present. It is also related that the Prophet was once seized with such emotion and clapped his hands so vigorously on account of what he heard that drops of blood appeared on his fingers. He is also reported to have said: "Whenever a dervish claps his hands while listening to music, he expels any sensuality within him; whenever he stamps his foot upon the ground, he ejects any lust inside him; and whenever he shouts out in praise of God, he drives away any desires remaining within him."

It is permissible to shout out in a musical gathering whenever one is inwardly overcome by ecstatic union, for one cannot help oneself in such a state. It is related that Moses was once saying something to the Israelites. Someone shouted out. Moses scolded him. When he was next in prayer, God said to him: "He was shouting out on account of his love for Me. You should not try to stop him or anybody else who weeps, cries out, or is comforted by being close to Me!"

Sheikh Abu Abdur Rahman has collected all these Traditions in a book on the topic of listening to music. Realize now that everyone who has some standing in these musical gatherings can have his standing measured according to how much he imbibes, and the taste that he develops for it, just as every penitent is helped to foster his grief and repentance by whatever he hears, while someone longing for God would experience a growth in his eagerness to see the face of God. A believer would be strengthened in his certainty; a disciple would want to continue his investigation of Truth; a lover would be further cut off from creatures, while an indigent one would experience the real foundation of his placing no hope in others.

It is said that listening can be likened to the sun, which shines on all things, but the measure of its effect on each creature depends on its quality and what is imbibed. One is burnt up, another is made to shine. One is helped to flourish, while another melts away. If anyone were to ask how it could happen that someone who has no knowledge or awareness of himself nevertheless manages to dance according to the beat of the singer and recognizes the voice and melody of the singer, the answer would be that when a man is no longer shackled by the strength of his animal soul and has no attachment to his own opinions and ideas, his heart becomes both more illuminated and strengthened. And when this weakening of the animal soul takes place, and the heart is illuminated, inevitably he will understand the beat of the music and the meaning of the singers.

If it is said that since they want to listen to God and for the sake of God, then it would be fitting that sitting in the company of those who are close to God should be for the purpose of hearing the recital of the Quran, not that of singers of songs of merriment. The reason for saying this is that the Quran is the Word of God, and that should come first. The answer to such an objection is that there are many gatherings where people do listen to the recitation of the Quran. It can happen that many individuals fall unconscious when they hear it, while many others have even given up their souls while listening to Quranic recitals, as is amply documented. The reason for substituting singers for reciters of the Quran, and songs for the Quran, is that the Quran, in all respects, is not suited to all the states of the lovers of God, for one finds in it stories about the infidels and commands concerning ordinary affairs and worldly matters, things such as this verse: "A mother is entitled to a sixth of the inheritance, and a half-share should be given to each daughter" (Q4:12). Or again, this verse could be recited: "If a woman's husband dies, she should remain in seclusion for four months and ten days" (Q2:234). These and similar verses scarcely serve to enkindle the fire of love and ardent longing. Nevertheless, anyone who is enraptured with the Final End of life hears Him whenever he listens to anything, even if the meaning of the words is far from Him. Such a person, however, would be rare!

A second reason to substitute songs for recitation of the Quran is that so many people already know the Quran by heart, while many others read it. Yet we know that, in most cases, we do not pay all that much attention to anything we hear frequently. Do you not see that when the Arabs first came and heard the Quran, they would weep and various states appeared in them? Abu Bakr said: "I also used to be like you, but now my heart has grown secure. It is now stilled by the Quran!"

The condition of listening properly, however, depends on the observance of three things: the place, the time, and the company. The place should be a hospice of the sheikhs, or some building that is clean and tidy, well ventilated and well lit. The company should consist of friends and dervishes, people endowed with discrimination, and able to converse properly. They should be people who practice austerities. As for the time, it should be when one's heart is completely free of all preoccupations. Moreover, proper conduct at such sessions demands that one should not take part until one's heart is actually freed from such things. Nor should you make a habit of it. You should participate only from time to time, lest the effect of its excellence upon your heart be lost. It is not fitting to try to look for an approving eye while in a charged atmosphere. If anybody renders assistance, he should not be hindered from helping. There should be no attempt to control what is happening to anyone, nor should a person be judged because of the particular verse being recited, for that is very distracting, and useless. It should also be noted that if the singer sings in a pleasing manner, one should not comment, "You sing very well!" Or, if he does not sing well, and his verses are not nicely balanced, one should not declare, "Sing better!" There should not even be any altercation with him in your heart! You should not permit him to come in the way at all. You should concentrate on listening attentively. If a group is seized by what is heard, but you are not granted a share in their rapture, it might be because, when you yourself were sober, you looked with disdain on their drunken state. It behooves you, on such occasions, to be full of supplication, and enable the Lord of time to shower His blessings upon you. If you are not granted the blessings mentioned, you should at least become closely attached to an experienced and favored man.

The second point to be observed is that all should bow their heads and not look at one another. They should not speak to one another during the session, nor have drinks of water. They should not look to the right or to the left, shake hands or heads, or disturb someone else by any untoward movement. Brother, they should be as composed as they would be when sitting on their heels during formal prayer. Every heart should be raised to God, Who is to be praised and glorified. Each one should wait patiently for Him, until the indescribable bounty is vouchsafed to him from the hidden world, on account of his listening.

When anybody overpowered by ecstatic union stands up, the others should support him by also standing up. If his turban falls off, they should put it back on his head. All of these are new practices, and are not found among the companions or their immediate successors. Nevertheless, not all innovations are to be reprehended.[107] The vast majority are good, as Imam Shafi used to say. The practice of listening to a recital of the entire Quran during the evenings of Ramazan dates from the Caliph Umar and is certainly a pious practice. A reprehensible innovation would be one that goes against the practice of the Prophet. However, when men have been inspired by a good disposition and heart, and rejoice in such a way that there is no belittling of the Law, then this is something laudable. It would be a bloody business to interfere in the traditional ways in which a particular people are accustomed to do things. The injunction of the Law is, "Deal with people according to their particular behavior and disposition," for people will be happy with what agrees with their behavior, but will be scared away by anything that goes against it. What is agreeable to them would be like a binding practice for them. You know, of course, that some of the companions were unhappy to see the Apostle dancing. The reason is that they detested such behavior. The culture of the Arabs is one thing, but that of the Persians is quite another!

Let the matter rest: we have said enough in this letter about musical sessions and the rules that apply to them.

*Peace!*


## LETTER 94: SECLUSION

*In the name of God, the Merciful, the Compassionate!*

Dear Brother Shamsuddin, may God grant you the grace of obedience! It is important for a disciple to enter into seclusion and to withdraw from people in order to be able to devote himself to the service of God. It has been related that a sheikh said: "I arrived at a gathering where an archery competition was in progress. I wanted to speak to one person who sat apart from the participants. He said: 'As far as I am concerned, it is good to remember God Almighty.' I said: 'Why are you sitting all by yourself?' He replied: 'My Lord is with me, and two angels as well.' He then got up and went off." At such moments creatures are a hindrance that prevents a disciple from devoting himself to divine service.[108] Moreover, he no longer enjoys their company, and is finally thrown into sin and destruction. What should he do? There is a story related about Hatim, who said: "I sought five things from people, but did not find them. I sought worship of God and austerities from them, but they do not practice such things. I said: 'Come, make friends with me!' but none did. I said: 'Be satisfied with me when I do something'—but they were not. I said: 'Don't be a hindrance for me!' but they rejected my plea. I said: 'Don't invite me to do those things that are not pleasing to God Almighty! Also, if I don't do such things, then don't blame me!' But they did just that! That was then I took leave of them, and became preoccupied with myself."

The Prophet has praised such behavior. It is also enjoined by the Law upon his people. He has commanded some to separate themselves from people. In this matter, there is no doubt at all that he must be wiser in such affairs than you or I, and also capable of giving us better advice about ourselves than we could ever give. When you come across a period like the one described by the Prophet, then take heed of his commands and accept his advice. If you do not take heed, you are simply destroying yourself.

What has been commanded is this, as Abdullah ibn Amr ibn al-'As put it: "I was close to the Apostle. He was describing a state of tumult. He said: 'When you see that men pay no heed to their promises, and have laid hands on things entrusted to them—' I interjected: 'What should I do at such a time, O Apostle of God?' He replied: 'It is necessary to keep to your house, and to maintain a watch over your tongue. Hold on to whatever you know, and abandon whatever you don't! It is for you to attend to your own work, and ignore the work of somebody else!' " It is related that the Apostle said, "It is a time of distress." The people said, "O Apostle of God, what time should be called a time of distress?" He replied: "It means a time when a man cannot feel secure with those who sit down beside him." Ibn Masud has related in another tradition that the Apostle said to Haris Amirah: "If you are granted a long life, a time will come upon you when there will be many preachers but few men endowed with knowledge; many who ask, but few who give. In such an age, following one's sensual appetites will be considered enlightenment." I said, "When will such a time arise?" He replied, "The very day when prayers are abandoned and bribery is embraced, and when the faith is sold for some merely worldly trinket. Flee from such an age, O blessed one! Yes, flee far from it!"

O brother, see with your own eyes all that has been described in this tradition. Study this very age itself in order to see what you ought to do. So many pious people of former times have been unanimous in their view that they should flee far from their own age and from worldly minded people, and embrace a life of seclusion. They have commanded their disciples to do likewise. There is no doubt at all that they were extremely wise and percipient in this whole matter.[109] Succeeding ages have not registered any improvement, but rather have deteriorated.

A venerable Sufi has said: "I heard from Sufyan Suri that he used to say: 'By the God apart from Whom there is no other god, seclusion has become lawful in our age.' If this is so in his time and age, then in our own it ought to be considered as being necessary—even a duty." It is also related to Sufyan Suri that he was seated facing Ibad Khass and said: "Realize that you are in such an age when the companions of the Apostle were seeking a refuge from what they found was happening then. And remember, they had a knowledge we don't possess! They also had helpers that we don't, as well as a power denied to us. What sort of state should we be in here and now? We have but little knowledge, less patience, and scarcely any helpers."

Khwaja Fuzail Iyaz has said: "This is an age when a person should keep a careful watch over his tongue. He should also live in a secluded spot. He should treat his own heart. He should keep quiet about what he knows and abandon what he doesn't." Daud Tai has said: "Fast from this world and break your fast in the next! Flee from people as you would from a lion!" Abid has said: "I have not seen a single wise man who did not charge me with this: 'If you don't want anybody to recognize you, realize that your work lies with God Almighty.' " And again, "Men will render vain what you have acquired through your devotion on account of what comes forth from them, from their hypocrisy, vanity, and artificiality." Khwaja Yahya Mu'az has said: "The attention of men is a carpet of hypocrisy. All the ascetics of previous ages from been afraid of it. Hence they have completely abandoned human intercourse and visiting one another, according to the practice of Haram ibn Hayan, who said to Khwaja Uways Qarani: "Oveis, come along with me so that we can be near each other, and visit each other from time to time!" Khwaja Uways replied: "It is better for us to pray for each other than to visit each other, for in visiting and meeting there is nothing but hypocrisy and artificiality." Now if this is the state of affairs with regard to meeting each other as observed by noted ascetics what then must be that of people filled with desires and vanity, to say nothing of the wicked and the ignorant?

Realize that the present age is completely given over to vanity—unless, of course, God wills otherwise! Men have become utterly depraved, even to the extent that they try to prevent you from performing your devotions. If they are unable to stop you completely, then even if you do something, they will strive to render it ineffectual. Hence it is necessary, in such an age, to seek seclusion, withdraw from men, and seek protection in God Almighty from the wickedness of the age.

O brother, remain continuously occupied with breaking in yourself! Quaff the cup of grief and empty vessels of sorrow and anxiety! Do not try, even for a moment, to be free from your own difficulties, since it is not the lot of anyone to have a happy countenance. Muhammad, the Apostle of God, the very purpose of both worlds, cried out in this manner from the very depths of the pain of his own being: "O would that the Lord of Muhammad had not created Muhammad!" Somebody said to Abdullah Masud: "O that I might be among the companions of the right!" Abdullah Masud said: "O that when Abdullah Masud turns to dust, his name might be wiped out from the register of existence! In no way can he lift up his head from the dust!"

There was one person who practiced devotion but hankered after its reward. There was another who sinned, but expected forgiveness. Yet another, out of shame at his own existence, did not lift up his head. It behooves you to remain far from self-praise and self-conceit. Recognize yourself among the rejected and those driven away. Wahb ibn Munabbih said: "A hypocrite is one who likes to praise himself by means of lies, and thus to pour scorn on the righteousness of his enemy."

*Peace!*

LETTER 95: SEPARATION FROM PEOPLE

*In the name of God, the Merciful, the Compassionate!*

Dear Brother Shamsuddin, may God grant you the gift of piety! There are two kinds of seclusion and separation from men. The first is in relationship to a man who is not at all needed by people, either for his knowledge or his religious instruction. Such a person should separate himself entirely from other men. He should have no inter-course at all with them, except on Fridays and in an assembly, or on big feast days, or on the pilgrimage, or in a learned gathering, or on some other unavoidable occasion. Except for these, he should conceal himself, so that no one might recognize him, nor might he recognize anybody else. If, however, such a person wishes to cut himself off ut-terly from people and his association with them, even on Fridays or in any assembly and so on, because of what he sees takes place on such occasions, it is not fitting for him to do so unless he does one of two things. He could go to some place where it will not be possible for him to come on Fridays or attend the congregational prayer, such as in some mountainous region,[110*] or on an island. Perhaps that is why some go to such distant places and remain there. On the other hand, he might know that the real harm that would accrue to him as a result of participating in the Friday congregation would be greater than the merit of such participation, due to his association with oth-ers. When sin is greater than merit, then certainly it is permissible to abandon Friday appearances and participation in congregational prayer.

It is said that a very learned old man in Mecca used not to be pres-ent in the mosque for the Friday gathering or congregational prayer, without any excusing factor perceptible by others. He was asked to explain his behavior. He said: "The sin that is my lot as a result of mingling with men is greater than the merit that accrues to me as a result of participating in the Friday prayer." The common opinion of the members of this group concerning this work, however, is that they should mix with the people during the Friday gathering and congregational prayer, as well as in charitable works, but, apart from these occasions, they should remain separate from others. If, howev-er, anybody resides in a city but does not take part in the Friday gath-ering or congregational prayer, he is doing something of great signifi-cance. It requires a very fine perception and a perfect knowledge. It is not allowable for everybody. Second, he should be a person who is so exemplary in his knowledge that men are in need of him in the work of faith. For example, he might discourse about God, reject some in-novation, or, by deed and word, incite men to some work of faith. It would not be proper for such a man to withdraw completely from the society of men. Rather, he should remain among men in order to give them advice and instruction about the life to come.

This is a practice dating back to the Prophet, who said: "If innovations begin to appear, and a learned man keeps quiet, let the curse of God be upon him." This is precisely when he should be among the people. It would not be right if he did not appear among them. If such a person were to separate himself from people, it would be in imitation of Master Abu Bakr Furak, who decided to go all by himself and give himself up wholly to devotion in some mountainous region. He heard a voice saying: "O Abu Bakr, since you have been enlightened by God Almighty about so many matters of advantage to people, why have you abandoned God's slaves?" He returned and once again began to reside among people.

It is related that Abu Bakr Ishaq said to the sages inhabiting the mountains of Lebanon: "O eaters of grass, how is it that you have passed by the community of Muhammad and fallen into the clutches of heretics, and are wholly taken up here with eating grass?" They replied: "We don't have strength to associate with men. God Almighty has given that strength to you. You have to give instruction to the people." Such a man, even though he is with the people in his person and in gatherings, and shows himself firmly rooted in all his duties toward them, then with all of this, what need does he have of building up a treasure for himself for the world to come? Consider what happened to Umar ibn Khattab, who said: "If I sleep in the night, it is my loss; and if I sleep by day, it is a loss to the people."

Living a kind of life in which one is bodily with the people, yet during which one keeps one's heart far from them, is very difficult indeed! Imam Ghazzali said: "When a wave of disturbances sweeps over the land, such a state of affairs arises that although people seek a learned man, yet they derive no profit from their quest, nor are matters of the faith of any concern to anybody." In such a time, a learned man is also excused. He may seek seclusion, fly far from men, and bury his knowledge, that is, he understands correctly the command to seek seclusion and fly from men, for its advantage will be considerable. It can also be extremely detrimental. Somebody might say that the Prophet said, "You should live with the group, for the mercy of God is upon the group. In addition, Satan acts like a wolf toward men, catching them when they are by themselves." Again it is said to be forbidden in these terms: "Satan is with the solitary, yet distant from any two people."

The answer to this is that the Apostle did say this, but he also enjoined seclusion and withdrawal from men in a wicked and disturbed age, and there cannot be any contradiction in his words. Also, he said: "You should be with the group!" In other words, "Do not fly from people on Friday or during the various assemblies!" I myself[112] have said that the duty of the recluse is to participate in all good works of the people, but to refrain from associating and taking part in their other activities, on account of the dangers inherent in such participation. Again, when he spoke thus: "You should be with the group," it was not a time of disturbance. Also, anyone who is somewhat weak is not advised to live by himself. A man of strength and insight into the demands of the faith can, however, as the Prophet himself said, separate himself from the people in an age afflicted with disturbances.

It is even said that this would be the best course of action for such a person. Except on a Friday and for the assemblies, he should not venture forth. Nevertheless, he should also participate in all good works so as not to be deprived of the merit contained therein—for there is a great merit to be derived from the group, even though some have been ruined by it. There is a Tradition about the great saints that says that they should be present on Fridays and in the congregation.

If anyone says that the Prophet said: "The leaders of my community are those who sit in the mosque," then this should be denied, for there they are not far from men. It may be remarked that this pertained to an age not suffering from disturbances, and also when there was no fear. If someone sits in the mosque, he should not mix with the people. If he does, then he is both with them in body, and not far from them in heart—yet the whole purpose of seclusion is to be far off in body.

O brother, if there is something expensive and you are too poor to purchase it, it is still quite permissible to desire it—but do not make a fuss about it! If you have water in your house, no grass will grow, but it will be cool. Also, if you gain a victory, it is no cause for astonishment. A poor cook suffers, wears blackened clothes, and has to bear the heat of the fire, while somebody else gets the food. Moses said, "Show Yourself!" and felt the sword of "You cannot see Me!" yet pieces of stone were granted this blessing—"When his Lord manifested His glory to the mountain" (Q7:143). If you do not find Him, it was simply not ordained that you should. Let your heart remain content! Moses was told: "If you were granted what you are seeking, there would be no diminution of My beauty, nor any loss of glory to

Me. On the contrary, this mountain without a heart would be effaced in the world of your grief. Still, I have something in store for you."

I cannot easily leave you,
Yet I have plans for your tresses and lips!

O brother, if Adam had not been ensnared by the wheat, there would not have been any blemish on His glory. And if Moses had been granted the vision of the Lord, there would not have been any loss in His beauty. The perfection of His beauty, however, makes it inevitable that thousands of lovers will lament and clamor after Him, yet remain caught in the chain of His wrath and in the net of separation—until the glory of His perfect Beauty appears!

On the night a pain arises in your head, give your complete devotion to it, for the headache He gives is no mere folly. It is related that Azir was granted a revelation. "O Azir, if, according to My measurement, I give you an apricot, thank Me for it! Also, do not look with scorn upon it! Take note that when I was parceling out the ages, I remembered you!"

O Beloved, my name is inscribed in Your register!
I am happy to be the least of Your soldiers!

*Peace!*

## LETTER 96: THE FORTY-DAY RETREAT[113]

*In the name of God, the Merciful, the Compassionate!*

Dear Brother Shamsuddin, as far as this group is concerned, there is no purpose peculiar to a forty-day retreat that cannot be attained outside it. Whenever, however, any repugnance arises for people in fidelity to the hours of prayer, then it is that they consider it good to abandon their normal occupations and make a forty-day retreat in the hope that the effect of the retreat might be extended to the rest of their lives, during which its healing quality might be experienced. What is specific to such a retreat is the remembrance of God Almighty himself! This has been expressed thus in the Law: "Springs of wisdom will appear on the tongue of anyone who sets aside forty dawns for the Lord!"

In the story of Moses we read about forty days having been set aside in order to cut oneself off more effectively from the world and all its concerns. The command runs like this: "We commanded Moses to set aside thirty days and nights; then We added another ten days, so that the appointed time of His Lord was a full forty nights" (Q7:142). These words refer, respectively, to the whole of the month of Zu'l-Qa'da and ten days of Zu'l-Hijja [the last two months of the Arabic calendar]. This story is very famous. It should also be realized that the fast of Moses did not mean simply that he refrained from eating during the day, but also did not eat during the night. No, he passed forty whole days and nights without eating anything at all. According to this example, keeping one's stomach empty of food is an extremely important element of the retreat. Moses attributed his talking to God Almighty to the fact that he had devoted forty days, in all sincerity, to Him, and had cut himself off from his worldly affairs, thus enabling him to take care of his soul, while his stomach remained light. God, the Exalted and Praised, showers much heavenly illumination upon such a person!

What is the wisdom that has led to specifying forty days? We really have no information about that. We can only say that the prophets must have known, for they were blessed with the fullness of the divine favor and illumination. Or again, some of the saints, who were especially selected by God for this knowledge, might have known. What has been stated in the *Awarif ul-Ma'arif* is this: God Almighty brought Adam into existence out of dust and then spent a long time kneading this dust, as the Prophet himself has explained. "God Almighty kneaded the clay of Adam for forty days without any instrument except the hand of His power!" When it is said "without any instrument," the correct interpretation is that He kneaded him without any intermediary for forty mornings until Adam acquired the capacity to dwell in both worlds. Just as he wanted to be an inhabitant of heaven, so too he requested God to allow him to dwell upon the earth. This was because he had been brought into existence out of dust and had been kneaded for those forty mornings in order to become thoroughly mixed and be further removed from God behind forty veils. In each veil there is some meaning that has been placed there and is suited for this inhabitation of earth. These veils act as checks on the way to God and the abode of nearness to Him for, if there were no delay, as is caused by these veils, then how could this world of ours be populated? It was because of this distance from the abode of nearness that the Lord established wisdom, the caliphate, and the vicegerency of His slave, Adam, for the sake of ordering this world of ours. By cutting oneself off from the world as an act of submission to God Almighty and then devoting oneself entirely to His service, while turning aside from all affairs of one's ordinary life, a person will daily emerge from yet another of the veils that have been placed with him. He will experience an attraction to God and progress in virtue in the measure that these veils fall away from him, and he will acquire a resting place very near to God Himself. It will be a place replete with many forms of knowledge. When the forty days have drawn to a close, all the veils will have disappeared and much knowledge and mystical illumination will simply be poured into him.

The sign of the integrity of the retreat and of its having had a fruitful impact, due to a person's fidelity to the requisite conditions of sincerity during the retreat itself, would be that a person begins to live a well-disciplined life, flees far from the abode of pride, and at the same time turns his face toward the threshold of the Divine Majesty. In this world, it should be noted, a life of self-denial is absolutely necessary if wisdom is to be manifested to anyone. Wisdom will not show its face to a person who does not lead such a life in this world. If, however, wisdom does not show its face to somebody who has completed a forty-day retreat, then it is clear that he has fallen into some negligence in observing its requisite conditions.

Now I would like you to know that there is a group that is greatly in error with respect to the path of seclusion and the forty-day retreat. The reason is that they enter into it without a properly constituted foundation, and so fall into the clutches of the Devil. This happens because they have heard that some of the sheikhs had retired into private communion with God and, while thus engaged, had many things revealed to them, experienced many things, and many strange and wonderful marvels were manifested to them. As a result, some people enter into seclusion for the sake of such experiences themselves. This is sheer pretense and the very consummation of error! They are ignorant of the fact that those people who have embraced privacy and intimate communion with God did so in order that their faith might rest more secure; that they might be enabled therein to discern the various states of their souls; and, finally, in order that they might be able to perform all their actions sincerely for the sake of God Almighty.

The mistake of the aforementioned group arises from the fact that they wanted to traverse this path without an outstanding religious leader to inspire them and without the necessary protection of an experienced spiritual guide. They tread this path assisted only by their own puny intellects. Mercy be upon the soul of Attar, who said:

> O Heart, if you go seeking along His Way,
> Look carefully in front and behind, and only then proceed!
> Look at the travelers who have arrived at His threshold,
> Generation after generation have arrived together!
> How do you know about which road to take?
> How can you know which one leads to His threshold?
> For every single particle there is a particular entrance:
> Yes, for each particle there is indeed a separate road to Him!

The wise have said that God Almighty requires steadfastness of you, and yet you yourself hanker after miracles. Much can be manifested to the righteous on account of the abundance of their devotion and the correctness of their discernment, and even future events can become illuminated for them. Yet it also happens that these secrets are not revealed to some. This is no reason for reproaching them for their state of soul. The time to reproach them would be if they were to turn aside from steadfastness. Also, it can be noted that whatever is made manifest to the righteous is for the sake of deepening their faith. It is also an invitation to correct self-struggle and to the development of such a disposition as would find expression in laudable behavior. Such things, if manifested to someone who lives beyond the pale of the Law, would draw him even further away from God and only serve to increase his pride and foolishness. This is why he would go on to consider men to be beneath him and even to despise them. In this way the halter of Islam would slip from his neck and he would deny all limits and commands, as well as any distinction, for himself, between what is lawful and what is not. He then considers that the object of worship is nothing except the remembrance of God. Hence he abandons the observance of the Law and ends up by becoming a complete heretic—may God forbid such a thing!

If some people engage for a time in austerities and become engrossed in seclusion yet remain rooted in pride simply because they have heard voices or have seen something in their imaginations as if in a dream, then in accordance with the effect all this has upon them, they begin to think that anyone who has been favored with such a condition has already arrived very close to God and that his actions have now become perfect. They call this "union with God," saying, "We have attained the fullness of our desire. Worship was necessary, as was the shunning of sin, in order to reach the stage we have now attained. At this stage what harm can there be for you if we sin or neglect our prayers?" They recite these lines in support of their contention:

> In the lane leading to the tavern, what distinguishes a dervish
>   from a king?
> Along the way to the Unique One, what is worship and what
>   is prayer?
> Before the lofty throne of God, what is the sun or the moon?
> Does it matter if a mendicant's face is all ashine or dark?

These foolish people are so contemptible and resourceless that if anyone does not publicly refer to their greatness or, in private, dares breathe even a word of criticism concerning them, then they will make of him a lifelong enemy. Or again, they claim to be both perfect and pure—but on the basis of their qualities of anger and pride. Enough! If such foolish people were in fact perfect men, they would not in the least be troubled by such things. As long as they are held captive by bad qualities like these, how can they claim to be perfect? If anyone claims that not even a trace of enmity, anger, or lust remains in him, he is deluding himself. The reason is that the rank of such a person could never be higher than that of the prophets, and yet they suffered from such blemishes. They were given to lamenting their own faults and lapses, while the righteous shun venial sins and, on account of a mere trace of suspicion, are ready to abandon even what is quite lawful. All tread the path of the fear of God. Because of the possibility that they might do something reprehensible, they continuously long for the security of their own annihilation. On the other hand, these foolish people think they are not at all entangled in Satan's snares but, on the contrary, have a more exalted rank than the prophets themselves had. The deluded ones think that what is a distinct defect in the prophets has been entirely subdued in themselves. They say that the prophets were like that, but whatever they did was for the instruction and benefit of the people. This group does not realize, however, that if things were like that, then why did they spit out of their mouths dates that had been given in alms? If they had eaten them, what harm would that have meant for the people—for alms are lawful for all? Yet we know that religious leaders have, from the very beginning, recognized the fact that one who fails to subdue his desires and keep them under control can be considered as a person of consequence!

O brother, the animal soul of man is very cunning and treacherous! It is forever making false claims and boasting that it has all its inclinations completely under control. If you seek from it some proof for this claim you should not be prepared to accept anything less than this: the fact that a person does not follow his own whims, but acts instead in accordance with the commands of the Law. Namely, whoever gives himself over completely to obeying the Law is the one who should be called "sincere." If, on the other hand, he is on the lookout for dispensations from the Law and interpretations favorable to himself, this means that he is still acting according to his own desires and inclinations and, to that extent, is still held captive by them! If he is a slave to anger, he is a dog in the form of a man. If he is a slave to his appetite, he is a wild beast. If he is the captive of lust, he is a pig. If he is a slave to convention in dress and is preoccupied with his personal adornment, he is a woman dressed up as a man.

The person who is both adorned with and tested by the commands of the Law, and who has given over the reins of his being into the hands of the Law, so that he turns in whatever direction the Law dictates to him, is the one who has brought his inclinations and desires under control. Those people who were renowned for their spiritual insight and good works saw things exactly as they are. Right up till their last breath they did not remove the halter of the fear of God from around the neck of their soul, so much so that when one of the venerable Sufis saw the Devil at the time of his death, the Devil said to him: "Go, you have escaped from my clutches!" The Sufi replied: "I still have one breath left!" The heroes of the faith and those renowned for their knowledge and faith have seen the future life in this light, and have understood the dangers accordingly.

O helpless one, this work is not within your power! You should, if you can, stay in the humble service of a spiritual master as long as breath remains in you. Otherwise, you might as well wash your hands of yourself, as has been said:

Anyone who has taken shelter in the shade of a man of God
Will never be put to shame as he travels toward Him.

Until the glance of such a man falls upon you,
How can you find out anything about your own being?

O brother, the boldness of spirit of the righteous melts along this path! The deluded ones, however, recline on the cushion of foolishness and pass their time in amorous playfulness. It is related in a tradition that Gabriel said to the Chosen One: "O Apostle of God, what do I know? If God Almighty had thought about me in the terms He chose to think about Satan, what would my present condition be?" A similar astonishment has struck one and all! For example, Jesus said: "You know whatever is in my heart, but I do not know what is in yours!" (Q5:116). It is said that the fear of the prophets and of the righteous stems from the fact that, although they are free from any worry about their final end, they are not free from reproach and censure. They are afraid and think like this: "It would not be right if we were to do anything that could make us deserving of reproach or censure, for any reproach or censure, within the abode of nearness to God, is harder to bear than the punishments and afflictions of hell itself!" The secret of this has been thus expressed:

I am preoccupied with thoughts, reflections and deliberations:
Both day and night, I am astonished at my state!

Hence it is that they say that the first stage of a Sufi is astonishment and also his final stage is that of astonishment. The first is experienced on the occasion of blessings conferred, just as when a man is extolled and raised up by some great person, he lowers his head, abashed. The second occasion for astonishment is when a person realizes this fact: "No matter how poor and needy I may be, this can never affect my union with God!" So the whole story begins with astonishment and ends on the same note, as one who knows about such things has said:

Of the reward of heaven's inhabitants and the punishment of
   hell's,
I know not which is mine!

*Peace!*

# THE HUNDRED LETTERS

LETTER 97: DEATH

*In the name of God, the Merciful, the Compassionate!*

Dear Brother Shamsuddin, men are of three kinds: The first are covetous and greedy; the second have begun to turn to God; and the third have attained the heights of mystical knowledge. Pleasure-prone people simply do not think about death and, even if they do, it is in order to pine for this world and to become further engrossed in its good things. The remembrance of death makes such a person move further away from God. A person who has begun to turn toward God thinks about death as a means of producing fear and dread in his heart, and thus be enabled to turn completely toward Him. If often happens that he has a great aversion to death out of fear that it might come before he has turned fully toward God and prepared the provisions necessary for it. Such a person would be excused for such an aversion, and would not come under this threat: "Anyone who has despised the vision of God Almighty does not rest in His favor." This is because he does not abhor death and the divine visage, but rather is afraid of losing that very sight on account of some fault of his. It is like a person who delays seeing his beloved, and remains engrossed in making preparations to meet her at the time and place that will be most to his liking. He does not bother to make a count of the labor involved in such preparation. The sign of his friendship is that he is always making some effort on her behalf, and is not preoccupied with anybody else.

The advanced Sufi is forever recalling death, for it is the time appointed for seeing the countenance of the Friend, and no lover can ever forget the time fixed for meeting his beloved. He would love to be swallowed up by death so that, being freed from this dwelling place of sinners, he might rise to the abode near his Friend, just as Huzaifa relates: "O God, You know that I prefer poverty to riches, sickness to health, and death to life. Make death easy for me, that I might arrive at my reward—You!" Now it will be understood why the novice is excused for shunning death and for desiring it, while, on the other hand, the advanced Sufi is also excused—for loving death and yearning after it! It is said, however, that there is an even higher stage than both of these, when a person makes use of nothing at all, but does his work purely for the sake of God. For himself, he chooses neither death nor life. This is the stage of resignation and acceptance, and it is the final point of those who have reached the summit.

A person has attained this stage when the remembrance of death makes blessings appear irksome, and changes the pleasure one derives from them into vexation, and when what normally renders insipid things pleasurable and desirable for man becomes something leading to salvation. Here is a hint about this: "Think more about the destroyer of delights [i.e., death], that your inclination toward them might be severed. Thus will you be enabled to turn toward God Almighty." It is related in a Tradition: "If animals knew as much about death as you do, then you would not be able to eat the meat of any fattened animal."

Aisha said: "O Apostle of God, who will appear together with the martyrs on the Day of Resurrection?" He replied: "Anyone who thinks about death twenty times each day and night." He also said: "Death is a present for the faithful, because the world is their prison, and they are always grief-stricken in it. Death is the release from all that, and release from prison is certainly a much-prized gift!" Again, he said: "Death is an atonement for every Muslim." Anyone who is a real Muslim, unlike you and me, is in quest of it. A genuine believer is the person from whose hand and tongue Muslims receive peace and security. The behavior of the believers should edify others. They should not be stained by sins, except for trifling ones. Death makes them pure.

Khwaja Hasan Basri said: "Death has dishonored this world. It has not allowed any sensible man to rejoice!" A wise man wrote the following to one of his brothers: "Be afraid of death in this abode before you go to the other dwelling place, for you will long for death therein, but will not find it." When Ibn Sirin was reminded of death, all his limbs became transfixed. Umar Abdul Aziz [a caliph] used to gather all the juris-consults together each evening and recall death, the Day of Judgment, and the last things, and also weep as though his bier were in front of them all. And Khwaja Rabih Tamimi said: "The pleasures of this world cut me off from two things: One is the remembrance of death, the second is standing in the presence of God." Kaab Ahbar said: "Everyone who realizes what death is finds that the trials and difficulties of this life become easy for him to bear!" It is related that Mutarraf said: "I saw in a dream that someone in the mosque of Basra was saying that the description of death tears to pieces the hearts of the timid." It is related that whenever Jesus was reminded of death, blood used to ooze out of his body.

O brother, it behooves you not to lag behind those who day and night used to recall death at least twenty times. As far as possible, remain steadfast in this practice and be ready for death to come, whenever that may be. Qaqa Hakim said: "I have waited thirty years for death to come, for I have no love for anything here." It is also related that Imam Suri said: "I saw an old man in the mosque of Kufa who said: 'I have waited for death for thirty years in this mosque, not knowing when it would come. When it comes, I won't have to wait for anything else. I don't want any delay. I have no claims on anybody else, nor does anyone have any claim upon me.' " One beloved of God wrote in a letter: "This world is a dream. After it, comes the awakening. Midway between them lies death. We are all perplexed with dreams."

O brother, even if there were no sorrow, grief, fear, or torment, still death and its pangs would be quite sufficient, for the whole of life is made miserable because of that moment. All pleasure is spoilt therein, while every blunder and foolish action will be changed completely at the awakening. Meanwhile, it is said that death is more painful than the blow of a sword or a cut from a saw, or removing the nails from one's fingers. Hence it is that the Apostle said: "O God, make the pangs of death bearable for Muhammad!" In a similar way, Jesus said to his followers: "O my apostles, beseech God Almighty to make death easy for me, for I am so much afraid of it that my fear itself is plunging me to my death!"

It is also related that a group of the sons of Israel was passing by a cemetery. They prayed to God Almighty that He might revive one of the dead so that they might question him. Lo, one dead man rose up from his grave and, between his eyes, was the mark of his repeated prostrations. He said, "O men, what do you want of me? It is fifty years now since I tasted death, but its bitterness has not yet departed from my heart!" Imam Auza'i has related this: "I was told that a dead man is afflicted by death till the moment he is raised from the grave." One man used to make great inquiries of sick people who were at the point of death, saying: "How do you find death?" When he himself fell ill, and was hastening toward death, some people asked him, "How do you find death?" He replied: "It is as though the sky were covering the earth, and as though my soul were being drawn through the eye of a needle."

It is also related that the Apostle said: "If even a single hair of a dead person were to be placed upon the inhabitants of the heavens and earth, then by the divine command all would certainly perish, because in each hair is contained the effect of death, and this effect simply cannot fall upon anything without causing it to perish." It is also related that he said: "If only a drop of the fear of death were to be placed upon the mountains of the earth they would certainly melt away." It is also said that when the soul of the prophet Moses reached the Divine Presence, God asked: "Moses, how did you find death?" He asked this question, even though He is fully aware of what it is like. Moses replied: "I found my soul was like a sparrow, and in such a state as though it had been fried in a pan but did not receive the relief of death, nor was it released so that it might fly away." Now understand that at the time of death the lover appears to pass away, that is, he is completely peaceful and at rest. Some appropriate words of witness will assuredly be found on his lips at that moment. In his heart there will be a good idea about God.

There is a tradition that the Prophet said: "A dying man's attention should be fixed on three things: He should be blushing with shame; tears should be flowing from his eyes; and his lips should be parched. This would all be due to God's mercy, which had been showered upon him. And when he makes a noise, it would be a choking sound; his color would turn red, and his lips became the color of dust. All this constitutes torments sent by God, which have now overwhelmed him. It would, however, be a good sign if his tongue still moved in witness to God." It is also related that the Prophet said: "Everyone who is dying, and knows that there is no other god but God, will go to heaven." It is also narrated how the Prophet went to a young man who was dying. He inquired: "What is your idea about God?" The youth replied, "I hope in God, but am afraid of my sins." He said: "At such a time, both these two sentiments cannot be present in a man's heart, namely, that God Almighty would not grant him that for which he hopes, but would change his fear into assurance."

O brother, the end of one and all is by this way alone, whether you are a beggar or a king, for here it is all the same with respect to the possessions of kings and the poverty of beggars, as has been said:

If your possessions were to stretch from earth to the moon,
Finally, they would all lead to this door!
When your jaw suddenly turns rigid,
Then all the World's wealth is no more than a chin!
If you are a Faridun or an Afrasiyab,
In this Ocean you are but a drop!

410

# THE HUNDRED LETTERS

All the creatures of this world are submerged in an ocean of
    blood:
Who knows what their condition is like beneath the dust?

If you say that in any particular state one of these two, that is,
fear or hope, should overcome the other, realize that when a slave is
strong and completely correct in his belief and practice, fear is what
should predominate. On the other hand, when he is sick and weak, especially when he is gripped by the pangs of death, that is when hope
should predominate. Scholars have said that the reason is because
God Almighty has said: "I am close to those whose hearts are broken
out of fear of Me!"

At the time of death, and while undergoing its pangs, hope is better because at that moment a person's heart is broken, due to the sins
committed while he was vigorous and healthy. If you were to say,
"No, one should have only a good opinion about God, according to
the traditions," then understand that one of the good opinions we
should have is to shun any sin whatsoever against God Almighty, as
well as fear the punishments of the world to come, while striving to
serve Him. Realize also that all works return to this one source,
namely, it is a point that breaks backs, turns faces pale, rends hearts,
and turns eyes into blood. Yet that very fear is the cause of mystical
knowledge. In other words, this is the limit and extremity of those
who fear God. A venerable Sufi has said: "There are three types of
sorrow: that of worship—has it been accepted or not? that of sin—
has it been forgiven or not? and that of the vision of God—will it be
denied or not?" The especially favored ones have said: "There is really only one sorrow—that of being denied the vision of God! Every
other sorrow, apart from that, is easy to bear, because it is not destined to last." Hence it is that the prayer of all the wise in this: "O
Lord, do whatever You wish, but don't cut us off from this!" The secret has been couched in the following verse:

The hearts of all are stirred
In expectation of seeing Your face!
Our bodies, out of fear of separation,
Cry out in the midst of pleasure and comfort!
Without Your beauty, flowers of desire
Turn to thorns in my hope-enkindled eyes!

*Peace!*

411

# MANERI

*In the name of God, the Merciful, the Compassionate!*

Brother Shamsuddin, for the body of orthodox Muslims, there is agreement that unmitigated threats are meant for the infidels, while boundless promises are for those who perform good works. If one of the faithful is a sinner, he does not become an infidel until he comes under the ban of the unmitigated threat of God. Neither does a person become given over completely to good works until he is caught up by the boundless promises of God. Otherwise, within himself some opposition would remain. The Mutazilites say that such a person belongs to the group that is under the divine threat. If he were to quit this world in the state of sin, he would remain eternally in hell. The religion of the orthodox, however, is that there is a suspension for him. Hence it is not a question of boundless promise or unmitigated threat. The command concerning him is connected with the will of God. If God so wishes, He can forgive him. That would be a sign of His grace. Or, if He wishes, He could punish him. This would be a sign of His justice. In no way at all could one of the faithful be said to be perpetually in hell, no matter how great a sinner he might have been. Abdullah Abbas is accredited with this saying: "Every believer who dies in a state of sin is treated in one of three ways by God Almighty: He, out of His immense mercy, may forgive him; or due to the intercession of the prophets, He might forgive him; or according to the measure of the man's sins, He might punish him and then set him free."

> If you are a sinner, the door of repentance lies open:
> Repent, for the door will never be shut!
> If you approach this door but once, in righteousness,
> A hundred victories will come rushing forward together!

All the followers of Tradition are agreed in this matter, namely, if God Almighty so wishes, He can punish a slave for both his serious and trifling sins; or, if He wishes, He can forgive a person's slight faults, and catch him for his serious sins. Or again, if He wishes, He can forgive his serious sins but catch him for his faults. It is fitting for God to forgive a slave's serious sins but punish him for his small faults. In short, it should be known that, no matter how great a person's sins might be, they cannot exceed the mercy of God. Also, although there may be some trifling faults, if He were to exercise His justice, they would not be considered small. Thus the wise have said: "When He bestows grace, no serious sin remains. And when He exercises His justice, no slight faults at all remain, for they are all changed into serious sins because of His justice, while His grace changes serious sins into trifling ones." The secret of this is given thus:

> If You bestow Your grace, we shall certainly be liberated.
> But if You exercise Your justice—alas, how humbled we shall
> be!

One group say that, even though this be true, that is, that every sin a slave considers to be trifling is in fact so, nevertheless it will become serious, while every sin a slave considers to be serious, even though this be true, it will become trifling. Hence it is that the wise refrain from calling any sin trifling. In short, the orthodox opinion is that all sins can be forgiven, except for that of polytheism.[114] "God Almighty will not forgive polytheism, but He will forgive any other sin" (Q4:116). The secret is contained in this:

> Come back at last, for I have opened the door.
> I stand ready to forgive you the moment you repent!
> Just look at the wisdom contained in Love's play.
> Man does his worst, but God displays His mercy!
> If there were none except those devoted to prayer,
> There would be no scope for His wisdom to play at Love!
> Without this, the work of wisdom would be incomplete;
> He cannot help being generous—that is the way He is!

The Lord Almighty conditionally denied forgiveness for polytheism or infidelity, and the forgiveness of whatever falls short of infidelity is also dependent on the will of God. Serious sins fall short of infidelity, but it is surely true that God's will to forgive extends to all, so that some benefit accrues to a person for clinging to God. Be filled with hope, no matter how poverty-stricken and resourceless you may be! One dear to God has said:

> If you stand empty-handed in His audience hall,
> Then nothing less than your own nothingness can be thrown
> before him!
> Not only the perfection of austerities is cash here:
> Absolute penury, too, has purchasing power in this hall!

The following is the story of how the revelation of the verse concerning Wahshi, the murderer of Hamza, the uncle of the Prophet, took place. A certain man promised to give a reward to anyone who murdered Hamza. The man did not keep his promise. Wahshi said to himself: "Although I cannot revive Hamza, I can at least seek a new lease of life for myself." He sent a certain person to the Prophet, saying: "I have committed all these terrible crimes. Is there any hope of reconciliation?" The reply came, "If you come, there is." Again Wahshi sent a message to the Prophet, saying: "I want some security!" The Prophet replied, "I am the security!" Again Wahshi sent a message, saying: "This is your own saying, 'You yourself are not included in any command.' Security should come from a person who possesses something." Then this verse came: "God forgives everything except this [i.e., infidelity]" (Q4:116). Again Wahshi sent a reply: "Forgiveness depends on the will of God, but I don't know whether He wants to forgive me or not. I want a better condition than this before I come for reconciliation." Then this verse was revealed: "And those people are forgiven who did not worship any other than God and have not killed anyone except in the cause of justice, and have not been guilty of fornication" (Q25:68). Wahshi sent back this reply: "I am guilty of all three crimes! Since they are not forgiven, why should I come? I shall come only if I receive a better request than this. Otherwise, I shall remain right where I am." The reply came: "[None is forgiven] except the person who repents and believes and does good works" (Q25:70). Again Wahshi sent a reply, saying: "The condition is a very difficult one. I accept that I have faith, but cannot offer any security for good works. How can I know whether I am able to do such works or not? I want a better condition than this." The command came: Say, "O My slaves, you have oppressed your own souls! Do not despair of God's mercy! God Almighty will forgive all your sins. He is certainly great in forgiving and showering down His mercy" (Q39:53). Then Wahshi came to the Prophet and became a Muslim. This is in order that you might know that the crimes of all sinners are no more than a drop in the ocean of His mercy, as has been said:

> His mercy is like an ocean without limit;
> At His door, sins are like a drop of rain!
> If anyone has experienced this kind of forgiveness,
> How can any change be a cause of defilement for him?

Now realize that when he said, "Undoubtedly God will forgive him all his sins!" the forgiveness of all sins is obviously meant, whether serious or trifling. It is related that the Prophet said: "Certainly God Almighty forgives all sins, small or great, hidden or manifest" (Q39:53). He also said, "He is surely one who forgives and displays great kindness" (Q12:98). People have said that this is a very reassuring saying. He said: "I do not forgive you because you are worth forgiving, but because I myself am forgiving and merciful." In other words, I act in this way because of My own attributes, not because of your worth. The meaning of the first verse he recited, "God forgives every sin except polytheism," is given thus: "When you become an infidel or polytheist, you put a substitute in My place. In friendship, however, there is no provision for any 'other.' Again, if you had committed no polytheism, no substitute would have taken My place. When you sinned, it was simply bad manners and rashness, and these are but passing conditions where friendship is concerned. In other words, Do not put any substitute in My place, because I will not pass over that! I will, however, overlook brashness and other excesses."

This point is absolutely fundamental in jurisprudence: When the faith of the heir is the same as that of the testator, no cause for disappointment can arise, except if the heir murders the testator, for the simple reason that murder means the destruction of the very source itself. The roots of a tree should be in place if branches are to grow from it. Polytheism is nothing short of the uprooting of the root of faith itself. The root of faith, however, must be in place if forgiveness is to grow from it.

One day, Shibli was going somewhere. He heard a voice saying: "All your sins have been forgiven, except that of turning your face away from Me." I also heard this verse from God Almighty: "God does not forgive polytheism but, apart from this, He will forgive all other sins to whomever He pleases" (Q4:116). What He is saying is this: "Do not turn your face away from Me. Do not put any substitute in My place! Anything else can be forgiven, but not this."

This group, however, has been overcome by fear. They live in fear. Whatever they say springs from fear. Anyone who observes them would think that they were living under the divine threat—but it is not so. Actually, in the secret recesses of their beings, any sins, even trifling ones, are considered as serious, for holding in contempt any injustice at all is to hold the divine command in little esteem; while considering injustice as something serious means that you hold the divine command itself in high esteem. Such people are always at war with themselves for the sake of God, but are not themselves at war with God. Advanced Sufis make no deals with their own souls.

How can their souls press forward any claim upon them, for God Almighty himself is their friend, while their soul is their enemy? They fight their enemy for the sake of their Friend; they most certainly do not fight their Friend for the sake of their enemy! It is clear that anyone who makes peace with his own soul is in conflict with Almighty God.

It is said that, even with all their purity and the persistence of God's claims upon their own souls, and despite all their virtues, still all their hope is in God Almighty, and is directed toward the good fortune of men, while the fear they show concerning their own fate is such that you would think that all the divine threats had fallen upon them, while all God's promises were for people other than themselves. The wise have spoken thus: "The faith of a slave becomes really complete when, if any calamity at all descends upon the people, he thinks that it is because of his own lack of generosity. On the other hand, if some goodness appears within him, he thinks that it must be the result of the activity of someone else." Hence one of them has said:

> We are Zoroastrians of old, not Muslims.
> We have earned a name for infidelity, and are a disgrace to the faith!
> When Satan comes to us, he puts a cap on our heads,
> For we can teach him about making evil suggestions!

Khwaja Fuzail Iyaz was asked, on the evening of the vigil at Mt. Arafat, how he saw the states of men. He replied: "They would all be forgiven if I were not in their midst. In other words, I am the worst of all men. If they are not forgiven, it is because of my lack of generosity." It is also related that a revelation descended upon Moses saying: "Seek out from among your people the holiest of all the sons of Israel!" He chose a certain man, who was adorned with austerities and devotion. The command came: "Tell him that he is to go in search of the worst of all the sons of Israel!" The man asked for three days' grace. On the fourth day he bound a rope around his neck, came to Moses, and said: "I have brought before you the worst of the sons of Israel." Moses said: "You are the most devoted ascetic from among them all. How can you of all people say such a thing?" He replied: "Because I am certain about my own sins, but in doubt about those of others. And anyone who is certain about his own sins is certainly worse than anyone whose sins are doubtful." A pronouncement appeared: "O Moses, this man is really the best of all the sons of Israel, not so much because of his great devotion, but because he considers himself to be the worst of all creatures."

Khwaja Sari Saqati said: "I used to look at myself several times a day in the mirror, out of fear that my face might have turned black!" This has been put thus:

If you advance but a hair's breadth in your own estimation,
You will find that you are even worse than an idol!
If praise or duty make any difference for you,
Then you are only an idol-maker, fashioning your own
    features!

O brother, it is said that in this world the light of sincerity and the oppression of hypocrisy appear on a person's face.[115] As a proof of this, the Lord said: "The sign of their prostrations is clearly visible on their foreheads" (Q48:29). But, as long as the beholder is himself blind, he cannot see anything. If there had been no prayer on the part of the Prophet, beseeching God to remove all diminution and deformation from among his people, then much ignominy would have made its appearance among them. Hence the wise have said: "Diminution and deformation appeared in previous communities, but have not done so in that of Muhammad." Also, Khwaja Sari Saqati said: "I don't wish to die in a place where the people know me, out of fear that the earth might not receive my body, and that I might thus become infamous." The reason for this doubt about himself was that he considered himself to be the worst of men, otherwise he would not have thought of himself that way. This is what happened to earlier peoples, but God Almighty has preserved this one from such a disgrace. The secret of this has been put thus:

Out of the pain of faith, all those long on the Way
Have dyed their beards with the blood of their hearts!
Because of this difficulty, all men of real faith
Have livers that are parched, and hearts that have been roasted!

O brother, become nothing in the world of His being, for being is His property. All you can lay claim to is nonexistence. Finally, you must have heard, "What exists between the two nothings is itself nothing." Cancel the entry of your own existence from the Book of

Destiny so that one day you might see the very face of Being Itself. It has been put thus:

Cease to be! Really, that is all your work consists of.
Lose yourself—union is nothing other than that!

If a moth had even the slightest touch of self-concern, it would never fling itself upon the fire the way it does. Every lover in this world yearns to be consumed like a moth or like a madman, but not a one follows their example!

When lovers remain crowding around Your door,
The reason is that none has found a road leading to You!

Intellects are lost in astonishment at His glory! The minds of men grow giddy at His beauty! Human understanding is utterly helpless and turned completely upside down by the faintest perception of His omnipotence! The secret is hinted at thus:

O You against whom thousands of pigeons don armlets.
O Deer who captures lions, how long can we escape from You?
Enough, for no one has ever found himself bound to You.
Yet, all taste sorrow and calamity on account of You!

*Peace!*


LETTER 99: HELL

*In the name of God, the Merciful, the Compassionate!*

Dear Brother Shamsuddin, you were told: "Fire is where all will end up" (Q19:71). Then the following verse was revealed: "Those who live lives of abstinence will be saved" (Q19:72). We are certainly heading toward hell, but there is doubt as to whether we are heading toward heaven or not. Take this opportunity now of looking at, and reflecting over, the valleys of hell and its various partitions, as described by the Prophet. "There are seventy thousand valleys in hell. In each valley there are seventy thousand caverns. In each of these there are seventy thousand snakes and scorpions. There will be no end to the torments of the infidels and the hypocrites until they have passed by them all." It is also related that he said: "We seek

God's protection from the pit and valleys of sorrow." The Apostle was asked what the pits and valleys of sorrow were. He said: "There is a valley in hell from which hell itself prays for protection seventy times a day. God Almighty has made this to help me remain steadfast."

[A number of traditions and stories—mainly in the form of a continued pictorial presentation of hell—follow.]

Khwaja Hasan Basri said: "There was a man who was released from the fire of hell after seven thousand years. O that I were that man!" On another occasion, he was sitting on a rubbish heap, weeping. He was asked why he was weeping. He replied: "I am afraid that I might be thrown into the fire of hell, and that it may not be able to purify me!" Here it can be said:

> Since no one is pure in My estimation,
> There is no possibility of dust being found in My world!
> Yet, entrust to Me your day of death for, in My presence,
> The killing of a pure person is no cause for fear!

If such was the state of Khwaja Hasan Basri, what will happen to a mere handful of dust? It is related that Khwaja Ahmad Harb said: "We all seek shade from the sun; why shouldn't we seek paradise as a refuge from hell?" It is related that Jesus said: "There are many in good health, with ruddy complexions and glib tongues who, on the morrow, will cry out in the various parts of the fire of hell." David used to say: "O God, how could I possibly endure the heat of the fire of hell, when I can't even bear the heat of Your sun? How could I bear the sound of Your torments, when I can't even bear that of Your mercy?" Look at this terrifying sight, and realize that God Almighty has created both this frightening fire and also people for it, whose number will not increase or decrease. This is something that has already been decided upon and marked down by God Almighty. In our foolishness, you and I are perplexed, for we have no idea what was determined for us from the very beginning. If you say, "If only I knew where destiny was calling me, and to what I am returning and what was determined concerning me from the very beginning!" understand that there is something that would serve as a sign for you. It might help you to love and, by means of this, your hope will become well founded.

Look at your own states and actions, for the purpose for which everyone is created is rendered easy for him. If the path of goodness has been made easy for you, rejoice, for you are far from the fire of hell! If, on the other hand, you cannot intend doing anything good without being surrounded by all sorts of impediments that prevent you from acting; and if it happens that, no sooner do you decide to do something evil, than everything is made easy for you, realize that it was destined for you! It is a sign of your final end, just as rain is an indication of vegetation, and smoke is a sign of fire. The Quran has this to say: "Undoubtedly those who do good are destined for the blessings of heaven, while evildoers are destined for the fire of hell" (Q82:13). Think of your soul with respect to these two verses if you wish to know where you stand in relation to the two abodes!

It has been reported that Khwaja Yahya Mu'az said: "I don't know which of these two sins is harder to endure—missing out on paradise, or going to hell. At any rate, it is easier to go without the blessings of heaven than to endure the torments of hell. Yet there is an even greater and more unbearable trial in hell than there would be if there was to be a release granted at some stage, namely, the fact that hell lasts forever. What heart could endure that? What soul could put up with that?" The secret is contained in these words of Jesus: "The thought of remaining forever in hell tears to shreds the hearts of the fearful." What you have heard is a mere introduction to what hell and its torments are like! There is a secret in this. At death, the veils of this world are removed; the soul remains sullied by the impurity of this world, and is not entirely separated from it, even though it is now really distinct from it. It is as though some dross and rust were to remain on some precious jewel. Or, again, it is like a mirror that is so covered with rust as to be completely spoiled. No amount of cleaning or polishing could have any effect on it. These are the people who have become entirely and eternally veiled from their Lord—may God forbid such a thing!

On the other hand, some jewels have not reached this stage and are still capable of being cleaned and polished. They are placed over the fire until they are cleansed of all dross and rust—for no longer or shorter time than that! It is commonly said about believers that, in three thousand years, no soul will depart from this world without any stain from the world remaining upon it, except perhaps for a very few. Now realize the secret meaning of this verse: "There is not one of you but who will have to come to it. Your Lord has required it!" (Q19:71).

*Peace!*

420

# THE HUNDRED LETTERS

*In the name of God, the Merciful, the Compassionate!*

Brother Shamsuddin, when the sorrows and evils of this abode have
been experienced, you should know that there is another abode that is
just the opposite of this one. Consider its blessings and pleasures! It is
inevitable that the further a person is from either of these two, the
closer he is to the other. Arouse both fear and hope within your heart!
You should be greatly afraid at the thought of hell, but full of hope at
the thought of the blessings of heaven! Your fear will enable you to
attain an exalted status, while your hope will enable you to escape the
divine torments! "Whoever is afraid of standing before his Lord has
two gardens destined for him" (Q55:46). [Some traditions about heav-
en are then quoted.]

When a person arrives at one of the doors of paradise, he will
find two trees nearby. Beneath the trunks of these two trees, two
springs appear and flow through the garden. He chooses one of these,
according to what has been ordained for him, and drinks from it.
Whatever fear or grief is within him is removed. He then goes to the
second stream and bathes in it. His face will shine with the freshness
of the divine blessings. Even his hair will no longer be capable of being polluted. No darkness at all can cloud his face—it will appear to
be shining with oil. He has reached paradise and is greeted with,
"Peace be to you, for you remained pure in the world! Enter herein
for all eternity!" (Q39:73). He will see himself surrounded by servants
just as a nobleman in this world is surrounded by his. They will be
waiting for him as he returns from his journey. They will say to him:
"Rejoice, for the Lord God has prepared all sorts of blessings for
you!"

One of his slaves will go to the damsel of paradise who is destined for him. He will say, "I saw so and so—using his earthly
name—coming this way." She will say, "Did you really see him coming?" He will reply, "I saw him, and he is following me." She will
rush to the door, beside herself with joy! She will be ready to greet
him when he arrives. When he does, he will see that his mansion is
built on a huge, precious stone, and that it is constructed of emeralds,
rubies, and yellow-colored gems. He will lift up his eyes to the roof
and there he will see a dazzling light like lightning. If God Almighty
did not give him a special strength, he would certainly lose his sight.
He will look hither and thither and see his wives. Everywhere he will

see glasses and pitchers. He will see couches and pillows aligned together, and a carpet spread on each floor. Then, seated on a large cushion, he will say: "Praise and thanks be to the bountiful Lord who showed me the way to this place! If He had not guided me, where else could I have found guidance?" Then a herald will come and proclaim, "Live forever! You will never die! Stay here, for you will never have to leave! Remain healthy, for you will never fall sick!"

Look carefully at the windows of heaven, noticing the different heights of each. Just as there is a clearly recognizable difference between the devotion and behavior of men, so also in heaven there will be differences in their reward. Hence, if you want to secure a high rank in heaven, you should not allow yourself to be outdone in worship of God. If your friends and neighbors get a bigger reward, or a more splendid mansion than you do, you will experience a certain heaviness of spirit, and your life will be rendered miserable. It will be much better for you if you fix your attention on heaven now, and not allow yourself to be outdone in the worship of God. Yes, fix your eyes on heaven, but do not allow yourself to feel secure about it, lest any group take precedence over you, for there is absolutely no comparison between the blessings that will be experienced tomorrow and those of this world! [Many traditions about the joys and delights of paradise are then quoted.]

A man asked the Prophet: "O Apostle of God, will there also be horses in paradise, because I have a great love for horses?" He replied: "If you like horses, you will be given a magnificent stallion to bear you swiftly wherever you wish to go in heaven!" Another asked him if there would be camels in heaven, for he was fond of them. The reply came: "O slave of God, if you go to heaven, you will find there whatever you want, as well as whatever pleases you." He also said that men will have children in heaven. Whenever they want a child, then in the twinkling of an eye the child will be born and, after but one hour, he will grow up into a young man. Also, if somebody wants to talk to another, his carpet will bear him instantaneously to wherever his friend is. They will discuss various events that occurred upon earth. [More traditions follow.]

O brother, what you have heard is fitting for you and me, for it describes our capacity. But what is this all about? It reminds us that, God willing, we should never be without hope! Now we come to what is the Desire of the righteous and the Object of the souls of the prophets and the saints. "There is more in store for those who have done well." This is the vision of God himself! It is such a source of delight that all the pleasures of paradise are completely forgotten therein![116] Jarir Abdullah said: "I was once in attendance upon the Prophet when a full moon was shining. He said: 'Undoubtedly, you will see your Lord without any veil, just as you see this moon!' "

It is related that when those destined for both paradise and hell have gone there, a herald will cry out: "O people of paradise, did God Almighty promise you anything?" They will reply: "Lord, didn't You create our faces white?" He will say: "That promise still remains." They will say: "O God, didn't You save us from hell and grant us paradise?" He will say: "That promise still remains." They will say: "Didn't You give us, in our right hands, the record of our good actions?" He will say: "Something still remains—the vision of My very Self!" Then all veils will be removed, and those people will behold their Lord!

You should realize, however, that in orthodox Islam the vision of God is not a recompense for good deeds. No, it is due, purely and simply, to the Grace of God! [More traditions follow.]

One Tradition says: "Come, I am your Lord! Look upon Me! Peace be upon you! You have been purified. Remain here for all eternity!"

Those who are especially close to God will remain at all times in His court. In comparison to the pleasures of being close to the Lord Himself, all the blessings of paradise weigh no more than a particle of dust! Khwaja Hasan Basri said: "When those destined for paradise arrive there, God Almighty will reveal Himself to them. They will remain in utter astonishment at His glory and beauty for eight hundred thousand years because, when they catch sight of His beauty, they will be overjoyed at What they see and, when they see His glory, they will simply melt away!" In other words, they will be beside themselves with joy! No pleasure of eating or drinking, of beautiful maidens or anything else will remain in them, even to the extent of the smallest particle.

It is also related that, when the believers go to heaven, they will hear this command: "Desire your great, exalted, and unique Lord!" The trouble is that they will not know how to desire Him! They will go to their teachers and tell them. While they were in the world, if they ever had any difficulty, they also used to go to them for a solution. "Now we have been commanded to desire. Tell us what exactly we should desire!" The scholars will reply: "DESIRE THE VISION

OF GOD ALMIGHTY HIMSELF!" The Prophet, it has been reported, was once asked about the vision that creatures have of their Lord. He replied: "Some will see their Lord once a month; some will see Him once a week; and others will see Him morning and evening, that is to say, day and night."

May all the believers through the protection of the prophets and saints experience the beneficence and kindness of God! May His peace be upon all the prophets and apostles, for there is no power nor strength but in God, the Exalted, the Mighty! [Concluding invocatory prayers.]

# NOTES

1. Each letter, after the greeting, begins with a phrase that, literally translated, would run, "let him know that. . . ." The phrase is generally omitted.

2. The hieratic classification(s) found here and elsewhere in *The One Hundred Letters* are not original to Sharafuddin. This one, for example, is found in *Awarif al-Ma'arif*, a thirteenth century Sufi text popular throughout Hindustan (see H. Wilberforce Clarke, trans., 1891, reprint ed., New York, 1970, pp. 62–65). Sharafuddin's originality consists in filtering somewhat academic divisions through the depths of his own inner, spiritual experience, and thus bringing them to life.

3. Q47:19 refers to the Quran, chapter (*surah*) 47, and verse (*ayat*) 19. The numbering followed here and in subsequent Quranic citations is that of Gustav Flügel, whose concordance is widely used in India. For a clarification of the full context of Sharafuddin's citations, the reader may refer to the Arabic original or to any standard English rendition of the Holy Quran.

4. This statement, carefully elaborated in the introductory letter, recurs from time to time in subsequent letters. Coupled with the whole tone of Sharafuddin's instruction, especially his insistence on divine grace, such a statement makes it difficult to imagine how anyone could classify the saint from Maner as a monist or pantheist in Islamic garb!

5. See the index of names for a brief note on Mansur al-Hallaj and other important Sufis mentioned in *The One Hundred Letters*.

6. Personages familiar to English readers are given their usual name (e.g., Abraham for the prophet), while others taken from the Islamic tradition are cited in their Arabic spelling (e.g., in this instance, the Sufi Ibrahim).

7. Occasionally Sharafuddin mentions the specific name of the poet

whose verse is being quoted. At other times the poetic citation is anonymous, though some of the couplets and quatrains were probably of Sharafuddin's own composition. The relationship of poetry to prose is one of the measured literary (and theological!) nuances that distinguish *The One Hundred Letters*.

8. A few stories have been omitted. Care has been taken, however, *not* to omit representative anecdotes that the modern reader might find uncongenial, e.g., the ants talking to Solomon, the prescient dog of the Companions of the Cave, etc.

9. Such quotations, given without any reference, derive from the vast body of Traditions linked to the Prophet Muhammad and enjoying a scriptural authority for Muslims second only to that of the Holy Quran. Their actual identification presumes a degree of specialized knowledge beyond the scope of this series, but it ought to be noted that Sharafuddin was among the foremost Traditionists of his age, and he is said to have pioneered the study of Tradition among the Muslim elite of Bihar. (The corpus of his writings, in addition to his recorded discourses and the letters of his chief disciple, Muzaffar Shams Balkhi, provides abundant evidence in support of this statement. See also M. Ishaq, *India's Contribution to the Study of Hadith Literature*, Dacca, 1955, pp. 66–71.)

10. It is worth noting what follows upon the phrase "O brother" because it implies a stress in *The One Hundred Letters* not dissimilar to the "Amen, Amen" sayings in the Gospels.

11. Pharaoh is the figure par excellence of the man who lays claim to lordship; by contrast, God in the Quran addresses man, even before he has come into existence, with these words: "Am I not your Lord?" (Q7:172).

12. The moral soundness of this and the preceding teaching, as well as its social value, are obvious.

13. Throughout *The One Hundred Letters* one comes across this formula, in an astonishing variety of expressions: Everyone and everything depends on God's grace, and yet He bestows His grace on the individual who makes an earnest effort.

14. In the Islamic tradition the forbidden fruit Adam ate was wheat; it had, however, an effect similar to the apple of Biblical lore.

15. The word *himmat* is a pivotal Sufi technical term for Sharafuddin, and it is variously translated as "spiritual resolve," "high resolve," "courage," and "magnanimity," in each case connoting that determination of will without which the seeker cannot proceed beyond the pleasures of this world or the delights of paradise to the only true and worthy goal, the vision of God Almighty Himself.

16. "Stages" (*maqamat*) refer to a person's habitual spiritual disposition on his journey to God, while "states" (*ahwal*) refer to the actual condition of his soul at any particular moment, whether it be one of consolation or desolation.

17. Sharafuddin is convinced, from his own spiritual experience, that a

disciple who earnestly seeks a guide will be provided with one by God Himself. The case of Maulana Jalaluddin Rumi and Shams Tabrizi, though not cited in *The One Hundred Letters*, aptly confirms Sharafuddin's testimony.

18. The threefold division here adumbrated occurs in numerous Sufi manuals and expository writings. Perhaps the earliest, and certainly the most condensed, reference is to be found in Khwaja Abdullah Ansari's *Munajat* (see W. Thackston, trans., in the The Classics of Western Spirituality, Paulist Press, New York, 1978, p. 215).

19. The Indian or Hindu context of *The One Hundred Letters* is oblique and inferential rather than direct and anecdotal. We hear nothing about individual encounters between Sharafuddin and yogin adepts, nor attempts at conversion, nor public debates, and yet in literary allusions to the Brahmin's thread and to idol worship Sharafuddin seems to be providing his readers with implicit guidance in their conduct vis-à-vis their fellow countrymen.

20. The Mutazilites were an eighth- to ninth-century group of speculative thinkers, principally located in the urban centers of Basra and Baghdad, who greatly influenced the nature and development of dogmatic theology in medieval Islam. By the end of the tenth century their influence was on the wane, but their views continued to be cited by Sufi and other speculative writers till the modern period.

21. It may seem obvious, but it is nonetheless worth noting that Sharafuddin shows great respect for the Divine Transcendent. The name of God is invariably written in red ink in manuscripts of *The One Hundred Letters*, and it is accompanied by at least one adjective, usually the "Most High" or "Almighty," but sometimes omitted from this translation. We have made liberal use of capitals for pronouns referring to God in order to convey in English something of the profound respect with which Sharafuddin took the name of God.

22. Letters 8 and 9 are addressed to the same senior disciple who was commended at the beginning of Letter 4 as an accomplished Sufi able to interpret the content of the earlier letters to Shamsuddin, who is the addressee for the remainder of *The One Hundred Letters*.

23. It should be noted that the Prophet Muhammad is always accorded a special blessing after the mention of his name. This blessing, reserved for him alone, as well as standard blessings for other prophets and saints, have usually been omitted in the translation.

24. The Kaaba is a cubic structure situated in the center of the great mosque in Mecca, and it is the specific point of orientation toward which all Muslims turn in ritual prayer.

25. Sharafuddin is convinced that an utter humility, rather than any miraculous power, indicates genuine saintliness.

26. The reader has to discern from the context to whom reference is being made by the word *group*. Sometimes it refers to the Sufis as opposed to the theologians; at other times it means the Sufis who follow the Law as opposed

to those who repudiate or neglect it; on other occasions it alludes to the Sufi brotherhood of which Sharafuddin is not only a member but the principal saint, viz., the Firdausiya. In the latter instance, which corresponds to the present instance, the reference is implicitly to Sharafuddin himself.

27. Pursuant to note 19 above, it ought to be added that many of the idols in Bihar are extraordinarily beautiful, especially the images of goddesses from the Shaivite tradition, and Sharafuddin is undoubtedly playing on the sensual delight of idols in linking them here so intimately with miracles, suggesting that the latter can become as tantalizing for Muslims as the former have been and continue to be for Hindus.

28. This poem is particularly delicate as an allusion, both literary and theological, to the point of this passage. Here Sharafuddin wants to suggest that God Himself is the only true "idol," i.e., he is no idol at all but the Beloved!

29. The central image exposited here, common to all Sufi speculative literature, is that of a veiled beauty tossing her veil back over her head and thus allowing people to catch a glimpse of her lovely countenance.

30. According to Islamic mythology, the *jinn* are intelligent, imperceptible creatures created out of smokeless flame (Q55:15).

31. There is a frequent delight in letter mysticism among Sufis (see, for instance, Annemarie Schimmel, *Mystical Dimensions of Islam*, Chapel Hill, N.C., 1975, appendix 1: "Letter Symbolism in Sufi Literature"), and the letter *alif* has sparked continual fascination because its calligraphic form (ı) suggests the stark oneness and uprightness characteristic of God, whose name in Arabic also happens to begin with the same vertical stroke!

32. Sharafuddin's discussion may have been based on his meeting with the famed ecstatic 'Bu Ali Qalandar of Panipat, near Delhi, although, according to Firdausi sources, Sharafuddin was unable to receive any help from his Punjabi contemporary.

33. Sharafuddin's affirmation of Islamic Law is consistent throughout *The One Hundred Letters*, and undoubtedly accounts for the persistent popularity of his most famous work during the later Mughal period.

34. The reference here is clearly to Mansur al-Hallaj. See the index of names.

35. The reader should note the inherent tension between Sharafuddin's exposition of Asharite theological views on predestination and his own experience of God as the Merciful and Compassionate One, echoed repeatedly in his citation of the Quranic verse: "Don't despair of God's mercy" (Q39:53)!

36. In this discussion the writer is consistent in maintaining the absolute supremacy of the Prophet Muhammad over every other human being, including saints. The conflict of sainthood and prophecy exercised Sufi speculative writers throughout the medieval period, and Sharafuddin's position on this issue links him to the moderate Sufis, as does his advocacy of the Law.

37. Of the numerous poets whom Sharafuddin does mention by name and whose verses he cites in *The One Hundred Letters*, none stands out as decisively as the bard of Nishapur, Fariduddin Attar, whose own masterpiece, *Mantiq ut-Tair* [The conference of the birds], will subsequently appear in English translation in The Classics of Western Spirituality series.

38. This is a very "compassionate" view of hell, which qualifies its permanence without diminishing its horror!

39. As in other passages of *The One Hundred Letters* where Sharafuddin is attempting to defend a theological viewpoint, as distinct from imparting spiritual teaching to aid a seeker on the Path, the argument is weak, its conclusion indecisive.

40. See notes 19 and 28 above.

41. Other Sufi theorists, past and present, have upheld the Prophet Muhammad as the first Sufi. (See, for instance, Martin Lings, *What Is Sufism?* Berkeley, 1977, p. 101: "Muhammad was, in fact, as the Sufis insist, the first Sufi Shaykh in all but name.") Yet Maneri's exposition is entirely consistent with his own view that Sufism originated with the human race, i.e., with Adam.

42. The most common word for the patched cloak of Sufis is *khirqa*, but in the present, eloquent passage Sharafuddin also uses the term *galim* and *jama-ye suf* to describe the earliest garb of Muslim mystics. He returns again to this important topic in Letter 91.

43. By now the reader will have realized that the citation of Biblical figures and incidents is to edify Sharafuddin's correspondent, and not to conform to canons of historical criticism. Nonetheless, it ought to be noted that some stories, e.g., the connection of Shu'aib to Moses, have a firm place in Islamic pietistic literature long before their inclusion in *The One Hundred Letters*.

44. When reading statements about the unconditional nature of divine mercy, one needs to keep in mind such passages as this where Sharafuddin emphasizes the exclusive nature of both Islam and Sufism. In every case, however, it is human "ignorance," and not divine contrivance which excludes.

45. The injunction about consuming poison is not to be taken literally, since suicide is strictly forbidden in Islamic Law. In Letter 71, on the topic of Service, Sharafuddin says of the adept, in less dramatic and more accurate language: "He [the disciple] gives preference to the group over himself in all circumstances. He does not refuse them in any matter, unless it be something forbidden by God."

46. Sharafuddin is very much aware of the "godmen" who claim to be "men of God." It requires keen sensitivity to discern the difference, and a person's ability to make such a discernment is itself a measure of the spiritual level he has attained.

47. Letters 25 and 26 treat one of the basic tenets of Sufi triadic divi-

sions—the Law, the Path, and the Truth. Sharafuddin's approach to all three parallels that of Hujwiri (*Kashf al-Mahjub*, Nicholson trans., pp. 383–84) but also amplifies it in certain important respects.

48. Contrast this passage with the earlier passage linked to note 44.

49. The balance between the Law and the Truth, so beautifully expressed in the present paragraph, is but one more example of the coincidence between man's action and God's crowning grace that becomes a recurrent theme in *The One Hundred Letters*.

50. Muhammad ibn Tughluq was the reigning Sultan of his dynasty in Delhi from 1325 to 1351.

51. The intimate relationship between mystical knowledge and love of God is as basic to the outlook of Sharafuddin as it is to that of other medieval Sufi theorists.

52. In Letter 28, as in Letter 26, Sharafuddin uses the strongest possible imagery to suggest the necessity of combining outer and inner facets of the truly spiritual life; even the wording is partially repetitious, though it never borders on redundancy!

53. For the authorship and date of *Qut ul-Qulub*, see the index of books cited at the end of this text.

54. It is important to note that in Sunni or Orthodox Islam the successor or vicegerent (*khalifa*) is the person who succeeds to an office initiated by Abu Bakr after the death of Muhammad in A.D. 632 and technically encompassing spiritual responsibility for the entire Muslim community, while in Sufism the *khalifa* is one (but usually more than one) person who succeeds to the spiritual domain of a sheikh and is authorized by the sheikh to communicate his teachings only to later generations of Muslims belonging to that Sufi brotherhood. The former *khalifa* is universal and single, the latter is restricted and multiple.

55. Letters 32–35 deal with the pillars of Islam. It is instructive to note how Sharafuddin communicates his deeply spiritual understanding of Muslim faith through expositing its pillars.

56. The reference here is to the Ascension of Muhammad, an event, with slim Quranic support (Q17:1) but massively documented importance in the popular history of Islam and Sufism; see, e.g., the visual spectacle set forth in *The Miraculous Journey of Mahomet: Miraj Nameh*, introd. and comm. by Marie-Rose Seguy, New York, 1978.

57. On *Sharh-i Ta'aruf*, see the index of books cited. Abu Bakr Kalabadhi (d. 995) is the author of the *Kitab ul Ta'aruf* (Eng. tr., A. J. Arberry, *The Doctrine of the Sufis*, Cambridge, 1935), on which is based the commentary noted by Sharafuddin.

58. See note 5.

59. For a full explanation of the forty-day fast, consult Letter 96, which is devoted to this subject.

60. The passage that follows expressed the very core of the Islamic faith.

61. It is worth noting that for Sharafuddin, as for most medieval Sufis, man is meant to rejoice in *all* righteous activity.

62. The sequence of topics treated in *The One Hundred Letters* also reveals the priority of their author: Saintly love is exposited after mystical knowledge, both because the former is superior to the latter and because the former presupposes the latter.

63. Once again, Sharafuddin is not as concerned to demonstrate the cleavage between love (*mahabbat*) and passionate love (*ishq*) as to indicate that the former is normative while the latter is extraordinary; for the adept both are necessary, but at different stages of the mystical journey to Truth.

64. A transformed heart, not one's outer garments, constitutes genuine conversion for the saint from Maner.

65. It is apparent that much of Sharafuddin's time has been wasted by such men.

66. A close study of this and the preceding sentence reveals the central role of the heart of man, as mentioned in this and the preceding sentence. Also consult Letter 80. Yet in the traditional scheme that follows, Sharafuddin subordinates the heart to the soul, a theosophical digression he cannot—and does not—integrate into his spiritual teaching.

67. Sharafuddin is referring to the extreme ascetical practice of inserting a needle into the genital organ to relieve sensual passions.

68. This, and similar expressions, is best understood in the light of the teaching set forth in Letter 1. Also see note 4 above.

69. Such meditative reflection, though highly praised, is distinguished from both ritual prayer (Letter 32) and the types of prayer described in Letter 36.

70. Due to the several years that he spent in the jungles of Bihar, especially in his cave near Rajgir, Sharafuddin can speak with great authority about solitude.

71. It is rather startling to say that "the Law changes from man to man," and yet it is a concept in keeping with traditional Islamic teaching.

72. On the supremacy of the heart, see note 66 and numerous other passages throughout *The One Hundred Letters*.

73. Yet again the author stresses that transformation occurs internally by the grace of God and not through human efforts, however vigorous and well intentioned they may be.

74. The important principle stated here and beautifully elaborated in the rest of the letter embodies a theological subtlety that would not be acceptable to formalist scholars of Islam.

75. See note 5 above.

76. A person's attitude toward God is an indication of God's attitude toward him. The reciprocity between creature and Creator is axiomatic to Sharafuddin's spiritual outlook.

77. Here is a crucial distinction for the traveler on the path to Truth.

# NOTES

78. This fine sense of discernment is required of people who have already made some progress in the spiritual life.

79. The polemic set forth here is of historical interest since Rajgir was a center for Buddhists, Hindus, and Jains. This reference and, even more so, a number of explicit statements in his recorded discourses about practices of the "Hindus" (probably a generic term for Hindus, Buddhists, and Jains) in Rajgir could prove to be of considerable historical interest.

80. The clear affirmation of this duty has to be kept in mind by those who are intent on abandoning worldly goods.

81. In other words, a person who has brought his soul under control is moved and guided by God's grace in all circumstances.

82. Here Sharafuddin is leaving room for intercessory prayers directed toward the Prophet and great saints. Such prayers, in his view, can be a vehicle for extolling God Almighty.

83. In choosing his company, a person is also making a statement about himself and his own model for exemplary living.

84. This letter contains some remarkably fine expressions of the profound dispositions requisite to anyone who, as a member of a religious group, sets out to devote himself entirely to the service of his fellowman.

85. Only someone who has been liberated can devote all his energies to the service of others.

86. Sharafuddin stresses both the dedication and the attraction of an affectionate heart.

87. This is the covenant of "Am I not your Lord?" (Q7:172), which is cited time and again in *The One Hundred Letters*. The significance of this single Quranic verse for Sufism can scarcely be exaggerated. It forms the metaphysical backdrop of the teaching set forth in almost all their speculative and devotional literature.

88. It is the tenth day of the Arabic month of Muharram, especially important to the Shi'a for commemorating the martyrdom of Husain at Kerbala.

89. It is necessary to stress that such detachment is the result of God's grace and not repeated austerities; see also note 13 above.

90. The reader will not find any solution to the problem of free will and predestination in this letter. Once again, one senses the tension between Sharafuddin's theology and his spiritual experience, though the large number of Quranic citations in this letter (nineteen in all!) indicate how anxious the saint is to convince his correspondent that the views expressed herein accord with sound Islamic teaching.

91. Sharafuddin's recurrent reference to "the dog of the Companions of the Cave" harks back to Q18:18, where mention is made of "their dog [which] stretched out his paws at the entrance." Many names and legends have been linked to this dog in the magical and mystical literature of Islam. The most popular name is Qitmir, the most widespread legend, that he became a man

as reward for his fidelity. See also W. Thackston's translation of Ansari's *Munajat* in The Classics of Western Spirituality Series, Paulist Press, New York, 1978, note 11, p. 223.

92. "Orthodox" is used to translate "the people of tradition and the community."

93. Letters 81–86, in particular, deal with the main task of "real men," that is, those of high spiritual resolve (*himmat*: see note 15). Their task, above everything else, is to bring their unruly animals souls under control.

94. Sharafuddin is quite alive to the dangers of pseudo-saints.

95. From the perspective of contemporary psychology and charismatic healing, portions of this paragraph would make very interesting, and also valuable, reading.

96. The strategy here outlined may be commended to every earnest believer.

97. Though a radical reinterpretation of Islamic faith, this point of view simply expresses the logical outcome of continued Sufi asceticism.

98. Once again (compare with notes 52 and 61 above), Sharafuddin underscores the primacy of love.

99. See note 4.

100. In all probability, the saint from Maner is here referring to himself.

101. Consult note 77, where it is explained that our attitude toward God is a touchstone of His toward us.

102. Eternal life, which is the only real life, for Sharafuddin, comes from God, not from our own human and transient existence.

103. Musical assemblies were a controversial practice among Sufis, and Sharafuddin has devoted a lengthy letter to the topic in order to make clear his own views on every aspect of Sufi conduct at such assemblies.

104. *Qalandar* as a literary term connotes that Sufi who completely disregards the norm of the Law in order to pursue the innermost Truth. He is frequently outrageous in his disdain for personal cleanliness as well as for the rubric of canonical prayer.

105. The balanced quality of Sharafuddin's discourse once more offers a prescriptive principle that may be commended to all genuine Path breakers.

106. The notion of "good innovations" would be a contradiction in terms for formalist scholars, but Sharafuddin has documented his point of view in providing fresh fuel for Sufi apologetics.

107. A distinction has to be made between "are" and "can be." Creatures, of themselves, lead a person to God. It is man's inordinate desires, as the saint from Maner never tires of saying, that draw him away from God.

108. One is struck by the inner tension between the teaching in this letter, bordering on self-justification, and the quite different teaching in Letter 70.

109. Sharafuddin is perhaps alluding to the Rajgir Hills where he spent several years of his life before settling in Bihar Sharif.

110. Sharafuddin's own life is a confirmation of his advice.

111. In only one other place in *The One Hundred Letters* does the saint say *'ma khud,'* i.e., I myself, thus indicating the heavy stress he wishes to place on this point.

112. The letter that follows is of particular interest and value to those acquainted with the Ignatian thirty-day retreat.

113. It is difficult for a person who has never known devout Muslims to understand the revulsion they feel at the prospect of a believer's lapse into infidelity.

114. The conviction that the state of a person's soul is mirrored in his face occurs often in *The One Hundred Letters*.

115. The vision of God Himself is the source of eternal delight. Such a vision sums up the teaching of *The One Hundred Letters*, even as it forms the crown upon the mystical knowledge and love of God nurtured by the dedicated seeker in this life. By comparison to the consummate vision of the divine Beloved, the pleasures of paradise are trite, and Sharafuddin, like every true Sufi, has no use for them.

# Index to Preface,
## Foreword, Introduction and Notes

437

# Index to Text

441

412, 413, 423; and prayer, 72, 112; of Prophet, 221, 252; of prophets, 80-85, 116; of saints, 80-85; and salvation, 286; and submission. 30.

Gratitude, 164-169.

Greed, 300-305.

Guide, 52, 125; and contemplation, 343; and disciple, 25-30, 31, 32, 91, 95, 96, 112, 114, 117, 121, 122, 123-124, 143, 144, 174, 187, 204, 206, 207, 208, 209, 210, 222, 226, 227, 230, 270, 271, 272, 290, 320, 347, 403, 405; and knowledge, 222, 230, 333, 379; Law as, 372; and music, 383; qualities of 25-30, 205, 226, 346; Quran as, 371; sanctity of, 32, 33, 94, 219; sayings of, 218, 245; and seclusion, 396-400; seeking of, 25-30; state of, 357; and Way, 13, 25, 26, 29, 36, 58, 62, 91, 95, 143, 145, 165, 204, 206, 261, 272, 333, 357, 403.

Gurgani, Abul Qasim, 96, 225, 332.

Haddad, Abu Hafs, 286.

Hakim, Qaqa, 409.

Hallaj, Mansur al-, 13, 27.

Haman, 277.

Hamza, 414.

Harb, Ahmad, 419.

Haris, 171.

Harisa, 59, 65.

Harut, 168.

Harvi, 153.

Hasan, 241, 270, 274, 360.

Hasan, Abul Fazl, 143.

Hatim, 221, 393.

Heart, 28, 224; and belief, 12, 146, 169; consoling of, 126, 153, 184, 185, 293, 294, 399; dead, 97; desire of, 34, 35, 74, 109, 192, 264, 299, 309, 327; and detachment, 309, 310, 354; and disciple (novice), 29, 32, 114, 230; and faith, 132, 188,

269, 357, 372; and favors, 259; and God, 259, 260; grief of, 54, 59, 154, 161, 196, 231, 245, 295, 318, 327, 329, 351, 363, 364, 366-371, 411, 417, 420; hardened, 20, 176; and hope, 41, 46, 308; illumination of, 56, 62, 76, 134, 169, 372, 373, 391; and insight, 244; and intention, 302; and knowledge, 31, 146, 178, 208, 230, 281, 298, 372; and light, 9, 56, 168, 169, 206, 216; and love, 185, 189, 192, 195, 200, 280, 304, 326, 327, 387, 389; of master, 270; and prayer, 138, 140, 269; purification of, 55, 56, 62, 63, 70, 74, 98, 100, 116, 117, 18, 123, 129, 230, 246, 268, 302, 354, 372, 377, 392; and religion, 168; and revelation, 59; secrets of, 316, 378, 382; of servant, 215, 309; and service, 302, 303; and sloth, 32; state of, 244, 330; transformation of 20, 232, 262, 287; treasure of, 327-330; turned to Lord, 19, 21, 33, 34, 38, 51, 53, 94, 138, 153, 157, 185, 235, 247, 264, 285, 327, 380, 392, 407, 408; and Way, 224, 228, 229, 247, 269, 403.

Heaven, 81, 175, 185, 202, 263; and Adam, 67, 119, 152, 201, 263; blessings of, 296, 299, 327, 420, 421, 422, 423; desire for, 41, 90, 276, 301, 328, 351, 419; destined for, 351, 420, 423; eight, 67, 203, 219, 224, 231, 234, 235, 259, 263, 304, 307; and elect, 265; first, 69; hope for, 301, 320, 410, 421; and knowledge, 108, 109, 146; liberated from 34, 82, 84, 120, 130, 150, 201, 276, 301, 304; nine, 212; pleasures of, 24, 119, 136, 297, 421-424, reward of, 406, 422; road to, 211, 234, 299, 330, 410, 418;

seven, 129, 144, 147, 168, 199, 213, 235, 261, 292, 359, 361, 363, 364; and spirit, 332; vision of, 82, 135, 145, 186; and worship, 142.

Hell, 12, 24, 34, 76, 82, 83, 84, 93, 100, 104, 108, 109, 118, 120, 127, 130, 136, 142, 145, 150, 151, 155, 167, 169, 199, 200, 201, 214, 219, 222, 231, 234, 235, 250, 251, 257, 258, 259, 276, 282, 297, 303, 307, 311, 313, 316, 320, 324, 329, 330, 332, 340, 349, 357, 368, 377, 406, 412, 418-420, 423.

Heresy, 80, 95, 104, 114, 134, 220, 222, 249, 324, 325, 326, 341, 398, 403.

Hijaz, 287.

Hilal, 359, 360.

Hindus, 383.

Holiness, 24, 80, 416; and disciple, 125, 220, 300; of God, 193, 314; in guide, 26, 28, 33, 300; and miracles, 47; of Muhammad, 219, 314; ranks of, 374; of saints, 352; and secrets, 59; world of, 372.

Hope, 96, 113, 114, 133, 136, 139, 140, 141, 160, 162, 164, 202, 213, 248, 255, 276, 278, 279, 296, 308, 311, 316, 319-322, 328, 329, 342, 346, 352, 364, 375, 410, 411, 413, 416, 419.

*Hud*, 317.

Hujwiri, Ali, 388.

Humility, 41, 98, 116, 155, 293, 377, 381.

Husain, 241, 274, 360.

Huzaifa, 407.

Ibn Abbas, 245, 377.

Ibn ᶜAiniyah, Sufyan, 140.

Ibn al-ᶜAs, Abdullah ibn Amr, 394.

Ibn ᶜAli, Suhail, 244.

Ibn al-Qattan, Yahya ibn Saᶜid, 138.

Ibn ᶜAuf, Abdul Rahman, 285.

Ibn Balkhi, Muhammad, 336.

Ibn Fazl, Muhammad, 136.

Ibn Hayan, Haram, 53, 395.

Ibn Husain, Umran, 211.

Ibn Khattab, Umar, 398.

Ibn Maqla, 121, 122.

Ibn Mas ᶜud, 140, 394.

Ibn Muᶜaz, Saᶜid, 215, 216.

Ibn Saiyad, 60.

Ibn Sirin, 408.

Ibn Tughluq, Muhammad, 254.

Ibrahim ibn Shaibani, 292.

Idols, 15, 24, 35, 36, 40, 42, 43, 50, 52, 73, 74, 86, 100, 102, 104, 153, 160, 176, 181, 205, 220, 221, 225, 231, 237, 245, 253, 272, 278, 317, 319, 327, 335, 336, 369; worship of, 37, 61, 85, 119, 177, 199, 217, 219, 251, 258, 302, 314, 320, 333, 357, 417.

Ignorance, 72, 74, 76, 92, 93, 96, 106, 109, 136, 144, 157, 167, 172, 191, 203, 204, 206, 209, 220, 221, 222, 223, 233, 262, 268, 312, 314, 330, 340, 349, 361, 386, 395.

Illumination, 53, 237; and attitude, 275, 276; and concealment, 63; divine, 31, 62, 63, 64, 66, 134, 194, 195, 206, 401; and faith, 76, 357; of heart, 56, 62, 76, 134, 169, 372, 373, 391; and knowledge, 223; lacking, 379; and mystics, 9, 12, 402; and righteous, 403; of soul, 9, 12, 27, 51, 55, 62, 63; of wisdom, 77; and witness, 63.

India, 139, 273.

Infidelity, 384.

Infidels, 16, 40, 49, 50, 55, 60, 75, 85, 86, 89, 104, 110, 139, 140, 160, 198, 212, 219, 220, 222, 231, 236, 251, 274, 275, 278, 282, 283, 293, 339, 391, 412, 415, 418.

449

451

Way, 200, 201; and worship, 192.

Service, to brothers, 122, 143, 230, 241, 295; of disciples, 10, 29, 218, 234, 293-297, 393, 405; false, 271; to God, 92, 94, 145-152, 173, 190, 271, 288, 301, 302, 303, 304, 306, 310, 316, 355, 369, 393, 402; of hearts, 333; and intention, 310; and love, 64; to Prophet, 321; and prophets, 101; and salvation, 286; and Solomon, 369.

Shabih, Ibrahim, 52.

Shafii, 393.

Shafiq, 287.

Shame, 161, 184, 190, 377, 396, 405, 410.

Shamsuddin, cf. *passim*.

Sharafuddin Ahmad ibn Yahya Maneri, 10.

*Sharh-i-Ta'-aruf*, 125, 196.

Sharih, 244.

Sheikh, and disciples, 27, 222, 289, 295, 333, 376; dress of, 377, 379; miracles of, 117; and music, 391; need for, 25; of the Path, 228; perfection of, 72; and prophets, 78; and purification, 118; qualities of, 30-34, 68, 95, 329; and Quran, 387; and revelations, 402; and sanctity, 32, 61, 94; sayings of, 93, 47, 107, 129, 193, 196, 197, 226, 228, 244, 269, 287, 291, 311, 318, 320, 326, 337, 341, 349, 351, 393.

Shibli, 115, 131, 157, 211, 221, 236, 287, 293, 318, 338, 358, 415.

Shish, 91.

Shuaib, 91, 216, 285.

Sin, causes of, 161, 233, 306, 330, 339; continual, 237, 283, 340; 416; and error, 71; existence is, 255; expiation of, 306-308; and fasting, 345; and fear, 123, 141, 410; forgiveness of, 17, 19, 21, 29, 41, 42, 84, 85, 88, 90, 133, 139, 141,

147, 154, 227, 263, 297, 302, 311, 312, 315, 329, 352, 353, 362, 396, 411, 413, 415; and grace, 15, 413; and guide, 36; and ignorance, 312, 314; intercession for, 53; keeping from 38, 79, 83, 190, 193, 253, 254, 276, 311, 341, 404, 411; kinds of, 18; and misery, 312-315; and negligence, 360-366; and pardon, 16, 17, 88, 111, 141; and predestination, 317; and prophets, 38, 41, 85-89; punishment for, 19, 20, 46, 197, 222, 263, 265, 299, 312, 338; and purification, 41, 42, 115, 330; and repentance, 15-18, 19, 20, 22-25, 38, 78, 141, 162, 188, 253, 255, 329, 330, 362, 363, 412; results of, 231, 330, 386; sorrow for, 20, 21, 54, 88, 139, 162, 174, 362, 404; transformed, 46.

Sinai, Mt., 18, 115, 251, 300.

Solomon, 15, 27, 76, 148, 162, 242, 285, 298, 310, 355, 356, 369.

Soul, appetites, 103; and awe, 164; control of lower soul, 330, 332, 333, 335, 337, 339-347, 375, 377, 378, 405; creation of, 323, 325; desires of, 39, 109, 212, 219, 277, 281, 282, 308, 317, 337, 367; and favor, 167, 260; glory of, 61; and grace, 159; grief of, 196, 253, 264, 308; guide for, 19; illumination of, 9, 12, 27, 51, 55, 62, 63; and knowledge, 174, 175, 287; liberation from, 347-353, 384; light of, 56, 57, 60, 66, 356; and love, 54, 55, 58, 129, 192, 194, 195, 247, 273, 304, 326, 327; lower, 196, 201, 203, 204, 233, 282, 325, 330-334, 336, 369, 378, 384, 391; Object of, 299; and prayer, 172, 189; purification of, 59, 62, 73, 117, 194, 212, 241, 283, 357, 377, 380, 389, 420; and salvation, 168; and

proficiency in, 9, 65, 93, 160; and
Prophet, 252; seeking of, 93, 146,
208, 218, 221, 234, 241, 282, 283,
329, 330, 331, 342, 372, 390; and
soul, 229; and Sufism, 89; and
veils, 158, 228; and Way, 92, 102,
104-107, 114, 202, 203, 224, 228;
world of, 329, 357.
Turkey, 273.
Tustari, Suhail, 17, 146, 223.

Uhud, Mt. of, 298; battle of, 334.
Umar, 119, 122, 211, 231, 258, 284,
319, 360, 363, 367, 377, 393.
Umru, 173.
Unity, and conflict, 249; covenant
of, 302; crown of, 214; of faith,
169; formula of, 152-156; of God,
10, 12-15; 24, 38, 43, 54, 60, 85, 93,
101, 102, 104, 105, 117, 118, 123,
134, 145, 153, 155, 158, 170, 171,
173, 174, 175, 203, 204, 251, 256,
262, 279, 284, 303, 317, 349, 357,
370, 381; and mysticism, 9, 215;
ring of, 378; and self, 353; stage
of, 99; Unconditioned, 229; way
to, 153, 201, 303; world of, 145,
153, 157.
Uns, 389.
Usamah, 342.
Usman, 285, 321, 360, 380.
Uzza, 258, 314.

Virtues, 24, 43, 46, 60, 87, 119, 124,
140, 144, 151, 289, 416; of disciple,
220, 227; praiseworthy, 238-242,
384; progress in, 402; of righteous,
16, 298.
Vision, cf. also God; 143; divine, 71;
and faith, 155; inner, 153, 206;
and intellect, 59; special, 58.

Wahb ibn Munabbih, 396.

Wahshi, 414.
Waki' ibn Jarrah, 351.
War, holy, 102, 124, 186, 231;
against soul, 225.
Wasi, Muhammad, 244.
Wasiti, 137, 208.
The Way, cf. also Path; 28, 231;
blessings of, 113; and blame, 379-
382; die for, 181; difficulties of,
142, 153, 156, 165, 166, 197, 201,
204, 226, 247, 261, 267, 333, 356-
360, 377; and ecstasy, 67-69; and
error, 69-73, 74; following of, 15,
23, 31, 32, 39, 54, 58, 64, 71, 93, 97,
98, 110, 114, 115, 118, 122, 153,
166, 168, 175, 177, 183, 191, 197,
203, 225, 226, 241, 242, 249, 264,
271, 272, 281, 320, 336, 338, 349,
350, 355, 364, 369, 372, 417;
fundamentals of, 97-101; goal of,
369; to God, 203-207, 208, 223,
228, 230, 271, 272, 275, 294, 316,
327, 354, 355, 369, 378, 401, 404,
405, 418; and guide, 13, 25, 26, 29,
36, 58, 62, 91, 95, 143, 145, 165,
204, 206, 261, 272, 333, 357, 403;
and heart, 224, 228, 229, 247, 269,
403; and inner purification, 102,
354; and knowledge, 10, 68, 72, 74,
76, 99, 110, 148, 152, 158, 179, 241,
272, 370; and Law, 70, 92, 101-104,
114, 202, 224, 228; and light, 60,
206; proficiency in, 9, 28, 93, 102,
200, 230, 265; purposefulness in,
34, 35, 361; and Quran, 371;
secrets of, 37; seeking of, 67, 92-
96; and sheikhs, 196, 197; and
silence, 365; stages of, 36, 61, 68,
153, 196, 200, 209, 219, 228, 229,
356-360, 378; and Truth, 92, 102,
104-107, 114, 202, 203, 224, 228.
Wisdom, 59, 72, 77, 90, 239, 283,
372, 400, 402; of God, 78, 105, 153,

154, 280, 313, 338, 353, 379, 413; of
Muhammad, 326.
World, both, 66, 109, 115, 142, 146,
148, 154, 155, 157, 159, 166, 195,
199, 200, 201, 213, 215, 239, 243,
249, 269, 280, 284, 293, 310, 313,
332, 347, 364, 374, 378, 401; to
come, 74, 93, 94, 120, 131-132, 135,
143, 157, 186, 189, 196, 213, 225,
226, 234, 250, 251, 265, 272, 281-
284, 290, 305, 306, 307, 309, 312,
329, 341, 343, 361, 373, 379, 395,
411; creation of, 243; and desire,
35, 99, 120, 131, 309-311; Divine,
66, 67, 84, 238; end of, 105;
explanation of, 306-308; hidden,
69, 158, 171, 183, 232, 392;
intelligible, 59; Lord of, 131, 146,
153, 155, 168, 174, 256, 284, 308,
329, 334, 340, 357, 372; Master of,
155, 238; numbers of, 58; present,
94, 130, 143, 165, 186, 189, 196,
213, 225, 226, 234, 236, 250, 251,
265, 272, 277, 293, 305, 309, 318,
329, 341, 361, 373, 379, 395, 409,
420, 421, 422; Pride of, 91, 124,
201, 239, 261; Prophet of, 210; of
purity, 293; separation from, 65,

83, 102, 114, 118, 120, 142, 172,
197, 237, 280, 309-312, 342, 368,
374, 401, 402; slaves to, 172, 173;
united to, 35, 65, 83, 206.
Worship, of God, 21, 23, 34, 45, 73,
83, 94, 98, 108, 115, 120, 123, 124,
142-145, 148, 149, 150, 151, 162,
166, 170, 172, 173, 174, 189, 190,
194, 208, 219, 220, 235, 243, 264,
271, 292, 304, 309, 310, 316, 328,
337, 362, 366, 375, 393, 411, 414,
422; of idols, 37, 61, 85, 119, 177,
199, 217, 219, 251, 258, 302, 314,
333, 357, 374; and Law, 403; and
love, 147, 192; and prayer, 22, 137,
138; and Prophet, 22, 243; of self,
45, 54, 98, 136, 160, 161, 201, 203,
205, 255, 259, 272, 278, 304, 373,
375, 422.


Yemen, 181, 240, 287.


Zachariah, 149, 152.
Zahid, 341.
Zaid, .173.
Zoroastrians, 133, 275, 329, 416.
Zulaikha, 197, 198, 275, 336.